# Visions of Glory

# SLAVICA NORVEGICA V

*In memory of*
*Aleksej Ansberg and Sigurd Fasting*
*Slavists and friends*

Jostein Børtnes

# Visions of Glory
## Studies in Early Russian Hagiography

English Translation
Jostein Børtnes and Paul L. Nielsen

Solum Forlag A/S: Oslo 1988
Humanities Press International, INC.: New Jersey

First published in 1988 in Norway by SOLUM FORLAG A.S.
and in the United States of America by
HUMANITIES PRESS INTERNATIONAL, INC.,
Atlantic Highlands, NJ 07716

© Copyright 1988 by Jostein Børtnes.

Cover design: Radek Doupovec.

Financially supported by Norges allmennvitenskapelige forskningsråd (The
Norwegian Council for Science and the Humanities).

**Library of Congress Cataloging-in-Publication Data**

Børtnes, Jostein, 1937-
    Visions of glory.

        Bibliography: p. 281
        Includes index.
        1. Hagiography. 2. Church Slavonic literature—
Soviet Union—History and criticism. 3. Russian
literature—To 1700—History and criticism. 4. Soviet
Union—Intellectual life. 5. Russkaia pravoslavnaia tserkov' —Biography—History and
criticism. 6. Orthodox Eastern Church—Soviet Union—Biography—History and
criticism. I. Title.
BX394.B67    1988        891.7'09'382  .        86-20841
ISBN 0-391-03490-1 (U.S.)
ISBN 82-560-0462-2

Printed in Norway
by S. Hammerstads Boktrykkeri, Oslo
Type-set by typo-service a-s

# Contents

# List of Illustrations

# Preface

This book is about hagiographical patterns and their transformations. It is concerned with the ways in which writers of saints' Lives in Kievan Rus' and in Muscovite Russia took over the prototypes inherited from early Christian and Byzantine literature, adapting them to their own material in accordance with their own spiritual background and historical context. The book is partly an essay in the interpretation of some of the Lives which in my view represent the key-texts of early Russian hagiography, partly an attempt to see these texts in their relationship to the visual arts and to the political history of the time when they were written. My investigations have their origin in my study of nineteenth-century Russian literature. I found in the works of Leskov and Dostoevsky motifs and plots deriving from the Lives and legends of pre-Petrine Russia, and I realised that in order to understand the art of last century's great Russian writers, it is essential to know the literature of the Russian Middle Ages. I hope, therefore, that the book may offer something of interest both to students of medieval hagiography and to students of modern Russian literature.

Since the book is intended not only for scholars working in the field of Slavonic studies, I have translated the texts into English, giving the original passages in transliteration wherever this is required by my argument. In the absence of a universally accepted system of transliteration for Greek and Slavonic personal and place names, I have preserved original spellings and endings in some cases (Philotheos, Ključevskij), whereas English forms have been used in others (Theodosius, Dostoevsky).

All scholarship is dialogue and all dialogue involves conflicting views. Throughout my study of early Russian saints' Lives, my dialogic imagination has been constantly stimulated by the writings of Dmitrij Likhačev, whose interpretations of early Russian literature, although very often differing from my own, have been, together with the theoretical writings of Roman Jakobson, Mikhail Bakhtin, and Jurij Lotman, my greatest inspiration.

A Norwegian version of this book was published in 1975. I remember with gratitude my old teacher, Professor Christian S. Stang, who taught me Church Slavonic and Old Russian, and at whose lectures the idea of this work was originally conceived. At a later stage I was fortunate in being able to discuss many of its themes with Professor Carl Stief of Copenhagen, Professor Sigurd Fasting of Bergen, and Professor Erik Egeberg of Tromsø, all of whom gave me great encouragement and suggested that my book ought to be translated into English. In a perceptive review in *Die Welt der Slaven*, Henrik Birnbaum (1979) supported this idea. It is a pleasure to record my thanks to Professor Birnbaum for his encouraging assessment of my study.

In the process of translation, parts of the book have been completely rewritten, others revised and brought up to date. I owe a considerable debt to my English friends, Father Aelred Squire of the Camaldolese monks, the Immaculate Heart Hermitage, California, for his critical vigilance, and the late Lawrence Burton, who patiently read through the whole manuscript at an early stage, making numerous valuable comments. It is a pleasant duty to thank the Norwegian Research Council for their financial support, which has made the publication of my book possible, and my publisher, Knut Endre Solum for including it in his series, *Slavica norvegica*. My thanks also to the University of California Press for permission to include the chapter previously published as "The Function of Word-Weaving in the Structure of Epiphanius' *Life of Saint Stephen, Bishop of Perm*'," in *Medieval Russian Culture*, ed. by Henrik Birnbaum and Michael S. Flier (1984). But more than to anyone, I am grateful to my friend and co-translator, Paul L. Nielsen, who has used his time and extraordinary linguistic competence so generously in improving and correcting the text.

— *Amico fideli nulla est comparatio.*

# Introduction

## Hagiographical Genres in Early Russian Literature

It is the texts that have come down to us from Kievan Rus' that form the base of the study of early Russian literature. During this period early Russian literature acquired the schemes and formulae of the Christian canon, brought to Kiev by the Byzantine Church, when towards the end of the tenth century Kievan Rus' was converted to Christianity and became part of the Orthodox *oikoumene*. Like its art and architecture, the literature of the Kievan period is marked by the transmission and imitation of Byzantine models; the Byzantine prototypes were not simply copied, however, they were broken down into individual motifs and elements, which were then recombined in new configurations, and given an individual colouring by Kievan writers.

As early as around 862, Constantine-Cyril the Apostle of the Slavs, had provided the Slavs with a literary language, the so-called Old Church Slavonic. At the same time he and his brother Methodius had laid the foundations for a Slavonic literature with their translations of the corpus of Greek liturgical texts into the vernacular. Gradually a series of Orthodox cultural centres grew up among the Slavs in Eastern Europe: in Moravia and Pannonia, as a direct result of the Cyrillo-Methodian mission; in Bohemia, where the Benedictine abbey of Sázava near Prague was a leading centre of this culture throughout the eleventh century, until it was closed in 1097; and in Bulgaria, which during the reigns of tsar Boris I and his son Symeon (852–927) enjoyed a cultural growth similar to that of Kiev a hundred years later.

Bulgaria seems to have been the most important intermediary in the process of transmitting Byzantine literature to Kiev. According to the Russian *Primary Chronicle*, however, Kiev already had its own translators and scribes, under Prince Jaroslav (reigned 1019–1054), monks who copied the Old Church Slavonic manuscripts and translated from the Greek. Today their work is referred to as the "translated literature" of the Kievan period. Hagiography, representing the lives of the saints, their spiritual battle, and heroic death for the true faith, holds a prominent position in this literature.

What is a saint? The Bollandist Hippolyte Delehaye (1930) defines a saint in relation to what he calls the two "hagiographical coordinates," as a person whose burial place has become the object of a special cult and as one who is commemorated with an annual feast day. In connection with this cult of saints there emerged a literature which in the Middle Ages was equally popular in Western Europe and in the Orthodox East. Its functions were the same everywhere: hagiographical texts were designed to be read out in church and to the monks during their communal meals, and designed also for private contemplation.

In the first centuries the cult of saints and hagiographical literature were not yet bound to any process of canonisation. Either a *cultus ab immemorabile tempore* had established itself, and was sufficient legitimation, or congregations and monasteries began to commemorate their own local saints. This cult demanded a written account of the saint's life story, following conventional hagiographial patterns. Once the saints' *vitae* had been written down, their fame soon spread beyond the local communities where their cult had first originated (Beck 1959:274).

Hagiographical heroes fall into three main categories: the Apostles, who were the first witnesses to the Christian faith; the martyrs or "blood witnesses", who suffered death for Christ's sake; and the confessors, revered for their quest for individual perfection and for their "bloodless martyrdom."

Hagiographical texts may be classified in a similar way: a martyr story focuses on the arrest, interrogation, and death of the hero. The central part of a martyr story is a dialogue between the hero and his antagonist, the pagan interrogator, be it the emperor himself or one of his deputies. After this dramatic verbal duel, in which the martyr defends his faith and is sentenced to death, he is handed over to the emperor's soldiers, tortured, and put to death. A martyr story, Latin *passio*, was called *athlēsis* or *marturion* in Greek, and rendered as *strast'* or *mučenie* in Old Church Slavonic.

The stories of the Apostles deal with their acts, *praxeis*, and their journeys, *periodoi*. These accounts acquired a paradigmatic significance for the subsequent literature about the lives of the confessors, the *vitae sanctorum* proper, which represent the struggle of the holy heroes to gain eternal bliss through a pious life, in contrast to the sanctification of the martyrs in the blood-baptism of death. A Life, Greek *bios*, Church Slavonic *žitie*, usually consists of a continuous story about the life of the saint, from his birth until his death, entombment, and posthumous miracles.

The miracles form a basic constituent in all hagiography. In the representation of a saint's life they indicate his participation in the divine power acting through his figure, whereas the posthumous miracles are a sign of the apotheosis of the saint, his deification. Passions as well as *vitae* may culminate in an exaltation of the hero, a *laudatio*, Greek *enkōmion*, *pokhvala* or *pokhval'noe slovo* in the Church Slavonic

translation. Sometimes the entire *vita* or passion is written in the form of
a laudation, characterised by a panegyrical, encomiastic style. Texts
marked by this style are distinguished from texts belonging to the
narrative hagiographical genres, such as the accounts of the lives of the
confessors and passions of the martyrs. *Vitae* and *passions* therefore lead
to a further subdivision into a narrative and an encomiastic variant, into
biographies relating the lives and deeds of the saints, and encomia to
their eternal glory.

By the time the Greek *bioi* and Acts of the Martyrs were translated into
Old Church Slavonic, they had already been collected in various
compendia for liturgical purposes. In the process of translation, however, titles and contents were often confused, so that the Slavonic
versions do not always correspond to the Greek originals. This has led to
terminological uncertainty and to inaccurate descriptions of the
contents and functions of the Byzantine originals in relation to their
Slavonic counterparts. The Greek *Menaia (ta Mēnaia)*, for example, do
not correspond to the early Russian *Čet'i minei*. Whereas the latter is a
collection of expanded Lives, today referred to as *rasprostranennye
žitija*, arranged by the months of the ecclesiastical year, the former
consisted of a series of twelve volumes, one for each month, beginning
on 1 September and comprising the Proper of the Saints, the Offices com-
memorating the saints. The *Menaia* contain the lives of the saints,
hymns, and prayers. The office or *akoluthia* of each saint consists primarily of a hymn to his praise, the so-called *kanon*, whereas the
hagiographical section generally takes the form of a condensed narrative
inserted between the sixth and seventh odes of the canon. This short note
was called a *Synaxarion*, a term used also for a collection of such short
hagiographical texts, which when collected were often expanded. A
third type of liturgical compendium is the *Menologion*, originally a collection of extensive Lives. The title *Menologion* was sometimes used
instead of both *Menaia* and *Synaxarion*. In Kievan Rus' the collection of
short synaxarial narratives was known as the *Prolog*, due to a misunder-
standing of the introductory "prologos" of the Greek original. The
*Prolog* found a development of its own within the literature of the
Kievan period, when a large body of heterogeneous hagiographical texts
were inserted into it. The *Prolog* became one of the most popular works
of early Russian literature, a thesaurus of motifs and subjects for such
modern Russian writers as Herzen, Tolstoy, Leskov, and Remizov.

Besides these collections which arose in connection with the codificati-
on of the liturgy for individual saints' feasts, early Russian hagiography
inherited from Byzantium the so-called *paterica*, or Lives of the fathers,
Russian *pateriki* or *otečniki*. A *patericon* is a kind of anthology
consisting of brief, often novella-like stories with a strong admixture of
the fantastic. The recurrent subject is the hard-working life of the monks
in the Egyptian or Palestinian wilderness. The stories deal with their

struggle against the demons both in themselves and in their inhospitable surroundings; their miraculous encounters with great sinners, heretics, and infidels; God's blessing and his wrath.

Palladius of Hellenopolis wrote his *Lausiac History* at the beginning of the fifth century. Another famous Byzantine *patericon* is the *Leimon pneumatikos*, or "Spiritual field," of Saint John Moschus, from c. 600 A.D. It contains the story of Saint Gerasimus and the lion, today known especially through Leskov's adaptation of the Slavonic translation. Both these works form part of the translated literature of the Kievan era.

However, it was not only by way of anthologies that Byzantine hagiography came to Kievan Rus'. Some of the larger independent Lives were also known at this time. The Russians had their own copies of a number of large Byzantine *vitae* in Slavonic translation even from the eleventh and twelfth centuries. Among these should be noted the *Life of Saint Antony*, the founder of Egyptian monasticism, written about the middle of the fourth century by Athanasius, Patriarch of Alexandria. This *vita* became a model for saints' Lives in both Eastern and Western Europe and has therefore a particular significance in the history of the genre. The works of Cyril of Scythopolis from the second half of the seventh century form an important new phase in the history of Byzantine hagiography. Cyril is the great hagiographer of the Palestinian monks. One of his major works is the *Life of Saint Euthymius*, the founder of a monastery near Jerusalem where Cyril lived as a monk before moving to another great monastery nearby, founded by the man whom Cyril glorified in his most important work, the *Life of Saint Sabas*. The protagonists in the *vitae* written by Saint Cyril are not anchorites like Saint Antony. The Palestinian monks organised their lives differently from the way of Saint Antony and his disciples in the Egyptian desert. These men led an anchoretic life marked by an idiorrhythmic form of asceticism, whereas the monks Cyril writes about were builders of monasteries, who organised their communities according to rules that were already partly coenobitic—these monks divided their lives between communal life in the monastery and solitary contemplation and prayer either in their cells or in the desert. Cyril depicts both Euthymius and Sabas as active participants in the ecclesiastical struggle of their times, and this wider historico-political perspective contributes to the specific character of his works.

The *vitae* written by Saint Cyril had a decisive influence on early Russian hagiography. The monk Nestor, the great Kievan hagiographer, used Cyril's works as exemplars for his own major work, the *Life of Saint Theodosius*, which contains long excerpts from the *Lives* of Euthymius and Sabas.

Among other great individual *vitae* that were early incorporated into Russian literature we may mention the anonymous *Life of Saint Alexis*, widely renowned throughout the Middle Ages, and the great Slavonic *vitae* such as the *Lives* of Cyril and Method, Apostles to the Slavs, and the Czech saints Ludmila and Wenceslas.

One of the foremost experts on Kievan literature in this century, the Russian scholar I. P. Eremin, called attention (1966) to a remarkable aspect of the earliest translations: they may generally be traced back to Greek originals from the second to the sixth centuries, to the period Krumbacher (1897) called "early Christian." The texts the Byzantine Church translated into the written language of the Orthodox Slavs belong to the "classical" canon of the Christian Church. On the other hand, Byzantine literature from the eleventh and twelfth centuries was practically unknown in Kievan Rus'.

Another essential feature in the translation of Byzantine literature is that non-Christian literature, which Greek authors continued to cultivate in direct imitation of Classical Greek and Hellenic models, had no impact at all in early Russian literature. It is therefore doubtful whether we can talk of a transmission of the Byzantine system of genres, as contended by Stender-Petersen (1963). It was, rather, the system of liturgical and paraliturgical genres of the Byzantine Church that were transmitted to the Slavs. The translations made the Orthodox system of genres a model for the development of indigenous variants among the Slavs. One such type of text is the *vita*. As mentioned above, there were already Russian variants in Kievan times, and in the following centuries the *vita* became one of the most productive genres in early Russian literature. It was a living literary form up to the end of the seventeenth century. After the adoption of the Western European genre system from the second part of the seventeenth century onwards, the Lives of saints, like icon-painting, were to become "gesunkenes Kulturgut." Icon-painting has, however, come into its own again, thanks to the combined efforts of art historians and restorers. Nothing like this has yet happened to the Lives of saints, even if Russian scholars have repeatedly emphasised their importance for the understanding of early Russian literature. A main reason for the slowness of their rediscovery is no doubt to be found in the relative absence of adequate methods of analysis. A survey of hagiographical studies as they have been pursued since V. O. Ključevskij's fundamental work, *Drevnerusskie Žitija svjatykh kak istoričeskij istočnik* (1871), will demonstrate how the methods used in trying to uncover the distinctive character of the *vita* were taken over from the study of history. The avowed aim was historical, with the result that the aesthetic character of the *vitae* remained hidden.

# Means and Ends in the Study of Early Russian Lives of Saints

Since the turn of the century early Russian saints' Lives have been studied from a number of different angles, which I shall briefly explain here. The approaches of individual scholars and their results will be dealt with in a more detailed discussion of the individual *vitae*.

The scholarly study of early Russian hagiography began with Ključevskij's seminal work of 1871, which is still a standard reference for the emergence of saintly Lives in Northeastern Russia, particularly for the growth of Muscovite hagiography from the fourteenth to the sixteenth centuries. Ključevskij says in his foreword that he had originally begun to examine the Lives hoping to find in them the "most copious and the freshest" source for the study of the part played by the monasteries in the colonisation of Northeastern Russia. He soon had to change his mind, first, because the source proved to be far less fresh and copious than he had believed, and second, because its "poor historical content" could not be used until the whole of the material had been critically examined. Relying on his vast historical knowledge Ključevskij tries to separate fact from fiction and place the individual Lives in their historical context by dating them, tracing the author, establishing his relationship with his saintly protagonist, and identifying his sources, his intellectual background, and his reading. The starting point for Ključevskij's analyses of Muscovite hagiography is the conception of form and content as two clearly definable and separate entities, where the form, being specifically literary and hagiographical, encompasses a core of historical facts. It is the scholar's task to extricate or prise out this historical core from the framework of hagiographical conventions.

This, however, turned out to be much more complicated than Ključevskij had at first thought:

> it will be very difficult to find any literary genre where the form prevails to a greater extent over the content and subjects it to its fixed, unchangeable rules. This appears as the most serious barrier between the scholar and historical fact as contained in the *vita:* a critical analysis of the *vita* has to start with a study of its form. (1871:358)

From his critical studies of the Lives of saints Ključevskij concluded that the *vitae* have no historical source value. The hagiographer's task had not been to represent historical facts; it had consisted in elucidating "ethical paradigms" derived from the alien world of Eastern monasticism through the accounts of Russian saints' lives. This, according to Ključevskij (1871:432), explains the hagiographer's indifference to biographical fact "v ego dejstvitel'noj prostote."

Because Ključevskij regarded formal complexity and historical truth as inversely proportional factors, he concluded that the miracle stories were the most reliable element of the Lives. The miracles had a more documentary character than the other parts of the *vita*, as in this part of the Life the discourse is "least marked by the hagiographer's conventional devices, *loci communes* and stereotyped conceptions: judging by its literary form it is mostly a faithful rendering of naive tales told by the healed themselves" (1871:438).

Ključevskij undertook his analysis of the early Russian saint's Life presupposing a dichotomy between its form—the literary, that is, conventional and artificial, imported elements—and historical facts, which are excluded, hidden, or distorted in the hagiographer's endeavours to adapt his historical material to hagiographical schemes. In Ključevskij's conception form becomes a clearly negative element, while the value of the Lives is represented by historical facts, their core of reality. This was to become the prevailing view in subsequent investigations of the Lives of saints and their place in Russian literature. Scholars continued to examine the hagiographical texts to try to trace possible historical facts. Their aim was to isolate all extraneous matter, everything that the early Russian hagiographers had taken over from other sources. Thus, the *vitae* have been subjected to extensive textual criticism with a view to uncovering and identifying borrowings and quotations from Byzantine and Slavonic sources (e.g., Šakhmatov 1896, Bugoslavskij 1914, Tschiževskij 1950, and in particular Siefkes 1970:149-271). Another objective was to clarify the relationship between extant variants of the same work, or between different versions of the same theme in works belonging to different genres (e.g., Müller 1954, Fennell and Stokes 1974). At the same time there have been scholars who tried to overcome Ključevskij's negative assessment of the historical value of the Lives; this could be done by placing them in their historical contexts and analysing their significance in the history of ideas (e.g., Kadlubovskij 1902, Fedotov 1931, Likhačev 1962), and by trying to find traces of the politico-historical development in the hagiographical texts (e.g., Adrianova-Peretc 1947b).

However, it has proved to be the case that the Lives of saints cannot be understood even as documents in the history of ideas or as contributions in the political power struggle without prior analyses of the specific modes of expression belonging to the genre.

Like their colleagues in other parts of Europe, medieval Russian hagiographers worked with a set of stereotyped formulae that they applied in conformity with conventional rules prescribed by the genre, without necessarily conforming to historical reality. Ključevskij (1871) warned against confusing the hagiographer's *loci communes* with factual information about the historical lives of the saints.

The *loci communes*, or *koinoi topoi*, of hagiography must be regarded as a supplementary rhetorical repository from which the individual hagiographers selected their phrases, combining them into continuous accounts of their saints' childhood, adolescence, ascetic achievements, death, and glorification, according to the rules of the genre. Inspired by Western European *topos* research Tschiževskij (1956c), especially, studied the use of *koinoi topoi*, or "expressional constants" in early Russian saints' Lives. He based his studies on the Lives of the saints Stephen of Perm and Sergius of Radonež written by the monk Epiphanius the Wise, the most distinguished Russian hagiographer in the years around 1400.

An inventory by Tschiževskij (1956c) of the different introductory *topoi* in Epiphanius' Lives shows that his introductions were composed of such stock phrases, intended for this particular section of the *vita*. Observations of this kind form an important corrective to the many naive attempts to construe the hagiographers' conventional expressions of self-abasement, their references, their invitations to their audience, and similar devices as direct vehicles for the private thoughts, wishes, and moods of the individual author. That references in the *vitae* to an historical reality outside the text so often turn out to be pure convention makes it difficult to infer anything about the hagiographer's personality and the genesis of a *vita* on the strength of its text alone. Corroboration from other, more reliable sources is always necessary.

Present-day *topos* research must be regarded as a special field in what is usually called "stylistics" in the study of the Russian *vita*. This field is not limited to hagiography, but relates to other genres as well (see Tvorogov 1964). "Style" is not an unambiguous term in the study of literature as understood by the Russians. It is used differently by different scholars. For Adrianova-Peretc (1947a) it signifies primarily the means of expression used by the various genres, which she has studied in a number of works. By the term "hagiographical style" Adrianova-Peretc (1964) understands a system of specific hagiographical means of expression, seen as a "religious shell" covering a "kernel," the hagiographer's representation of reality. This "shell" is not compact. In the various texts the hagiographical style is crossed by other systems, and at the points of intersection historical reality shows through the idealising idiom of the hagiographer. This background of historical reality is the object of Adrianova-Peretc's stylistic analyses. Deviations from the hagiographical norm become particularly significant, because we here "discover a departure from the abstract religious ideal, elements of psychological analysis, of truthful description of social background, which uncovers existential situations behind the religious shell—be it in man's struggle with himself or in his clashes with the environment, and

with the background he has abandoned to enter a monastery" (1964:70).
In this view the hagiographical style of the *vitae* becomes important
mainly as a stage in the development towards a realism Adrianova-
Peretc (1958) finds to be characteristic of early Russian literature in the
seventeenth century, a stage which was negated and overcome in the
course of historical progress. It could be said that Ključevskij's negative
evaluation of the formal elements of the Lives has here been superseded
by a dialectical conception of the history of early Russian literature as
moving towards an increasingly realistic and truthful image of reality.
An evolutionary approach also underlies the analyses of the hagiographical style of the early Russian *vita* undertaken by D. S. Likhačev
(1958, 1967, 1970, 1973). It is no longer a question of style in the sense of
specific means of expression belonging to a particular literary genre, but
of style in a sense used by art historians, the style of an epoch. In the concept of style thus defined, the various styles of the language of literature
and the stylistic conventions of different genres become subordinate
factors in the representation of reality, of man's inner and outer
qualities, of his social conditions, his relationship with nature, and so
forth. Style in this sense, of the predominating stylistic principle of an
epoch determines not only the forms of literature, but of the visual arts as
well, according to Likhačev (1970:4, 1973:11f.).
Likhačev's style of an epoch comes very close to Jagoditsch's (1934)
use of the term *Gesamtsystem* and to the attempt by N. S. Trubetzkoy
(1973) to describe systematically the place of literature within early
Russian culture. However, there is a significant difference between the
two Vienna Slavists on the one hand and Likhačev on the other. The
former operate with an undifferentiated and static notion of epoch,
whereas Likhačev has introduced a dynamic concept of early Russian
culture as a series of consecutive stages, each with its own stylistic
dominant.
In his analysis of what he calls the "expressive-emotional" style in
Russian hagiography around 1400, Likhačev (1958) compares the *vitae*
written by Epiphanius the Wise, the foremost representative of this style
in its verbal aspect, with icon-painting of the same period. The method
had been anticipated by Trubetzkoy and Jagoditsch in the 1920s and 30s
with direct reference to Oskar Walzel's slogan of a "mutual illumination
of the arts" (*wechselseitige Erhellung der Künste*) (Jagoditsch 1934:65).
The same comparative method finds expression in the works of art
historians such as M. Alpatov and N. Brunov. In their *Geschichte der
altrussischen Kunst* (1932:325ff.) they devoted a chapter to the comparison of icons and saints' Lives. The discovery, at the beginning of our
century, of the aesthetic value of the once much-neglected early Russian
icons brought to the attention of scholars the possibility that similar
values might be hidden in the *vitae*. In contrast to the synchronic
approach of his predecessors Likhačev operates with a diachronic series

of stylistic systems which take predominance over, displace, and replace each other in a hierarchy of genres, where some genres, marked by the prevailing style of a period more clearly than others, emerge as "typical" of their time (Likhačev 1970:4, 72). The early Russian *vita* becomes in Likhačev's view the representative genre of the "expressive-emotional" style around 1400 (see Likhačev 1970:Ch. IV).

On a cursory view it would appear that Likhačev has tried to work out a methodology on the basis of Russian Formalist theories of literary evolution, especially those of Tynjanov (1929). But this impression dissipates as soon as we go further into Likhačev's intentions and methods. In his pioneering work on the concept of man in early Russian literature, *Čelovek v literature drevnej Rusi*, Likhačev tried to demonstrate how the style of "monumental historicism" in the twelfth and thirteenth centuries was superseded by the "expressive-emotional" style of the fourteenth and fifteenth centuries, which in its turn was followed by an idealising biographical style, prevalent in the sixteenth century, until its dissolution in the seventeenth century, when early Russian literature, in a time of transition, produced its first heroic figures of some complexity. This periodisation of early Russian literature on the basis of its image of man is in fact a far cry from Formalist theories of an immanent literary evolution. Likhačev's scheme represents in the last resort a much more conventional view of stylistic development. He sees it as a continuous progression from the schematic rendering of the "immortalised" features of the heroes of monumental historicism, through the "surface psychologism" of the expressive-emotional style, to a realistic portrayal of human character, freed from the literary conventions of the Middle Ages, in the seventeenth century.

This idea of stylistic evolution has been widely accepted in art history. Even at the turn of the century Emanuel Loewy claimed that the history of Greek art could be explained in terms of a development from archaic schematism to the victory of naturalism, in consequence of a gradual approach of *schemata* to perceptible reality. This evolutionary theory was taken over and elaborated by Heinrich Schäfer, who applied it to Egyptian art, and it was soon extended to all fields of art history, where, however, its explanatory value has today come to be regarded with scepticism (see Gombrich 1972). There is thus every reason to view Likhačev's account of stylistic evolution in early Russian literature with similar scepticism, especially as in this case we are dealing with a literature that cannot be traced back to an archaic phase, but which originates in the literary system brought from Byzantium to Russia by the Orthodox Church. A distinctive feature of Likhačev's method is his concentration on the emotive impact of the *vita* as a demonstration of the author's attitude towards his subject. In this respect he differs from both Adrianova-Peretc, who is primarily interested in tracing an historical course of events in the texts, and from Trubetzkoy (1973), who lays particular emphasis on the hagiographer's didactic intention. Likhačev's concentration on the emotional elements as well as his comparison of the Lives with icon-painting was quite plainly anticipated by Jagoditsch (1934), for example in the following characteristic statement: "Both the icon and the *vita* of the fifteenth century are marked by a unique style determined by the religious attitude of mind striving to find expression in them." What is problematic in this method becomes apparent if we compare Likhačev's and Jagoditsch's descriptions of the same style and its emotional meaning.

Although each of these scholars takes Epiphanius the Wise and the style of contemporary icon-painting as a starting point, Likhačev maintains that the style expresses the hagiographer's emotional exaltation, while Jagoditsch interprets it as an expression of a serene inner calm, which he finds also in icon-painting, where Likhačev, on the other hand, sees a reflection of the artist's highly strung emotions in his shimmering strokes. A method that leads to such conflicting conclusions about the same object is clearly based on an inadequate theoretical foundation. In this case the theoretical failure consists in a confusion of form and meaning, of the *signantia* and the *signata* of the two different media, and in the direct comparison of isolated formal components, verbal and visual. Both scholars have based their conclusions on immediate impressions of texts and pictures, instead of analysing their structure in order to define the principles underlying the selection and combination of stylistic elements in Lives and icons respectively. Likhačev and Jagoditsch are both content to interpret the emotional meaning of the style on the basis of their own emotional responses to the texts. They rely on empathy rather than on analysis.

This approach will necessarily lead to subjectivism. A comparison between hagiography and icon-painting with regard to common emotional content cannot rely on a mere collocation of more or less randomly selected elements. Comparisons of this kind call for systematic analyses of the expressional value of the constituent components within the structure of the given texts and pictures. This requires a thorough knowledge of the codes governing the individual hagiographers' and icon painters' artistic means of expression. A very interesting attempt at a comparative approach has been made by Konrad Onasch (1977), who has tried to decipher a selection of early Russian saints' Lives and icons with the help of the Byzantine *Urbild-Abbild-Aesthetik*. Comparisons between hagiographical texts and icons require that image and word express a meaning that remains constant when translated from one medium to another, a problem we shall revert to at length in the discussions of the *Lives* of Saint Theodosius and Saint Stephen. It is particularly pertinent to the discussion of *vitae* and icon-painting in the period around 1400 and Likhačev's theory about the second South Slav influence in Russian culture.

With the exception of Onasch, what the scholars here mentioned have in common is that their analyses of early Russian Lives are primarily focused on extrinsic factors. They approach the texts from a stylistic angle, with a view to establishing their historical, psychological, or didactic values. As early as 1871 Ključevskij had shown how both the hagiographer's representation of a saintly Life and the expression of his emotional engagement are conditioned by the conventions of the genre and lose their meaning when taken out of their context. This has been further confirmed by recent topos research (Tschiževskij 1956c). Ključevskij explained the conventional character of the *vita* as a result of its didactic intention. In his overemphasis on the didactic function of the Lives, Ključevskij failed to see their aesthetic value. In the light of the last century's cult of genius and originality, the hagiographer's conventional devices came to be regarded as mere stereotypes. What is particularly striking in the various scholars' aims and methods is the correlation between their methodological basis and the results of their investigations. This is related to a more general phenomenon. We approach a work of art with our various backgrounds and expectations, which in their turn affect our observations and thereby also our experience of the work in question. Similarly, what psychologists call a "mental set" (Gombrich 1972) determines our choice of method and, ultimately, our conclusions. Depending on our orientation, different structures are foregrounded in our perception. It is possible that the set towards external factors, towards the author's emotions, the historical context of the saint, and the responses of the audience, is the reason why the structure and intrinsic value of the Lives have for so long attracted relatively scant attention.

A Russian scholar keenly aware of this problem was I. P. Eremin. In a number of papers on early Russian literature he criticised the one-sided emphasis on extrinsic factors, pointing out the need to rediscover the specific "system of aesthetic principles" in early Russian literature (1966:249). In his textual analyses as well as in his more theoretical works Eremin called attention to a feature in the writings of early Russian authors that may provide a key to their aesthetic function.

According to Eremin (1966:245-254) early Russian literature is marked by an antinomy between two different systems: we have on the one hand the factuality of official records which is in itself devoid of poetical meaning and on the other a system of literary conventions that permit of a "constant transformation of reality" on the model of a given set of ideals. This system can be used separately, along with, or projected onto the former. Although Eremin left us with only an outline of his method, his insight provides a useful starting point for an attempt to define the poetic value and distinctive structure of the early Russian Lives of saints.

Eremin's approach differs from the others we have discussed in his set towards the text as such, his focusing on the system of internal relations between its constituents. This is also the general basis for the hagio-graphical studies in the present work. But a more detailed theoretical foundation is needed. This brings us to Roman Jakobson's definition of the poetic function of language, and his opposition between *selection* (the paradigmatic axis of language) and *combination* (the axis of con-catenation) as the two cardinal operations of the speech act. The units of any discourse are selected from a given stock and combined with others according to codified rules. In the first case a "selection among alternatives implies the possibility of substituting one for the other, equivalent to the former in one respect and different from it in another. Actually, selection and substitution are two faces of the same operation" (1956). Selection is an internal relationship based on the *similarity* of substitution sets. On the paradigmatic axis the units are mutually con-nected by various forms and degrees of *similarity:* "likeness, similitude, equivalence, resemblance, analogy, diverse grades of specification, contrast" (1966a). Combination, on the other hand, is based on the external relationship of *contiguity*: "neighbourhood, proximity and remoteness, subordination and coordination" (1966a). Inflection, derivation, and predication are also based on the principle of contiguity. Moreover, any combination creates a context: "combination and contexture are two faces of the same operation" (1956). Selection thus "deals with entities conjoined in the code," whereas combination deals with entities conjoined both in the code and in the actual message, or only in the latter.

The polarity between selection, based on the principle of similarity, and combination, based on the principle of contiguity, manifests itself in a number of different and diverse dichotomies in the use of language, including the development of a discourse in which "one topic may lead to another through their similarity or through their contiguity" (1956). The first of these processes is the "metaphoric way," since it finds its most condensed expression in metaphor, whereas the second, the "metonymic way," can be demonstrated by metonymy (including synecdoche). In the normal use of language there is a constant interac-tion between these two modes of arrangement. But under the influence of such factors as cultural patterns, individual personality, and verbal style, preference is given to one of the processes over the other. This means that in a given message or text we shall find either a metaphoric or a metonymic structural dominance. This applies not only to verbal texts, but also to texts in a far wider sense of the word, as this bipolar structure is characteristic not only of language, but holds good for any semiotic system, for primitive magic, painting, and the modern art of the cinema (Jakobson 1956).

In the study of literature this theory of the bipolar structure of all semi-otic systems and of the predominance in a given text of one pole over the other may serve as a starting point for our analyses of individual works of art with regard to their structural dominant. Furthermore, the theory may provide us with a clue to the place of individual works in their wider context, given the oscillation between metaphoric and metonymic predominance, conditioned by external factors such as genre, personality, and cultural patterns.

For the study of literature the application of this method will imply that attention is focused on various forms of juxtaposition and repetition of identical elements in different contexts, and of elements similar or contiguous to each other. The concept of parallelism will be fundamental. In actual fact the concept of parallelism also underlies Jakobson's definition of the poetic function of language as the projection of the principle of equivalence from the axis of selection into the axis of combination, so that equivalence is promoted to the constitutive device of the sequence (1960:358). This definition implies that verbal art consists precisely in a systematic creation of paradigmatic relations between the constituents in a sequence, so that in this intentional variety of correspondences between the units an ambiguity is created which is typical of all poetry, in contrast to the cognitive forms of verbal communication, where "disambiguation" is the aim. A literary analysis concentrating on the poetic function of a text will thus first and foremost aim at tracing paradigmatic relationships between the constituents and at trying to establish their underlying systems.

In numerous analyses of individual poems from many literatures Jakobson (1981) has shown how fruitful his functional method may be for the study of subliminal structural patterns in the phonological and grammatical levels of these poems, and of the significance of these patterns for the poem as a whole. Jakobson's analyses of the poetic function of language have focused mainly on the systematic exploitation of the sound system of a given language in verse. In principle, however, nothing should prevent us from transferring this method of analysis to that category of verbal art in which the poetic function becomes manifest primarily on the *signatum* level, "the prosaic variety of verbal art" (Jakobson 1960:374), distinguishable from poetry in its narrower sense, that is, verse, through a higher degree of translatability.

In prose the referential function of language will usually be more preponderant than in pure poetry. The imitation of nonverbal forms of reality and other nonverbal sign systems becomes preponderant: kinship relations, ritual patterns, myths, ideological systems, etc., structures which have been called "secondary modelling systems" in Russian structuralist terminology (see, for example, Lotman 1965a). It is characteristic of these systems that they do not necessarily have their origin in language, but the information imparted by them remains embedded in language.

On the *signatum* level the projection of the axis of equivalence into the axis of combination may thus be assumed to manifest itself in a juxtaposition of segments from various secondary modelling systems in order to establish paradigmatic relations between them. As a result of a recoding, the *signata* of one system are expressed through another system's segments, which thereby in addition to their referential function now connote the meaning of those segments of which they are expressions. This means, in other words, that the *signans* and the *signatum* of the segments belonging to one system together function as the *signans* in a new, connotative system of meaning in which the segments of the other function as the *signatum*. What is achieved on the lexical level through metaphoric and metonymic constructions is at a higher level realised through selection and combination of textual segments on the same principles.

A definition of the art of prose as such a combination of textual segments from various secondary systems into a system of connotations will be particularly important for the study of hagiographical literature, where the heterogeneous character of the text has always been a stumbling block.

Further, this definition will take analysis in a direction diametrically opposed to traditional hagiographical research, where the professed aim has been to purge the tale of a saint's life of the load of quotations and loans from other texts, which have been regarded by modern hagiologists and literary historians as confusing and redundant elements, and even as evidence of the medieval hagiographers' low cultural level, poor taste, and primitive technique. The hagiographers' use of loans and quotations is conditioned by the genre and is a characteristic feature of this form of verbal art which cannot be removed without destroying the distinctive character of the *vita*. It becomes therefore a main task for hagiographical research to study the interplay between the author's own narrative and his borrowings from other texts, between narration and quotation.

My investigations focus on this interplay to show how it is conditioned by the bipolarity underlying the hagiographer's selection and combination of elements.

Both my method and my aim call for a limitation of the number of hagiographical texts to be examined. I have chosen, therefore, to examine in some detail three of the best-known Lives, from different periods but each representative of hagiography in its own particular era: Nestor's *Life of Saint Theodosius* from the end of the eleventh century, Epiphanius the Wise's *Life of Saint Stephen, Bishop of Perm*, written about 1400, and Avvakum's autobiographical Life, dating from the 1670s. These three *vitae* in turn stand for the three main periods in early Russian literature, the Kievan era, the early Muscovite age, and the era of transition in the seventeenth century. Of these works, the *Life of Saint*

*Theodosius* has received the least attention; the *Life of Saint Stephen* has been examined by a number of scholars, particularly from a stylistic point of view, and is today regarded as the apex of early Russian hagiography, while Avvakum's account of his own life is now more widely considered to be an autobiography in the modern sense of that word rather than a hagiographical work. Viewed thus it would represent a breach with the conventions of the *vita* genre, signalling a new form of literature, a view I shall discuss in some detail in my own analysis of the Life.

An investigation of these *vitae* from the point of view of genre presupposes an understanding of its invariant structural schemes. These cannot be deduced from early Russian texts alone, but must be established on the basis of a study of early Christian hagiography.

In my discussion of twentieth-century studies of early Christian hagiography I hope to establish the abstract invariant schemes underlying the structure of early Christian saints' Lives. Because of the markedly conventional character of the genre, we must assume that these schemes also underlie the works of early Russian hagiographers.

## Early Christian hagiography and Literary History

In our survey of translated Kievan hagiography we saw that the term refers not to a single type of text or genre, but to a number of interrelated genres, all centred around a saintly hero.

In Western Europe the hagiographical genres are collectively referred to by the medieval term *legenda*. One of the most popular anthologies of the late Middle Ages is the *Legenda aurea*, compiled by the bishop of Genoa, Jacobus de Voragine, at the end of the thirteenth century.

In the hierarchy of hagiographical genres, *vita* and *passio* are hybrid categories, combinations of lesser genres such as novella-like stories, dialogues, letters, encomia, miracle tales, visions, etc. strung together on a simple additive principle or integrated into higher, more complex structures. A brief biography may be added to a martyr story under the heading *Vita et passio, Bios kai marturion*. The eulogy of the saint, the *enkōmion*, may be enlarged through the addition of tales from the saint's life into a text of the type *Praxeis kai periodoi enkōmiō sumpeplegmenai*. Similar combinations were common in Kievan hagiography; combinations such as *S"kazanie i strast' i pokhvala, Č'tenie i pamjat'*, and *Mučenie i žitie* can all be found in the *Uspenskij sbornik*, the great collection of manuscripts from the twelfth and the thirteenth centuries.

The early Christian *vitae* as well as the medieval anthologies of hagiographical legends form a motley collection of highly heterogeneous texts, where the same plot or motif may occur in a number of variants, grafted on to the life-stories of saints from different backgrounds and ages. The legends of the saints may thus recall the oral genres of folklore, myth, and folk tales. They differ, however, from the folk tale by being clearly defined in space and time and by being put forward as true, and from myth by evolving not a single motif but usually combining several motifs and grouping them around a single hero. In this respect the saintly legend comes closer to the heroic tale (Gad 1961:3f.).

The use in the Lives of hagiographical devices, of current motifs, *topoi*, and plots is, from an aesthetic point of view, evidence of their poetic character, while to the historian all this is redundant and has to be cleared away before real research can start. The leading figure in this "tidying-up operation" was the Bollandist Hippolyte Delehaye. In a number of important studies he analysed early Christian and medieval hagiography precisely with a view to ridding it of all those fictitious elements that had in the course of time formed encrustations around the saints' historical figures. Through this methodical cleaning-up process he sought to uncover the historical core, if any, of the hagiographical texts under scrutiny.

Among Delehaye's works two, especially, are important for the study of hagiography: *Les légendes hagiographiques* (1905; see Delehaye 1962) and *Les passions des martyrs et les genres littéraires* (1921). According to Delehaye hagiographical legend presupposes as its theme or starting point an historical fact. This fact constitutes the first and most important element of the legend and is opposed to its fictitious element. The relationship between these two elements varies from one text to another. The texts may be classified accordingly as history or as legend in the narrower sense of a nonhistorical account or tale, depending on whether the predominant element is factual or fictitious (1962:8). A legend is born through a process of fictionalisation in which historical facts are transformed. This distortion of historical truth is effected in two ways (1962:II–III, 12–85). The former method has the character of a popular, collective, and unconscious transformation, while the latter represents a conscious literary revision. The former, whereby historical material is turned into folklore, transforms the saint's individual features according to typical patterns, ignores historical and geographical data, and elucidates abstracts through concrete images. The saint's biography is represented by a limited range of conventional motifs. This popular transformation is regarded by Delehaye as a corruption of the original. The work of the professional hagiographer consisted in writing a coherent work about a particular saint based on the material at his disposal and following a programme usually set out in the introduction to the *vita*. Only in exceptional cases did the hagiographer base himself on factual historical material. Moreover, his idea of history was different from ours, and he was of course ignorant of the methods used by present-day historians in separating facts from fiction and reconstructing the distinctive features of an historical personality or a particular era. In the Middle Ages history and legend overlapped. Everything that was told, everything that was read, was history. As emphasised by Gad (1961:5), the logical conclusion of Delehaye's studies must be that the "legend as an historical source is reduced ad absurdum," that it is fiction, "and ought to be examined as literature from the point of view of literary history."

A similar corollary was in fact drawn by Delehaye himself in both the introductory and final chapters of the 1927 edition of *Les légendes hagiographiques*. He concluded that the legends of the saints were a kind of verbal art, possessing in their unsophisticated way some of the sublime poetry of the old cathedrals, a divine beauty, shining more intensely when its transcendent radiance breaks through the hagiographer's simple devices. Against the background of Delehaye's original purpose this conclusion is quite paradoxical. Even if *Les légendes hagiographiques* earned its author the attribute "dénicheur des saints" from conservative Roman Catholic quarters, when the book first appeared, it must be remembered that it had been intended as an attack on the disrespectful study undertaken by literary historians of the literary, fictional aspect of the legends. From an apologetic point of view Delehaye's book still has this function (see Peeters 1962:207ff.)

A representative of the school attacked by Delehaye is Heinrich Günter, who studied the legends as an historian of religion and as a psychologist. He was almost exclusively interested in the miracle motifs and their connection with similar motifs in the literatures of non-Christian religions. In his studies Günter demonstrated that a number of these motifs are common to Christian, Hellenistic, and Hebrew literatures, which he accounts for by the theory that these basic motifs are *Menschheitswünsche,* collective expressions of human desire which remain constant throughout the series of historically conditioned variations (1949:5). In contrast to Delehaye and the Bollandists, Günter stressed the *Doppelsein* of the legends, their ambiguous position between history and fiction, instead of drawing systematic distinctions between these two elements. Günter's view seems more justified, because the writing of history and legend was generically closely associated in medieval times, when factual events acquired their historical significance only by being interpreted into a divine scheme. It is a characteristic medieval feature that "l'histoire particulière s'inscrit toujours dans l'histoire du salut" (Leclercq 1957:151). The value of Günter's method rests in his attempt to trace the multiplicity of legendary forms back to a limited number of constant motifs, provided that these motifs are no longer defined psychologically, in terms of *Menschheitswünsche*, but seen as literary invariants. In the individual legends such recurrent motifs will be realised in their contextual variants and integrated into larger narrative patterns. The identification of conventional motifs will therefore be less important than discovering the principles regulating their selection and combination into higher narrative units, allowing us to group the legends according to the patterns underlying their composition.

The modern study of hagiographical composition was inaugurated by German classical scholars well before the turn of the century, when men like Weingarten (1877), Usener (1879), Reitzenstein (1906), Mertel (1909), and Holl (1912) showed that neither the Christian veneration of saints nor hagiography represented anything wholly new, but that the cult of saints and its literary expressions have their roots in pre-Christian hero worship and in the literary genres of Late Antiquity. Early Christian hagiography took over genres and motifs from the pagan tradition, combining them in new ways and adapting them to fit its own aims, but not infrequently retaining the basic patterns of the older texts. The function of such literary patterns may be compared to the role of late-antique iconography in early Christian art. The choice of prototypes or compositional schemes influences the hagiographer's account of the life of his protagonist in much the same way as the icon painter's choice of iconographical models determines the holy image. Both the hagiographer and the icon painter perceive their subject through conventional patterns, transforming their saintly heroes according to forms inherited from a pre-Christian tradition. But in this process traditional schemes are in their turn modified and adapted to the material and intentions of the Christian artist, so that the individual *vita*, the individual icon, if it is a work of art, will be something more than a mere copy of the scheme. This is particularly true of early Christian hagiography, in which old forms had to be restructured in order to serve the purpose of the new faith. Consequently, there is also a moment of discontinuity in the transition from late-antique to Christian forms of expression. Recently there has been a tendency to stress this aspect of early Christian art and literature and to move away from the position of Usener and his school of comparative religion. Peter Brown (1981:6), for instance, has in a number of studies stressed the difference between the Christian cult of saints and pagan hero worship, between the art of the new religion and its Graeco-Roman models, going so far as saying that to "explain the Christian cult of martyrs as a continuation of the pagan cult of heroes helps as little as to reconstruct the form and function of a late-antique Christian basilica from the few columns and capitals taken from classical buildings that are occasionally incorporated in its arcades." It is characteristic of Brown's critique, however, that he is more concerned with individual details than with patterns and structures, ignoring the fact that the early Christian basilica was connected with pre-Christian architecture in a much more fundamental way than by a handful of spoils mounted into its arcades. In actual fact, the Christian basilica is an imitation of the Roman cult basilica and represents a direct continuation of an imperial building. Furthermore, its relationship to pre-Christian architecture has a parallel in the relationship of early Christian painting to imperial iconography: the Christian pictorial schemes are variants of types and patterns developed in connection with the cult of the Roman emperor, not images created spontaneously by representatives of the new creed. The correspondences between pagan and early Christian literature, described by Usener and his school, may be defined as the verbal aspect of this development. But whereas the school of comparative *Religionsgeschichte* focused on the pagan tradition and often tended to reduce early Christian literature to a kind of *gesunkenes Kulturgut,* it would seem to be more rewarding to try to find out how the old patterns were modified and given new values in the context of early Christian hagiography.

The research carried out by Usener, Reitzenstein, and others shows that hagiographical legends like the short anecdotal novellas found in early Christian anthologies represent, in the guise of an apparently artless naturalism, many of the action patterns underlying ancient myths and folk tales. In many of these narratives the same plot is carried over from one protagonist to the other with only slight alterations. Only a few stand out from the great mass of stories through a more individualised characterisation of the hero and his environment, attracting the attention of the modern reader by their depiction of everyday life in early Christian convents and monasteries. One such story, found in the early fifth-century *Historia Lausiaca* by Palladius of Helenopolis (1974:162-167), tells of the recluse Piterum and the mad nun at Tabennisi in the Upper-Egyptian Thebaid.

The only otherworldly element of the story is the angel who appears before the holy Piterum, bidding him to go to the convent at Tabennisi where he will find a nun wearing a diadem on her head who is more worthy than himself. Apart from this incident the modern reader is struck by the grotesque account of the nuns: Piterum arrives at the convent where the nun, pretending to be mad, is living in abysmal misery. She is despised by all the other nuns, who leave her to do all the most menial tasks in the convent kitchen, scorned and scoffed at in every way. Because of her madness, she is not allowed to wear a nun's *koukoulion,* or cowl, but has to walk about in penitential apparel, a rag wrapped around her head. The holy man demands to see all the nuns. None of them is the right one, and he understands that one must be missing. He demands that she, too, be present. The nuns reply that all of them are present except the mad nun in the kitchen. When Piterum wants to see her, she refuses to appear and has to be brought forth forcibly. Seeing the rag on her forehead he prostrates himself at her feet and asks her blessing, while at the same time she casts herself down before him asking his blessing. The other nuns come running along, shouting: "Abba, do not let yourself be fooled, she is mad!" But he answers that it is they who are mad and that she is their "amma," their spiritual mother. They all go down on their knees and confess their sins against the mad nun. One has emptied the swill over her head, another has attacked her with her bare fists, a third one has smeared her nose with mustard ... Now they repent. But she cannot bear the honour and the fame. After a few days she vanishes. "Where she went and where she is, and how she ended her days, nobody knew."

Reitzenstein (1906) saw in this story a version of the Cinderella tale, but the interpretation thus suggested received no further development in his study, and in order to understand the Christian meaning of Palladius' story, it is not enough to define the mad nun as a Christianised Cinderella. Rather we must turn to Palladius' text and the religious message conveyed by the mad nun's story.

If we return to the opening paragraph of Palladius' account, we shall see that the central theme of the nun's feigned madness has been brought together with a quotation from Saint Paul in a way that draws our attention to the analogy between the words of the narrator and those of the Bible. The nun, "pretending to be mad [*hupokrinomenē mōrian*] ... fulfilled in deed that which is written: 'If any man among you seemeth to be wise in this world, let him become a fool [*mōros genesthō*], that he may be wise'" (1 Cor. 3:18). We see that the aesthetic effect of this juxtaposition is greatly diminished in the English translation, where *mōrian* and *mōros* are rendered by "mad" and "a fool" respectively, with the result that the sound similarity between the two closely related Greek words is lost. In the Greek text this similarity underlines the semantic parallel between Saint Paul' gnomic paradox and the nun's behaviour, thereby transforming the story into an image of the truth concealed in the quotation. The relationship between her apparent madness and the higher wisdom hidden underneath it corresponds to the relationship between the rag of cloth she has wrapped around her forehead and the diadem the angel says she is wearing. The diadem is the heavenly counterpart of the rag. The whole story is based on an inverted symbolism where life on earth in its most humble and despised forms serves as the visible analogue of an invisible glory transcending the world of the senses. What to the modern reader would at first seem to be an instance of grotesque naturalism was to an early Christian audience a profoundly symbolic tale, representing the nun's life in the convent in negative analogy to her real, "upperworldly" existence.

Another example of this negative, or inverted, symbolism in early Christian literature, this time with a male protagonist, is found in the story of Euphrosynus, a Byzantine *mini-vita* dating from some time between the fourth and the seventh centuries.

When he was shorn a monk and "clothed in angelic habit," Euphrosynus was filled with the "meekness of Christ" and, being an unlearned man, had to spend all his time in the kitchen of the monastery, scorned and humiliated by the other monks. His face was always grimy with soot, his clothes wretched and dirty. One night the abbot's most fervent prayer is granted and he is carried away in spirit to a wonderful garden whose guardian is none other than the cook Euphrosynus. In reply to the abbot's question what kind of garden this is, Euphrosynus tells him, repeating in full the verse from Saint Paul already quoted by the abbot: "Eye hath not seen, nor ear heard, neither have entered into the heart of man, the things which God hath prepared for them that love him" (1 Cor. 2:9). The next morning the abbot relates his experience to the brethren. But before he has finished, Euphrosynus slips through a side door and leaves the monastery "to flee human fame, and has not turned up again to this day."

Euphrosynus' story, like that of the mad nun, is based on the antithesis of heaven and earth which "runs obsessively through the literature of the period" (Brown 1978:16). His sooty appearance is the earthly, negative image of his inner divine self, much as the nun's madness is a symbol of her wisdom.

This art of representing the divine and the lofty in the idiom of inversion and travesty has a long tradition in pre-Christian literature, reaching back to the symbolism of archaic regeneration myths and rites. In these symbolic representations of death as rebirth and new life, the god and the divine ruler would descend into the nether world and be transformed into a slave, a criminal, a fool, or a cook. All these lowly and base figures are "death metaphors," to borrow Olga Frejdenberg's term (1936:235). In her studies of ancient Greek comedy she has shown how the comic genres grew out of archaic representations of death, as parodic inversions and outrageous mockery of the divine in its sublime and serious aspect. Death was conceived as the wrong side of life, as life turned inside out, so to speak. In Olga Frejdenberg (1978:282ff.), this "other side" of life and of the divine is referred to as its *hubristic* aspect, a concept I should like to adopt and apply to such phenomena as feigned madness and self-abasement in Christian hagiography. In pre-Christian literature this *hubrism* will be known to modern readers from Plato, in particular from Alcibiades' speech in the *Symposium*, where Socrates is compared to the figures of Silenus found in statuaries' shops, in which he is represented holding flutes and pipes, but which conceal little figures of gods that are revealed when the statues are taken apart. The legendary figure of Socrates, hiding his insight underneath the popular mask of the bewildered fool, is Plato's version of the ambivalent image of wise ignorance, which re-emerges in early Christian literature in such figures as Euphrosynus and the mad nun at Tabennisi.

By defining their humiliation as the *hubristic* side of their holiness, we are able to bring out the metaphorical meaning of the grotesque naturalism found in Christian hagiography. The saints' lives on earth have a symbolic function, representing life in the "nether world" as a temporal inversion of their divine, "upperworldly" existence. The art of this literature is grounded on the principle of contrast, reducing the points of similarity between the "earthly" and the "upperworldly," the visible and the invisible, to a minimum, so that the earthly lives of the saints are seen as negative parallels of their eternal glory. This paradoxical art corresponds to the negative theology developed in the writings of Dionysius the Areopagite. In his system the cataphatic, affirmative way of knowing God, and the negative, apophatic method, are complementary. In aesthetic terms this means that God can be represented in both "similar" and "dissimilar" images, the latter being, however, more suitable than the former to the representation of the transcendent reality of the divine: "If then, as far as the divine is concerned, the negations are true, while affirmations are inadequate to the secret character of the mysteries, it is more appropriate that the invisible should be revealed through dissimilar images" (CH, II, 3, 141 A).

Another early Christian genre where ancient forms have been given a new function is the apocryphal Acts of the Apostles. In spite of many similarities in design and motifs, these works differ considerably from the canonical Acts and in many ways recall the four Gospels. Like them they consist of a number of stories about the protagonist's words and acts combined with a final passion story (see Hägg 1983, in particular 154–165).

The apocryphal Acts of the Apostles represent their individual adventures in the form of a travelogue. The Apostle's sermons alternate with miracle stories about his healing of the sick and resurrection of the dead, with descriptions of his struggle against idolatry and warlocks. When in peril, he is rescued by a miracle: imprisoned but released by divine intervention, thrown into the arena but untouched by the wild beasts, or saved in other ways, until he is put to death in the concluding passion sequence. The chastity motif is much in evidence, but usually in connection with piquant erotic situations and a religious teaching of a marked gnostic slant (Gad 1961:73). This combination points not only to the Hellenistic Graeco-Oriental novel as a generic parallel, but also to non-Christian aretalogies of philosophers and prophets and similar genres (Reitzenstein 1906; Kerényi 1927:207). Again, it is not the superficial similarities between the apocryphal Acts and late-antique genres such as the Greek novel that are important; the correspondences are interesting from a literary point of view because the stories of the Apostles and of the separations, quests, and recognitions of loving couples or family members in the Greek novel may be seen as transformations of a plot that also underlies the representations of cyclical death and renewal in myth and ritual (cf. Kerényi 1927, Frejdenberg 1936). The correspondences at this level between different types of text show that neither the late-antique novel nor early Christian hagiographical literature is pure entertainment or even entertainment with an additional didactic function, as has often been maintained. Rather, they are the verbal expressions of a mythical world-view in which conceptual contrasts such as life and death, affirmation and negation, deification and abasement, are not absolutely opposed to each other, but are complementary: life is fraught with death and death with birth, affirmation implies negation, humiliation is the other side of *theosis*. Both the Christian protagonist of the Acts of the Apostles and the Isis-*mustes* in Apuleius' *Golden Ass*, conquer death through their suffering and prove worthy of deification through the god for whose sake and in whose image they have undertaken to suffer.

The hagiographical genre of imitative suffering *par excellence* is still not the apocryphal Acts of the Apostles, but the *passio martyrum*, in which the story of the protagonist's deeds is displaced by an account of his suffering. Martyr Passions are traditionally divided into two categories, the first comprising a handful of texts written down by truthful witnesses and believed to be historically reliable, the second consisting of works in which fiction and fantasy have been substituted for the historical facts of the original records. The "genuine" martyr Passions are regarded as "documents of the first order" (Delehaye 1921:182), deriving directly from Roman court records and documents from the trial proceedings against Christians, from stenograms and eyewitness accounts of their imprisonment, interrogation, execution, and burial. The texts of the second category, the "fictitious" martyr Passions, compiled and expanded by later editors, are supposed to represent the influence of popular religion on what were originally the works of the enlightened leaders of the Church. Although this "two-tiered" model of early Christian hagiography has been severely criticised by Peter Brown (1981:12ff) and others, those scholars whose interest in hagiography is mainly historical still see it as their main task to "distinguish 'literature' from history in order to keep editor and witness apart" (Delehaye 1921:9). The aim of their research is to recover the factual nucleus of the "genuine" Passion from the layers of fictitious elements added to it in order to satisfy more popular tastes. This nucleus is as a rule confined to the dialogue between the martyr and the Roman judge, together with a note about the sentence. These dialogues are official Roman records and would not as such belong to hagiographical literature, were it not for the fact that they have hardly ever survived in a pure state, but have come down to us as parts of larger narratives, either in combination with other documents, strung together by an editor, or as part of eyewitness accounts of the whole passion sequence. In its hagiographical context the dialogue between the Roman magistrate and the Christian defendant assumes the character of a *pars pro toto,* presupposing a knowledge of the whole trial in order to be understood. At the same time this dialogue, when reproduced as a written record, constitutes a literary genre in its own right, a juxtaposition of two interlocutors representing the opposite poles in a *pro et contra* about life's ultimate questions. This genre, termed *dialogic syncrisis* by Bakhtin (1963:147f.), is well known from the New Testament, where it is found in a number of variations: as a dialogue between the tempted (Christ, the righteous man) and the tempter, the believer and the nonbeliever, the righteous man and the sinner, the beggar and the rich man, the follower of Christ and the Pharisee, etc. In the martyr Passions, the martyr as the tempted follower of Christ is confronted with the emperor or with one of his deputies, usually the proconsul. In this syncrisis the emperor and his men stand for the powers of evil and the kingdom of this world, whereas the martyr represents the divine powers of Christ and the Kingdom of Heaven. In the context of the martyr Passion the dialogic syncrisis is combined with the corresponding *provocative anacrisis,* the creation of an extraordinary plot situation in order to test the martyr and everything he stands for as an embodiment of the new creed.

That the dialogue between martyr and judge can be seen both as an official Roman document and as a literary genre, depending on the reader's context and point of view, shows that it cannot be adequately decribed exclusively as a legal document and a record of historical fact. When read in its hagiographical perspective, it reveals a different meaning, which transcends mere factography. As part of a *passio* the dialogic syncrisis has become a segment of a whole sequence, where several structures and points of view overlap, with the result that new meanings are generated within the text which do not exist outside it as objective historical facts.

A famous Passion in which this process is particularly evident is the story of Polycarp, the bishop of Smyrna who was martyred in the second half of the second century, probably in 177 A.D. (Camelot 1951:227). The *passio,* written soon after, takes the form of a letter from the Christians of Smyrna to their brethren in Philomelium. The account of Polycarp's martyrdom is told from an eyewitness point of view and written down by a certain Marcion. It is the oldest of the extant Passions and the first example of the genre. It describes how Polycarp tries to escape from his persecutors, how he is seized in his hideout after having been forewarned in a vision three days before that he will be burnt alive. He is taken to town riding on an ass, and finally to the arena, where an excited populace attends his interrogation. As Polycarp enters the stadium, he hears a voice that tells him to take courage. According to the narrator no one could see the speaker, "but those of us who were present heard the voice." In the syncrisis that follows, the proconsul tries to persuade Polycarp to swear by the *genius Caesaris* and thus implicitly to accept the divinity of the emperor. Instead, Polycarp openly declares himself a Christian and is sentenced to death. The spectators, and especially the Jews among them, clamour for his death at the stake. The condemned Polycarp says his last prayer, in which Biblical and liturgical reminiscences are woven together into praise of God for having deemed him worthy of becoming a martyr and thus of sharing in the chalice of Christ. The pyre is lit and the flames blaze up, but the martyr remains unhurt in the middle of the fire, "not like flesh being burnt but like bread being baked." Finally the executioner has to stab him with his dagger. The fire is put out by the martyr's blood. To prevent the Christians from getting hold of his body, it is burnt. The charred remnants of the saint are then reverently collected by the brethren and preserved in a place where the congregation will now come together at the anniversary of Polycarp's death, "the day of his birth, in memory of those who have suffered before us, and in order to prepare those who will have to suffer in the future."

As we can see even from this résumé, the dialogue between Polycarp and the proconsul has been integrated into the sequence of events that together represent the complete action pattern of the trial: arrest, interrogation, and death preceded by suffering are the constant elements of this plot, which unfolds according to its own rules, superimposing on the protagonist its own system of restraints, its own rhythm. But as we can also see, the meaning of the action is different from different points of view: in a legal perspective the events are all part of a judicial examination in which Polycarp proves his guilt by confessing that he is a Christian. To the enraptured crowd Polycarp is the main actor in a true "theatre of cruelty" on a par with the protagonists of the gladiator fights and pantomimes performed in the Roman arena. From this point of view the "genuine" *marturion* is but a transcription of a dramatic spectacle in which the contrast between life and art is obliterated, and the martyr, indistinguishable from his role, suffers a real torture and dies a real death according to a pre-established pattern. From the Christian point of view of the eyewitness narrator, however, this spectacle of cruelty has a different function. To him this sequence of extreme situations serves the task of provoking and testing Polycarp and the truth he embodies "so that the Lord once more could show us a martyrdom in accordance with the Gospel"—*to kata to euangelion marturion*. This is the explicit intention of the author of the *passio Polycarpi*: to represent the events leading up to the account of the martyr's death at the stake in parallel to the Passion story of the Gospels. This is the idea determining both his selection of historical facts and his combination of them into a coherent whole. To the Christian reader, Polycarp's Passion conceals a hidden, esoteric meaning that can be deciphered only by those who are able to see its points of similarity with the Passion of Christ. To the initiate, Polycarp is like Jesus in that he does not give himself up but waits until he is betrayed. He takes refuge in a place outside town like Jesus in Gethsemane, and is betrayed by one of his own servants as Jesus was betrayed by Judas. The police magistrate is called by the name of Herod. It all happened on a Thursday before supper, and like Jesus, Polycarp spends a long time in prayer before he is arrested and taken back to the town, riding on an ass, as Christ once did.

Underlying the *passio Polycarpi* is the idea that Christ is "the model of the Christian" and that his perfect imitator is "the martyr who follows him in his suffering and reproduces his passion in himself" (Delehaye 1921:19). By the juxtaposition of his own text with the text of the Gospels, the author of the letter has produced a new text, which no longer conveys only the historical facts of the martyrdom, but generates a new meaning, representing the martyr as a *mimetēs Christou,* "whose martyrdom *kata to euangelion* everybody wishes to imitate." By turning the news of Polycarp's cruel end into a re-enactment of Christ's Passion, the hagiographer creates a cathartic effect, overcoming the feelings of pity and fear in the reader. For by his "patient endurance" the martyr has triumphed over the "unrighteous magistrate," and having thus received "the crown of immortality" he is now "rejoicing with the Apostles and all the righteous, glorifying God, our Father the Almighty, and praising our Lord, Jesus Christ." By bringing into his account elements that positivist historians seek to remove in order to retrieve the message of the text, the author of Polycarp's Passion has transformed it into a dramatic sequence of events whose ultimate aim is the resurrection and deification of the protagonist in conformity with the divine prototype of Christ. In its basic structure, therefore, the Passion is but another variation upon the pattern that we have found in the apocryphal Acts of the Apostles and in the tales of the mad nun and the monk Euphrosynus. In all these texts the protagonists' humiliation and abasement correspond to the death phase of their existence and their temporal sojourn in the nether world, depicted as an inversion and negative analogy to the divine, eternal upperworld, to which they are reborn through their suffering and death in conformity with Christ.

The paradigmatic function of the Passion of Christ in the Gospels may be shown more clearly if we try to establish a sequence of those events that are common to all four versions. This would give us the following pattern:

1. A confrontation in the form of a trial between Christ, the Son of God, and the representatives of the earthly authorities, the Jewish priests and Pontius Pilate, the Roman governor.
2. The sacrificial death of Christ, the incarnate Godhead, as a mock-king and scapegoat or *pharmakos,* who goes voluntarily to His doom in order to save humanity.

3. The determination by the centurion that Jesus is dead and the laying of His dead body in a tomb.
4. The mourning of the disciples.
5. The recognition or *anagnorisis* of the resurrected Christ, followed by His ascension and *apotheosis* or *theophany*. The moment of recognition coincides with the *peripety*, the sudden reversal of sorrow into joy.

This sequence is practically identical with the framework of traditional incidents underlying some of the great works of ancient Greek drama, such as Euripides' tragedy the *Bacchae* and Sophocles' plays about King Oedipus. It is an action pattern that has its origin in myths and rituals celebrating the death and rebirth of Dionysus, "the dying God whose defeat is victory, the ironical Buffoon whose folly confounds the pretence of wisdom" (Cornford 1934:XXX).

In the Passion of Christ we have the archetypal Christian counterpart to this drama, in which the Son of God appears as the Son of man and *pharmakos* in order to save the world. As if to reinforce this parallel, the Evangelists have inserted into their Passion story a scene in which the high seriousness of the main events are repeated in a grotesque variation. Forming a "passion within the Passion," as it were, this scene occurs when Jesus is handed over to a band of Roman soldiers, who set up their own "theatre of cruelty," dressing Jesus up in a scarlet robe, putting a crown of thorns on His head, giving Him a reed to hold for a sceptre, falling down before Him in sham obeisance, and hailing Him as King of the Jews. Having performed this mock-rite, they spit upon Him, strike Him with the reed on His head, take the robe off Him, and lead Him away to be crucified. The incident corresponds fairly accurately to the crowning and decrowning of the ephemeral king of the Roman Saturnalia. Elected by lot, this mock-king represented the god in his terrestrial image, enjoying all the prerogatives of a real king during the festival, a period of extreme dissipation and licentiousness, until at the end he was dethroned and, according to some sources, killed as a sacrifice to the god. But when the mock-ritual of the Roman soldiers is transposed to the Gospels its meaning is determined by the new context. Here, the crowning and subsequent decrowning of the mock-king form an inverted parallel to the main sequence, where Crucifixion and death precede the moment of *apotheosis*. What from the Roman soldiers' point of view was the mocking of a criminal soon to be executed has become, in the larger context of the Passion story, a representation of the death phase of Christ, the divine King and Son of God, who conquers death by His descent into the nether world and whose defeat is victory. In this context it is the soldiers and everything they stand for that are ridiculed: the whole myth of the divinity of the secular ruler and the whole rhetoric of imperial power in the cult of the Roman emperor are implicitly rejected. Instead, a new image of man is projected, based on the idea of individual salvation and deification through imitation of Christ.

The fundamental device employed by early Christian hagiographers in order to bring about this transformation of historical records into ever-new variations of Biblical paradigms is the juxtaposition of their own historical accounts with Biblical quotations and allusions. In this way they created a parallelism between their own narratives and the Gospels, between their own protagonists and Christ. The product of this operation was the Christian saint, the new hero, whose individual life story is transformed into a *mimēsis Christou* and a revelation of the other, suprahistorical reality that became manifest in history through the mystery of the Incarnation. This other reality is diametrically opposed to the reality of earthly life, in relation to which it represents *das ganz Andere*, the Wholly Other, to use the term introduced by Otto (1917) in order to designate everything holy and sacred in contradistinction to the profane. This device of transforming a story about the present into a re-presentation of a divine pattern revealed in the past and handed down in Holy Writ is a method early Christian hagiographers were able to take over from the New Testament, where the story of Christ is constantly juxtaposed with the Old Testament so as to bring out the similarity between the past and the present. We all recall stock phrases inserted into the Gospels in order to make explicit these parallelisms: "And he came and dwelt in a city called Nazareth: that it might be fulfilled which was spoken by the prophets, He shall be called a Nazarene" (Matt. 2:23), "But all this was done, that the scriptures of the prophets might be fulfilled" (Matt. 26:56), "And the scripture was fulfilled, which saith" (Mark 15:28), "and all things that are written by the prophets concerning the Son of man shall be accomplished" (Luke 18:31), "And Jesus, when he had found a young ass, sat thereon; as it is written" (John 12:14), "But this cometh to pass, that the word might be fulfilled that is written in their law" (John 15:25), "For these things were done, that the scripture should be fulfilled" (John 19:36).

In this context events and figures depicted in the Old Testament in addition to their historical meaning take on a function as *prefigurations* or *tupoi* of events and figures in the New Testament. The Jews in the desert were, according to Saint Paul, *tupoi hēmōn*, "our examples" (1 Cor. 10:6). By means of this method of Biblical typology or "figural interpretation," an equivalence is established between two events or persons, "the first of which signifies not only itself but also the second, while the second encompasses or fulfills the first" (Auerbach 1973:53). In this way a system of parallelisms is superimposed on the chronological course of contiguous events, corresponding to the transformation of historical events and persons *kata to euangelion* in early Christian literature. Prefiguration and imitation are two versions of the same basic device, pro-

jecting into the infinite stream of historical events a finite, Christocentric pattern of parallels and equivalences, beginning with the
Creation and Fall of man, reaching its apogee in the mystery of the Incarnation, and progressing towards the Second Coming of Christ, when
history will come to an end. Christ is the centre and at the same time the
generative model of this pattern, in which events and persons are seen
as representations of the model, as images of the archetype. This means
that the second half of the pattern, the history of the Christian Church, is
similar to but not identical with the first part, the history of the chosen
people of God. The history of the Church is both imitation of Christ and
prefiguration of the transhistorical reality of His heavenly Kingdom
which is the goal of all history. Life in the Christian Church is a re-
enactment of the mystery of the Incarnation and also progress in time.
This antinomy is reflected in the unity of cyclical and linear time in the
liturgy of the Church, which is a revelation of the eternal reality of the
*aion* in the transient moment of *chronos*. This coincidence of time and
eternity in the liturgy is an important factor in the development of
Christian art and literature, in particular in the Byzantine period (see
Byčkov 1977: Ch.1).

Byzantine theology took over the Christian aesthetic of *mimēsis
Christou* from the early Church Fathers and further elaborated it,
although some modern Orthodox theologians claim that imitation of
Christ "is foreign to Eastern spirituality," that the "way of the imitation
of Christ is never practised in the spiritual life of the Eastern Church"
(Lossky 1957:215, 243). This view has been convincingly refuted by
Hausherr (1948), whose research has shown that the idea of the
Christian as an imitator of Christ is prevalent in Orthodox theology
throughout its history, finding its fullest philosophical treatment in the
writings of Maximus the Confessor (d. 662). According to Maximus, to
imitate Christ is to follow Him in His humiliation and suffering in order
to reach a state of conformity with Christ, a *Christoeidēs katastasis*. In
Byzantine monasticism life is explicitly defined as an imitation of Christ
in the Instructions of Basil the Great, where Christ is referred to as a
model of piety and virtue, as the archetype whom the monks strive to
reproduce in themselves, each according to his individual faculties. By
their constant *mimēsis* of the archetype, the monks internalised the
archetypal features of the model, thus themselves becoming worthy of
imitation as images of the divine archetype. This is reflected in
Byzantine hagiography, where the *mimēsis Christou* is a constructive
idea, determining the selection of historical data and their combination
into a Life. Although we know too little about Byzantine hagiography
to be able to define in detail the significance of the motif for the development of the genre, we may follow Hausherr (1948) in emphasising the
role of the *mimēsis-Christou* motif in the *Life* of Symeon the New
Theologian, the great mystic who died in 1022. In the words of his

biographer, Symeon was "faithful to the image of the Apostles and an imitator of Christ" who "when he suffered never menaced," and who "when persecuted, endured." Through his imitation of the humiliated Christ, Symeon was "spiritually united with God in the divine light, in the company of the angels in heaven," one who might be called "a terrestrial angel or a heavenly man." Symeon, says Hausherr, "experienced that one *ascends* in deification, following the way of *descent*, the kenosis of God made man," and he quotes the words of Gregory of Nyssa that humility is "a descent towards the heights" (1948).

The Edict of toleration, issued under the Emperor Constantine the Great in 313 A. D., legalised the Christian religion within the boundaries of the Empire, and fourth-century hagiography is clearly marked by this new situation. The Church could now without any danger glorify her heroes in words, images, and architectural forms. Whereas the martyrs' feasts had in the past been celebrated by simple commemorations at their graves, churches were now being built over these graves, and the feasts turned into popular festivals. The commemorative speeches delivered at these feasts were modelled on the pre-Christian *encomia*. The great fourth-century Church Fathers, Basil the Great, Gregory of Nyssa, Gregory of Nazianzus, and John Chrysostom, all wrote their *encomia* in conformity with the rules of classical rhetoric, despite their assurances to the contrary. According to these rules, the martyr is represented as a superhuman hero, and individual features, even down to names, were suppressed (Delehaye 1921:183ff.)

The heroisation of the martyrs is possibly a cause of the increasingly heavy emphasis on their sufferings in martyr stories throughout the Middle Ages. Even while the passion stories retain their character of a dramatic struggle between the representatives of Christ and those of the devil, between the martyrs and the rulers of this world, they become also, through the growing number of torture scenes, a representation of the martyrs' heroic courage and gradual perfection. Thus seen, they have a parallel in the spiritual perfection portrayed in the Lives of the confessor saints, which now emerged as the major genre of hagiography. The prototype of the early Christian *vita* and the model for its subsequent development in both Eastern and Western Europe is the *Life of Saint Antony*, written by Athanasius, Patriarch of Alexandria, probably as early as 357 A. D., i.e., one year after the saint's death (Migne, *Patrologia graeca:* 26, 1887, 835–976).

The question of the literary significance of this *vita* began in earnest to engage scholars when Hans Mertel (1909) claimed that Athanasius had composed the *Life* according to a wholly conventional pre-Christian pattern: "Athanasius relates the *Life of Saint Antony* in a rhetorically coloured language, following the scheme of Plutarch and the peripatetic tradition. His use of this scheme is marked by a certain degree of independence. Because of the edificatory tendency of his tract, however, he failed to create a well-ordered and integrated work.— Plutarch represents a character, Athanasius a type" (Mertel 1909:19).

Mertel's interpretation of the *Life of Saint Antony* as a realisation of a conventional biographical scheme was an attempt to demonstrate that the *vita* is not a genre created by Christian biographers, but one taken over from classical literature. His own conclusions, however, assuming a static view of the relationship between scheme and realisation, are of somewhat limited value. This view leads to a negative evaluation of the *Life of Saint Antony*, precisely because the *Life* is something more than a mere copy of a pre-existing pattern, containing as it does a number of elements not predicted by the scheme. Mertel's analysis led to the paradoxical conclusion that the specifically hagiographical elements of the *Life*, for instance, its concluding miracle stories, are nothing but arbitrary additions, which have only a confusing effect and no aesthetic function in the totality of the *vita*. The discrepancy between Plutarch's biographical scheme and Athanasius' text contributed to calling into question Mertel's thesis. Karl Holl (1912) refuted it categorically, maintaining that Plutarch's biographies were without any significance for the shaping of the Christian *vita*, which in his opinion has its origins in quite different models. Holl traces the *vita* back to representations of Socrates and to biographies of philosophers representing the sage in a life-long struggle with his own low nature and with the agents of false wisdom. His life takes the form of a gradual ascent to ever more perfect stages culminating in his deification. The intermediate link between this genre and the *Life of Saint Antony* would be the portrait of the perfect gnostic in the writings of Clement of Alexandria (Holl 1912).

The account of the protagonist's inner development as a struggle and a gradual ascent leads to a shift of emphasis towards the end, where the tales of his miracles show that he has reached the highest stage attainable in this life and has become an instrument of higher, divine powers. As a representative of these eternal powers the philosopher is contrasted to the emperor, the incarnation of the highest secular power—"the philosopher as *sōtēr* is the secret rival of the emperor" (Holl 1912:418). This opposition was likewise to become a constituent element of the Christian *vita*, where, however, it is no longer identical with the juxta-position of two irreconcilable principles in the martyr passion, repre-sented by the saint and the emperor respectively. In a Life the emperor and the saint no longer represent two different principles, but rather the same principle in contiguous spheres. One of the hagiographers' tasks after the Edict of toleration, and particularly when Christianity had be-come the state religion, was precisely to express the Church's view of the ideal relationship between the emperor and the representatives of the Church. Athanasius does this in the *Life of Saint Antony* by depicting the old Antony as adviser and teacher to the emperor and his sons.

Holl's comparison of *vita* and philosopher biography was originally meant as a refutation of Mertel's theory. Today it should rather be viewed as complementary and corrective. Holl attacked the attempt to trace the composision of the *vita* to Plutarch and the peripatetic tradition of classical biography, shifting the whole analysis onto a plane different from the external structure of the text. Holl was primarily interested in uncovering models for the "inner form" of the *vita*. Characteristic of Holl's comparative method is the itemisation of individual similarities between the *Life of Saint Antony* and other, earlier texts. The method has its value when used by a man of Holl's tact and erudition, even if it unavoidably leads to a demonstration of superficial correspondences with no basis in the structure of the different works.

On similar lines, the question of late-antique models for the *Life of Saint Antony* was broached by Reitzenstein (1906, 1914), who found in the different parts traces of a variety of literary models. The first part (Chapters 1-48) was identified by Reitzenstein as an imitation of a lost Pythagoras biography; the second part (Chapters 49-66) has an aretalogy as its exemplar; and the third (Chapters 67-88) follows a biographical scheme arranged in *praxeis, aretai,* and *epitēdeumata.* Owing to this mixture of heterogeneous exemplars and models Reitzenstein saw the *vita* as an artistic failure, in form as well as content. The confusion produced a saint marked by strident inner contrasts: Antony is represented now as an ascetic and a miracle worker, now as a subtle philosopher, a combination Reitzenstein found unacceptable.

The only appropriate conclusion to be drawn from this kind of comparison is that the *Life of Saint Antony,* indeed, the whole genre, was probably produced through a combination of various genres.

For the structural analysis of the *vita* the question of textual origins is, nevertheless, of secondary significance. Far more important are the mutual relationships between elements stemming from the different types of text that have left their traces in the *vita,* and the principle governing the selection of preformed elements and their combination into a new totality in Athanasius.

The scholar who has most convincingly argued that the *Life of Saint Antony* is an integral whole and not a textual conglomeration is J. List (1930). Unlike earlier scholars, List went back to literary theory in Athanasius' time. He called attention to a characterisation of the *Life of Saint Antony* given by Gregory of Nazianzus who composed an *encomium* or *euphēmia* of Athanasius. In Gregory's terminology the *Life* is a *historia,* and more generally a *diēgēsis.* The difference between *euphēmia* and *historia* is a matter of size. Whereas a *historia* relates everything about the person whose praises it extols, the *euphēmia* is concentrated on the qualities necessary to prove his virtue, his *aretē,* in its various manifestations.

An interesting aspect of this distinction is that the two ways of representation, *vita* and *encomium*, are not essentially different. They are both eulogies. The distinction between them lies in a different accentuation of the protagonist's exploits. In the composition of a *diēgēsis* and consequently of a *vita*, chronology plays the predominant role. In the *euphēmia*, or *encomium*, on the other hand, the exploits of the protagonist are not arranged chronologically, but according to the various forms of *aretē* they represent. The primary factor here is the catalogue of virtues, while the chronological course of events is secondary. This difference in the mode of representation does not, however, constitute a principle, according to List (1930:8). In both cases the protagonist's exploits are merely "signs of virtue," expressions of his *aretē*. Furthermore, Gregory's definition of the *Life* as a special version of the *encomium* implies that it was not intended to depict the saint's psychological development through a chronological account of the separate events of his life. In this it differs radically from the modern art of biography, which all too often has become our yardstick for the *vita*. Like the *encomium*,the *vita* is a product of Greek rhetoric, coloured by a logical and systematic attitude to the empirical world, characteristic of the Greeks. Their attention was focused primarily on the logicality of things, while the chronological connection between empirical data came second. Instead of biography the Greeks cultivated the art of "demonstrative character drawing" (List 1930:9). According to Aristotle and the tradition on which he built, man's exploits have no intrinsic value as an object of rhetoric. Nor do they have any significance as an illustration of man's historically conditioned psychological development. The encomiastic representation of the protagonist's exploits serves to prove the ethical definition of his character. His achievements are signs of his moral habit—*sēmeia tēs hexeōs* (Aristotle, *Rhet.* I, 9, 137b, 33; see List 1930:9).

The rules governing the composition of an *encomium* followed a fairly fixed scheme and were part of the rhetorical study that Athanasius had passed through during the course of his education. According to this scholastic tradition the *encomium* is divided into the following chapters (see Delehaye 1921:196f.; List 1930:10ff.):

1. Prenatal: ethnic origins—parents, family, nation, country.
2. Birth.
3. Childhood: education and predisposition.
4. Studies.
5. Manhood: exploits, development.
6. Death: duration of life, way of death, after death, final comparison.

The biography proper is framed by a foreword, *prooimion*, and an afterword, *epilogos*, both of which are equally constructed according to fixed rules. In the *Life of Saint Antony* the frame takes the character of a letter to the "monks abroad" whom the writer first addresses by means of conventional introductory *topoi*, and finally apostrophises anew in the epilogue, in which the *Life* is rounded off by means of concluding *topoi*. *Topoi* are also used extensively in the biography proper, where traditional encomiastic "expressional constants" are replenished with fresh, specifically hagiographical formulae, which later became part of the repository of hagiographical rhetoric.

When, for instance, Athanasius praises the addressee in the introduction to the *vita*, emphasising that he is able to record only a small part of all he knows about the saint, or when in his *prothesis* he gives a brief review of the ensuing biography, this is all part of school rhetoric and subsequently also of the common hagiographical stock of introductory *topoi* (see Curtius 1954:89ff., 1960:58-80).

In the beginning the *Life of Saint Antony* follows the compositional rules of the *encomium* fairly faithfully. The tone changes, however, when Athanasius proceeds to describe the saint's exploits, his fight with and victory over the demons. In this part Antony's life is rendered as a sequence of events that are only loosely strung together chronologically; at the same time, the biography also differs from the traditional encomiastic device of representing the protagonist's virtues through his achievements. The predominant principle for the representation of the saint's life in this part of the *Life of Saint Antony* was first uncovered by List (1930:16ff.): the individual episodes are selected and combined in order to represent the saint's spiritual ascent and perfection as a gradual intensification of his ascesis, corresponding to the five stages in the initiations of the mysteries.

The first stage of Antony's ascesis takes place at home, the second in a tomb far outside the village where he is harassed and tormented by demons, until at the age of thirty-five he has his first vision. This leads to the third stage, when Antony leaves his old teacher and sets out for the desert. Here he shuts himself up in a deserted fort, where he spends the next twenty years fighting the demons until, finally, he gives in to his disciples' entreaties and emerges from the fort "as from a sanctuary, initiated into the sacred mysteries, and divinely inspired" (*memustagōgēmenos kai theoforoumenos*), an expression that clearly points to the initiation rites. Antony has now passed through his purification process. His soul, we are told, has become pure, and he is ready for the fourth stage, at which he emerges as teacher, training others in the art of ascesis. He founds a number of monasteries, while withdrawing periodically to solitude, practising his ascesis to even stricter rules than before, until he completely abandons the coenobitic life in the monastic community and withdraws to the mountains, where he remains until his death. Life in these mountainous areas, the fifth and last stage of Antony's life, differs from the preceding in that it is no longer dominated by the saint's struggle with the demons, but rather by his visions and miracles.

With his account of the visions and the miracles the hagiographer has reached the highest, theoretical stage in the spiritual perfection of his saint, where he is about to attain the goal of his life's struggle: deification. Antony emerges as the sign and instrument of God, and incarnation of the *Wholly Other*. God has made him partaker of his power and lets it work through Antony's person, so that he is endowed with prophetic gifts, and his fame finally reaches even the imperial court. It is in this part of the *vita* that Constantine and his sons approach Antony and ask his advice. They are reported to rejoice in the answer, when the saint reminds them that Christ alone is the true and eternal king.

In his dynamic account of the saint's ascent Athanasius deviates from the encomiastic writer's static enumeration of virtues and achievements. He combines the compositional rules of the *encomium* with a scheme we know from the initiation rites of the mystery cults, where the postulant is led through purification—*katharsis*—and illumination—*phōtismos*—to beholding—*epopteia*. The same scheme underlies the Neo-Pythagorean and Neo-Platonist ways of ascent (see Reitzenstein 1914; List 1930). The most important feature distinguishing the *Life of Saint Antony* from non-Christian versions of this scheme is the number of Biblical quotations. These have not only a didactic function in transmitting the Christian message to the readers, but also a distinct poetic function in the text of the *vita*. By inscribing the Biblical quotations in his own account of Antony's life Athanasius adds a new dimension to the saint's spiritual struggle.

One example of this is the introduction to the paragraph about the saint's miracles at the end of the *vita*. Through a series of quotations this aspect of the saint's work is interpreted as a fulfilment of the prophecies and promises of Christ, that nothing shall be impossible for the true Christian, and as testimony to the saint's realisation of the command given by Christ to His disciples and to all Christians: "Heal the sick ... cast out devils: freely ye have received, freely give" (see Matt. 10:8).

The juxtaposition in Athanasius' work of various pre-Christian types of text with Biblical quotations, is in principle identical with the device we have demonstrated in other hagiographical texts, as in the tale of the mad nun of Tabennisi and in the story of Polycarp's passion *kata to euangelion*. The difference lies in the far greater complexity of the *Life of Saint Antony*. Whereas in the earlier texts the process was based on a simple juxtaposition of segments from two different contexts, the *Life of Saint Antony* comprises elements from several contexts. Through a number of recodings the story of Antony's life has finally been transformed into a Christianised initiation. The life of the Christian saint has acquired meaning as an initiation into eternity.

The three types of hagiographical text described thus coincide in their vision of the saint's earthly life as preparing for deification and rebirth in the life to come. Their common aim is to resolve the opposition between life and death. Their modes, however, are different.

In the Passion of Polycarp the protagonist's path of suffering is systematically compared to the Passion of Christ in the Gospels. The parallels are emphasised in order to transform the story of Polycarp into an image and re-enactment of the archetypal suffering, death, and resurrection of Christ. The Passion of Christ is reflected in Polycarp's martyrdom and he emerges as an *imitator Christi*, a metaphor of Christ. In the *Life of Saint Antony*, on the other hand, contiguity prevails over similarity. In contrast to the *marturion*, Antony's sanctification takes the form of a gradual approximation to the divine. His *Life* describes a covering of the distance to the *Wholly Other*. When at the end of the *vita* he has attained the highest stage in his ascent, and is already on the threshold between life and death, his figure has become part of a larger, divine whole and is filled with God's miracle-working power.

It is clear that sanctification is here represented in two different modes: in the *vita* the structure is determined by metonymic relationships of contiguity, chronology, distance, and approximation, whereas in the *passion* it is dominated by the metaphoric relations of similarity and contrast.

This is the theoretical beackground against which we shall try to examine various texts from early Russian hagiography. At the same time we shall try to place these texts in a wider historical context. We may assume that the individual author's choice of either the metaphoric or the metonymic way is conditioned not only by a strictly personal preference, but also reflects a particular attitude to reality determined by his times and historical environment.

# Nestor's *Life of Saint Theodosius*:
# Imitation of Christ and Mystagogia

## The Frame

In the foreword to his *Life of Saint Theodosius*, Nestor says that he began writing it after the completion of his account of Russia's first saints
and martyrs, the brothers Boris and Gleb (*Čtenie*). Theodosius was the
third abbot of the Kievan Monastery of the Caves, where Nestor himself
became a monk only after Theodosius' death in 1074. He never knew the
saint personally. In his own words the *Life* is based on oral traditions in
the monastery, the first part, dealing with the saint's childhood, going
back to what Theodosius' mother related to the cellarer Theodore. The
*Life* was probably written in the 1080s (Poppe 1965). The oldest extant
manuscript is that of the twelfth-century *Uspenskij sbornik*.[1]

Textual criticism from about the turn of the century (Šakhmatov 1896,
Abramovič 1898, Bugoslavskij 1914) contended that Nestor to a great
extent reproduced Greek sources, with particularly copious quotations
from the *Life of Saint Sabas* by Cyril of Scythopolis. Nestor's extensive
use of quotations from Greek sources did not, however, prevent a scholar
like Šakhmatov (1896:48) from counting the *Life of Saint Theodosius*
among those early Russian works that distinguish themselves through
their high literary quality. It was only later that the *Life* acquired a
reputation for being unoriginal, at a time when comparative textual
criticism had in actual fact become an obstacle to an unbiased study of
the literary value of our *vita*. This prejudice was not removed until
Fedotov (1931:32ff.) put forward a new interpretation of the *Life*,
claiming that in contrast to the austere and rigorous ascetics of
Byzantine hagiography, Nestor's Theodosius is conceived after the
humbled, human figure of Christ, and represents a distinctive, typically
Russian saintly ideal. It is clear today that Fedotov's exclusive emphasis
on the "kenotic" features of Saint Theodosius suppressed other aspects
of Nestor's account (Børtnes 1967). The Russian scholar's emphasis on

---

[1] *Msca maija. Vb .g. dnb žitije prpdbnaago oca našego Theōdosija igoumena
pečerъskago.* Pp. 71–135 in: *Uspenskij sbornik XII–XIII vv.* / prep. for publ. by O. A.
Knjazevskaja, V. G. Dem'janov, M. V. Ljapon, ed. by S. I. Kotkov (Moscow: Nauka,
1971). Except where otherwise noted, my references to the *Life* are to the numbered
columns of this edition, given in parentheses after my quotations. All translations are my
own.

the saint's imitation of the humbled Christ may in retrospect seem like a projection of Tolstoy's and Leskov's ideals onto early Russian hagiography, and in a wider context as an interpretation conditioned by Fedotov's own Christian socialism as well as by the concern in modern theology with the human figure of Christ, to the neglect of His divine nature.

After Fedotov the *Life of Saint Theodosius* has been examined by a number of scholars and from different angles (Tschiževskij 1950, Eremin 1966:28–41, Børtnes 1967, 1972, Siefkes 1970, Kossova 1984). There seems today to be broad consensus about its high literary qualities. To quote Tschiževskij (1950:85), it is "one of the most influential, most popular, and aesthetically most valuable monuments of early Russian literature."

Hagiographical conventions demanded that the biographical part of the *Life of Saint Theodosius* should be preceded by an introduction and followed by a conclusion that together constitute the frame story of the *vita* (Børtnes 1967). The hagiographers themselves gave much attention to the frame. Both introduction and conclusion were composed of *topoi* culled from the texts of other hagiographers and recombined according to rules laid down by the genre. It was particularly important to follow the rules for the introduction, whereas in the conclusion one was at greater liberty. The introduction was to contain the basic idea for the biography proper, a *prothesis* with a brief summary of the ensuing representation of the saint's life. Nestor's *prothesis* combines the idea that the Russians had been Christianised at the eleventh hour with the notion that in Theodosius they had received a saint who surpasses all other Church Fathers, Christ Himself having chosen him as His collaborator (*s"del'nik*) and shepherd for the "last, frail generation." These *topoi* form the core of the introduction and anticipate one of the main themes of the biography: the representation of the saint as abbot among the monks of the Monastery of the Caves in the image of the Good Shepherd. As shown by Siefkes (1970), the imagery of the *Life of Saint Theodosius* has its origin in the Bible and belongs to the rhetorical repertoire of Byzantine hagiography. The image of the Good Shepherd is no exception. The originality of Nestor's art lies in his ability to apply this imagery to the life story of Saint Theodosius, thus bringing out the essential features of his saintly figure. In the introduction the other parts are grouped symmetrically around this nucleus according to the following plan:

1. The hagiographer begins with a brief invocation of God, with thanksgiving.
2. The hagiographer introduces himself, his protagonist, and the occasion for the *vita*.
3. The hagiographer justifies his task through introductory *topoi*.

4. *The centre of the introduction* is the description of Theodosius as the S"*del'nik* of Christ and a shepherd for the "last, frail generation."
5. The hagiographer addresses his audience, repeating his *captatio benevolentiae*.
6. He continues the presentation of his own person.
7. The introduction is concluded with a renewed invocation of God and a prayer for inspiration to complete the *vita*.

This plan shows how the introduction is composed according to a concentric pattern around the idea that Theodosius is the s"*del'nik* of Christ, His *sunergos* or collaborator, an idea which is central also to the *Life* proper. By means of conventional *topoi* Nestor constructed his introduction so that the second part not only repeats the individual paragraphs of the first, but at the same time elaborates their themes.

The symmetrical structure of the introduction expresses a will to balance and harmony characteristic of the *Life* as a whole, especially in its representation of the saint's figure.

From a literary point of view, the function of Nestor's frame story is to represent the process of narration. The primary elements constituting this process are the narrator, who tells the story, the audience, to whom the story is told, and the story. These elements, always implicit in narrative discourse, are externalised in the form of the frame story. In the role of narrator Nestor addresses as his ideal audience the brethren of the Caves Monastery and all the future generations of monks who will read the *vita* in its written version. After having introduced himself, he presents his theme, situating his act of narration in a "Here" and "Now": "having girded myself with faith and hope that all things are possible unto Thee, I began to write down the story of the life of the Holy Theodosius, the former abbot of this monastery of Our Holy Lady the Mother of God. For today we are observing the anniversary of his departure by holding a service in commemoration of his death" (26b). The saint's feast is the anniversary of his death, when he was reborn to eternal life. The date is the third of May, according to the heading of the *vita*. With these lines at the very beginning of his introduction Nestor has situated his act of narration within the holy precincts of the Caves Monastery and incorporated his *Life of Saint Theodosius* into the sacred *nunc* of the liturgy. With this liturgical *nunc*, the *sēmeron* of the Byzantine hymns, Nestor's act of narration has been transferred from the transitory flow of historical time to the sacred time of the Church's year with its cycle of ever-recurring feasts. Before putting forward his *prothesis*, Nestor has in actual fact established a fictitious narrative situation in the frame story.

Having created a liturgical setting for his narration, Nestor propounds his main idea, anticipating the central theme of his narrative: the representation of Theodosius as the *sunergos* of Christ. This idea is introduced in a series of periphrastic passages in which Theodosius is compared to the Holy Fathers of bygone ages. His great example was, says Nestor, Saint Antony, the founder of monasticism. The culminating point of this glorifying comparison is reached when Nestor interprets Theodosius' work as the fulfilment of that which is written in the books of the Fathers about the last, frail generation: Christ Himself has chosen Theodosius as His collaborator and shepherd for His flock.

The second part of the introduction takes the form of an amplifying repetition of the first. It concludes with a prayer carrying over from the *nunc* of the frame story to the past of the biography. For while the act of narration is presential in relation to the narrator and his audience, the story of Theodosius' life is perfective and will have to be told from a retrospective point of view. Moreover, Theodosius' life story is not Nestor's own, but a story he has heard from other monks. His own account does not directly refer to the life and deeds of the saint, but to the words of others about him. It would therefore be naive to try to seek the meaning of he *Life* in its reference to an historical reality. Its meaning is to be found in a structure of sense within the *Life* itself, created by Nestor in the act of remembering what others have told him about Theodosius and transforming his knowledge into a proper saint's Life and an expression of the Wholly Other. In order to achieve this, Nestor will have to bridge the gap between the Life and the frame story. For it is by being incorporated into the latter that the Life is integrated into the liturgical *nunc* of the commemoration. This connection is brought about when in the process of narration Nestor interrupts his story by such phrases as "the Monastery was famous and is so to this day"; "Antony dug a cave where he dwelt and never left, the same in which his revered body rests to this day"; "on the right-hand side of the church, where his grave is still visible" etc. By means of adverbs such as "now," "still," "to this day," the perfective past of the life story and the *nunc* of the frame are combined in a temporal continuum. The references to the *nunc* of the frame story throughout the narrative also serve to link up introduction and conclusion. And when Nestor has completed his account of Theodosius' life and posthumous miracles, he abandons his retrospective viewpoint and resumes his direct address to the audience: "With the help of many witnesses we have now completed our tale; let us leave it" (67a). With another reference to his sources and with a fresh sequence of humility *topoi*, Nestor concludes his *Slovo* about the life of Saint Theodosius.

Nestor's ample use of conventional modesty *topoi* serves a function comparable to his use of stories told by others in his representation of the saint. With the help of *topoi* he creates a self-portrait in which the reference to historical reality is subdued. As the "unworthy narrator," "ignorant" and "unpolished," Nestor transforms himself into an image of the prototypical hagiographer. His only hope is that God will "enlighten his heart" and enable him to record the story of Theodosius'

saintly life, and through it to proclaim the glory of God. Like the poets
of Classical Antiquity, medieval writers regarded their task as sacred and
their talent as a divine gift.

This portrait of Nestor as the humble vehicle of the Word of God
acquires its full significance only in the light of the saint. Through his
self-abasement he models himself in the likeness of his hero. And when
at the end of his introduction he turns towards his audience with an
appeal "to follow and imitate the life of Saint Theodosius and his
disciples," frame story and Life proper are brought together in a process
of imitation whose aim it is to transform the audience, too, into
individual representations of the prototype embodied in the figure of
Saint Theodosius.

The retrospective viewpoint of the frame story is necessary for Nestor's
intention, which is to represent the life of the saint from his birth to his
death, as a concluded and completed sequence of events.

Equally necessary from a hagiographical point of view is the
apotheosis of the saint. It is only with this event, which transcends the
saint's earthly life, that the history of his life can be interpreted according
to a hagiographical pattern. The glorification of the saint's figure will
have to be included in the *vita* somewhere and in some form or other.

In Nestor's *Life* the glorification takes place at the point where the
narrator leaves the introduction and turns to the life proper. The
account of the saint's birth, naming, and baptism is interrupted twice
by digressions culminating in the vision of Theodosius' ascension and
union with Christ, the *sol iustitiae*, who crowns him with the crown of
victory. Only in the transcendent light from this *visio Dei* can Nestor
begin to transform his biographical material into a representation of
Theodosius' sanctification. The combination of biographical facts and
visionary elements in the account of the saint's birth is an instructive
illustration of Nestor's method. The events of the saint's biography are
here combined with quotations from the Scriptures and other sacred texts.
Correspondences are established between other texts and Nestor's own
story, so that in the interplay between them a new, poetic totality is
created.

The passage begins with a brief, abstract description of the saint's
hometown and of his parents. The town is characterised by its distance
from the capital city of Kiev. The parents were Christians—a *topos* in a
saint's Life. Then, as the narrator proceeds to the naming, an almost
imperceptible shift of levels is effected: the saint was named Theodosius
(= the gift of God), because the priest, "when he beheld the boy, perceived with the eyes of his heart that he would devote himself to God
even from infancy" (27a–b). By a metaphor quoted from Ephesians 1:18,
"the eyes of your understanding", Nestor translates the historical event
of the naming into a figurative level of meaning. This figurative sense is
further explored in the description of the saint's baptism, when "God's

grace was with him and the Holy Spirit dwelt in him" (27b). This statement contains in embryo Nestor's account of the saint's life as a gradual transfiguration, until in the vision of his apotheosis Theodosius is united with the glorious figure of Christ. After this account of the descent of the Holy Spirit into Theodosius at his baptism, the narrator erupts into an *excessus*, in which he turns away from the past and describes an opposite, ascending movement. *Remembering the future,* he describes Theodosius' apotheosis in connection with his birth.

"And who can express the mercy of God!"—with this emotional rhetoric, in poignant contrast to the detached style of the *narratio*, Nestor introduces his vision. "For behold! he did not choose one of the wise philosophers or one of the lords of the cities as pastor and teacher to the monks, but so that the name of the Lord may be glorified in this also: he who was ignorant and without learning proved wiser than the philosophers" (27b). One of the main themes of the frame, the idea of Theodosius as teacher to the monks, has been used as an introduction to the vision.

"O hidden mystery! A brilliant morning star shone before us where nobody dared to hope for it, that people in all countries shall see its light and run towards it, despising everything else, and quench their thirst by its light alone" (27b). Here, in the second paragraph of the vision, Nestor has taken a further step by representing Theodosius in the metaphor of the Morning Star. His figure is thereby removed from the historical plane into a cosmic allegory.

In the third paragraph Nestor reverts to the image of the shepherd, which is now directly combined with the Monastery of the Caves: "O divine clemency! In the beginning you selected and blessed the place where you wanted the herd of your spiritual sheep to graze, until you had chosen their shepherd" (27b). Through the traditional sense of "shepherd" = "leader," Nestor has represented life in the Monastery of the Caves in a pastoral allegory.

At this point the vision comes to a temporary halt. It has a distinctly tripartite composition—an indication of the theme, followed by two allegories on different levels: the star allegory, which elevates the saint to the astral plane, and the pastoral allegory, which interprets life in the Monastery of the Caves under his leadership in the image of the Good Shepherd. In both allegories the saint is represented in the image of Christ; in the star allegory as an imitation of Christ, the Morning Star of the Apocalypse (22:16), in the pastoral allegory as the Good Shepherd of the Gospels.

The allegories are kept in a sustained rhetorical, emotionally excited style. Each paragraph is introduced with an invocation of God in the form of a metonymic periphrasis. The Almighty, indescribable, is referred to by his attributes, whereas the divine totality defies hagiographical description. This emotive accentuation of the impotence of language faced with the Wholly Other is in telling contrast to the appearance of the Godhead in the glorified figure of Christ, in the final paragraph of the vision, where the two allegories are united. In order to effect this union, however, the pastoral allegory has first to be brought into harmony with the light metaphors of the Bible. The narrator has to revert to the historical plane before he can bring his vision to its climax:

"By order of the Prince, the saint's parents had to move to Kursk, or as it would be more correct of me to say"—and here the historical narrative is again brought to a halt, this time by a *correctio*, the narrator interrupting himself with a self-correction—"thus God willed that the brave youth's life should begin to shine there, as it behoved, in order that our morning star should rise in the East"—we are once more back in the star allegory—"attracting many other stars" (= brethren) "in expectation of the Sun of Justice, Our Lord Jesus Christ" (27c).

Having incorporated the pastoral allegory, the star allegory culminates in a vision combining the saint's ascension with the eschatological motif of the Bible, the Sun of Justice, the *sol iustitiae*, a symbol which in Nestor's allegory equals the representation of the Pantocrator in icon-painting.

While the pastoral allegory wherever it occurs in the *Life* likens Theodosius to the historical Christ, the star allegory elevates him to the presence of Christ the Pantocrator. At the entrance to this hidden Empire of the triumphant Christ, the vision shows the beatification of Theodosius in the form of a dialogue between Christ and His saint at the gate of the Kingdom. This dialogue places the allegory on the plane of Biblical reality, ending as it does with scriptural quotations:

> "Here I am, my Lord, with my children, whom I have nourished with your spiritual food. Here, my Lord, are my disciples. I have brought them to you, having taught them to despise all earthly things and to love you alone, our Lord and God. Behold, O God, the blessed sheep, whose shepherd you have chosen me to be. I have tended them on your divine pastures. I have brought them hither pure and innocent." And God will answer, "Good servant, you have faithfully increased the talent which was entrusted to you. Therefore, receive your crown and enter into the joy of your Master." And he will say to the disciples: "Come, good flock; come, blessed lambs of the good shepherd: you who have thirsted and suffered for my sake, inherit the kingdom prepared for you from the foundation of the world." (27c)

The vision is concluded, as we have seen, with a string of Biblical quotations. Nestor represents in his own discourse the Wholly Other Word, the *Logos* of the Bible. Through this juxtaposition Nestor's account no longer refers merely to Theodosius' life story, but connotes at the same time another story, the Wholly Other as it manifests itself in Holy Scripture. Carrying the Holy Spirit in his heart, the saint from the very beginning participates in this Wholly Other, divine reality. Nestor's account of his childhood shows how the Holy Spirit is gradually hypostasised and reflected in the saint's visible features, through his *imitatio Christi.* The hagiographer sees it as his task to represent Theodosius' way to sainthood as the metamorphosis of his figure into a verbal icon, an image of the divine prototype of Christ, against the background of heavenly glory that even from the opening vision frames and illuminates his biography. Only against this gold background is it possible to grasp the full import of Nestor's Theodosius. Its aura surrounds and illuminates his *kenotic* figure with the luminosity of a promise, and reveals the purpose of his abasement; he who belittled himself in this earthly life shall sit down with the first in the Kingdom of Heaven. Each trait in his portrait holds a hidden sense which is revealed only in the celestial radiance of the *sol iustitiae.* The historical Theodosius is transfigured, and emerges as a holy image in which the archetypal traits of Christ have once more become visible. This verbal icon takes the form of a *diptychon,* that is, it consists of two main parts. The first comprises Theodosius' life until he enters the monastery and takes the vow. The second deals with his monastic life as abbot of the Caves Monastery. The account of Theodosius' tonsure and investiture forms a caesura between the two parts, which are, incidentally, so different that most scholars have concentrated their attention on Nestor's childhood story and been content to characterise the second part of the *Life* as a sequence of episodes of varying length devoid of any unifying principle except that the saint is the protagonist and appears in practically all of the nearly hundred episodes (in the *Uspenskij sbornik*). In what follows we shall see that the *Life of Saint Theodosius* is composed according to a structural principle that not only arranges the constituent episodes of the second part into a coherent pattern, but also combines the two main parts of the *Life* into a poetic totality.

# The Saint's Childhood

Nestor's story of Theodosius' childhood and adolescence contains a number of traditional *topoi* that one would expect to find in this part of a Life. The saint's disgust at the other children's games, his joy in church-going, and his desire to learn to read the Scriptures are such typical elements, inherent in the genre. However, we cannot expect to reach a real understanding of Nestor's *Life* by itemising its individual *topoi.* It

is far more important to try to establish the system whereby the individual elements are brought together in a coherent picture of the saint's childhood.

What makes this part of the *vita* so different from most similar stories
is the account of the saint's struggle with his mother after the death of his
father. The conflict is already evident while his father is still alive. The
occasion is the boy's refusal to wear the clothes his parents think
appropriate for a boy of his class. Instead he insists on walking about in
garments that are both worn and wretched, contrary to his parents'
wishes. He does this because he would rather be like one of the "poor"—
*jako edin ot ubogykh*—than obey his parents. In early Russian the word
*ubogij* had religious overtones, now lost, connoting meanings like
"god-forsaken," "far from God," "unhappy," and other similar senses
(see Ivanov 1973:6 n.6). The struggle between mother and son becomes
really serious when, after his father's death, Theodosius starts going
with his serfs into the fields, working with them "in all humility." Later
we find him baking the Host for the church. He buys the corn, grinds it,
and bakes the bread, and thus abases himself in the eyes of his mother.
On the other hand, we hear that it "pleased God that the pure bread of
the Eucharist should be brought to the church of God by a youth without sin and without reproach." In order to escape the scorn of his fellows
and his mother's fury, Theodosius flees to a priest in a neighbouring
town, where he continues his baking of the Host. The key to a deeper
understanding of the saint's humble field work, his grinding of the corn,
and baking of the bread is given in a dialogue with his mother. She is
furious with her son for having brought shame upon their family.
Moreover, she cannot bear to see him sitting black and sooty from the
stove. Theodosius submits patiently to his mother's fury and defends
himself "humbly" by referring to the example of Christ:

> Listen, Mother, I pray you, listen! The Lord, Jesus Christ, has
> abased and humbled Himself and given us an example, that we, too,
> shall humble ourselves for His sake. Also, He was scorned, spat upon,
> and beaten. And all this He suffered for our salvation. Must we not
> then with even greater cause suffer in patience, so that we shall gain
> Christ! And as for my work, Mother, listen: when Our Lord, Jesus
> Christ, reclined at the Last Supper with His disciples, He took the
> bread, brake it, and gave unto His disciples, saying: "Take and eat,
> for this is my body, broken for you and for many others for the
> remission of sins." But when Our Lord Himself has called it His
> flesh, shall I not then rejoice, that He has made me worthy of being
> partaker of His flesh? (29c-d)

Stylistically these lines differ from the *narratio* in a number of rhetorical
outbursts, repetitions, and parallelisms, and through their strong

admixture of Church-Slavonic elements. These are all features that link the lines with the highly strung style of the opening vision.

Thematically, however, Theodosius' speech forms a contrast to the opening vision. His description of his own abasement and humiliation after the example of Christ and of his partaking of the body of Christ through the baking of the altar bread forms, as it were, the opposite to the allegorical vision of the saint's encounter with Christ, the *sol iustitiae*. But we are not talking here of absolute opposites. Abasement and glorification are complementary. The saint's imitation of the humbled Saviour and his assimilation to the radiant figure of the Pantocrator in the light allegories should be interpreted according to the two natures of Christ, human and divine, and the deification of man through Christ, in imitation of His suffering: "Who shall change our vile body, that it may be fashioned like unto his glorious body, according to the working whereby he is able even to subdue all things unto himself" (Phil. 3:21).

Fedotov (1931:39f.) has rightly emphasised the significance of this speech for our understanding of Nestor's *vita*. By overlooking the complementary relationship between abasement and glorification, however, Fedotov's definition of the saint's *imitatio Christi* becomes a one-sided description of Theodosius' humiliation. This in its turn led to the theory of Theodosius as the founder of Russian kenoticism. Fedotov's conclusion that Theodosius embodies a national, distinctively Russian saintly ideal is based on a comparison with Greek hagiography, where he found no parallels to the story of the young Theodosius' baking of the altar bread and of his imitative self-abasement.

The idea that the childhood story of the *vita* is unique in hagiographical literature was challenged by Tschiževskij (1950), who drew attention to a number of striking parallels between Nestor's account and Chapter 8 of Gumpold's Latin *vita* of Saint Wenceslas of Bohemia (d. 929). More recently, other scholars, and in particular N. W. Ingham (1984), have convincingly argued that the hagiographical representation of Saint Wenceslas as the righteous prince whose innocent death is an imitation of Christ's Passion served as the immediate model for Nestor's account of the martyred brothers Boris and Gleb, thus indirectly supporting Tschiževskij's hypothesis.

In the passages quoted by Tschiževskij (1950:78ff.) we learn of Saint Wenceslas that he

> when the time of harvest had come rose in the middle of the night, stealthily, and went barefoot into the field with the above-mentioned youth, cut the wheat with his own hands, binding it in sheaves, lifting it up himself onto his own and the youth's shoulders, and hid it in a secret corner of the house … and there he threshed it and ground it on the millstone … sprinkled it with water

in the name of the Holy Trinity, and alone, only with his retainer …
he mixed in a bowl flour with water that he himself had fetched
from the well in a pail, blessed it by invoking the Holy Trinity,
kneaded it with the work of his own hands, and having baked the
altar bread, he sent the loaves to the priests in their churches, in
order that they should be sacrificed during Mass to Our Lord, Jesus
Christ.

One has to agree with Tschiżewskij that the correspondences suggest
more than accidental similarities, even if there is no question of
verbatim repetition. On the evidence of Ingham's research (1984) we may
assume that Nestor knew the hagiographical interpretation of
Wenceslas' martyrdom as an imitation of the sufferings of the Lord and
that he carried this pattern over into his own Legend (the *Čtenie*) about
the *strastoterpcy* Boris and Gleb. Yet Nestor's representation of Saint
Theodosius according to the same scheme shows that in early Kievan
hagiography the idea of sainthood as re-enactment of the fate of Christ
was not confined to the cult of the martyred prince but has to be seen in a
wider context.

In Nestor's *Life of Saint Theodosius* the motifs of the saint's field
work with his serfs, his grinding of the corn, and baking of the altar
bread have been combined with the account of Theodosius' struggle
with his mother. This struggle is rendered in a number of individual
episodes that together constitute the childhood part of the *vita*. The
saint's reply to his mother about the aim of his self-abasement is part of
one of these episodes, constituting what we might call the *epiphany* of
the childhood story, the moment where its *quidditas*, "its soul, its
whatness leaps to us from the vestment of its appearance," to apply
James Joyce's definition of epiphany in a work of art.

Theodosius' field work leads to the first critical confrontations
between him and his mother. Later these confrontations are repeated
regularly as critical climaxes in each episode that follows. These scenes
between mother and son follow a set pattern: Theodosius starts an ascetic
exercise, a *podvig*, which in his mother's eyes causes disgrace to himself
and to the whole family. She forbids him to go on like this, and when he
refuses to obey, she is furious; he tries to run away, she pursues him, and
when she gets hold of him, beats him, tears him by his hair, throws him
to the ground, ties him up, and brings him back to the house, where he is
locked up for several days without food, his feet in fetters. All this the
saint submits to "in joy," and every time a crisis ends, "he praises God."
In more general terms, the boy's *podvig* gives rise to the struggle between
him and his mother, followed by the account of his suffering, and, finally, by a reversal of the action when the boy goes to church to praise God
for all he has gone through.

A comparison of the humbled and sooty Theodosius with the mad nun of Tabennisi and the monk Euphrosynus reveals a striking resemblance between them. Like them, Theodosius is represented in his *hubristic* aspect, his sooty, humiliated appearance being the earthly, negative image of his inner, divine self. Seen in its hagiographical context, Nestor's account of the saint's childhood turns out to be an early Russian counterpart of the inverted symbolism of Christian literature from the first centuries. Furthermore, the basic motifs of Nestor's childhood story coincide with some of the central motifs of late-antique and early Christian literature: disguises, field work, strayings, beatings, and imprisonments are stock elements in this literature, in which the wanderings of the heroes (the *plane* motif) almost inevitably end in serfdom (*douleia*). The heroes are represented as prisoners (*aichmalotoi*) and as enchained (*desmioi*) at a very early stage on their road of suffering, and the accounts of the tortures of someone incarcerated and starved have their parallels in the episodes where Theodosius is beaten up, brought home "in chains like a criminal" (28d), locked up, and kept without food.

Kerényi (1927:125ff., 198), who traces this *topos* back to the *marturia* of pagan philosophers, the prototype for the torture scenes in both the Graeco-Oriental novel and in the Christian martyr passion, maintains that the whole situation, and in particular the total passivity of the hero, points to its ritual character, the passivity of the hero being that of a postulant. In Nestor's childhood story the ritual character of the hero's sufferings is supported by the whole context. By letting the young Theodosius go through this series of trials, all following the same basic pattern, Nestor is testing the faithfulness of his calling, gradually assimilating his figure to the divine prototype of Christ, showing at the same time how the saint through his works becomes partaker of the divine essence of the prototype, symbolically present in the altar bread. The Theodosius who emerges from Nestor's childhood story is not a product of heredity and background, as with the protagonists of the modern biography, but a hypostasis of the divine energy of the Holy Spirit. To his secular surroundings, represented by his mother, he becomes an outsider.

In his characterisation of the saint's mother, Nestor has emphasised her masculine appearance: "for she was large and strong like a man, so that one who heard her speak without seeing her would believe she was a man." From a literary point of view this virago is so atypical that most scholars have taken her to be a realistic portrait of the historical figure of Theodosius' mother. Like Stender-Petersen (1952:51), they regard her as "an obstinate and domineering matron who sticks at nothing to prevent her son from becoming a monk." Only Eremin (1966:30) has taken a differing view, seeing in the saint's mother "an incarnation of the tellurian, material principle," thus suggesting a mythical interpretation of the story of mother and son. However, it is also possible to define the masculine figure of the mother in more functional terms, as the saint's adversary in a tale where he, the "divine youth," represents the bright forces, in contrast to his mother, who, according to the narrator, acts at the instigation of an evil power that has possessed her. Carrying out the schemings of the devil, she opposes her son's ascesis and his endeavours to bring new life to the "last," "frail" generation.

From a literary point of view, the struggle between mother and son follows a traditional pattern, according to which the relationship between the champion and his adversary is temporarily inverted: the champion is defeated by his adversary and prevented from carrying out his task; he violates the interdiction, and in consequence must suffer for it. When finally he conquers, Theodosius' mother gives in to her son's entreaties and follows his example: taking the veil, she enters a convent in Kiev. Symbolically reborn in the image of the Holy Virgin, she is healed and restored to true womanhood, mother and virgin in one.

At this level of abstraction, the virago figure of the saint's mother may be defined within the pattern of the *combat tale*. As Walter Burkert (1979:18f.) has observed,

> the combat tale, the ending of which is victory, will not introduce two medium-sized, medium-minded, average people to fight—they would rather shake hands. The prospective victor and the antagonist are made opposites in every respect: the victor will be bright, handsome, nice, young, perhaps slim and small, but tough and virtuous, while the adversary will be dark, ugly, repulsive, old, big and powerful... Thus the principle of contrast may give color to the peripeteia of a tale: the champion may be heavily underprivileged at the beginning, to make his victory all the more overwhelming... A combat of men with women is a startling inversion—the Amazon myth, or the wife killing her husband; worse still is the father killing his daughter, or the son killing his mother, perverting in addition the bonds of family descent. These then are most concise and memorable narrative structures...

Such a structure may also be discerned in Nestor's childhood story.

The revelation of the saint's *imitatio Christi* in the dialogue with his mother leads to a shift in the account of his suffering: whereas it has a passive character in the first episodes, in which the saint "patiently submitted to everything," it acquires a more active colouring in the remaining episodes. Through voluntary suffering the saint prepares for the symbolic act of immolation represented in taking the vow as a monk. In the story of Theodosius' service in the governor's house he appears in "shining garments," which he has always refused to wear but now wears "as a heavy burden," until he gives the clothes away to the poor, dons his old rags, and replaces the shining burden given to him by the world with a voluntary burden hidden to the world: iron chains with which "he girded his loins," and which "drew blood from his body."

The bestowal of clothes to the poor and the wearing of the chains are complementary gestures in the representation of the saint's childhood ascesis. As part of his *imitatio Christi* and preparation for the monastic life, they have a symbolic meaning in Nestor's account.

The *Life of Saint Theodosius* contains a marked admixture of Christian Neo-Platonism, which becomes manifest not only in the description of the descent and incarnation of the Holy Spirit in the saint's figure and the corresponding description of his spiritualisation and ascent, but is also reflected in the love motif. This Nestor represents in its two aspects, as an emanation of *Agape* and as erotic longing for God.

The saint's gift of his clothes to the poor is a typically illustrative gesture, an expression of the divine energy which has filled his figure as the partaker of Christ and which in the form of charity emanates into his surroundings. The representation of his charitable work gives body to the *Agape* motif in the story of his life. His penance on the other hand, expresses how Theodosius "by his soul drawn to the love of God" (27d)—a phrase of unmistakably Platonic overtones—strives to free himself from the world of the senses and to fulfil the command implicit in the words of Christ to His followers: "He who does not leave his father or mother and follow me, is not worthy of me." These words introduce the story of the saint's flight to the monastery. The wearing of the chains is an outward sign of Theodosius' inner torment as long as his soul is separated from the object of its erotic desire, and an image of the saint's struggle to keep his virginity. In suffering, the ascetic expresses, in infinite passion, his relation to eternal bliss. Self-torture becomes a negative symbol of the saint's erotic striving.

Both the *Agape*-motif and the *Eros*-motif are carried over into the account of Saint Theodosius' life in the Caves Monastery and are further developed there. For the time being, however, these penitential exercises spark off the final confrontation between the saint and his mother after she finds out about the chains he wears beneath his clothes. The scene between them takes place as he is about to change into clean clothing to go and help during a feast at the governor's house. His mother is present while he is changing:

> He was of a simple mind and felt no shame before her. She regarded him attentively and noticed blood on his shirt. Looking more closely, she found that the blood was caused by the gnawing iron. It kindled her fury against him, she rose in anger, tore his shirt, beat him, and wrenched the iron from his loins. (30c)

Both the saint's "shining garments" and service in the governor's house here bring in connotations of Christ before Pilate, to which the episode also corresponds in the Biblical subtext of Nestor's narrative. After this the saint is ready to renounce his previous existence and start a new life in the monastery. Now he flees to Kiev, where on the "wings of the spirit" he hurries to the cave of Antony, the hermit, is shorn a monk, and disappears from the eyes of the world. The initiation mystery takes place out of sight, but from its place in the childhood sequence we can understand its ritual significance.

His mother searches for her son, in vain. "She grieved deeply over him and beat her breast as if he were dead" (31c), as Greek women have bewailed Christ on Good Friday down to our own times. The mother's lament corresponds to the *threnos* of the rites.

The separation lasts for four years, until some travellers are able to report that Theodosius is said to be in Kiev. His mother immediately goes there and finds him in Antony's cave. In the beginning he refuses to appear before her, but emerges finally after several days during which she has been waiting and wailing at the gate of the cave. They are reunited, and his mother takes the veil. Theodosius has triumphed over the "old" time, saved by him now in his mother's figure, and reborn to a new life. He emerges as "conqueror of the evil spirits" (33b), and the light symbolism of the opening vision for the first time breaks through in the *narratio* of the *vita*:

> And three radiant figures could be seen in the cave, dispelling the devil's darkness with prayer and fasting—I mean the Holy Antony, the Blessed Theodosius, and the Great Nikon. They dwelt in the cave, praying to God, and God was with them. For He has said: "Where two or three are gathered in my name, there I am in the midst of them." (33c)

This cave, in which the three holy men, illuminated by a divine presence, triumph over the darkness of evil, is a symbol with a deep resonance in Orthodox art and literature. In the Eastern tradition Christ was born not in a stable but in a cave, from which He shone forth to the world. And in another cave, the cave of death, He conquered the powers of darkness. Symbolically, the two have been fused into one double cave of birth and burial (Onasch 1981:345). This holy cave of light is a symbol of birth and death, burial and rebirth, a place of initiation and mystery. In the liturgy, the virgin figure of the Mother of God and the illuminated interior of the church are both representations of this symbol. In Nestor's context, Antony's holy cave clearly has the same symbolic value. It is the place where Theodosius is initiated into the mysteries of monastic life and dies away from the world in order to start a new life as a monk. This transition from one world to another represents a rite of passage in which the process that began with the indwelling of the Holy

Spirit at his baptism culminates in Theodosius' rebirth. What we can now see, however, is that the intermediate stage, the episodes describing the saint's struggle with his mother, are variations on the same pattern, repeating the basic scheme of a rite of passage in a sequence of different contexts. Taken together, this alignment of parallel episodes describes the progressive metamorphosis of the saint, whose imitation of Christ's human figure culminates in ritual death, whereas in the cave scene the saint's illuminated figure re-emerges as a foreshadowing of the glorified Christ of the opening vision.

It is this idea of the saint's metaphoric significance that dominates the *Life of Saint Theodosius* and determines Nestor's use of Biblical texts and Orthodox symbolism. By introducing these elements into his own narrative in the form of quotations and allusions, he creates a new super-structure on the basis of the historical narrative, transforming the saint into an image of the divine prototype, given by Christ *in illo tempore*. This concept of sanctification as an image of the incarnate Godhead forms the basis of Nestor's poetics. It is a concept well known in Byzantine icon-painting, and also in the *Urbild-Abbild* aesthetic of Byzantine Neo-Platonism, the *cult aesthetic* (Onasch) of the Orthodox Church. This poetics could be described as a form of allegory, in which the content of the image is conventional, in contrast to the unexpected and unconventional use of metaphor by modern poets. Yet Erich Auerbach (1946, 1967) has tried to distinguish between the *Urbild-Abbild* structure found in Christian art and conventional allegory, maintaining that in contrast to pure allegory the *imitatio Christi* of Christian literature establishes a similarity relation between historical events and persons in which one individual event or person refers not only to itself or himself, but also to the other, whereas the other comprises or fulfils the first. The two poles of the figure are separated temporarily, but are contained within time as real events or figures; they are both comprised by the flow of history, and only the understanding of their connection, the *intellectus spiritualis*, constitutes a spiritual act (1967:77). It is to this method that Auerbach has given the name *figural interpretation*. It is a method widely used by early Christian Church Fathers to explain events in the Old Testament. In the Middle Ages it came to be used also to explain events that had taken place after the completion of the historical mission of Christ. Through the *intellectus spiritualis* of figural interpretation an analogy was established between the prototypal acts of Christ and subsequent historical events. Auerbach has examined the use of this method in his article on Saint Francis in the *Divine Comedy*:

> Now the existential following of Christ with which we are dealing here in the mystical marriage of Francis with Poverty is so to speak an inverted figure; it repeats certain characteristic features of Christ's life, renews them and invests them with a bodily form for all to see,

thereby renewing the office of Christ as the good shepherd whom
the herd must follow. ... Together figure and imitation form an
image of the closed teleological view of history whose centre is the
appearance of Christ. (1967:53; Eng. transl., Auerbach 1973:97, is
unfortunately, inadequate.)

Figural interpretation as a literary method has its origin in the idea that
historical events have significance not in themselves, but only as
repetitions of an archetypal model, revealed by the Godhead *in illo
tempore* (Eliade 1966). This idea of history, which transforms an
historical person into an exemplary hero and an historical event into a
ritual re-enactment, is typical of a mythical world vision: "On the one
hand the myth always refers to events alleged to have taken place long
ago. But what gives the myth an operational value is that the specific
pattern described is timeless; it explains the present and the past as well as
the future" (Lévi-Strauss 1967:205). The liturgical year of the Christians
is based on the concept of history as such a periodic repetition of the
birth, suffering, death, and resurrection of Christ, and on everything that
this mystical drama means for the individual Christian: an annual
renewal of individual man and of creation through a re-enactment of the
Passion of the Saviour *in concreto*.

A fresh element entered the archaic regeneration rites with Christianity. This lies in its eschatological belief that history will reach its close at
the Second Coming of Christ on the Day of Judgement. To a Christian
in medieval times this repetition, therefore, had as its aim to imitate the
incarnate Godhead in His suffering and death, in order that through a
complete *metanoia* in the union with Christ he could begin to realise the
Kingdom of God among his fellow men even in this life. For those who
through the mystery of the Eucharist had become partakers of the eternal
*nunc* of the divine reality, history had come to an end. By constantly
realising himself in the image of the humiliated Son of God, the
Christian was able to anticipate the world to come, even in this life. The
*imitatio Christi* of medieval monks thus had as its model both the
humiliated Christ who once *came* to earth and the triumphant Christ
who *will* once *come*. In their work to cultivate the "sinful" and "fallen"
nature and inhabit the wilderness they wanted to recreate the lost
Paradise and transform the earth into an image of the Heavenly
Jerusalem, to lead creation back to its original *status naturae integrae*.

The figural interpretation of biographical space and time in the *Life
of Saint Theodosius* transforms the historical narrative into an image of
eternity. Borrowing a concept from Bakhtin (1975:234ff.), we could say
that figural interpretation determines the "chronotope" of the *Life,* "the
fusion of spatial and temporal indices in a meaningful and concrete
whole." With the transfiguration of Theodosius in the symbolic time-
lessness of the holy cave of light, begins the account of his life as a monk

and abbot in the Monastery of the Caves. Nestor, however, inserted a brief, novella-like story of the young boyar Varlaam's investiture between the first and second parts of the *vita*, a story whose function in the *Life* presents the reader with a puzzle that must first be solved.

# Epic Integration and Inserted Novella

The holy cave of light is in the centre of Nestor's story of Saint Theodosius, the symbolic borderland between life and death, both grave and womb. Here the "descending movement" of his transfiguration reaches its lowest point, and he begins his ascent back to the heavenly abode of the Holy Spirit. But once a year, during Lent, he would disappear from the brethren and return to the cave in order to conquer the demons anew, only to re-emerge on Good Friday at Evensong (37d). Through this yearly re-enactment of the saint's symbolic descent the cyclical continuity of the new era is ensured in his monastery.

The visionary transfiguration of Saint Theodosius has, however, set him apart from Nestor's audience, the monks apostrophised in the frame story. He is divine or godlike, and they in their human striving are admonished to become like him.

A possible interpretation of Varlaam's story is to see it as an illustration of the narrator's *tropological* aside in the frame story: "Therefore, brethren, let us also strive to become zealous imitators of the life of Saint Theodosius." Nestor introduces Varlaam as an example of such imitation. This he does by the traditional narrative device of epic integration, repeating the central motif in a thematic variation that takes the form of an "inserted novella." In this novella the significance of the *Life* for the individual members of the audience becomes evident. Varlaam's story serves at the same time as a retarding element at the turning point. The meaning of the account is thus emphasised and the attention of the audience roused as the narrator proceeds to the second part of the *Life* proper.[1]

The "inserted novella" deals with the young boyar Varlaam's struggle to get away from the courtly life around Prince Izjaslav in order to become a monk in the Caves Monastery, a conflict which takes the form of a juxtaposition of two contrasting codes of behaviour within the same context: chivalry and monasticism. A life modelled on a knightly code of

---

[1] In the *Uspenskij sbornik* the leaf containing the beginning of Varlaam's story has been excised. For the missing passage I refer to Abramovič's edition of the *Life* in the *Patericon of the Caves Monastery* (see Tschiževskij 1964:32ff.).

behaviour will appear meaningless from a monastic point of view, whereas the monastic way of life will seem absurd when measured against the codes of chivalry. On this level the two codes of behaviour are contrary. Still, it is not a question of absolute contrasts, of two completely different systems, but of an opposition within what is essentially one cultural system (Lotman 1967:32). Varlaam's story describes the transition of the hero from one extreme to another, from the knightly sphere to that of the monastery.

The background to the story is the dispute between Prince Izjaslav and the monks because they tonsure his knights. Izjaslav's eunuch has become a monk along with Varlaam and has taken refuge in the monastery. The Prince has a grudge against the monastery because more and more young men are leaving the ranks to become instead "soldiers of the heavenly emperor" in the Caves.

Varlaam's conversion follows the familiar pattern of the initiation rite: from action through suffering to insight. The stages are represented in a scenario whose symbolic meaning is expressed in significant gestures.

The theme is suggested, by way of introduction, through the Biblical quotation that "It is easier for a camel to go through the eye of a needle, than for a rich man to enter into the kingdom of God" (33c-d).

Events are triggered off by Varlaam's solemn *exodus* from his house: surrounded by his retinue, with their horses dressed up for parade, he arrives at the cave on horseback, "in shining garments." At the gate he is received by the fathers, who "bowed down to him as it behoves to noblemen."

Thus far, the transition has been depicted in accordance with the ceremonies of chivalry. It all has a secular character. The hidden meaning of the procession is revealed only in the portrayal of Varlaam's answering gesture: he descends from his horse, bows down "to the earth" before the fathers, takes off his boyar clothing, places it at the abbot's feet, and surrenders his horse to the abbot, saying: "Behold, father, all this is the beautiful vanity of the world. Do with it as you like, for I hold it in contempt and wish to become a monk and live together with you here in this cave. And never will I return to my house" (Tschiževskij 1964:32f.).

In Varlaam's gesture of self-abasement the norms and values of chivalry are annihilated, viewed as they are from the monastic codex. The incident at the gate expresses in significant gestures that *Umwertung aller Werte* which has brought about Varlaam's breach with worldly society and his transition to the sacred society of the monastery. By climbing down from his horse Varlaam surrenders his lordly rank and prepares to begin a monk's struggle for the heavenly wreath of victory. Through his divestment, the ceremony at the gate becomes a ritual act.

The incident may be compared to a similar episode in the *vita* of Saint Francis of Assisi, the account of his exposure in the marketplace of his hometown, when he put off his secular garments, giving them back to his father in order to be able to pray, "Our Father, which art in heaven, not father Pietro Bernardone." He stood there stark naked, according to the legend, until the bishop covered his shame with a flap of his cloak and by this gesture anticipated his investiture. In each case the shedding of the clothes represents a stage in the conflict between father and son, and symbolises the son's death to the "world" and rebirth to new life by a spiritual father's maieutic aid.

The story of Varlaam's struggle and suffering in the conflict with his father follows the incident where he has divested himself of his knightly apparel, expressing thereby his intention to abandon the world.

The father appears at the monastery, takes his son home with him by force, tears off his habit, and throws it "into the abyss" together with the "helmet of salvation," i.e., the hood. He clothes his son in "shining garments" as "it behoves noblemen," puts him on horseback, and leads him through the city, hands bound. "With his soul glowing in ardent love of God," Varlaam succeeds in getting free, throws the "shining garments" into a "muddy ditch," and jumps into it himself. Trampling the clothing into the mud, "he trampled on the cunning schemes of the evil fiend" (34a).

The description of Varlaam's *pathos* ends with a three-day imprisonment at his father's house. Closed up in solitary confinement, he sits "in a corner," "without moving," "without tasting food or dressing." We see him hungry and half-naked, in the typical posture of the initiate, on the borderline between life and death. In this situation temptation appears before him in the guise of his wife, who at his father's command requests her husband to "sit down on the bed," as Nestor puts it. But Varlaam answers by turning in prayer to God, who "has power to save from such folly." And finally, on the fourth day, "God beheld the youth's patience" and fulfilled the prayers of Varlaam and the monks of the Caves: He "changed the father's hardened heart," and the father released him. To the laments of his relations "as over one dead," he hastened back to the cave "like a bird freed from its snare, like a hind let loose from its net." The reunion with the monks concludes the story (34c–35a).

This "inserted novella" may also be interpreted in a different way, without excluding its function as a link between the saint and the audience of the *vita*. Seen in relation to the childhood story, the novella may be read as the transformation of a motif already suggested in the incident of the iron chain, when the saint's mother tore off his bloodstained shirt, especially since Nestor not only stresses the significance of Varlaam's sexual abstinence, but combines this motif with the story of Izjaslav's eunuch. The knight and the eunuch thus double the saint.

# The New Era

Our analysis of the childhood story has shown that it is structured according to the Christian idea of death and rebirth. This idea forms the basic pattern, embracing the individual episodes in one major action. At the same time the individual episodes are themselves variations on this fundamental scheme.

The question is now whether Nestor's account of the saint's life in the Caves Monastery follows a similar principle of composition. The traditional view has been that this part of the *vita* is more rambling and less coherent than the childhood story, which accounts for a mere tenth of the hundred chapters of the *narratio*.[1] "Of Theodosius' deeds, of his actions, and his spiritual character, Nestor writes in a fragmentary way," maintains even so sympathetic a scholar as Fedotov (1960:118). "Assembling the scattered facts, one may form an idea of the ascetic type of Theodosius." The expression used by Fedotov is symptomatic of his professed aim. He wanted to "form an idea" of Saint Theodosius as a type on the basis of Nestor' representation. His primary intention was not to investigate Nestor's own idea of the saint's exemplary significance. From the "scattered facts" of the *vita* Fedotov created the idea of Theodosius' kenotic figure. His reconstruction of the saint, however, recalls Nesterov's nineteenth-century portraits of medieval Russian saints more than it does early Russian icons. Likewise, in Eremin's description (1966:28–41) Nestor's Theodosius is seen more as a portrait than as an icon. His analysis of the second part of Nestor's *narratio* rests on the assumption that its structural models are to be found in the Chronicles. Defining the account of Theodosius' pastoral work "as an integral part of the history of the Caves Monastery," Eremin concludes that Nestor, in a number of chapters, adopts the factual appproach of the Chronicles, whereas the hagiographical representation proper is limited to giving a "portrait-like characterisation of Theodosius as man and abbot" (Eremin 1966:35). Compared with portrait-painting in modern literature Nestor's representation of the saint seems "extremely simple": "He started by enumerating all of Theodosius' virtues and spiritual merits ('of a gentle disposition,' 'of a peaceable mind,' etc.) at times in a rather arbitrary order, not without repetitions, and this enumeration was accompanied by numerous explanatory examples" (1966:35).

Eremin's structural comparison of the second part of the *vita* to the Chronicles begs the question of an underlying pattern in Nestor's

[1] The number of "episodes" or chapters varies in the extant manuscripts. In the *Uspenskij sbornik*, where our *vita* has been copied by two different hands, the first scribe has consistently omitted to number the chapters, whereas the second divides his part into chapters numbered from 61 to 100.

account: "The outcome is that Nestor's *vita* has in this part disintegrated into a number of stories, individually meant to show Theodosius in crucial situations, has been transformed into a collection of stories connected through their protagonist" (1966:35). This theory about the chronicle-like structure of the *vita* is not convincing. In the first place, as noted also by Eremin, only two dates are referred to in the oldest extant copies: 6570 (1062), when the monks moved from the cave and settled in Theodosius' new monastery, and 6582 (1074), the year of the saint's death. Second, and more important, chronology has a somewhat different function in Nestor's *vita* from that of the Chronicles. By means of such temporal adverbs as "after this," "at that time," "when," and "then," Nestor establishes an inner chronology in his account. The fragmentary accumulation of heterogeneous elements in the Chronicles, on the other hand, is effected by means of continual references to an extra-textual, historical course of events. The chronicler's main task consisted simply in recording actual events. The hagiographer's task, however, was to immortalise historical events by taking them out of the irreversible flow of time and transforming them into images of archetypal models. Only thus could the account of the saint's life be incorporated into the Church's unchangeable, ever-recurring festival calendar.

One of the devices used to achieve this effect in the second part of Nestor's *vita* is to concentrate the individual episodes in thematic cycles:

> Some stories duplicate each other, reproduce an identical theme in different variations ... are built on the same typical scheme by means of the same stylistic figures. Such stories are those which tell of Theodosius' power to curb demons, of the robbers who try to rob the monastery, of Theodosius' singular modesty and his faith that God would never let the monastery suffer hardship, but always provide the necessaries in due time. (Eremin 1966:36)

These stories are all expressions of what we might call the saint's charismatic gifts, and although Nestor builds on similar accounts in earlier hagiography, among them the *Life of Saint Sabas* (Adrianova-Peretc 1964, Eremin 1966:35), the episodes illustrate the idea of the divine *Agape* that emanates from the saint's figure and fills the monastery with the grace of God. Nestor's account of the saint's life in the monastery springs from his idea of Saint Theodosius as *novus Christus* and pastor to the "last," "frail" generation. Within the sacred precincts of the monastery he emerges as the new *aion* personified.

The story of the new era in the monastery starts with the tale of the saint's nocturnal grinding of the corn, as a newly consecrated priest. In this episode he makes his first appearance in the second part of the *Life*: "of a gentle disposition, a peaceable mind, of simple intellect, and filled

with spiritual wisdom and above all with pure love for all his brethren"
(35c). In conformity with the rules of the *encomium*, the depiction of the
saint takes the form of an enumeration of abstract, typical qualities. The
saint's "spiritual body" defies description by means of concrete details,
for it is invisible, hidden beneath his monastic cloak. It can be referred to
only by means of this abstract catalogue of *topoi*, and then illustrated by
examples from his life.

One such example is the tale of how he used to grind the brethren's
grain for them. At night each monk received his portion to be ground for
the baking of the next day's bread. While the others slept the saint went
around to them, took the grain, ground it for them, and left the flour in
its place.

The *Agape* motif has here been thematically linked with the bread
symbolism of the childhood story. The nightly scene from the life in the
monastery is at the same time a figural interpretation of the saint as the
collaborator and imitator of Christ. The image of a person grinding
grain for others forms part of the pictorial representation in medieval
times of the Biblical world of symbols. Émile Mâle (1924:167) gives a
description of such an image from the cathedral at Vézelay: a figure is
grinding grain on a mill, while another bends to receive the flour. The
typological or figural significance of this image emerges through a comparison Mâle has made with a no longer extant medallion in a window
at Saint-Denis mentioned by Abbot Suger. It represented a number of
men carrying grain to a mill where a figure is turning the grindstone.
The hidden meaning is uncovered in Suger's Latin lines beneath this
scene:

> Tollis agendo molam de furfure, Paule, farinam,
> Mosaicae legis intima nota facis;
> Fit de tot granis verus sine furfure panis
> Perpetuusque cibus noster et angelicus.

Common to this depiction of Saint Paul's mystical mill and Saint
Theodosius' grinding is the representation of their synergism in the
same metaphor: as partakers of the body of Christ they are both shown in
the figure of the Provider, as makers of the "living bread."

The tales of Theodosius as the provider of the Caves Monastery form a
thematically homogeneous cycle in the second part of the *vita*. They are
modelled on a common pattern and may be summarised as follows: one
of the brethren, usually the cellarer, informs Theodosius that they have
run out of flour, oil, or mead. The saint asks him to look again, but the
result is the same: the oil jar is empty, in the flour bin there is only a
handful of bran left. The saint asks the cellarer to be firm in his faith, and
retires to pray. Suddenly, after a while, whole carriageloads arrive before
the monastery gates with all the necessities for the brethren. Noble givers

have remembered them, now a rich boyar, now an unknown benefactor. The story ends with Theodosius calling the brethren together to a feast in order to celebrate the day when "God visited the monastery."

Factually viewed, the miracle stories are "wrought in the natural order of things" (Fedotov 1960:122), with "the economic welfare of the monastery as the only aim" (Eremin 1966:39). However, the cycle of miracle stories opens with an account of Prince Izjaslav's frequent visits to the monastery, where he would confess to Theodosius and return home "nourished by his spiritual words," an expression that from the outset gives the provider theme a metaphorical dimension.

The miracle stories representing the golden age of the Caves Monastery are all variations on the provider theme: the saint emerges in the image of Christ the Provider, *XC krъmitel* as this prototype is called in Slavonic Orthodox art (Hamann-MacLean 1976:70). Within the context of the *Life*, the provider theme represents a further development of the baking of the altar bread in the childhood story. Moreover, the miracle stories illustrate Theodosius' demand that the monks must not collect material property or care for tomorrow, but have faith in God. Likewise, the festive abundance of the miracle sequence anticipates the heavenly riches that will be theirs at the end of the road, when they shall reap the fruits of their toil.

Here, as everywhere in the *Life*, its poetic pattern becomes evident only through its symbolic meaning. Taken out of context the miracle stories appear as a number of independent incidents, linked together according to a simple principle of addition. This apparently primitive composition of our *vita* has been seen as an anticipation of the *Patericon of the Caves Monastery*, written by Simon and Polycarp about 1120 (Eremin 1966:35). However, the symbolic connection between the individual episodes of the *vita*, and its predilection for thematic cycles, testify to a structural principle very different from Simon and Polycarp's collection of stories about life in the Caves Monastery. The *Patericon* has its generic models in the early Christian Books of Fathers and consists like them of short stories depicting the struggle of individual ascetics in the lists of life. The *Life of Saint Theodosius* differs quite clearly from this genre by its tendency to arrange its component parts into a hier-archical composition by means of what we might call, with a term from art history, *übergreifende Formen*—the framework, the light visions, and the mythico-ritual scheme which form the basic pattern in Nestor's account of the saint's life.

How, then, does this tendency to a hierarchical arrangement become manifest in the second part of the *vita*? The answer can be found only if we are willing to abandon the traditional factual point of view and see Nestor's account as a symbolical representation of the saint's ascent, as it has been allegorically anticipated in the opening vision.

What has usually been interpreted as a deficiency in Nestor's account, namely, the relative independence of its components and the constantly changing viewpoint of the narrator, may also be viewed positively if we can manage to free ourselves from the demands for a unitary perspective for the whole account.

The difficulty in Nestor's account of the saint's pastoral work consists especially in that it has lost the strongly dramatic character of the childhood story. The saint is depicted from a number of different viewpoints, now seen by a brazen and ignorant coachman, now as the prince's equal, or even his superior, now celebrating the liturgy with the heavenly host.

If the term "perspective" as used by art historians is to be transferred to literary criticism, it must be treated as an historical concept. In the same way as the central perspective of the Renaissance signifies only one possibility of perspective representation, literary historians will have to realise that the naturalistic tenet of a fixed standpoint is only one of a number of possibilities. Another possibility is represented by Nestor's fluctuating viewpoint in the account of Theodosius' life in the Caves Monastery. This technique recalls the use of shifting angles in Byzantine mosaics and fresco cycles and the reversed perspective of icon-painting that opens up the world of the image to the space in front of it. A Byzantine pictorial cycle is not represented from a fixed optical standpoint, but is meant to be viewed from shifting angles. Its individual figures meet the eye of the viewer gradually as he moves about in the church, and should be viewed from the angle where their symbolic meaning as integral parts of the whole is clearest. This fluctuating perspective emerges clearly in the decoration of the church. The figures are represented with consummate artistry to give the spectator the intended impression, as he proceeds slowly and solemnly into the interior of the church. Moving along in a rhythm corresponding to the movements of the eye he will have a feeling of being accompanied by the figures in the church vaults. No static technique of reproduction can do justice to this art form. Maybe the possibilities of cinematic art would be more apt to convey it (see Mathew 1963, Likhačev 1967:212–363, Uspenskij 1973).

The unity of the iconographic programme is recreated in the spectator's mind, when during his progress through the church he views the pictures as part of the symbolic representation of God's cosmos: moving from the Last Judgement over the entrance, his eye is struck by the image of the Son of God incarnate, represented in the central apse as He dispenses the holy gifts of the Eucharist to His disciples.

Beneath this picture he sees standing the row of Holy Fathers. Above it the Mother of God with upraised arms intercedes for humanity before her Son, Christ the All-Ruler, in the sun-lit dome, viewing His church on earth, surrounded by angels, prophets, and Apostles. With an upward glance from the lowest registers to the symbolic sky of the dome the spectator catches this cosmos as his eye moves across the mediating figures of Christ the Saviour in the central apse and His Mother in the conch. The final aim of this *mystagogia* is, through the contemplation of the *kosmos aisthetos* of the icons, to obtain a vision of the *kosmos noetos* of the divine prototypes.

A similar *mystagogia* is achieved by Nestor in his *Life of Saint Theodosius*. By describing the saint's deification in the form of a vertical progress through ever higher architectural structures he creates a spiritual movement from the atectonic room of the cave, the symbolic netherworld of the *vita*, to the *porta coeli* anticipated in the opening vision.

Theodosius leads the monks away from their subterraneous life in the cave, from all the "distress and hardship of that thronged place," to which "God alone was their witness and which human lips are unable to express" (35d), continuing the work of Varlaam, his predecessor as abbot, who built a "little church to the Holy Mother of God above the cave, in order to gather the brethren there for prayer" (35d). By his ever larger and more splendid buildings Theodosius transforms the Caves Monastery into an image of the heavenly Kingdom. At the same time he is himself described in the words of the Book of Psalms as the "righteous" who "shall flourish like the palm tree" and "grow like the cedar of Lebanon" (36d), an image that echoes the upward movement of the saint's building activity in the representation of his own figure. As the builder of the Caves Monastery Theodosius becomes more and more like the illuminated Christ in the dome of the Byzantine church, the Pantocrator and Creator of the universe, the *sun of justice* of Nestor's initial light allegory.

The anagogical interpretation of life in the Caves Monastery is achieved by a combination of the building theme with the light symbolism of the opening vision. It takes the form of a sequence of reported visions of how the saint and his monastery were illuminated by a mystical light in the middle of the night. This light theme, brought back into the narrative with the vision of the three holy men in the illuminated cave, is taken a step further in Abbot Sophronius' nightly vision of the monastery:

> You could see men who in their life on earth were like angels. And the monastery was like heaven, where our blessed Father Theodosius shone more brightly than the sun through his good works. And thus he appeared also to the abbot of the Monastery of Saint Michael the Archistrategos, Sophronius by name, when one night he was on his way home. And behold, he saw a light only above the monastery of our blessed Father Theodosius. And he wondered, praised God, and said: "O how great is thy kindness, Lord, that thou hast shown this light, this godlike man, in this place, he who by shining thus has illuminated his cloister." (39d)

Sophronius' vision is followed by the accounts of how a band of robbers was prevented from attacking the monastery by the miraculous light and the sweet smell that emanated from the church, where they heard the voices of angels singing, and of the boyar who suddenly saw the church of the monastery lifted up to the clouds. Then follows a variation of the vision reported by Sophronius, this time seen by an anonymous passer-by, a pious Christian:

> There is a little mount above the monastery. And one night this man came riding across it. And lo, he beheld an awesome miracle: a wondrous light in the dead of night, right above the monastery of the saint. And lo, when he raised his eye, he saw the godlike Theodosius in that light, standing before the church in the middle of his monastery, with his arms upraised towards heaven, in devout prayer to God. And while he stood there wondering what this meant, behold, a new wonder appeared to him: a mighty flame came forth from the dome of the church, in the form of a bow reaching across to another height, and remained standing with that end on the spot which our blessed Father Theodosius picked, and where he later started building the Church. (55d–56a)

This time Nestor rounds off the vision with a quotation from the Old Testament (Gen. 28:17), thereby bringing out its deeper significance: "It therefore behoves us to say with the divine Jacob that the Lord is in this place. And this place is holy, and this is none other but the house of God, and this is the gate of heaven" (56a). Nestor's audience would remember these lines from the consecration ritual, where they signify the symbolic meaning of the church building as a *hieros topos* and a *figura* of Jacob's ladder. Only against this symbolism can we understand Nestor's further commentary. He explains the vision by mounting into his own narrative a passage from the *Life of Saint Sabas* about the pillar of fire that the saint one night saw rising from earth to heaven, how he found a cave in the place where the pillar had appeared and built a monastery there. This parallel leads to the following conclusion:

> In the same way this is to say that God has selected this place where today we see this glorious monastery, which is still flowering through his prayers. For such was our blessed Father Theodosius' prayer to God for his flock and for this place, and such his watchfulness and vigilance, and thus he shone like a brilliant light in his monastery. (56b–c)

The pillar of fire—*stulos puros*—is already a symbol of Christ in the *Acta Philippi* and occurs frequently in ascetic literature as an image of the spiritual figure of the fulfilled saint: "A pillar of fire connecting heaven and earth" (Evdokimov 1965:212).

It is, however, typical of Nestor's poetic vision that the pillar of fire, which had no figural function in its original context in the *Life of Saint Sabas*, acquires this function in the context of Nestor's *Life*. Moreover, in Nestor the image of the fiery column anticipates the final vision, when Prince Svjatoslav at the death of the saint sees above the monastery a pillar of fire reaching to the sky and remarks to his retinue: "I think the blessed Theodosius has died today" (64c).

From the pious Christian's anonymous story the visionary representation of the Caves Monastery as a bridge between heaven and earth is taken a step further in the account of the saint's mystical liturgy. One night, some men in the neighbourhood heard "innumerable voices singing," rose, went out, and climbed up to a "high place" in order to see what it might be:

> A brilliant light shone above the saint's monastery. And lo, they beheld a multitude of monks who emerged from the old church and crossed over to the spot mentioned. At their head they carried an icon of the Holy Mother of God. And all who followed sang, and carried burning tapers in their hands. But before them went their godlike Father and Leader Theodosius. When they had reached the place, they celebrated with hymns and prayers. Thereupon they returned to the old church whilst the others looked on. (56d)

The meaning of this, says Nestor, is that "these were angels who appeared, whom none of the brethren was supposed to perceive."

It is significant that in this vision of the saint celebrating with the angels there is a reference to the "hymns and prayers" of the divine service. In these texts is found the clearest expression of the idea that the liturgy of the Orthodox Church is an analogon to and an echo (*apēchēma*) of the celestial liturgy, celebrated in communion with the angels. Thus we read in the "Cherubic hymn," sung by the choir at the Great Entrance:

> We who mystically represent the Cherubim (*ta cheroubim mustikōs eikonizontes*)
> and sing the thrice-holy hymn to the lifegiving Trinity
> let us lay aside all worldly cares
> That we may receive the King of the Universe
> invisibly attended by the angelic order
> Alleluia, Alleluia, Alleluia.

These liturgical images of men and angels in communication with each other represent the symbolic universe underlying Nestor's visionary transformation of life in Theodosius' monastery into a diaphanous

House of God opening up on the other world. The representation of the saint is given a vertical dimension, transferring the events of his life from the terrestrial world to the celestial, to which his figure has been transposed.

The descent of the Holy Spirit into the saint at baptism, and the account of his abasement in the childhood part of the *vita*, constitute a downward movement which has its counterpart in the visionary representation of his ascent in the second part, where the saint's life story is gradually assimilated to the transcendental reality prefigured in the opening vision. Thus, the allegorical vision of the saint's deification in the story of his birth, and Prince Svjatoslav's symbolical vision of his union with Christ in death, form the two extreme elements of an "inner framework" in the *Life*, consisting of the visions which elevate Theodosius to the presence of Christ in His Glory. The allegorical components of the *vita* are part of its structure, and cannot be removed in the hope of getting to the core of historical facts. On the contrary, the *Life of Saint Theodosius* can be placed in a wider historical context precisely on the basis of Nestor's light symbolism and its function in his account of the saint's life as an ascension *per lumina vera ad verum lumen*, to use an expression from Nestor's contemporary, Abbot Suger of Saint-Denis.

The spiritual verticalism of Nestor's *Life*, his representation of the saint's gradual ascent towards the eternal light, may recall Dante's *Divine Comedy*. In all its perfect complexity, Dante's poem, too, takes the form of an account of the hero's abasement and gradual ascent through the symbolic cosmos of the Middle Ages. Clearly, Nestor's modest *Life of Saint Theodosius* does not bear comparison with Dante's work from a purely aesthetic viewpoint. But just as there is an ideal similarity between the great medieval cathedrals—Hagia Sophia in Constantinople, the German Kaiserdome, and the Gothic cathedrals of France and England—and the small, modest parish churches throughout the poorer parts of the Christian world, because they all image symbolically the same prototype of the Heavenly Jerusalem, in the same way there is a connection between Dante's *Comedy* and Nestor's *Slovo*. In both of them we find man's road to salvation depicted as a gradual liberation from the darkness of this world, until he reaches and is united with the Heavenly Light of Christ. "Dante's main concern in the *Divine Comedy* is not the unfolding of a tremendous eschatological panorama, but rather the account of his own gradual illumination, which we are to relive as we read his poem" (von Simson 1964:129).

However, Nestor's Theodosius is not only an image of a divine prototype. He has also kept his human features. Composed of finality and infinity he exists in the span between these two poles, in his struggle to transcend the finite and become immortalised. The saint's striving towards the heavenly goal of his ascesis is thus seen as a manifestation of his spiritual struggle to liberate his soul from matter in a movement *de materialibus ad immaterialia.* Of this *moto spiritale,* to use Dante's own term, the immovable, God himself, is part. He is the goal of Theodosius' aspiration, its *telos,* and at the same time its *metron:* Christ is the model for his ascesis and its end.

The saint's spiritual struggle is expressed most directly in the stories of his nocturnal penance, his *vita passiva,* which runs parallel to the stories of his charitable work, his *vita activa,* in the second part of the *Life.* The stories of Theodosius' penitential exercises follow immediately after the tale of his nocturnal grinding of the grain. From it Nestor goes on to describe how Theodosius at times, when the night was full of mosquitoes and other insects, went outside, bared the upper part of his body, and remained thus sitting throughout the night, singing the Psalms of David. Not until matins did he go inside again, bloodstained with mosquito bites, attending Mass as if nothing had happened.

In the stories of his penance Theodosius' striving after God is represented as suffering, in analogy to the story of the chains he wore about his loins in the first part of the *vita.* In contrast to the open manifestations of the saint's *Agape,* Nestor significantly emphasises the hidden, inner character of the *Eros* motif, which is realised in the image of the penitent saint: Theodosius hides the hair shirt beneath his habit and hides his nocturnal vigil from the brethren. In order to be at all able to represent this aspect of the saint's life, Nestor has recourse to such devices as describing his hero as observed by the monks when he thought he was alone: one night one of the monks came to him to obtain his blessing. He heard Theodosius "praying and weeping unrestrainedly and beating his head on the ground." But as soon as he heard somebody approaching, he fell silent. Again, when he lay dying and had sent all the brethren away, one of them made a "little chink" in the door, and "behold, the saint had risen and was kneeling, and praying with tears for God's mercy upon his soul." The weeping and wailing is in odd contrast to Theodosius' elated mood in community with the brethren. "He then rejoiced in spiritual merriment," and "nobody saw him sit at table with the brethren in a despondent and downcast mood."

The contrast between the saint's carefree mood and his contrition has its roots in a serio-comic conception of life in this world, a conception that we have already observed in early Christian hagiography: life is tragic when viewed from a human standpoint, but comic seen in the supernatural perspective of a saint, whose glorious end is assured even from the beginning.

The hidden significance of the penitential exercises is revealed in the saint's own words to his brethren:

> For it behoves us who call ourselves monks daily to atone our guilt with repentance; for repentance is the road which leads to the King-

dom of Heaven. Penitence is the key to the gates of the Kingdom of
God. Nobody is admitted without it. It is the road to Paradise.
Brethren, we will keep to this road, set our foot and our sole on it.
For the evil serpent will never come near this road. The walks on
this road are tiresome, but afterwards full of joy. Therefore,
brethren, we will fight until the day when we are to receive the prize
and stay away from all those who in their overweening pride refuse
to live in penitence. (39c)

The interpretation of the penitential exercises as part of the struggle to
achieve the transcendent aim of ascesis belongs to the Platonist system of
ideas of the *Life of Saint Theodosius*. The same view of poverty and
penitence is to be found in Dante's praise of Saint Francis of Assisi, who
through his symbolic marriage to poverty gained the "hidden riches and
true good" of heaven: "O ignota ricchezza, o ben verace!" (*Paradiso*
11:82). Cervantes varied this motif in his own way, in the account of Don
Quixote's penitential exercises in Chapter XXV of the novel. Although
Don Quixote's penitence takes the form of a parody of the ancient *topos*,
we can still grasp its figurative significance as an inverted expression of
erotic desire. The classical representation of a hero obsessed with erotic
desire is, of course, Plato's Eros as portrayed by Socrates in *The
Symposium*:

In the first place he is always poor, and not at all tender and
beautiful as most people believe, but hardened and haggard, rough
and squalid, an unshod and homeless down-and-out, always
sleeping on the ground and uncovered in the open, before the doors
and on the roads— with want as his fellow.

This ostracised *Eros* figure is clearly modelled on the postulant in the
transitional situation between the "old" and the "new," "midway
between wisdom and ignorance," to quote Socrates. Plato's use of the
idiom of the mystery cult is one of the links connecting this cult with the
intellectualised, contemplative mysticism of Neo-Platonism and
medieval mysticism.

The negative realisation of the *Eros*-motif in Nestor's *Life* has passed
unnoticed. "Theodosius seems to ignore *Eros* in the sense of passionate
and mystical love of God as celestial Beauty. *Agape* remained for him the
only type of Christian love. That is why there is nothing mystical about
him. Contemplation was not his business" (Fedotov 1960:129).

The erotic significance of Theodosius' penitential exercises does not
harmonise with Fedotov's idea of the saint. Faced with this motif in the
story of the saint's iron chains he interprets it as "a temporary device in
his struggle with the passion of youth," an interpretation that seems

rather trivial and even less convincing in the context of Fedotov's subtle analysis of the *kenotic* element in the *Life*.

The attempt to explain away the erotic element in Theodosius' ascesis may be the result of Fedotov's wish to find a specifically Russian saintly ideal in Nestor's *vita*. Fedotov establishes an artificial distinction between Theodosius and his Western counterpart: "This lack of Eros, in the mystical as well as esthetic sense, constitutes the main difference between Theodosius and Francis of Assisi. Otherwise, the Russian apostle of poverty and kenotic love has his nearest Western counterpart in the Umbrian Poverello" (1960:129f.).

By overlooking the hidden side to Theodosius' figure, Fedotov excludes the possibility of pursuing this connection between Nestor's image of the Russian saint and the Western monastic ideal of the late Middle Ages. He contents himself (1960:130) with emphasising the notable fact that

> Saint Theodosius preceded Saint Francis by some one hundred and fifty years. In the Western Catholic world, the revival of the Christ of the Gospel was a great discovery of the twelfth century. Saint Francis closed the movement, not as a precurser but as a fulfiller. The Russian saint, alone, without any support of tradition, himself began the tradition, not a fulfiller but a founder.

The thesis that Theodosius represents a Russian type of saint without any historical background cannot be deduced from the *Life* without violating its structure. This structure, it will be remembered, is generated by the representation of Theodosius' abasement and ascent according to the pattern of Orthodox mystagogy.

Viewed as a whole, Nestor's account of Theodosius' *imitatio Christi* is closely related to the saintly ideal of the late Middle Ages in Western Europe, to both the Franciscan version and the one conveyed in the writings of Saint Bernard of Clairvaux:

> When our Lord and Saviour, Jesus Christ, wanted to teach us how to ascend to heaven, he himself did what he taught: he ascended to heaven. But as he could not rise without first having descended, and as his simple, divine nature, which can neither be diminished nor increased nor subjected to any changes, neither permitted him to descend nor ascend, he assimilated in the unity of his person our nature, that is human nature. In this he descended and ascended and showed us the road on which we, too, were to ascend. (Nygren 1966:546)

According to Saint Bernard, God has implanted in man his striving for ascent and glorification. But in his attempt to glorify himself, natural man ends up on the false road of pride and arrogance, and sinks only deeper. Solely through the example of Christ may man be saved for the right road by following His call and becoming His imitator. Even if in our earthly life this mainly and primarily means to follow Him in lowliness and abasement, our imitation of Christ must comprise both abasement and glorification. To the question "cur Deus homo?" Bernard replies that through His descent Christ wished to teach us how we were to rise to heaven. If we are exhorted to follow Him on the road of humility and abasement, the aim is that we shall finally, and like Him, rise to the Kingdom of Heaven—*per humilitatem ad sublimitatem* (see Nygren 1966:546f.). In Saint Bernard's writings we find the same idea of monastic life as an image and prefiguration of Paradise as the one we have discovered in Nestor's *Life*. It was the abbot of Clairvaux who coined the phrase *paradisus claustralis* when describing monastic life. In the same connection he quoted the words from Genesis (28:17) used by Nestor to describe Theodosius' monastery: "Quam terribilis est locus iste! non est hic aliud nisi domus Dei, et porta caeli."

The idea of sacred architecture as a symbolic image of the Kingdom of Heaven produced the church buildings of the Cistercians as well as those of the Orthodox monks. And it will be remembered that Abbot Suger of Saint-Denis, the founder of the Gothic, belonged to the order of Saint Bernard. The Bernardine idea of a connection between building and edification has been dealt with in detail by Jean Leclercq in his introduction to the French translation of Suger's work *De consecratione*, where he also emphasises the synthesis of contemplation and action characteristic of the ascetic ideal of the Cistercians. Otto von Simson (1964:128) gives the following summary of Leclercq's views:

> The goal of monastic life is sanctification. The monk's daily work in the service of this ideal may be described as "edification." Ascetic writers like to dwell on the ancient image of the soul as a temple, and to describe the work of sanctification as an act of building. Recalling the ancient architectural overtones of the word "edification," Leclercq suggests that the Benedictine concept of labor as a process of edification may find its perfect realization in sacred architecture, designed and constructed as an image of the Celestial City, and thus requiring the vision of divine glory for its design but physical labor for its material construction. Hence the church cannot be completed without the assistance of grace, which illuminates the builder's intellect as well as his moral and artistic powers.

By drawing this parallel we may place Nestor's *vita* in a larger context. Both the account of Theodosius' active work and mystical self-contemplation, and the *anagogical* interpretation of life in the Caves

Monastery as an image of Paradise, have parallels in the contemporary monastic art of Western Europe. This correspondence indicates that Nestor's saintly ideal was not unique, devoid of any traditional background, but that his Theodosius is a representation of the monastic ideal which the monks of the High Middle Ages also strove to emulate in the West.

If we seek the common source of these different versions, we shall find that the traces lead us back to Byzantium. The relationship of the Caves Monastery to Constantinople is a feature underlined by Nestor. As soon as Theodosius had moved the monks from their subterranean caves and established his new community, he sent for the rules from the Studios Monastery in Constantinople, and these became the basis of his own order. Nestor's *Life* agrees essentially with the historical facts and suggests one of the sources for his interpretation of the saint as an imitator of Christ. The Studios Monastery was well known for its tenacious opposition to iconoclasm, and at a later date also for the monks' predilection for a typological interpretation of Biblical history (Dempf 1964:234). Saint Bernard's Christocentric mysticism, too, may be traced back to Byzantium, to the *mystical theology* whose most prominent representatives were Dionysius the Areopagite, Maximus the Confessor, and Symeon the New Theologian (see Dempf 1964:214f., von Simson 1964:126–7 *et passim*).

The connection between this tradition and the *Life of Saint Theodosius* may best be established on the basis of its light visions, for in Greek *mystical theology* the light is the highest perceptible manifestation of Christ Himself, the *lux mundi*.

# Nestor's Light Visions in their Historical Context

Our analysis has shown that Nestor's *Life of Saint Theodosius* is a complex work, reflecting its author's familiarity with a number of different sources, ranging from the Scriptures and the books of the divine Liturgy to early Greek hagiography and the Life of the Bohemian Prince Wenceslas. In the *Life of Saint Theodosius*, however, this heterogeneous material has been redistributed according to Nestor's idea of the life of Theodosius as an imitation of the life of Christ and gradual transfiguration in the image of the glorified Saviour. This idea of the saint's glorification has its origin in the light metaphysics of Christian Neo-Platonism, developed in the writings of the early Fathers of the Eastern Church. This metaphysics of light found its clearest expression in the cult aesthetic of the Orthodox Liturgy and in the theology of the icon.

The origins of Orthodox light metaphysics are to be found in Dionysius the Areopagite's synthesis of Neo-Platonist philosophy and the light theology of the Fourth Gospel. The metaphysics of light expounded in the *Corpus areopagiticum* is grounded on the idea that material light is an image of the pure, intelligible Light, which is God in His transcendent glory. The light we perceive through our senses is the self-revelation of the transcendent godhead. Therefore, according to Neo-Platonist aesthetics, light is the highest and most perfect manifestation of beauty, the reflection of divine beauty, truth, and goodness, which never reveals itself directly to man, but which "sends forth a ray, incessantly and continuously produced in itself, and transforms this ray through its goodness into natural radiance, which corresponds to individual finite beings. It raises those who are hit by the Holy Spirit up to itself according to their possibilities, lets them behold its reflection and partake of it, and teaches them to resemble itself as much as possible" (Dionysius the Areopagite, DN I, 2:588 CD).

The experience of God underlying this aesthetics of light is difficult to apprehend from a modern angle. It presupposes the medieval concept of analogy, implying that all things have been created in the image and likeness of the Creator, being in various degrees "manifestations of God, images, vestiges, or shadows of the Creator" (von Simson 1964:54). As observed long ago by Ostrogorskij (1928), the holy icons represent only a single case in this context:

> Saint John of Damascus quite consistently views not only the holy icons as "eikōn," but Holy Scripture as well ... In the same way the prophetic symbols of the Old Testament are also "icons" to him. Furthermore, the Son is the icon of the Father, and, indeed, each individual created in the image and likeness of God is God's icon. And throughout the creation there are icons of the Creator. For, as the Patriarch Nicephorus says, all things are "icons" in a certain relationship to the prototype and product of the first cause.

This relationship of similarity between things created and their divine Creator is a symbol of God's presence, giving each thing its place in the hierarchic order of the universe. But whereas in the Areopagite the opposition between the noetic reality of the divine and the world perceived by our senses is absolute, this is no longer so in post-iconoclast Byzantine light aesthetic. Here, Christ through His Incarnation has become the mediator between the two spheres. This Christocentric reinterpretation of Dionysian light mysticism was carried through by Saint Maximus the Confessor, the seventh-century theologian, according to whom Christ is the prototype transforming each individual believer into

His image and filling him with His energy, thus assimilating him to Himself. This process of assimilation, the return of the image to its prototype, of the thing to its logos, is what is meant by the term *theosis*, or deification. It is a process begun and prefigured by Christ in the mystery of His Incarnation, when He became His own image. The interpenetration of image and prototype in Christ is the model and aim of all *theosis* (see Živov 1982).

This *Urbild-Abbild* aesthetic, which found expression in the divine Liturgy of the Orthodox Church, is the historical background of Nestor's *Life of Saint Theodosius*. His account of the saint's mystical illumination and ascent is determined by the conception that light is the highest perceptible expression of the transcendent God in whom everything has its origin. The light that illuminates Theodosius' figure, like the gold illuminating the saints in medieval paintings, is a visible symbol of Christ, "the true Light, which enlightenth every man," according to Saint John. By becoming light, all men, indeed, all things, are transformed into images, or icons, of the Uncreated Light which is God Himself. This is the anagogical meaning of Nestor's opening vision, where the saint is finally transfigured in the light emanating from Christ, the Sun of Justice, and the two are united in a luminosity symbolising the glory of divine transcendence.

Byzantine light aesthetic in the Christocentric version found in Maximus the Confessor had a decisive influence, not only on Orthodox art and literature after the victory of the iconodules in 843, but also on theology and sacred art in the West. Under the Carolingians the *Corpus areopagiticum* and the writings of Saint Maximus reached Western Europe, where the Monastery of Saint-Denis in the Île-de-France became a centre for the study of Greek Platonic theology. In the ninth century the writings of the Areopagite were twice translated into Latin by abbots of the monastery, first by Hilduin, and then by John Scottus. Scottus also translated Maximus the Confessor's *Ambigua*, which he dedicated to the Emperor Charles the Bald, and his *Quaestiones ad Thalassium*, whereas excerpts of the *Mystagogia* were translated by the great scholar Anastasius the Librarian of Rome, who sent his translation, supplied with a summary of the whole work, to Charles the Bald, stressing the close relationship between Maximus and Dionysius, "whom you love and who loves you," as he put it in his dedicatory epistle to the emperor (von Simson 1964:127).

Contemporaneously with this interest in Byzantine light aesthetic in the West, the mystical theology of the Greeks became known to the Slavs. According to his *Life*, Saint Constantine the Philosopher was well versed in the writings of Dionysius, his favourite thinker. When arriving in Rome in 868, the Apostle of the Slavs was able to quote from memory one of the Areopagite texts to Anastasius, who had it written down and brought to Saint-Denis the same year. Roman Jakobson's analyses of the

Philosopher's own writings (1954, 1963, 1970) show that both in his choice of concepts and in his spiritual outlook he was deeply influenced by the theology of the Areopagite and by the idea so central to the Byzantine Fathers, that man conquers his own transience and is deified through his participation in and imitation of Christ.

In Russia there are no extant Dionysian writings from the times before the Tartar invasions. It is therefore generally assumed that their Neo-Platonist ideas first came into evidence in Russia in the fourteenth century in connection with the so-called second South-Slav influence. Nestor's *Life of Saint Theodosius* demonstrates, however, that the mystical theology of Orthodox Neo-Platonism was known in Kiev even by the eleventh century.

To the light mystics the highest form of enjoyment was the contemplation of things in order to discover their "light" and thus behold the divine Logos, the Uncreated Light of Orthodox mystics, as it is reflected in matter. This contemplation was an act of salvation, a restitution of wholeness in "disintegrated nature." In his commentary on *Super ierarchiam coelestam Sancti Dionysii*, I, 1, John Scottus writes:

> This is why the universe becomes one great light, composed of many parts as of many lamps, in order that the pure images of cognition of intelligible things be revealed to and perceived by the eyes of reason. Divine grace and the power of reason thereby cooperate in the hearts of the initiated faithful. (Hinc est, quod universalis huius mundi fabrica maximum lumen fit, ex multis partibus veluti ex multis lucernis compactum, ad intelligibilum rerum puras species revelandas et contuendas mentis acie, divina gratia et rationis ope in corde fidelium sapientum cooperantibus.)

For John Scottus, contemplating the place of all things in the divine totality, every stone, every piece of wood, becomes a light: "Lapis iste vel hoc lignum mihi lumen est."

Only against this background is it possible fully to appreciate the significance of Nestor's light visions, his account of the saint's building of the monastery as an image of the Kingdom of God, and his representation of the saint as an *imago Christi*. By contemplating Theodosius' metaphorical meaning as an image of the True Light, Nestor interprets and illuminates his figure and his life on earth. By integrating the audience in his account, he raises them in spirit from the shadowy world of the senses to the contemplation of the transcendent, the inscrutable, of God himself, who is reflected in the gold background of the *vita*.

In this way, the *Life of Saint Theodosius* bears witness to the aesthetics which in the High Middle Ages became victorious throughout Christendom, and which had also an impact in Kievan Rus'.

One of the earliest manifestations in the West of Areopagite aesthetics is the light symbolism of the Ottonian Renaissance in Germany, which reached its apex around 1000 A. D. In the "Uta-codex," an eleventh-century Regensburg manuscript, there is a reference to *De coelesti hierarchia* in John Scottus' translation. The way in which colours are perceived in Ottonian painting also testifies to Dionysian influence. They are "anti-naturalistic, in order to lend transcendent essence to the light of the image ... the colour serves to represent the light as the true being" (Schöne 1954:21).

In the Cologne "Hita-codex," another Ottonian manuscript, a representation of the *Majestas* is explained in terms that might well have served as an epigraph to Nestor's light allegory: "Hoc visibile imaginatum figurat illud invisibile verum cuius splendor penetrat mundum" (see Jantzen 1963:84). The reason why Dionysian light metaphysics found this early expression in Ottonian art is not least the contact with Byzantine culture during the reign of Otto II, who married a Byzantine princess.

The Golden Age of Areopagite light metaphysics in the West is, however, the Gothic, as it developed on the model of Abbot Suger's new church at Saint-Denis, consecrated in 1144, half a century after the *Life of Saint Theodosius*. Otto von Simson (1964:133) in his study of Suger's *ars nova* concludes that "the transformation of Norman and Burgundian models in the design of St.-Denis can really be explained as the artistic realization of ideas actually taken over from the Pseudo-Areopagite." Erwin Panofsky (1955:108–145) in his analysis of Suger's writings has shown that they, too, are a faithful reflection of Dionysian light theology. Indeed, Suger's world vision is based on the *Corpus Areopagiticum* in the translation of his predecessor, John Scottus. It emerges from Suger's writings that he was himself perfectly aware of the significance of his new church as a mystical image of the Heavenly Jerusalem. In an inscription above the entrance portal, everyone who entered the church was exhorted not to be content with a superficial admiration of its splendour, but to let his mind, enlightened by its luminous brightness, ascend to the True Light, to which Christ is the door. And the legend on the gilded portal explained why: through material things the dull mind rises to the Truth. In contemplating the perceptible *claritas* of the church, the mind is raised from its submersion in matter, from the world of the senses which keeps it prisoner:

Portarum quisquis attollere quaeris honorem,
Aurum nec sumptus, operis mirare laborem.
Nobile claret opus, sed opus quod nobile claret
Clarificet mentes, ut eant per lumina vera
Ad verum lumen, ubi Christus janua vera.

Quale sit intus in his determinat aurea porta:
Mens hebes ad verum per materialia surgit,
Et demersa prius hac visa luce resurgit.

It was not only in the countries west of Kiev that artists and scholars were
stirred by Neo-Platonist ideas. In Georgia, about 1100, there grew up a
philosophical school that had a clearly Neo-Platonist, Dionysian
character. It is especially the dense gold background of Georgian miniatures of this period that distinguishes them from earlier miniatures, a
feature that underlines the connection of the period with the spiritual
current I have here tried to sketch (see Amiranašvili 1966, for examples).
One of the leading Georgian Neo-Platonists, Peter Petritsi (1050–1130),
was a contemporary of Nestor.

A common characteristic of these Neo-Platonist movements that
flourished in Byzantium after the victory over Iconoclasm in 843, and in
the following centuries spread to the Caucasus in the East and to France
in the West, is that they run parallel to the ambitious plans of ruling
princes to transform their lands into states on the Byzantine model. The
Ottonians, the Capetians, the Georgian Bagrations, all looked to the
Byzantine emperor as their ideal prototype. So did Jaroslav the Wise,
Prince of Kiev (1019–1054), and his successors. Jaroslav's new layout for
Kiev systematically imitated Byzantine architecture, and the princely
cathedral, the Church of Holy Wisdom, founded by Jaroslav in 1037 and
probably completed in the 1060s by his son, Prince Izjaslav, was, as the
name shows, symbolically meant to imitate the Hagia Sophia of Constantinople, the ideal model also for Suger's new church at Saint-Denis.
The political significance of the Caves Monastery recalls the part played
by the monastery at Saint-Denis under the Capetians. According to
Nestor's *Life*, Saint Theodosius acted as adviser to the Kievan ruler, as
did Suger at the court of Louis VI. But in contrast to the Western
Church, the Church in Kievan Rus' never managed to regulate this
relationship with the secular princes.

In the Caves Monastery we find the same imitation of the Greeks as in
Jaroslav's new city. Nestor relates how Theodosius introduced the Sta-
tutes of the Studios Monastery in Constantinople, organising the life of
the monks according to its coenobitic rules. The new church, the
Cathedral of the Dormition, founded by Theodosius in 1073 and consecrated in 1089 (destroyed in 1941), was modelled on the Church of the
Dormition at the Blachernae Palace in Constantinople and decorated,
according to the *Pečerskij Paterik,* by Greek masters. Although the
decorations have been lost, we know that like those of the Church of
Holy Wisdom and the mosaics preserved from the Mikhajlovskij
Monastery, these decorations followed the classical Byzantine picture
programme. Moreover, the circumstantial evidence produced by
Lazarev (1966c:68ff.) allows us to conclude that in style the decorations

of the Church of the Dormition were closer to the Mikhajlovskij Monastery than to the Church of Holy Wisdom, the main difference between them being that whereas in the latter the figures are illuminated by the external source of the gold background, the artists working in the Mikhajlovskij Monastery used gold tesserae to the extent that only the contours are drawn with coloured stones, leaving the images of the saints completely golden. The aesthetic effect of this is to make the figures seem diaphanous, radiating an inner light that makes them at one with the golden background.

When comparing Nestor's *Life of Saint Theodosius* with these monuments of early Kievan art, we see that the pattern underlying his account of the saint's *imitatio Christi* is identical with the iconographical programme representing the sacrifice and subsequent glorification of Christ. He translated into verbal art a spiritual content that found its visual expression in the murals and mosaics created by his contemporaries. These visual equivalents to Nestor's *vita* enable us to see it in a wider aesthetic context, thereby placing his "light-poetics" closer to the diaphanous art of the Mikhajlovskij Monastery than to the somewhat older mosaics in the Church of Holy Wisdom. That this has not been done before may mainly be due to the prevailing view that Orthodox light mysticism was created by Gregory Palamas, the leader of the Hesychast movement in the fourteenth century. The idea that Orthodox light mysticism originated in the theology of fourteenth-century Hesychasm has prompted scholars like Likhačev and Tschiżewskij to link its appearance in Russia with the new wave of influence from Byzantium and the Balkans around 1400. In our assessment of Hesychasm, however, we have to take into account the fact that as a mystical way of knowing God it had existed for centuries when Palamas created his version of it. Instead of seeing in Palamism a wholly new spiritual trend within the Orthodox Church, we are more inclined to regard it as a continuation of the Neo-Platonist tradition that has always formed an undercurrent in Orthodox theology. From the eleventh century onwards the Neo-Platonist world-view was predominant in the Orthodox Church. It became the system of ideas that determined the individual believer's conceptions of the world in which he lived. These ideas were decisive for the development of art throughout the Christian world.

Nestor's *Life of Saint Theodosius* is an outstanding monument of this age, when Kiev, not only politically, but also by virtue of its works of art, was one of Europe's most prominent cities. Adam of Bremen named it "the most brilliant adornment of Orthodox Christendom":

CLARISSIMUM DECUS GRAECIAE

# Hagiography and History
# in Russia about 1400

## The Second South Slav Influence in Russian
## Culture and the Theory of
## an Eastern European pre-Renaissance

By the end of the fourteenth century Russian culture was being strongly influenced from the south, particularly by the Orthodox Slavs in the Balkans. This influence is usually referred to as the "second South Slav influence" in Russian culture, in contradistinction to the earlier Bulgarian influence in Kievan Rus'.

Since the end of the last century this influence and its historical origins have been the object of a number of studies starting with the works of Petrov (1876), Sobolevskij (1894), Radčenko (1898), and Syrku (1901). In both methods and aims these works are characterised by the positivist approach of their authors, more concerned with the collection of facts than with the question of their historical meaning. They considered their task completed when the facts had been recorded and their origins given a plausible explanation (the emergence of the *poluustav* in writing, Graecisms in the orthography, word formation and syntax, Bulgarian and Serbian elements in literature and painting). The result was the gradual accumulation of material demanding further analysis. The time had come for a systematic examination of it based on new methods and new approaches to the problems.

The reassessment of the second South Slav influence in Russian culture was initiated by D. S. Likhačev's paper to the Fourth International Congress of Slavists, *Nekotorye zadači izučenija vtorogo južnoslav-janskogo vlijanija v Rossii* (Moscow, September 1958).

From Likhačev's point of view the second South Slav influence was not merely a question of some few isolated instances of South Slav culture in Russia at a time when many artists and men of letters fled northwards from the Ottoman advance, as had been maintained in the past. Likhačev saw the South Slav elements in late fourteenth-century Russian culture as signs of a *new style,* and in his paper he proposed to regard this new style as an expression of a larger current within late medieval thought and culture in Eastern Europe, hoping in this way to shed new light on the complex network of cultural interrelations and influences between Byzantium, the Balkans, and Russia, going back even to Kievan influences on the literatures of the Bulgarians and the Serbs.

From these approaches Likhačev built up his own view of the second South Slav influence, focusing on two areas: stylistics and the history of culture. These areas are described and analysed side by side, while at the same time he attempts to create a synthesis between them. Hagiography, the most prominent genre in Russian literature at the time, has a special significance in Likhačev's conception of the new style, which he thinks reached its peak with the *Lives* written by Epiphanus the Wise.

Epiphanius was a contemporary of the icon painter Andrej Rublev. Both had their background in coenobitic monasticism, which had been reintroduced in Russia by Saint Sergius of Radonež in the middle of the fourteenth century, after a decline during the preceding century. Epiphanius wrote the *Life of Saint Sergius,* a work he started soon after Sergius' death in 1392 and on which he was engaged for more than twenty years. It was probably completed around 1417, but it is extant only in later copies and in a radically revised form. Epiphanius' other main work is the *Life of Saint Stephen, Bishop of Perm,* dated to 1397, the year after Stephen's death. Although here, too, Epiphanius' autograph has been lost, it is thought to be preserved in its original form. The works of Epiphanius become key texts for Likhačev's definition of the new style in Russian literature, a style he finds also in the painting of the time, and the origin of which he seeks in each case in the second South Slav influence. Literature and painting are seen as expressions of the same spiritual trend (1958, 1962, 1973). For Likhačev the most important thing was not to define the new style by formal criteria. The new style is characterised not only through the description of its predominant technical devices, but also by means of the ideology that Likhačev (1958) postulated as its moving cause. His analysis is thus based on a combination of formal elements and ideological content. In itself this method is not new, but it heralded something new in the study of Russian literature from the time around 1400.

On the whole, the literature of this period had previously been negatively assessed, since Ključevskij (1871) had characterised it as an exaggerated, empty panegyric, in which the style had become a superficial ornament and an aim in itself. Borrowing an expression from Epiphanius, the style had become known as *word-weaving (pletenie sloves),* a term with largely negative connotations in positivist scholarship. Literary historians came to regard it as an unnecessary complication in their attempts to ascertain and verify the historical content of the texts. Word-weaving was reduced to "artificial rhetorical effects," to a style marked by its "artificial, pompous, and laborious character," "hopeless-

ly idiosyncratic, long-winded, full of recherché linguistic contrivances"
(Ključevskij 1871, Glubokovskij 1892, Orlov 1945).

What was new in Likhačev's 1958 paper was his attempt to find a
meaning, a poetic intention in word-weaving. This in itself signifies a
departure from the traditional, unsympathetic attitude of previous
scholars. Likhačev places word-weaving in the system of early Russian
literature according to his concept of its three different stylistic
"spheres" or strata. This classification is based on both generic and
stylistic criteria. It is not absolute, and the boundaries between the three
spheres fluctuate. Nevertheless, it is possible, according to Likhačev, to
project onto medieval Russian literature the tripartite stylistic scheme
known from classical theory. We thus get a high, Church Slavonic style,
comprising Lives of saints, homiletic literature, instructions, etc., a
middle style closely related to the style of the chancelleries, comprising
chronicles, historical tales, travelogues, etc., and, finally, a low style distinguished by the authors' use of elements taken from colloquial language and by their parodying of other, higher genres, and known to us
only from relatively late texts. It is characteristic of word-weaving that
this style is confined to the high genres (1958:27).

Another important presupposition for Likhačev's analysis is the
concept of *abstraction (abstragirovanie)*, a concept typical of all
medieval literature, which nevertheless acquired a special function in
word-weaving. This abstractifying trend originates in the authors'
striving to find what is general, absolute, and unchangeable in the
particular, concrete, and temporal, the immaterial in the material. This
was not only an ethical, but also an aesthetic principle, and should be
seen as diametrically opposed to what Likhačev (1958:26ff., 1967:109ff.)
calls "the urge for concreteness" in modern art and literature. The high
genres of early Russian literature differ from the literature of our own
and of the last century through their orientation towards symbolic contexts and theological interpretations. The use of Church Slavonic
separates the high genres from daily life, elevates the representation
above its sphere, makes it abstract. The high style gives expression to
that which is holy, the *other* reality, and becomes comprehensible only
to the chosen few. It is a learned style with a complicated orthography
seeking to avoid concrete designations for things and conceptions belonging to historical reality, current political, military, and economic
terms. When referring to actual historical events or persons, the author
will deconcretise them by substituting other, vaguer terms for those one
would normally use, by employing periphrastic constructions,
Graecisms, etc. This is a stylistic feature Likhačev traces back to Kievan
literature, but whose origins must be sought in Greek rhetoric.

The constant use of scriptural quotations is also seen as part of this
process of *abstragirovanie*. With the aid of such quotations the writers
were able to create analogies emphasising what is general in the lives of

their saints, thus accentuating the didactic purpose of their life stories. This emphasis on the didactic function of the quotations points to a certain one-sidedness in Likhačev's definition of word-weaving. As we have seen, the use of scriptural quotations in early Russian hagiography is a manifestation of an *Urbild-Abbild* aesthetic inherited from the Greeks. Furthermore, it is connected with the "probative character drawing" of the Greek encomium, taken over by early Christian hagiographers in their striving to reveal in the representation of their heroes the archetypal features of their Biblical models.

The use of *topoi,* of traditional comparisons, metaphors, and epithets, is allotted the same abstractive function in Likhačev's definition of the new style. Rhetorical devices of this kind are not supposed to have the same innovative function in medieval literature that they have in our own time (Likhačev here refers to the theories of the Russian Formalists). Precisely in their capacity as stereotypes, expressional constants became means of representing the immovable, divine order revealed by theology once and for all.

To sum up, on the one hand Likhačev by his use of *abstragirovanie* (abstractifying) wishes to describe a basic feature in all the high genres of medieval literature, whereas on the other hand he maintains that word-weaving in Russian hagiography around 1400 differs from hagiographical style before and after this period through its particular version of abstractification.

What defines word-weaving as a specific form of abstractification is that it is charged with an extraordinary emotional excitability. It is a question of an "emotionality carried into exaltation, expressivity linked up with abstractification, abstraction of feelings combined with the abstraction of theological thought" (1958:31). All the stylistic features that are characteristic of word-weaving, its accumulation of synonyms, long sequences of synonymous comparisons, periphrases, antitheses, repetition of the same root in different forms and of the same form with different roots, all the rhetorical play on semantic and formal similarities and dissimilarities, in Likhačev's reconstruction become manifestations of an emotionality strained to the breaking point, a will to squeeze the expressive possibilities of language to their last drop, a virtuoso play on shades of meaning that change all static relations into a shimmering dynamism, dissolving the surface of things, transforming them into expressions of the emotional life of the saint, and of the author's and his audience's hyperconscious, even excited attitude to the representation of his life. The hagiography that emerged under the second South Slav influence is in Likhačev's view marked by an "abstract psychologism," abstract because the writers depict states of mind without seeing their true cause. They dissolve the surface into a constantly changing psychological play, but do not penetrate to the human character as the origin of the emotions. Nor are they able to depict mixed emotions, but follow the traditional scheme—either devotion, contemplation, and elation, or passion, wickedness, fury, envy, etc.:

> Emotions and passions, evolved and exaggerated to extremes, in a way lead their own lives, may be developed independently, and change suddenly. They are carried to a degree of expressivity where all individual nuances are blurred. All the more or less fine distinctions between various states of mind which may be clearly discerned when contemplated in the character of the individual, have gone. (1958:39)

When the representatives of this new style in Russia describe such highly strung states of mind, they are interested not so much in an exact rendering as in conveying the impression that these emotional eruptions make on themselves. They constantly emphasise the mystical significance, the inexplicable in their own feelings, their span. They burst into lamentations, then fall silent, but cannot suppress their enthusiasm and urge the audience to be carried away.

Thus interpreted, the typical stylistic features of word-weaving become a vehicle for a certain mental attitude in the authors who under South Slav influence took over its characteristic idiom. The devices of this new style are seen in direct relation to a particular attitude to reality, which Likhačev has defined from the point of view of "abstract psychologism." He has thereby moved one step closer to his objective: to connect word-weaving directly to Russian icon-painting in the fourteenth century, when it, too, was strongly influenced by South Slav, especially Serbian, art. Likhačev argues that we are here faced with the same interpretation of reality expressed through different media.

The closest parallels to word-weaving in contemporary icon-painting are, according to this thesis, the fresco paintings in the Novgorod and Pskov regions: in the Church of the Dormition in Meletovo and the Snetogorskij Monastery near Pskov, the Volotovo Church of the Dormition and the Skovorodskij Monastery near Novgorod, the Church of the Transfiguration in Novgorod, and a number of others. In the view of some art historians, all these fresco decorations represent a Russian version of the "Palaeologan Renaissance" in Byzantine painting, the style that evolved after the Emperor Michael VIII Palaeologus had recaptured Constantinople from the Latins in 1261.

In the execution of these frescoes and in their range of motives, Likhačev (1958:40ff.) recognises the same extreme emotionalism that he has found in the *Lives* of Epiphanius. He is particularly struck by the resemblance in scenes depicting the Birth of the Virgin, the Assumption, the Deposition from the Cross, and the Entombment, as they have been described by Russian art historians, on whose interpretations Likhačev bases his own comparisons. His own account of the emotional content of word-weaving corresponds to their characterisation of the paintings, even though there are no direct thematic parallels between the Lives of saints and the frescoes he refers to. By drawing these parallels with the art of painting Likhačev approaches the high-water mark of his revaluation of the second South Slav influence in Russia.

Fresco painting in Novgorod from the end of the fourteenth century, especially the famous frescoes by Theophanes the Greek in the Church of the Transfiguration on Elijah Street, executed in 1378, has repeatedly been interpreted as a visual expression of mystical Hesychasm. Disclaimed as heresy at the beginning of the fourteenth century, Hesychast theology nevertheless spread throughout the Orthodox world, and by the middle of the century, having defeated the opposition, Hesychasm became the official doctrine of the Eastern Church.

The question of how Hesychasm influenced Russian culture around 1400 has only recently come to the fore in modern scholarship. The point of departure has usually been precisely the Novgorod frescoes of Theophanes the Greek (Lazarev 1961, Golejzovskij 1964, Alpatov 1972).

Hesychasm (Greek *hēsuchia*, silence, inner quietude) in the fourteenth century meant a resumption and further development of the mystical theology of the *Corpus Areopagiticum*, Maximus the Confessor, and Symeon the New Theologian. The spiritual centre was Athos, the monastic community on the Aegean, which in the fourteenth century found itself in the domain of the Serbian king. But Constantinople and the Hesychast monasteries in Bulgaria had an important role to play as well, for the propagation of the movement. According to tradition, the first and most distinguished representative of Hesychasm in Russia was Sergius of Radonež. His Trinity Monastery outside Moscow, the Troice-Sergieva Lavra (today Zagorsk), became the nursery of Hesychasm in Russia. Epiphanius was Sergius' pupil and biographer. Andrej Rublev appears to have been close to the Troice-Sergieva Lavra (Kuz'mina 1971). The links between hagiography and icon-painting uncovered by Likhačev thus seem to rest on an historical foundation.

The connection between Hesychasm and the second South Slav influence becomes manifest also in translated Russian literature of this period. Besides the writings of Gregory of Sinai, the first leader of the Hesychasts in the early, militant period before 1350, and Gregory Palamas, their foremost theorist, other writings that were translated include those of the representatives of the triumphant Hesychasm from the second half of the century, the Ecumenical Patriarch Philotheos Kokkinos and the autocephalous Bulgarian Church's last head, the Patriarch Euthymius of Trnovo. Also, the mystical theologians of the Orthodox Church were translated at this time, among them Dionysius the Areopagite, Maximus the Confessor, and Symeon the New Theologian (Sobolevskij 1903:15ff.).

Likhačev (1973:101) in his interpretation of Hesychasm stresses especially its connection with Neo-Platonist "mystical individualism" and interest in the "inner man." Like so many other scholars he sees in Hesychast contemplative technique features recalling yoga. The technique was meant as an aid to concentrating the mind, so that the Hesychast through contemplation of the divine could be carried away in an ecstatic vision of the "uncreated light." This light was identified as that which was revealed to the Apostles at the Transfiguration of Christ. In Gregory Palamas' terminology it is identical with the energy emanating from the invisible, absolutely transcendent Godhead, different from, but nevertheless identical with the Godhead. In this mystical doctrine of man's union with God in the ecstasy of the light vision Likhačev (1958:22ff., 1962:83ff., 1973:93ff.) finds the origins of that "abstract psychologism" that gives Russian icon-painting and hagiography their distinctive stamp from the end of the fourteenth into the fifteenth century.

This connection enables him to take another step in his attempt to place Russian culture of this epoch in a wider context. With its strong admixture of Neo-Platonism, which Hesychasm has in common with all Orthodox mysticism, its emphasis on the ability of individual man to know God through mystical self-contemplation, sometimes even at the expense of Church dogma, and its connection with heretical sects like the Bogomils, Eastern European Hesychasm ceases to be an exclusively Orthodox phenomenon and becomes instead part of the complex of contradictory spiritual currents which Likhačev calls the Eastern European pre-Renaissance *(Predvozroždenie)*, a term borrowed from Italian art history, where it describes the new trends emerging around 1300, represented by Giovanni Pisano and Arnolfo di Cambio in sculpture, Giotto in painting.

The introduction of the term pre-Renaissance instead of the traditional Palaeologan Renaissance to signify the last phase in Byzantine art history, and the extension of the concept to literature, form part of Likhačev's comprehensive vision of unity in the cultures of Eastern and Western Europe during the fourteenth and fifteenth centuries.

The "abstract psychologism" of mystical Hesychasm and its stylistic counterpart in word-weaving and in the emotionalism of icon-painting are explicitly linked with Giotto's frescoes in the Arena Chapel in Padua (1306), the only work of art of the Italian pre-Renaissance mentioned by Likhačev, and in his vision of this epoch seen as the link between East and West (1958:42). In order to place Russian culture in the context of such an all-embracing Eastern European pre-Renaissance, Likhačev employs the concept of "distinctive national characteristics," a concept common in Russian art history, which in Likhačev's reconstruction serves to establish an indigenous Russian version of the pre-Renaissance, whose main characteristic is the grafting of new Byzantine and Balkan elements onto pre-Mongolian traditions. The use of pre-Mongolian models in early Muscovite literature, so obvious in the *Zadonščina*, is typical also of Epiphanius the Wise, whose *Lives* contain numerous quotations from early Kievan literature. In architecture this interest in the traditions from before the time of the Tartar invasions was reflected in the restoration of the churches in Vladimir-Suzdal, carried out under the son of Dimitrij Donskoj, the Grand Prince Basil I, who in 1408 sent Andrej Rublev and his painter friend Daniil to Vladimir to restore the frescoes of the Cathedral of the Dormition. The old churches of Vladimir were imitated in fifteenth-century Moscow, where the Grand Princes modelled their own sacred architecture on them, as did their rivals in Tver, Rostov, and Novgorod (Likhačev 1958:59f.). What Likhačev defines as a specifically Russian pre-Renaissance is thus seen by him as the result of two interacting factors: influence from the South, from the Balkans and from Byzantium, and the reawakening of cultural traditions from pre-Mongolian times.

The preponderance of the latter factor in the works of Andrej Rublev and Epiphanius the Wise gives them, according to Likhačev (1962), a typically national character, in contrast to the frescoes by Theophanes the Greek and the *Lives* of saints written by Pachomius the Serbian, a professional hagiographer working in Russia in the second quarter of the fifteenth century, and after Epiphanius the most important representative of word-weaving in early Russian literature. Likhačev stresses that these foreigners brought their own techniques and skills, and unlike their Russian colleagues remained relatively uninfluenced by the national tradition.

The Russian pre-Renaissance, or pre-Renaissance components, as Likhačev puts it more cautiously at times, are assumed to have resulted from a number of factors of a social and economic nature, such as the growth in the means of production, the emergence of cities and urban society, of the craft industries, and of internal commerce, as well as the first victories over the Tartars, which led to a heightened national self-assurance (1958:60f.).

With this description of a national Russian pre-Renaissance Likhačev concludes his paper. In the course of his argument a barely perceptible shift of focus has taken place. The problems of the second South Slav influence and its effects in Russia have given way to a reconstruction of the historical situation in Russia around 1400 *on the analogy of* the situation in those parts of Europe where the rediscovery of Classical Antiquity led to a break with the Middle Ages and to the emergence of Humanism.

This presentation of cultural life in Russia at the end of the fourteenth century is, to say the least, highly problematical, since early Muscovite culture lacked precisely the factor which enables us to talk of an Italian pre-Renaissance around 1300, and subsequently in those countries that came under Italian influence, namely a new humanist culture. Instead of a "rediscovery of Classical Antiquity," Likhačev (1973:113) is forced to have recourse to phrases like "obraščenie k svoej antičnosti" ("a turning to one's own antiquity,") in order to make the early Muscovite restoration of Kievan culture fit the picture. But this terminology cannot warrant giving Muscovite culture the classical humanist element it never had.

Likhačev's own account of how the legacy of the pre-Mongolian era was transferred to Moscow in order to create a Muscovite culture on the basis of this heritage, conveys a clear impression of the restorative character of early Muscovite culture. It is a question of whether Russian culture in the time from Dimitrij Donskoj's first victory over the Tartars in 1380 down to Ivan III's consolidation of Moscow as the Third Rome, after the fall of Constantinople in 1453, should not rather be seen as a restoration of the Orthodox tradition together with the *translatio imperii* of the Grand Princes of Moscow, the translation of the traditions of the Second Rome, the Eastern Empire, to Moscow. After the defeat of the Nemanja dynasty in Serbia, and the Bulgarian tsars, at the hands of the invading Turks, Moscow emerged as the principal contender for the imperial legacy.

This view, that the second South Slav influence represents restoration rather than "renaissance," is supported by the criticism that has been raised against Likhačev's attempt to define it on the theory of an "Eastern European pre-Renaissance."

This criticism has been voiced most sharply by Viktor Lazarev (1970:310ff.) who denies all scholarly value to the concept of a pre-Renaissance in Eastern Europe. For this term to become at all meaningful, it will have to be reserved for the phenomenon it has traditionally designated in art history: the break with medieval conventions, and the rediscovery of classical models in architecture and in sculpture by Nicolò Pisano and Arnolfo di Cambio, while at the same time the basis for a new realistic art of painting was being laid by Giotto and Pietro Cavallini. Lazarev sees these new trends in Italian art at the end of the thirteenth and the beginning of the fourteenth centuries in connection with the emergence of a new class—the bourgeoisie—and the rudiments of early capitalist social conditions in an age when Marsilio of Padua advocated a popularly elected government, and literature entered a new phase with Dante. It is this chronologically and territorially well-defined phenomenon that the term pre-Renaissance should continue to designate if, in Lazarev's opinion, it is to be used as a scholarly concept. It has its function as a designation for the early seeds of the new humanist philosophy and realism of the Renaissance, based on the application in art of a newly won scientific insight. Seen from this angle, Likhačev's concept becomes synonymous with the use of "renaissance" in compounds like "Carolingian," "Ottonian," "Macedonian,"

"Comnenian," or "Palaeologan" Renaissance, where the term "renaissance" has been reduced to mean simply a "cultural flowering," or "rebirth," that is, a flowering within the framework of medieval feudal culture.

It is true that some art historians use the term "pre-Renaissance" in a wider sense than that used by Lazarev. It occasionally designates a movement in the South of France, in Spain, and in Italy—the "pre-Renaissance of the twelfth century." However, in this context also, the use of the term is prompted by the presence of the remains of classical monuments of art, by the knowledge of Latin and of classical literature, in other words by influence from classical Antiquity (Panofsky 1965:55). Any such influence is, however, out of the question in Russian culture at the end of the fourteenth century and in the following century.

Both in the light of this wider definition of the pre-Renaissance, and even more if we use Lazarev's definition, art and literature in Russia during the second South Slav influence appear to be almost a negation of what the term usually covers. Here there is no direct contact with classical Antiquity, either with its visual arts or with its literature, nothing to indicate that the citizenry of the towns had a leading role to play in cultural development, or that the old social structure was weakened. On the contrary, the old feudal structure was reinforced and the development went in the direction of curbing the freedom of the individual. The Church consolidated her power and her cultural hegemony. The literature of the period is devoid of humanist elements, and art developed quite independently of the newly won knowledge of Antiquity elsewhere in Europe, unmoved by the new scientific attitude to the problems of the visual arts (Lazarev 1970:311).

Likhačev's characterisation of art and literature during the second South Slav influence as "abstract psychologism," a characterisation that Lazarev accepts with certain reservations, shows that what was new in Russian hagiography and icon-painting around 1400 should rather be seen in direct contrast to the new elements in the Italian pre-Renaissance. It is not abstract space and emotional high tension that mark the latter, but experiments with the representation of three-dimensional space, and human figures marked by a spiritual equilibrium and tranquillity. The heretical currents that Likhačev emphasises as a spiritual background to art in the Byzantine Commonwealth under the Palaeologans did not contribute to producing the new trends in Italian art. The Italian pre-Renaissance could evolve only when the radicalism and intolerance of the heretics had been overcome. Otherwise the new secular urban culture would have had no chance (Lazarev 1970:313).

As to the significance of Hesychasm for cultural life in the Balkans and in Russia in the fourteenth century, Lazarev warns against overestimating it. He rightly points out that it reached Russia in a highly modified form, and touches thereby on a crucial problem in connection

with Likhačev's definition of Hesychasm. It is a static definition which
does not take account of how Hesychasm developed from being virtually
a heretical movement at the beginning of the fourteenth century into representing the teaching of the official Orthodox Church in the second
part of the century. Lazarev dismisses Likhačev's claim that pre-Renaissance ideas should have become manifest in Byzantine Hesychasm and
that Palamas' psychological theories should have amounted to a clearly
progressive phenomenon in the fourteenth century. In Lazarev's
opinion it was, on the contrary, Palamas who integrated Hesychasm
into the official Church, systematically nipping in the bud any
Byzantine "humanism." Lazarev, much more than Likhačev, is here in
accord with the views proposed by other scholars respecting the significance of Hesychasm for the development of Byzantine culture, even if he
is admittedly somewhat too negative in his evaluation of its impact. The
struggle between Palamas and his opponents in the 1340s, which ended
with victory for Palamas and the Hesychasts, meant a complete defeat
for the Party of Union and the Greek humanists who favoured a
rapprochement with Rome and saw the West as a possible heir to their
own culture. The Party of Union represented a political and cultural
orientation that traditionally met with opposition from the mass of the
monks and the people. For them the Unionists were Latinisers and
defilers of Orthodoxy. The Hesychasts sided with the monks and the
people, and the consequence was that Byzantium was excluded from the
new humanist culture emerging in the West (Meyendorff 1964:133,
1981:99–107; Mathew 1963:140).

In the second part of the fourteenth century, when the Hesychasts had
captured the leading positions within the Orthodox Church, in
Byzantium, in the Balkans, and in Russia, these areas developed in a
direction that only widened the gap between Orthodox culture and the
Humanism of the Renaissance.

Let us take a closer look at the background to the differing views of
Likhačev and Lazarev with regard to the pre-Renaissance. We may start
by examining their respective approaches to the historical situation.

Lazarev views the pre-Renaissance retrospectively. For him it signifies
primarily an anticipation of the Italian Renaissance. He is mainly interested in those features of Italian art that mark its difference from the art
of Byzantium. In this respect his view is in full accord with traditional
interpretations of the Renaissance ever since Vasari's famous *Vite*, where
the term *rinascità* refers to the art of Giotto and his age, when Italian art
broke away from the flat, rigid, and lifeless travesty of painting that
Vasari associated with the Byzantines. In Vasari's scheme Giotto marks
the first of three stages. The second is represented by Masaccio, the third
by Leonardo, Michelangelo, and Raphael. Lazarev's emphasis on
Giotto as the only true representative in painting of the pre-Renaissance
shows that his definition in actual fact constitutes a more modern

version of Vasari's scheme. It is in their characterisation of Giotto's art that the two scholars' different approaches are most clearly expressed. Lazarev (1970:312) is prepared to accept Likhačev's characterisation of late Byzantine painting as "abstract psychologism," but he dismisses categorically Likhačev's attempt to view Giotto's painting in this context. Likhačev (1958:42) for his part sees in Giotto's frescoes a manifestation of the same emotionally tense style that characterises late Byzantine painting.

Lazarev's definition of Giotto's art as an expression of the pre-Renaissance is one-sided but logical, as it is based explicitly on an analysis of those elements in Giotto that were later integrated into the idiom of Renaissance painting.

Likhačev's (1958:42) attempt to use the similarity between Giotto and late Byzantine painting in making out a case for an Eastern European pre-Renaissance rests, however, on a faulty logic, as his comparison stresses aspects of Giotto's paintings other than those that anticipate the Renaissance. The elements that Likhačev especially notes in Giotto are in themselves equally essential for his art, but they do not point forward to the Renaissance. While Lazarev emphasises the differences between Giotto and the Byzantine painters, Likhačev stresses the similarities between Giotto's frescoes in the Arena Chapel and Byzantine frescoes like those of the Chora Monastery in Constantinople, Macedonian and Serbian frescoes, the frescoes at Volotovo near Novgorod, and others. The basis of comparison are the scenes from the legendary life of the Virgin Mary, common to all these frescoes. But they can hardly be said to anticipate the innovations of Renaissance art.

Despite their differences both Likhačev's and Lazarev's views of the relationship between late Byzantine art and the pre-Renaissance are marked by their conception of the Renaissance as a unique epoch in history, the historic moment when "man discovered himself." Their interpretation of the Renaissance should be judged against the background of the significance that this concept acquired since Jules Michelet's *La Renaissance* (1855) and Jacob Burckhardt's *Die Kultur der Renaissance in Italien* (1860). In both these works the term Renaissance represents a total reawakening from the darkness of the Middle Ages to a new, anthropocentric view of life, which is seen in opposition to the theocentric view of preceding centuries. For Lazarev this leads to an absolute divide between the pre-Renaissance and the Middle Ages, whereas Likhačev is led to try to give Russia and the other countries within the Orthodox *oikoumene* a "pre-Renaissance," even if Russia never experienced a true Renaissance in the sense which this term has acquired in European cultural history.

Likhačev's theory of an Eastern European pre-Renaissance presupposes an admiration for the Renaissance that is traditional in Russian cultural history. At the beginning of our century this admiration for the

Renaissance induced Ajnalov and other art historians to explain the Old
Testament Trinity attributed to Andrej Rublev, now world-famous, as a
product of the influence in Russia of Italian Renaissance painting.
Ajnalov (1913) traced Rublev's icon back to Sienese art from the time
around 1300, as we know it through the paintings of Duccio and the
Lorenzetti brothers.

This theory has now been abandoned. The resemblances between
Rublev's icons and Sienese painting are explained on the basis of a
common source in Byzantine art. It has gradually become clear that
Byzantine art had a far greater significance for Italian art in the
fourteenth century than was previously assumed.

The study of Byzantine painting has established an ever-increasing
number of connections between art in Byzantium and Italian art
even after Giotto. The divide between the pre-Renaissance and the
Palaeologan Renaissance can therefore no longer be drawn so sharply as
by Lazarev (1970:310), not even in Giotto's case. Gervase Mathew
(1963:9) sees the great difference between Giotto and his predecessors not
in a break with Byzantine art, but in his departure from the formalised
and at the time old-fashioned, provincial version of *arte bizantina* for the
new art developing in Byzantium.

It is to Likhačev's great credit that he has established a number of basic
similarities between Eastern European icon-painting in the fourteenth
century and Giotto's Padua frescoes, and at the same time outlined the
problems raised by these connections for the study of the relationship between Eastern and Western European art in the late Middle Ages, and for
the development of Byzantine painting among the Orthodox Slavs. It is
clear that the new conception of the relationship between Giotto and
Byzantine art also implies a new view of relations between the art of
Orthodox Slavs in the fourteenth century and Western art influenced by
Byzantium. We can no longer regard these trends as absolute contrasts.
They emerge as versions of a common style.

A striking instance of this is to be found precisely in Giotto's frescoes
in the Arena Chapel. What was new in Giotto's art in relation to Western
art in the thirteenth century finds a clear expression in his Lamentation over the body of Christ, often used by art historians to illustrate
Giotto's break with the old.

Giotto's figures are no longer confined to the picture surface and the
abstract play of lines. They are grouped behind each other in different
planes, the main figures in the foreground, the others behind them. A
suggestion of a landscape, in the form of a rock, constitutes the middle
distance, the blue colour of the background fills the space with air and
creates an illusion that the figures can move about within this space.
Tensions arise between them. To the left in the picture the Mother of
God kneels holding the body of her Son in her arms. Her eyes gaze into
the half-closed eyes of Christ as if to find there a sign of life. In the middle

of the picture, with his eyes directed towards Christ and His Mother, the Apostle John bows down towards them, spreading out his arms in a movement which gives a contrary emphasis to the movement of his torso, which is repeated and varied in the figures of the wailing women in the foreground and reflected in the group of grieving women behind Mary. All the figures in the picture express their grief over the body of Christ, in their gestures, from the contorted movements of the angels towards heaven, to the women hiding their faces and disappearing in the cubic mass of their mantles, whose shrouds even become a sign of grief.

If we regard Giotto's gestural expressionism from a Byzantine point of view, however, it cannot be described as a revolution in painting, as is done by those art historians who view the picture exclusively in the light of the Western tradition (e.g., Gombrich 1967:146). We recognise the same expressive gestures in a Serbian fresco painting from the second part of the thirteenth century, the representation of the lives of Mary and Jesus in the church at Sopoćani. Here, too, the figures are placed so that the space between them is charged with tension, and the tragic content in their dramatic gestures is emphasised. In the Deposition from the Cross the body of Christ is crouched on the Cross, His head drooping onto His shoulder, lifeless, the soldier with the spear in a twisted posture, and the Virgin Mary falling down in a faint towards the Apostle John. As in Giotto's painting the bodily outlines are hidden by the voluminous draperies, inscribed in their massive blocks.

The striking resemblance of these frescoes to Giotto was first explained on the theory of Italian influence, as was the case with Rublev's icons. In Sopoćani this explanation seemed even more likely, given the existing trade intercourse between the cities on the Adriatic at the time when the frescoes were painted. However, the dating of the frescoes to the 1260s excludes this explanation: they are about forty years older than Giotto's frescoes in the Scrovegni Chapel at Padua.

The possibility of an influence in the opposite direction was first put forward by N. Okunev (1928:1). Subsequent research seems to corroborate his theory. Today it looks more and more as if the "Italianisms" in Serbian painting may be traced back to Macedonian art in the eleventh and twelfth centuries (Radojčić 1956:68); in other words, it was Giotto who sought his models in the East, and not the reverse. This applies not only to his emotional style, but also to his spatial effects, traditionally regarded as the most revolutionary element in his *stil nuovo*. Giotto's spatial effects have, according to Mathew (1963:152), a long prehistory in Byzantine painting. Mathew goes so far as to maintain that Giotto's new style was "at its most Byzantine in the use of a 'box-space' perspective to contain the dramatic tension of its figure work."

The style represented by the Sopoćani frescoes forms a highly emotionalised version of Palaeologan painting. Elements of this style are found even from the Comnenian age—that is, from the time before the raids of the Crusaders and the establishment of the Latin Empire in Constantinople in 1204. Lazarev (1947:122) has established a close relation both iconographically and stylistically between the high emotional pitch of late thirteenth-century Byzantine painting and the frescoes in the Church of Saint Panteleimon at Nerez in Macedonia, executed by a Constantinopolitan master in 1164 at the behest of a member of the Comnenian dynasty. These frescoes are a unique testimony that the style known as "Palaeologan Renaissance" was already developing in the twelfth century. In the saints by the master of Nerez, Lazarev finds a parallel to the Novgorod frescoes by Theophanes the Greek, and in the former's cycle of Gospel scenes Lazarev sees a dramatisation of the narrative element typical of the thirteenth century.

In the Lamentation at Nerez the body of Christ lies almost horizontally in the arms of the kneeling Virgin. At Christ's feet we see the figure of the Apostle John, his head bent down towards the left hand of Christ, which he holds up as if to press it to his lips in a parting kiss, while Mary, as in Giotto's picture, bows down towards her Son's head, searching with her gaze for life in His eyes. The draperies have not yet received the swollen form they have in Sopoćani and in Giotto, where they hide the contours of the figures. But the emotionalised gestures are there, the pathos emphasised by Likhačev as a distinctive feature of Russian painting at the end of the fourteenth century. It is this pathos that in his view has found a verbal equivalent in the word-weaving style of Epiphanius the Wise, which will be dealt with below. For the time being we will content ourselves with recording that Theophanes the Greek in no way represents a new style in Orthodox icon-painting. His Novgorod frescoes are rather to be seen as a late phase in the development of the emotive style, which is in the process of breaking up. It can no longer be regarded as a probability that Theophanes brought this style to Novgorod, as maintained by Lazarev. On the contrary, it seems most likely that Theophanes acquired this style from the school of fresco painting in Novgorod and Pskov (Amiranašvili 1971:175ff.)

The Nerez style can be recognised in the far more provincial version of the Spaso-Mirožskij Monastery near Pskov, from the middle of the twelfth century, where the narrative element is much in evidence, and where the lamentation over the body of Christ also finds its expression in the dramatic gestures of the mourners. But the execution is more schematic and lacks the elegance of the Nerez frescoes.

This discrepancy is easier to understand if we bear in mind Gervase Mathew's definition (1963:142ff.) of the emotional style as a synthesis of Constantinopolitan court art and the narrative conventions of a more provincial, monastic school of painting, marked by its brutal and dramatic realism and its emphasis on the emotional aspect of the theme, transformed into a pictorial narrative immediately comprehensible to the spectators. The traditions of court art are displayed in superior technique, sense of rhythm, and a sure eye for the effect of contrasted colours and for the modelling of the figures. The other tradition provides the style with an emotional depth and dramatic tension that were new in Byzantine art. This emotionalism sprang from the spirituality that grew up in Byzantium even in the eleventh and the twelfth centuries, but which Western medievalists have associated with the Cistercian and Franciscan schools. This spirituality is dominated by a Christocentric devotion emphasising each physical detail of the Incarnation, from the crib to the Cross and the Resurrection. As examples of this Christocentric spirituality in pictorial art Mathew (1963:145) mentions Our Lady of Vladimir, the twelfth-century icon now preserved in the Tretyakov gallery, the Nativity in the Peribleptos Church at Mistra, a late fourteenth-century representation of the Virgin beneath the Cross from Thessalonica, now in the Byzantine Museum of Athens, the twelfth-century Christ in the dome at Daphni, and the Judgement scenes at Torcello and Sant' Angelo in Formis. These, in Mathew's opinion, are pictorial parallels to the Franciscan hymns of the Stabat Mater and the Dies Irae.

Our discussion of Likhačev's theory of a new style in Russian icon-painting at the end of the fourteenth century has thus led us back to the Christocentric spirituality underlying Nestor's *Life of Saint Theodosius.*

In the dramatic Passion scenes of late Byzantine fresco painting, the mythical story of the suffering, death, and resurrection of the godhead has been translated into pictorial modes of expression. The Lamentation scene should not be isolated as an image of purely human grief, but must be viewed as an integral component in the sequence of pictures representing the stages of the Passion story according to the invariant schema of ritual regeneration: Our Lady's lamentations over the dead body of her Son already anticipate His resurrection and reappearance in the new, glorified figure of the apotheosis.

The comparison of different versions of the Lamentation in the emotional style of late Byzantine painting shows that there is no basis for Likhačev's theory of a new style in fourteenth-century Eastern Europe. What he has called "abstract psychologism" represents in fact a late, final phase in the development of the emotional style in Orthodox art, where it suddenly and inexplicably disappears, whereas in the West representations of the Passion undergo a gradual transformation and the style reaches a new stage. The emphasis shifts to the human features of Christ and the story of His life on earth. This development culminates in the *pietas Christi* pictures of the Renaissance (Lazarev 1970:249).

Judging by what has survived, the Russian variant of the expressive style culminated in fourteenth-century Novgorod. In the region of Novgorod and Pskov the ground was well prepared for this style, as is demonstrated by the extant frescoes in the Cathedral of the Transfiguration of the Saviour in the Mirožskij Monastery. The Snetogorskij

Monastery is another testimony that this region had long been familiar with the expressive style when Theophanes arrived in Novgorod in the 1370s. Its frescoes, dated to 1313, resemble those of Theophanes the Greek to such an extent that Lazarev (1973:56) assumes that Theophanes studied them before proceeding with the decorations in the Church of the Transfiguration at Novgorod, executed in 1378.

Next to Theophanes' frescoes, the frescoes in the Church of the Dormition on the field of Volotovo and the Church of the Transfiguration at Kovalevo were the most important monuments of the expressive style until they were destroyed during the Second World War.

The chronological relationship between the extant monuments of Novgorodian fresco painting is not quite clear. Lazarev (1973:60ff.) dates both the Volotovo and the Kovalevo frescoes to around 1380, even if the Volotovo Church, according to the chronicle, was decorated as early as 1363. Lazarev's dating has not, however, been universally accepted. Amiranašvili (1971:178f.) takes as his starting point the year given in the chronicle for the decoration of the Volotovo Church, and maintains that its frescoes preceded the works of Theophanes and determined his style. An analysis of their content comes out in favour of Amiranašvili's dating.

The Gospel cycle at Kovalevo is strongly influenced by Serbian painting, iconographically and stylistically (see Lazarev 1970:234-278). The connection with Serbian and Macedonian fresco painting is most obvious in such scenes as the Lamentation and the Deposition from the Cross. But this is not the painting we know from the Gospel cycle at Sopoćani; the style has become drier, more stereotyped, and according to Lazarev (1970:276) is closer to the Morava style in Serbian painting, so called because it is best represented in the area on the river Morava, in the churches of Ravanica, Kalenić, Ljubostinja, and Manasija. In these frescoes, too, the central theme is Christ's life on earth. The dramatic element has, however, become subdued. The human figure of Christ is depicted as an image of His heavenly beauty, which has superseded the representation of His abasement in the Son of Man. The figures have become slim and elongated, with soft movements and a sophisticated sensitivity in the expression. With the Kovalevo frescoes, Novgorodian art under Serbian influence has moved away from the dramatic expressionism characterising the Volotovo frescoes and Theophanes' paintings in Novgorod.

The dramatic expressionism of late Byzantine painting reached its peak in Novgorod with the Volotovo frescoes, most probably executed in the early 1360s. We find here the same tendency to hide the human contours behind the geometrical patterns of the draperies, so characteristic of Giotto's Arena frescoes and the frescoes of Sopoćani; and the same tendency to place the figures in different planes, thereby creating a spatial effect, as in Giotto. In the Volotovo master's representation of Joseph and the shepherd, the seated Joseph is inscribed in a geometrical figure that bears a striking resemblance to Giotto's Joseph. The master of Volotovo, however, achieves his spatial effects not by the "box-space" perspective, but by the "crystalline character" (Alpatov) of its forms. The lines meet in a point in front of the picture.

In terms of their content the Volotovo frescoes differ from those of Kovalevo primarily in that unlike the latter they do not represent Christ's glory in His human figure, but concentrate on depicting man's way to deification through Christ's abasement. At Volotovo we find what to my knowledge is the only image in early Russian art of Christ disguised as a wandering beggar. This motif occurs in a sequence of pictures with scenes from Saint John Chrysostom's tale of the prior who did not recognise Christ when, in the guise of a poor beggar, He knocked on the gate of his monastery. The last scene of the composition shows the repentant prior following Christ with hands outstretched. Above the sequence are scenes from the life of Jesus, and a third register shows the Descent of the Holy Ghost and the Souls of the Righteous in God's Hands. Together, the three tiers of pictures represent three stages in man's way to salvation, whereas vertically they may be read as variations on a common theme, where the divine and human meet.

In retrospect the Volotovo frescoes appear as the summit of dramatic expressionism in the Russian school of late Byzantine icon-painting. They convey a religious fervour beyond the reach even of Theophanes the Greek. A term like Likhačev's "abstract psychologism" becomes quite inadequate when applied to this enthusiasm.

After Volotovo it is difficult to visualise a further stage in the development of this mode of expression, where movement and gesture are charged with a tension that threatens to burst and dissolve into a shimmering play of colours and abstract lines. It is just imaginable in the fragments that remain of Theophanes' frescoes in the Church of the Transfiguration on Elijah Street, built, according to the Chronicle, in 1374, by the "noble and pious boyar" Vasilij Danilovič and the inhabitants of Elijah Street. Four years later the interior of the church was decorated by Theophanes, and these frescoes are the only monumental works by the Greek artist that have come down to us. Covered by layers of whitewash and plaster, the frescoes were discovered in the years before the First World War, and restored in the following decades. During the Second World War, however, the frescoes were devastated by fire and damaged beyond repair. What we see today are only the restored ruins of Theophanes' original paintings. The combination of white garments and terra-cotta-coloured faces with shining highlights, which strikes us as incredibly modern and "expressionistic," is, in fact, a result of the fire. Recent discoveries of frescoes unaffected by the fire show that originally Theophanes' figures in the Church of the Transfiguration were much

more colourful than they appear today (Alpatov 1979:45). This is something we should keep in mind when trying to interpret the paintings,
since it is thus well-nigh impossible to say anything about Theophanes'
colouring, apart from his habit of painting his figures on a neutral background, applying first a basic layer of terra cotta and ochre, onto which
he would then superimpose bright highlights and dark shades, creating
a kind of clair-obscure. Furthermore, we are unable to reconstruct the
iconographic programme underlying the frescoes on the basis of the
existing fragments. The Eucharist in the apse and the frescoes on the
walls, columns, and arches are half-obliterated. In the dome the image of
the Pantocrator is preserved, together with four archangels and four
seraphs. Beneath them in the drum are represented the Old Testament
patriarchs Adam, Abel, Noah, Zeth, Melchisedek, and Enoch, the
prophet Elijah, and John the Baptist, the Forerunner. The best-
preserved frescoes decorate the chapel in the northwest corner of the
gallery, to which only boyars had admission. Here the frescoes ran
horizontally along the walls, one register above the other. The top
register is the best preserved, with five stylites, the Old Testament
Trinity or Three Angels appearing to Abraham, and medallions with
John Climacus, Agathon, Acacius, and Macarius of Egypt.

There is a marked stylistic difference between the images of the saints
in the chapel and the patriarchs and prophets in the drum. The figures
in the drum are motionless and elevated. Together with the celestial
powers of archangels and seraphs they belong to the Heavenly
Hierarchy ruled over by the dark and awesome Pantocrator in the dome.
Looking up towards these figures, the spectator is confronted with the
unchangeable and timeless reality of the beyond.

In contrast to the patriarchs and prophets in the drum, the saints in
the northwest corner chapel have been caught in the moment of spiritual
struggle, their gaze either absorbed in introspective contemplation or
wide open in mystical ecstasy, their hands lifted upwards in prayer or
directed towards the spectator in a traditional speech gesture. Whereas
the Old-Testament figures in the drum appear in their eternal glory, the
saints in the chapel have been depicted in their fight to free themselves
from the prison-house of their earthly bodies. In spite of their individual
characteristics Theophanes' saints are united in a common experience of
the Wholly Other. It is therefore in the representation of this Other that
we must try to discover the religious mentality underlying his ecstatic
art.

In Theophanes, the divine Other is reproduced in the form of white,
bluish, grey, and red highlights, applied to the reddish-brown flesh of
the figures without regard to the laws governing the distribution of
empirical light and shade. The highlights on Theophanes' saints
cannot be traced to any natural light source. They have no naturalistic
function, but illuminate the figures with a supernatural radiance that

distorts their human features.

It is a generally accepted opinion that Theophanes' use of highlights must be interpreted against Hesychast light theology (Lazarev 1961, Golejzovskij 1964, Alpatov 1972, Plugin 1974). The highlights are seen as synecdochic reflections of the immaterial light which, according to Palamas, is the perceptible energy of the transcendent, suprasensible godhead. But this interpretation is not without problems, for whereas in Palamas the divine energy causes the glorification of those struck by its beams, the earthly bodies of Theophanes' saints are distorted in the reflection of this divine light. Their emaciated figures may be described as "tragic caricatures," giving expression to a perpetual struggle between the worldly and the otherworldly.

This antinomy gives the art of Theophanes its keynote. The supernatural light reflected in his saints signals the *absence présente* of the divine in the earthly setting of the saints. The idea of a "hypostatic union" of divinity and humanity in imitation of Christ's human body seems to have no place in the world of Theophanes. This conception presupposes a fundamental closeness and similarity between the human and the divine, whereas in Theophanes the relationship between the two is marked by distance and dissimilarity. In their earthly strivings the saints find themselves infinitely far from God, and it is only by negative analogy that their distorted apparitions can be interpreted as "unlike likenesses" of their heavenly archetype, which is Christ in His eternal glory.

Returning to the comparison of Theophanes' art to the Volotovo frescoes, we now see that the stylistic parallels are the result of a formal resemblance hiding a fundamental difference in content. The master of Volotovo represents Christ as the mediator between the human and the divine. Here, sanctification is understood as the imitation of the human figure of Christ. For Theophanes, on the other hand, the aim is not to reproduce the figure of Christ, but to overcome the distance that separates man from God. The absence of Christ as mediator becomes as decisive for Theophanes' frescoes as is His presence in the Volotovo frescoes. Within the Christian cosmos of Theophanes the Greek, as we have tried to reconstruct it from the ruins of his art, we are tempted to interpolate as mediator between God and man the ecclesiastical hierarchy of the historical Church, which is so clearly prefigured in the images of patriarchs and prophets underneath the Pantocrator in the dome.

Against this interpretation of Theophanes' frescoes one might argue that it is determined by their fragmentary state. On the other hand, the best-preserved part of his iconographic scheme, the decorations in the dome, supports this interpretation. Its dark, terra-cotta-coloured Pantocrator, illuminated by Theophanes' characteristic flashes of light, is inscribed with a quotation from Psalm 102:19–21 (101 in the Russian numbering), which emphasises the distance between God and man: "from heaven did the Lord behold the earth; To hear the groaning of the prisoner; to loose those that are appointed to death; To declare the name of the Lord in Zion." The use of quotations from the Psalms around the Pantocrator of the dome was not unusual in late Byzantine art. Plugin (1974:96) cites examples from Kondakov's iconographic studies of Psalm 80 (Russian 79):14-15: "Return, we beseech thee, O God of hosts: look down from heaven, and behold, and visit this vine; And the vineyard which thy right hand hath planted." In connection with our interpretation of Theophanes' frescoes it is, however, worth noting that he exchanges this common quotation from the Psalms, which goes on to speak of "the son of man whom thou madest strong for thyself," for another in which there is no mention of God returning, but which refers to the Lord who from the height of his sanctuary beheld the earth "to hear the groaning of the prisoner; to loose those that are appointed to death."

Lazarev (1961:29, 1973:58) explains the dualist tendency in Theophanes' pictures as expressions of a subjective, individualist art, marked by the heretical currents of his time. The Russian art historian maintains that the Greek master's Novgorod frescoes ideologically signify an overcoming of and emancipation from Hesychasm.

This view is hardly tenable. It may be said against it, first, that the frescoes in question are to be found in an Orthodox church and that they were commissioned by prominent men in Novgorod and recorded in the chronicle, which suggests nothing of their heretical content. Second, the depiction of the godhead as an awesome, omnipotent authority, beyond all human comprehension, is wholly traditional in the Orthodox Church.

What strikes us in Theophanes' art is the preponderance of metonymical relationships between the human and the divine, combined with a rejection of the former for the sake of the latter, a stance which, ideologically, might be interpreted as an affirmation of the mediating function of the Church, in rejection of the heretical movements of the time, with their exclusive emphasis on personal experience. Such an interpretation, which to me does not seem at all unwarranted, would place Theophanes' art in a much more conservative context, in spite of its "expressionist" technique, which today gives it a distinct "avant-garde" flavour.

Whether the ideological content in Theophanes' frescoes really justifies placing them in opposition to Hesychasm is a different question, however. Such a conclusion would seem premature. As with Likhačev's attempt to explain the emotionalism of Russian art and literature around 1400 as a product of mystical Hesychasm, it appears to be based on a much too static view of Heysychasm, an ideology which in actual fact signifies a dynamic trend in Eastern monasticism. In the course of the fourteenth century it developed from being an esoteric movement among Orthodox monks into becoming the official teaching of the Orthodox Church whose supporters in the second half of the fourteenth century occupied the leading positions in the different national Churches of Orthodox Christendom, filled them with their own candidates, and consciously strove to propagate their ideology throughout the Orthodox *oikoumene.*

An analysis of the significance of Hesychasm for Russian culture during the second South Slav influence presupposes, therefore, a clear conception of its historical development and a definition of Hesychasm in its Russian recension.

# The Development of Hesychasm in the Balkans and in Russia

The fourteenth century was a critical time for the Orthodox Church. The Byzantine empire was in a state of disintegration from both inner conflicts and external pressures. In the northwest the Nemanja dynasty had built a Serbian empire; in the southeast the Turks advanced. Brussa was captured in 1326, Nicea in 1329, and Nicomedia in 1337. During the civil war in the 1340s the Turks invaded Thrace and the Balkans.

The Church was unable to counteract the spiritual and moral decline spreading among the clergy, and was thus also unable to deal with the discontent and uncertainty among the people. The upper clergy could no longer maintain discipline, and the Zealots, the party of the radical monks, came into direct opposition to the official Church and the wealthy monasteries. They headed a socio-revolutionary movement that led to open revolt in Thessalonica. In this excited atmosphere, full of anxiety and confusion, the heretical teachings of the Bogomils flared up again unabated. The Bogomils preached a radical dualism between the reality of God and the world of evil, between man's divine soul and his body, which belongs to the devil. With their traditional resistance to the cultural patterns of Byzantium, which were imposed on the people by the ruling classes, and their struggle for social justice against innocent suffering, the Bogomils joined the Zealots in their fight against the aristocracy, and this led to an emphasis on iconoclastic and anticlerical elements in their struggle.

Bogomilism came to Thessalonica probably from Macedonia, its original home (see Obolensky 1948, 1971:121ff., Goleniščev-Kutuzov 1973:17-37). From Thessalonica it penetrated to the monasteries on

Mount Athos, at the time when Hesychasm was gaining ground among the monks there. The Hesychasts met with strong resistance on Athos, where the leaders of this resistance tried to incriminate Hesychasm by identifying it with Bogomilism and linking it with the Messalians, another heretical sect in the Balkans which in the fourteenth century no longer seems to have differed from the Bogomils. Today most historians refute this accusation. We know Hesychasm primarily through the writings of Gregory Palamas, who with his teaching of the glorification of the body even in this life, by the grace of the Holy Spirit, takes a direct stand against the dualism of the Bogomils, at the same time as he attacks the Messalians for believing that those among them who are worthy behold the essence of God (Obolensky 1948:254).

Nevertheless, scholars such as Obolensky and Meyendorff have established several points of contact between Hesychasm and the heretics which show that the accusations cannot have been completely unfounded. The first Hesychasts were active in the same environment as the heretics. Their emphasis on inner recollection and private prayer was compared by their adversaries to the Messalian view of prayer as the only means open to man to get clear of the devil. Their distinction between *theoria* or *hesychia,* inner quiet or peace of mind, which is the ultimate goal of contemplation, on the one hand, and *praxis,* which has only a relative value, on the other, could be construed as a rejection of Church discipline and the sacraments. It could further imply an attempt to gain individual salvation independently of Church authority. Their incessant recitation of the Jesus prayer—"Lord Jesus Christ, Son of God, have mercy on me"—designed to aid spiritual concentration, had its parallel in the Bogomil teaching that all prayers except the Lord's Prayer are "babble." From an anti-Hesychast point of view, the Hesychasts' contemplative life could be seen as a reflection of the heretical opposition to manual work, and their austere attitude towards church decoration as an iconoclastic tendency.

The similarities between Hesychasm and Bogomilism have induced some scholars to interpret Palamas' exposition of the Hesychast doctrine as an exposition "in the spirit of Bogomilism" (Goleniščev-Kutuzov) or to emphasise the Hesychast teaching about the "inner way" to salvation as an indication of their anticlerical attitude. This interpretation is, however, without foundation in the historical material, both in what we know of their activity and of Hesychast writings.

In the first place, it was no new doctrine that was preached by the monk Gregory of Sinai, when at the beginning of the fourteenth century he came to Athos after his years of wandering in the Eastern Mediterranean. His teaching that man must overcome his passions and strive to reach a state of recollection and inner silence, and through prayer attain a true knowledge of God, in essence goes back to the traditional mysticism of fifth-century Orthodox ascetics.

From Athos, Gregory went to the remote region of Paroria in southeastern Bulgaria, where in 1330 he founded his own monastery, which until his death in 1346 was an important centre for the rejuvenation of Orthodox monasticism. From his monastery Gregory's teaching was spread by a number of Slav and Greek disciples, highly educated men of birth, who preached Hesychast ideas in writing and in speech, and introduced them to monasteries and royal courts throughout the Orthodox world. After Palamas' victory over the anti-Hesychasts, Gregory of Sinai's disciples rose to prominent positions in the different Orthodox communities, in Byzantium, in the Balkans, and in Russia. Among them are to be found two future ecumenical Patriarchs, Callistos and Philotheos, the Archbishop of Thessalonica, Gregory Palamas, and Theodosius of Trnovo, the founder of the Kilifarevo Monastery on the northern slopes of the Balkan Mountains, which became the centre of Hesychasm in the Balkans after the closing down of the Paroria house.

The foremost theorist of Hesychasm was Gregory Palamas, who defended their light mysticism in his writings as well as in his disputations with Barlaam the Calabrian, the spokesman of scholasticism in Constantinople. Palamas showed that light mysticism could be traced back to the writings of the Greek Church Fathers. He developed the distinction between God's essence, which is absolutely transcendent, unknowable to all human thought, and the energies or operations of God, which permeate the universe and which surrounded the transfigured Christ on Mount Tabor.

Palamas' doctrine is a synthesis of different versions of Orthodox Neo-Platonism, which was again brought into the forefront through his interpretation.

Many of the ideas he took up and developed can be traced to the Areopagite, especially the latter's teaching about the Divine Light that illuminates the universe; further to Symeon the New Theologian and his light mysticism, to the apophatic theology which was developed by the Neo-Platonists in fifth-century Athens—the transcendent essence of the phenomena defined as silence and absence—and finally to the patristic doctrine of *theosis*, man's deification and union with God through imitation of Christ and participation in His body in the mystery of the Eucharist and in contemplation of His Passion.

By means of the patristic tradition Palamas succeeded in providing Hesychasm with a sound dogmatic basis, at the same time infusing new life into this tradition, in contrast to his adversaries, who attacked his doctrine from a stereotyped literalist position.

Palamas' Christocentric theology shows that he conquered the dualism of the heretics by means of the patristic *theosis*, so that Hesychasm in his version acquired the character of a mysticism that resembled, but was still fundamentally different from, the ideas of the heretics.

After the Hesychast victory this resemblance was of considerable importance for the Hesychasts in their efforts to bring the apostates back to the fold. They had created an ideology which enabled them to integrate into the official teaching of the Church the spiritual rejuvenation which the Bogomils had been monopolising. In the second part of the fourteenth century the fight against the heretics became the Hesychasts' major concern. This campaign was fought throughout the Orthodox *oikoumene*. In Russia it was led by men such as Sergius of Radonež, Stephen of Perm, and the Metropolitan Cyprian. It also left its impress on Epiphanius' hagiographical accounts of Sergius and Stephen as embodiments of the ideal held up by the Hesychasts to counteract the accusations levelled against the clergy by the heretics, for not living in conformity with Holy Scripture (see Klibanov 1960:160, Dane 1961:72–86).

With the victory over its adversaries around 1350, when Hesychasm passed from being a movement in opposition to becoming the prevailing theology in the Orthodox Church, a new era began for its leaders. This period is marked by a consolidation of Hesychast ideas in Orthodox theology, philosophy, dogma, and church life, as well as by the endeavour to propagate the new teaching throughout the Orthodox world. The mystico-contemplative individualist aspect, which had been the predominant feature of Hesychasm in its first stage, when Gregory of Sinai was its leader, now becomes subordinated to political objectives. This is also the case with Hesychast theory as it was voiced in Gregory Palamas' writings. The theoretical aspect was subordinated to the political activity of the Hesychast leaders, who in the second half of the fourteenth century made the Orthodox Church a greater power than the Imperial court, both nationally and internationally.

The most discriminating and historically the soundest appreciation of Hesychasm as a fourteenth-century movement, is still the one given by G. M. Prokhorov (1968). Whereas, like previous scholars, Likhačev is content to define Hesychasm as a mystical school in Orthodox theology, and to explain the second South Slav influence in Russian hagiography and pictorial art as an expression of this mysticism, Prokhorov describes the development of Hesychasm in its three main phases: (1) the esoteric, introspective Hesychasm, as preached by Gregory of Sinai at the beginning of the fourteenth century; (2) the theoretical Hesychasm, represented by Gregory Palamas in the 1340s; and (3) the political Hesychasm of the second part of the century, after the victory over clerical opposition, when Hesychasts had captured the leading positions in the administration of the Church.

The Hesychast leaders in this final, political phase are good proof that mystical contemplation is easily combined with strategic shrewdness and organising talent. Members of this "Hesychast international" held the most important positions in the Church and in the large monastic communities in the second half of the fourteenth century. At the same time they were often distinguished theologians, hagiographers, calligraphers, and icon painters, who led the cultural *renovatio* which was manifested in Russia as the second South Slav influence (Prokhorov 1968:99). It was the monasteries on Mount Athos and in Byzantium, together with the Kilifarevo Monastery, that became the nurseries for the diffusion of this spiritual revival among the Orthodox Slavs. In these monasteries monks from various parts of the Orthodox world received a homogeneous schooling under the tutelage of competent teachers. Thence they returned to their respective homelands to practise what they had learnt.

A typical representative of political Hesychasm is Philotheos Kokkinos, the second Hesychast on the patriarchal throne in Constantinople, Callistos I's successor. He had two periods of rule, the first in 1353–1354, when he was overthrown together with the Emperor John VI Cantacuzenos, the second from 1364 to 1375. Like his predecessor he had been a disciple of Gregory of Sinai. With his Russian policy Philotheos had a decisive influence on the development of Muscovite Hesychasm. It was he who in his first reign managed to appoint Alexis, the Muscovite candidate, as Metropolitan of Kiev and All Russia. By rejecting the rival candidate of the Lithuanian Grand Duke, Philotheos granted the Grand Prince of Moscow a victory in the rivalry of the two princes for political hegemony over Russia. At the same time Philotheos sent envoys to Sergius of Radonež, the central figure in the revival of Russian monasticism, with a request to introduce the coenobitic rule into his Trinity Monastery, which was destined to become the stronghold of Russian Hesychasm.

The Russian Hesychasts were thereby organised on the same community principle as the one on which Theodosius had built his Monastery of the Caves, and not on the idiorrhythmic principle characteristic of Hesychasm in its first, esoteric phase. Idiorrhythmism was reserved for senior, experienced monks.

Philotheos' aim was to unite all Orthodox Christians in a common defence against both the Turks in the East and the Roman Church in the West. This occasionally led him into rather suspect intrigues, not unusual for the representatives of political Hesychasm in the second half of the fourteenth century.

In his attempt to strike a balance between Moscow and Lithuania and make the most of the rivalry between the two principalities, Philotheos, in his second incumbency, ended up by consecrating the Bulgarian monk Cyprian, the candidate of the Grand Duke Olgerd of Lithuania, as Metropolitan of Kiev, Lithuania, and All Russia, in the lifetime of Alexis. The Muscovites were just as embittered at this appointment as they had been satisfied with the appointment of Alexis. The machinations thus started continued for fifteen years until 1390, twelve years after Alexis' death, when the Grand Prince Basil I acknowledged Cyprian as metropolitan. In the meantime Olgerd's son Jagiello was baptised into the Roman Church and married the queen of Poland in 1386. He thereby moved outside the orbit of Byzantium, although Kiev, the old centre of Orthodoxy in Russia, was still the holy city to a large Orthodox population within the borders of Lithuania.

The Patriarch Philotheos was known in Russia not only through his political activity, but also as a theologian and an author. He codified the teaching of Palamas, whom he canonised in 1368, nine years after Palamas' death. It was above all in this codified, dogmatic form that Hesychast doctrines were propagated in Russia, where its more subtle theories had practically no impact. As far as we can judge, it was as a combination of contemplative *hesychia* and Church politics that Hesychasm became known in Russia from the middle of the fourteenth century (Prokhorov 1968:107f.).

Philotheos was, moreover, a prolific hagiographer. In Russia, where he was the best-known Byzantine author of the fourteenth century, he is, however, particularly famous for his hymns and prayers, translated into the Slavonic language by Euthymius, Patriarch of Trnovo, by Cyprian and the Abbot Theodore of the Simonov Monastery, later Bishop of Rostov, a close relation of Sergius of Radonež. No less than forty of the writings of Philotheos were known in old Russia (Prokhorov 1972).

The first advocate of Hesychasm in Russia was probably Sergius of Radonež, but the paucity of primary sources makes it difficult to reach any firm conclusions about his religious ideas. The *Life of Saint Sergius,* written by Epiphanius the Wise, is dated to about 1417, that is, to twenty-five years after Sergius' death in 1392. It has survived only in later copies, based on the version by Pachomius the Serbian from the middle of the fifteenth century, thus being rather a literary document of the age of Basil II than a primary biographical source.

A characteristic representative of Hesychasm during the second South Slav influence at the end of the fourteenth century is, however, to be found in the Metropolitan Cyprian. He combines its esoteric, introspective element with its active, political aspect in a way typical of Hesychast leaders of this period. Cyprian was politically active both before and after his arrival in Russia, where he was finally accepted as metropolitan in 1390, a position he held until his death in 1406. The contemplative, introspective Hesychasm is expressed in the words of the chronicle that he "loved solitude," and in the words he himself wrote on his deathbed, a lamentation on the vanity of this earthly life:

> Why am I distressed and agitated in vain, knowing the end of life, seeing the way it works, how we all in the same way proceed from dark-ness into light, and from light into darkness, from the maternal womb into the world, from the sorrowful world with tears into the

grave! And what is in between? A dream, a phantasy, the beauty of
this world. Alas and alas for the passions! In the great web of life
everything will pass away like flowers, like dust, like a shadow.
(transl.from Alpatov 1972:201)

About Cyprian's childhood and youth we know nothing for certain.
According to the most recent account of his life, he was a Bulgarian who,
having spent some years on Mount Athos, entered the service of
Patriarch Philotheos and soon became a member of his immediate
entourage, while at the same time preserving his personal connections
with Bulgaria (see Obolensky 1982: XI, Meyendorff 1981:201f.).

After Cyprian had at last been lawfully acknowledged as metropolitan
in 1390 under the Grand Prince Basil I, he worked incessantly for the rest
of his life and with shrewd political sense to make Moscow the spiritual
and political centre of the Russian Church. At the same time he fought
continuously to keep the Orthodox Church of Lithuania under his rule,
in spite of the policy of the secular princes.

In addition to his administrative activity Cyprian was an ardent
advocate of the revision of the liturgical books which his friend
Euthymius had started after becoming Patriarch of Bulgaria. Cyprian
copied in his own hand the new South Slav translations of the Greek
liturgical texts. Similarly, he copied the Slavonic translations of the
Greek Fathers. He composed messages and instructions, wrote a *Life* of
Peter, the first Metropolitan of Moscow, and took the initiative in the
compilation of the first Muscovite chronicle of 1409.

Among the works Cyprian copied are, characteristically, writings by
Dionysius the Areopagite and the *Ladder to Heaven (Klimax)* by John,
called Climacus after his work.

By making these authors known in Muscovite Russia, Cyprian
contributed to the propagation of Hesychast mysticism among Russian
monks, who were in this way integrated into the spiritual current which
managed in the fourteenth century to unite the Orthodox Church. This
work of integration is also seen in Cyprian's introduction of the new
South Slav liturgical books to Russia and in his adaptation of the
Bulgarian orthography of Euthymius.

Through this activity Cyprian emerges as a typical representative of
the Hesychast higher echelons of the fourteenth-century Orthodox
Church, of men who with their supranational Church policy made the
Church into a political force at a time when the Byzantine Empire itself
was already on the wane.

Cyprian's endeavour to make Moscow a centre of the Russian Church
was associated with his efforts to create a closer contact with the
Churches in the Balkans. It was he who included the *Lives* of the South
Slav saints in the Russian Church's Synaxarion, so that the Russians,
too, hereafter commemorated Cyril the Philosopher, Ivan of Rila, Sava,

Symeon, and other Bulgarian and Serbian saints on their feast days
(Kuev 1962:309).

Cyprian's own works are marked by being part and parcel of his
general activity to strengthen the Church, to re-establish discipline and
order, and to combat heretical movements. They are an exponent more
of the political than of the mystical Hesychasm. However, in his main
work, the *Life* of Saint Peter, Metropolitan of Moscow, the mystical,
esoteric elements of Hesychasm are combined with a clear political
intent in a way that makes it, to my mind, a characteristic expression of
political Hesychasm.[1]

# Mysticism and Power Struggle:
# Cyprian the Hagiographer

Cyprian's *Life of Saint Peter* is the second *vita* of the Metropolitan Peter.
The first was written probably in 1327, the year after Peter's death.
Ključevskij (1871:74ff.) ascribed it to Bishop Prokhor of Rostov. The
attribution is at best doubtful. There is much to indicate that the earlier
*Life* was written by an anonymous Muscovite around 1327 (Kukčin
1962).

Although Cyprian does not mention that he has used the earlier *Life*
as a source for his own work, the latter does in some passages coincide
almost verbatim with words and phrases in the earlier *Life,* which
suggests that he has in all probability based his own account of Peter's
life on this text (Ključevskij 1871:83).

Nevertheless, the two *Lives* are very different works. The first has the
character of a sober contemporaneous biography of the saint. In its form
it is a short *vita (proložnoe žitie),* a condensed account of the most
important events in Peter's life chronologically arranged, and concluded by the tales of his posthumous miracles.

Cyprian's *Life of Saint Peter* went through at least two redactions:
the shorter one, published by Prokhorov (1978), which may have been
written as early as 1381, during Cyprian's first, very brief tenure in
Moscow. The longer, published in the *VMČ*, mentions the death of
Emperor Andronicus IV in 1385, and must therefore have been written
after this event. It may have been published by Cyprian himself after
1390 (Meyendorff 1981:208, n.26).

---

[1] The *Life* has been printed in the *Velikie Minei Četi, I, dekabr' dni 18-20* (Moscow,
1910), col. 1620-1646, and in *Kniga stepennaja carskogo rodoslovija, I* (PCRL, XXI) (St.
Petersburg, 1913). I have made use of the VMČ edition. A shorter, earlier version was
published by Prokhorov (1978).

Both in form and content Cyprian's second version differs from the
simple story of the anonymous *Life*. Cyprian elaborates on the
individual events and has added some information that was especially
attuned to his intentions in writing the *vita*, for instance, the detail about
the saint's Volynian origins. At the same time the *Life* proper was
furnished with a frame containing both an introduction and a concluding eulogy, where the novel, "artificial style" was for the first time
evolved in Muscovite hagiography, according to Ključevskij (1871:84).
Ključevskij's emphasis on the "artificial" element in Cyprian's style is a
characterisation that recurs in practically all subsequent descriptions of
it. The *Life of Saint Peter* has acquired its place in Russian hagiography
as an example of the "Neo-Slavonic style of Patriarch Euthymius'
school" (Bugoslavskij 1946:234); the *Life* is said to represent "a new type
of saintly legend whose objective was no longer merely to captivate its
readers through a reliable and sober account, but also, and above all, to
glorify the saintly protagonist through a nicely calculated rhetorical
embellishment" (Stender-Petersen 1952:126).

Thus it has become customary to regard the *Life of Saint Peter* as an
intermediary link between the Neo-Slavonic style in fourteenth-century
Bulgarian hagiography and its Russian version as we know it from the
*Life of Saint Stephen*, written by Epiphanius the Wise.

However, this definition of Peter's *vita* as having a special significance in the history of hagiographical rhetoric in Russia comes up
against one main difficulty: Cyprian's style is far too different from both
that of Euthymius of Trnovo and that of Epiphanius the Wise for the
*Life of Saint Peter* to fall into line as an intermediary link in an
evolutionary sequence.

There can be no doubt that Cyprian mastered the individual stylistic
devices of word-weaving. A number of them occur in his *vita*: composite
nouns translated from Greek, repetition of the same root with different
suffixes, or of different roots with the same suffix, or different predicates
of identical form at the end of the clause, so that a sequence of clauses
form a rhythmic unity; these are all typical devices of word-weaving.
And yet, the use of these devices is very different in Cyprian's writing
from that in Epiphanius'—much more subdued and sober. Cyprian's
style is devoid of the accumulation of long sequences of equivalent
segments that are characteristic of Epiphanius' word-weaving. Similarly, the feature emphasised by Likhačev (1958:39) as the basic
hallmark of word-weaving is lacking: the emotional exaltation of the
discourse, the emphasis on the writer's own high-wrought emotions
remembering the saint, and his endeavour to express his feelings in its
stylistic idiom. This basic difference between Cyprian's style and the
style prevalent in fourteenth-century South Slavonic hagiography had
been observed by Golubinskij (1900:353), whose view, however, passed
unnoticed. Golubinskij sees Cyprian in connection with what he calls

the "Serbian school" in South Slavonic literature. He includes Cyprian in this school, but at the same time he points out that Cyprian differs in many ways from its other representatives, who "distinguish themselves by an unusual rhetorical prolixity and were able to compose extensive Lives even where the factual material was lacking." This "Serbian prolixity, which contains nothing praiseworthy, but was regarded as something very praiseworthy," is, according to Golubinskij, "totally lacking in Cyprian."

The discrepancy between Ključevskij's and Golubinskij's characterisations of Cyprian's style is probably due to a different use of the concept of style, for although Ključevskij (1871:84) speaks of Cyprian's artificial style, the context shows that what he means is not the elaborate use of grammatical devices in word-weaving, but Cyprian's extensive use of conventional hagiographical *topoi*. An example cited by Ključevskij is the story of the seven-year-old Peter's reading difficulties, which he did not overcome until a priestlike figure appeared to him "as in a dream" and touched his tongue, after which he surpassed all his classmates in reading proficiency. This is a *topos* we know in a slightly different version from the *Life of Saint Sergius of Radonež*. For Ključevskij the admixture of such legendary motifs represents redundant, even confusing elements in the biographical narrative. Quite clearly he much prefers the plain tale of the anonymous Peter's *vita* where the young saint was sent away to learn to read and "had soon acquired all wisdom."

The use of hagiographical motifs was not, however, a complete innovation in Cyprian's version. Already in the 1327 *vita* we find, for instance, a description of a vision which the saint's mother had when she was pregnant with the child. According to this vision she saw a "lamb carrying a tree full of different flowers on its horns."

This motif is taken up and embellished by Cyprian in his account: "she thought she was holding a lamb in her arms. Between its horns a tree grew up with beautiful leaves, adorned with many flowers and fruits, and many lights shining among its branches and sweet fragrance emanating." The representation of the saint as a lamb in this vision is an obvious allegorical allusion to Christ in the image of the lamb, an allusion that is amplified by Cyprian through his addition of the many shining lights in the mother's vision.

Cyprian's allegorical vision of the saint receives its explanation in the central episode of the *Life*: the consecration of the saint as Metropolitan of All Russia in the Church of Holy Wisdom at Constantinople. When the saint entered the church during the consecration ceremony it was filled with fragrance and became luminous with the radiance from his face, which shone like the sun during the service, according to Cyprian's description.

What was new in Cyprian's account was not the hagiographical motifs in themselves, but that these motifs had become subordinate to an overall Hesychast view of Peter's life and career. Cyprian draws a parallel between the story of the saint's gradual rise in the ecclesiastical hierarchy and the portrayal of his inner, spiritual ascent and trans-figuration in the first part of the *vita*, and later amplifies his account with a visionary illustration of how higher, divine powers side with Peter in the struggle for the metropolitanate.

The Hesychast element is especially in evidence in the story of the saint's years of monastic apprenticeship, where it forms its own con-ceptual level in the narrative:

> ... day after day he spent in meditation, setting up a ladder of ascent in his heart, as it were, according to the instruction and teaching of Saint John Climacus, submitting himself to his superior in every-thing ... through his humility and meekness and stillness a worthy model of a virtuous life for everyone ... but he felt an urge to acquire the art of icon-painting, and soon he had learnt the painting of Holy Icons ... and he painted the image of the Saviour and of His immaculate Mother, and also the figures and the faces of the saints. And through this all his spirit and mind were carried away from earthly things, and in spirit he was wholly deified, and he strove to become like their figures, and he devoted himself with even more zeal to a virtuous life, and he turned in his mind towards tears. For many people are so disposed that they will turn in their minds towards tears in love, as soon as they remember the face of the beloved. And so did this divine priest, lifting his mind from these painted images to the archetypes ... (*VMČ*, cols. 1622f.)

In the passages I have omitted Cyprian describes the saint's industry in the monastery in conventional phrases, and on the whole follows his source. But with Cyprian's depiction of the saint's icon-painting an unmistakable note of Hesychast mysticism has entered the story; it is apparent already in the emphasis on the saint's spiritual ascent during the reading of the *Lestvica*—the Russian term for the mystical treatise of John Climacus—and in the emphasis on his *molčanie*—the Russian word for *hesychia*. But the mystical teaching of the Hesychasts is particularly evident in Cyprian's portrayal of Peter's veneration of the Holy Icons: he turned his spirit and mind away from earthly matters—*um vsjak i myslь ot zemnykh otvodja*—and was wholly deified in spirit—*vesь oboženь byvaaše umom*—lifting his mind from the perceptible images of the icons to their divine prototypes—*ot sikh šarovnykh obrazov k pervoobraznym um svoi vozvožaše.*

Cyprian's explanation of the hidden significance of Peter's icon-painting shows that his recension of the earlier *vita* cannot aptly be char-acterised as a mere amplification by means of purely stereotyped fea-

tures, with a few new biographical items added, as maintained by
Ključevskij (1871:83ff.). Nor is it a question of anything as general as a
"really lifelike exposition" (Dmitriev 1963:243).

Cyprian's commentary on the story of the saint's icon-painting can be
characterised much more precisely: it is an interpretation of the cognitive function of the Holy Icons in accordance with the apologetic
iconology of the Greek Fathers, with their teaching, which was basically
Platonic, of the ascent of the spirit through the contemplation of perceptible images to the suprasensible reality of their prototypes. This
doctrine was taken up by the Hesychasts and integrated with their theory
of spiritual ascent, illustrated by Cyprian's account of the saint's reading
of John Climacus.

The story of Peter's spiritual ascent concludes the account of his
apprenticeship in the monastery. Characteristically, this stage in his
spiritual development is a prerequisite for his further activity. He has
reached the stage where he can go and teach others, first as a leader of the
monastic society he built up on the river Rata in Volynia, later as Metropolitan of All Russia, consecrated by the Patriarch in Constantinople.

Cyprian's representation of Peter's way to holiness thus falls into
three principal parts: first, a description of his gradual rise through
various stages of the monastic hierarchy, concurrent with the portrayal
of his inner, spiritual ascent, culminating in his *theoria* and *theosis* in
contemplation of the Holy Icons. Then follows the story of how the
saint is reluctantly persuaded to go to Constantinople after the death of
the Metropolitan Maximus, to forestall the high-handed attempts by
Gerontius, the rival candidate, to be consecrated. His mother's dream is
fulfilled: Peter, who even before his birth had appeared in his mother's
vision in the guise of the lamb, is transfigured in the light radiating from
his face. The presence of the Holy Spirit becomes manifest in the
fragrance emanating from his figure as he enters the church. The
voyages of the two rivals and their arrivals at Constantinople are
represented as parallel but antithetic courses of events: Gerontius'
arrival is a narrow escape after a turbulent voyage, whereas Peter's ship
rushes forth "rapidly as in a dream," favoured by a following wind.
Again, a vision is used by Cyprian to illustrate his intentions: one night
during the gale the Mother of God appears to Gerontius in a dream, in
the image of the very icon that Peter has painted of her, and makes it
clear to him that all his efforts will be in vain; a higher authority has
already elected Peter as metropolitan:

> Peter, the abbot of Rata, the servant of my Son and God and mine, is
> the one who will be elevated to the high throne of the glorious
> Russian metropolitanate. And he will adorn the throne, and proper-
> ly tend the people for whose sake Christ, my Son and Lord, poured
> out His blood, borrowed from me. And having thus lived in a

manner pleasing to God, he will, in venerable age, go joyfully to the
Master of his longings and First Priest. (*VMČ*, col. 1627)

This vision functions not only as a miraculous prediction of coming
events; as an analogy to Peter's spiritual ascent and transfiguration, it has
also a function in the underlying Platonic scheme that determines
Cyprian's Hesychast revision of the *Life* of his predecessor: first the
ascent to the knowledge of the Wholly Other, then the way back to active
work in the service of this Other reality, for Christ the Pantocrator as the
supreme head and heavenly High Priest of the Church. (For a diagram of
Plato's far more complex version of this paradigm, see Wyller 1970:111.)
   Cyprian's image of Christ the Pantocrator and High Priest has an interesting parallel in art history, where it corresponds iconographically
to a variant of the type "Christ as priest," known for instance from the
mosaics in Kiev's Cathedral of the Holy Wisdom and from Neredica.
The particular variant that is reflected in Gerontius' vision developed in
the Balkans in the fourteenth century (see Lazarev 1970:234-278). What
distinguishes this variant is its representation of Christ in the vestment
of a bishop, which early on was combined with the image of Christ as
the King of Kings. In this combination it occasionally replaced the traditional figure of the Pantocrator, for instance in the Church of Peter
and Paul at Trnovo, from about 1400, where Christ is depicted in a
*deesis*, or intercessionary group, in the guise of a bishop, between the
Mother of God and John the Baptist, with the headings *Carъ
carstvujuščim* and *Velikij Arkhierej* (The King of Kings and Great High
Priest), a sure sign that the two types have been combined.
   In Russia this figure is known from the Kovalevo frescoes, where it is
found in a version called *Predsta Carica odesnuju tebe*, a representation
of the Virgin as the Queen of Heaven standing before her Son, the King
of Kings and High Priest. This type probably arose in Serbia, where the
oldest surviving examples date from the second part of the fourteenth
century (Lazarev 1970:260).
   Christ and Mary in Gerontius' dream correspond so closely with these
figures that the parallel seems unavoidable. It is likely that in Gerontius'
dream Cyprian has translated the message conveyed by the new iconographic figures of Christ and Mary into hagiography, a possibility
strengthened by the hypothesis put forward by Lazarev (1970:268) that
the Kovalevo frescoes were executed by monks from the Balkans, brought
over or recommended by Cyprian when he first came to Russia in 1373-
1374.
   The iconological significance of the *Predsta Carica* type is still uncer-
tain. We must therefore try to decipher the meaning of Cyprian's figures
within the context of the *Life*. In Gerontius' vision Christ emerges as the
divine prototype and supreme head of all primates of the historical
Church, who in turn, in accordance with the metaphorical structure of

the *vita*, become historical representatives of this divine prototype. This conception determines Cyprian's version of the *Life of Saint Peter*. He has transformed the story of Peter's life into an exemplary account where sanctification is achieved through assimilation to the divine prototype of Christ. In this context the story of Gerontius has its function in the semantic universe of the *vita*. His attempt to attain the metropolitanate by the aid of secular powers marks an anti-holy act. His conduct is strongly condemned in Cyprian's quotation from the Patriarch's admonitory speech in Constantinople: "for laymen are not allowed to carry out the election of bishops, nor may anyone dare to reach out for such a title on his own, not before he is elected by the Holy Assembly, and first of all marked by the sign of the Most Holy and Lifegiving Ghost" (*VMČ*, col. 1629). The Patriarch's admonition is not only part of the story of Gerontius' unsuccessful journey to Constantinople, but is equally an expression of Cyprian's own view of the metropolitan's status, and a contribution in his own struggle to assert the independence of the Church of secular princes and to retain its unity in the face of their rivalry and conflicts.

The combination of heavenward mysticism and practical church politics that marks the *Life of Saint Peter* is a feature it shares with the *Lives* written by Cyprian's close friend, the Patriarch Euthymius of Trnovo. In his *Life of Ivan Rilski*, Euthymius gives first an account of the saint's ascetic life, then of the relationship between Ivan and Tsar Peter, with clear allusions to the author's relationship with Tsar Ivan Šišman, which is also described in terms of the supremacy of the Church over the Prince and secular powers. In this part of the *vita* the ideological tendency emerges quite clearly. Euthymius' intention was not restricted to recording the story of Ivan Rilski's life; he wanted at the same time to express his own view of the political significance of the Patriarch and to demonstrate that the Church was above the secular powers (Dinekov 1962:295).

The same tendency is reflected in the third part of Cyprian's *Life of Saint Peter*: the tale of his struggle with and victory over his adversaries, secular as well as clerical, after the return from Constantinople. The *vita* depicts Bishop Andrew of Tver as Peter's most formidable enemy, which is not surprising when we know about the struggle between Moscow and Tver for the ascendancy in fourteenth-century Russia. However, Bishop Andrew is not alone in this struggle. The *Life* also refers to "certain others," who at the devil's instigation opposed Peter when metropolitan. Who these others were does not emerge from the *vita*. The real historical antagonisms have been blurred and must be reconstructed from other sources, which according to Dmitriev (1963) provide reason for assuming that the reference must be to Prince Michael of Tver.

The climax in this part of the *vita* is the account of the removal of the metropolitanate from Vladimir to Moscow. This event is explained by the Muscovite Princes' devoutness and love of churches and monasteries. The picture given of the relationship between the Metropolitan and "his son," Prince Ivan Danilovič, idealises it in a way that quite obviously intends to demonstrate that the latter is subordinate to the primate of the Church. Compared with the earlier *vita*, Cyprian's version has few alterations in this section, apart from his emphasis on the saint's importance for the development of Moscow as Russia's new political and cultural centre. Peter's part in the development of the new capital is shown in the description of the new Cathedral of the Assumption, built at the saint's behest, and the place where he himself was buried.

A characteristic detail has, however, been suppressed by Cyprian: that on his deathbed the saint designated his own successor. To Cyprian this procedure must have seemed too high-handed and arbitrary, for in other writings he condemns it outright. The political Hesychasts' work to build a spiritual empire, which was to unite the single Orthodox Church communities under their leadership and the supremacy of Christ the Allruler, had no room for Peter's separatist procedure; they had to insist that the Metropolitan of All Russia should be appointed by the Patriarch of the undivided Church.

Through small alterations and omissions and through the addition of an allegorical level of visions, Cyprian in this way reworked Peter's life story into an illustration of the political programme of the Hesychasts; the saint was seen as the ideal Church Prince, i.e., an image of Christ and the vicegerent of the Allruler and High Priest.

This metaphorical representation of Peter is a prerequisite for the parallel finally established between the life of the saint and Cyprian's own life. In his concluding eulogy of Peter, Cyprian recapitulates the most important events of his own life in a way that emphasises the correspondences between himself and his protagonist. The eulogy thus becomes a key to the interpretation of Peter's *Life* as an autobiography of Cyprian. The parallels drawn by Cyprian between his own life and that of Peter were emphasised by Ključevskij (1871:86) as a distinguishing mark of this *vita*. This analogy between author and protagonist is close to the one found in Euthymius' parallel of his relationship to Šišman with Ivan Rilski's relationship to Tsar Peter. Both *vitae* thus acquire an autobiographical level of meaning. The *Life of Saint Peter* finally turns out to "deal with Cyprian himself just as much as with Peter" (Dmitriev 1963). Similarly, in his eulogy Cyprian shows how the Emperor, by opposing the Hesychasts and high-handedly appointing one of their adversaries, "the mad Macarios," as Patriarch, after having removed Philotheos, brought misfortune and affliction upon himself and all his Empire, which is approaching its downfall, "the sea held by the Latins, the lands conquered by the infidel Turks" (*VMČ*, col. 1644). This description of Constantinople is set against the scene of Moscow under the Grand Prince Dimitrij Ivanovič, as Gerontius has earlier been seen in opposition to Peter. The eulogy ends by depicting the Russian princes at Peter's tomb. Cyprian regards them from the metropolitan's exalted standpoint, picturing them as they devoutly kneel and receive the blessing with all the Orthodox, "giving praise to the Life-giving Trinity, through which we shall all receive mercy in Christ our Lord, to whom the glory, the honour, and the power with the eternal Father, now and forever and for all time, amen" (*VMČ*, col. 1646).

So ends Saint Peter's *vita*. The secular Princes are depicted as humbly kneeling before the Metropolitan Cyprian to receive the blessing of the King of Kings through his supreme representative in Russia. Thus in Cyprian's version the *Life of Saint Peter* has acquired a completely different structure and ideological content from that of his source, where the single events were linked in a simple chronological sequence. On the one hand Cyprian has inserted into the story his own interpretation of the saint's "upward way" and his return from the meeting with the divine prototypes of the icons to his work in the service of the Church as the representative in Russia of these prototypes, whereas on the other hand he projects his own career into the story by emphasising in the final eulogy the similarity between his own life and that of the saint.

Author, protagonist, and divine prototype thus form a hierarchically ordered paradigmatic sequence in which the key figures in some respects resemble each other, while in other respects they differ. (In this sequence the anti-holy metropolitans, Gerontius and Macarios, have their parts to play as negative variants of the prototype they do not resemble but are contrasted to, representing the enemy, the power of evil.)

In his capacity of Russian metropolitan, Peter is represented after the example of the glorified Christ. He holds an intermediary position in the sequence. In his turn Cyprian emerges in the image of his predecessor and thereby as a representative of the historical Church's heavenly primate. Predecessor and successor, protagonist and author, both equate in their capacity of metropolitans the Christ-figure in Gerontius' vision. They appear in the *vita* as variants of the same ideal prototype, an ideal which must be seen in connection with the ideology of political Hesychasm and its thesis that the Church Princes are above secular rulers, having received their power from the Heavenly Ruler of their spiritual empire.

The difference between the three figures derives from the varying distance of protagonist and author from the prototype. The figure of Cyprian belongs to the frame level, and is related indirectly to the prototype. His assimilation to the prototype presupposes the interpretation of Peter's life story as an indirect autobiography of Cyprian himself, an assimilation of his career to his predecessor's fulfilled and glorified life. In order to emerge as a worthy representative of the transcendent head of the Church, Cyprian has to picture himself through his picture of the saint's life, so that his official function becomes not only a continuation but also a re-enactment of his predecessor's life. As a re-enactment or imitation of the completed and glorified past of the *vita* the frame story, too, is glorified.

It will be seen from the present analysis that Cyprian's *Life of Saint Peter*, like Nestor's of Theodosius, originates in the idea of sainthood as an *imitatio Christi*. Both *Lives* are dominated by the metaphor, that is, the principle of similarity. This basic similarity, however, does not prevent a marked difference in execution, as *imitatio* is grounded on two different conceptions of the prototype. In the *Life of Saint Theodosius*, *imitatio* was shown as a ritual re-enactment of the Passion until the saint emerged as a *figura Christi* prefiguring in the light visions his final *theosis*. The abasement depicted in the first part of the *Life of Saint Theodosius* has no parallel in Cyprian's *Life of Saint Peter*. In the latter the exposition of Peter's road to sainthood opens with the description of his spiritual ascent and *theosis*: not in the form of an anticipatory allegory, as in Nestor's introductory light vision, but as a tale of events in Peter's life, a stage in his spiritual progress. In the contemplation of the Holy Icons he beholds their divine prototypes and inscribes them within his own self. The "epiphany" in the *Life* occurs in the story of his consecration as metropolitan in Hagia Sophia: his face is transfigured in a supernatural radiance which in the context of Hesychast light metaphysics must be read as a hypostasis of the light within himself, of Christ (see Meyendorff 1964:150f.).

With Cyprian the Passion is not the object of *imitatio*, despite the fact that Philotheos' version of the Chrysostom liturgy, introduced by Cyprian in Russia, is marked precisely by its emphasis on the liturgy as a symbolic representation of the Easter mystery, when the priest, in donning his *epitrachelion*, symbolically takes upon himself the sufferings of Christ (Odincov 1881:129).

In Cyprian's *Life of Saint Peter* the shift of sanctification in the direction of an *imitatio* of the triumphant Christ should be seen as a reflection of the political function hagiography has acquired for Cyprian. The saving death of Christ is the historical basis for Cyprian's struggle, and that of political Hesychasm, to subordinate the secular powers to the supremacy of the Church. It is Christ's resurrection and victory, however, that provide the ideological basis for political Hesychasm in its attempt to create a powerful historical Church. In the image of Christ's omnipotent figure, both Peter and his successor, Cyprian, appear as representatives in history of this omnipotence. In Cyprian's *vita* liturgy and hagiography have acquired different functions, while Nestor in his *vita* transformed the life of the saint into a *mimesis* of the ideal scheme represented in the liturgical drama of Christ's suffering, sacrificial death, and resurrection.

With its persistent emphasis on the supremacy of the Church vis-à-vis the Prince, the *Life of Saint Peter* shows that the struggle between

Church and State that flared up unabated under Ivan III had already started at the end of the fourteenth century. In the history of Russian Church politics Cyprian has his place among the prelates who fought for the power of the Church under the watchword *"mirskaja vlastь estь pod dukhovnoju,"* to quote a tract from the end of the 1490s, written at the behest of Archbishop Gennadius of Novgorod. It was at this time, a century after Cyprian, that Iosif Volotskij fought to subordinate Tsardom to the Church, in complete agreement with the Church Princes of Novgorod (Zimin 1953). The last representative of this militant Church policy in Russian history is the Patriarch Nikon; for a brief period in the early 1650s it appeared that he would be able to implement his idea that *"svjaščenstvo carstva prebole estь,"* but like his predecessors he had to give in to the Tsar in the end.

Our analysis of Cyprian's *Life of Saint Peter* should be regarded as a corrective to the prevalent view that Nikon's militant Church policy had its ideological roots in Novgorod and in Byzantium (Onasch 1967:75). It had also, undoubtedly, Muscovite models; at any rate it can be traced back to Cyprian and late fourteenth-century Hesychasm.

We hope also to have demonstrated that Cyprian in his portraiture of the saint was not only superficially influenced by Hesychast mysticism, but that he employed mystical terminology and cognitive schemata in a way that shows this distinguished representative of political Hesychasm to have been fully familiar also with its esoteric aspect. At the same time, his style is characteristic in its lack of word-weaving. The *vita* is an indirect argument against the theory that the origin of word-weaving must be sought in mystical Hesychasm, indeed, that the style itself should be a linguistic medium for Hesychast mysticism.

Thus again the question arises whether Likhačev can be right in his conclusions about a causal connection between word-weaving and Hesychast mysticism in Russian hagiography during the second South Slav influence as we know it from Epiphanius' work.


## Word-weaving—a Reassessment

The theory that word-weaving is a product of and reflects Hesychast mysticism turns on the traditional view that this stylistic device was inspired by the linguistic reform believed to have been implemented by Patriarch Euthymius in the years between 1375 and 1393.

According to Likhačev and the scholars on whom he based his theory, in particular Sobolevskij (1894), Radčenko (1898), and Syrku (1901), Bulgaria was at this period a centre for the diffusion of Byzantine culture on Slav territory; it was here that the Greek originals were translated into Church Slavonic, here that the Patriarch and his disciples allegedly developed the new style of word-weaving in their endeavour to find an equivalent in their own Church Slavonic for the mystical literature that followed in the wake of Hesychasm (Likhačev 1958:14ff.).

This view of Bulgaria as the centre for the dissemination of Byzantine culture during the late Middle Ages, a view still held by a number of scholars in both Russia and the West, should be rejected as too undifferentiated. According to Mulić (1975) it is a view closely connected with certain Slavophile ideas and with the official Russian attitude towards Serbia in the 1880s and 1890s, when the Serbian king tried to counteract Russian domination by seeking closer ties with Austria, while Bulgaria remained within the Russian sphere of influence and became the centre for Russian expansion in the Balkans. This is the general ideological background against which the overemphasis on Bulgaria's role in the second South Slav influence to the detriment of early Serbian literature should be judged. Nor should it be forgotten that in the late 1950s, when Likhačev published his paper, Russia's relations with Yugoslavia were even more strained.

To obtain a more balanced view, we have to go back to the 1870s, the heyday of pro-Serbian feelings in Russia. In his address to the Kievan Theological Academy, *Istoričeskij vzgljad na vzaimnye otnošenija meždu serbami i russkimi v obrazovanii i literature,* N. Petrov (1876) draws the attention of his audience to the "age-old, uninterrupted relations between Serbians and Russians, of which Russia's public opinion in favour of the Slavs suffering from the Turkish yoke serves as the brilliant climax." Petrov goes on to demonstrate how in the fourteenth century Serbia experienced the influence of Byzantine culture both directly, in the form of new translations from the Greek originals, and indirectly, through new transcriptions and recensions of earlier Bulgarian manuscripts. The centre of this literary activity was the Serbian monastery of Hilandar on the Holy Mountain of Athos. By the middle of the fourteenth century, when the monastic community on Mount Athos had been incorporated into Stephen Dušan's Serbian Empire, and Bulgaria had become a Serbian vassal state, it was Serbia rather than Bulgaria that emerged as the centre for the propagation of Byzantine culture among the Orthodox Slavs.

What is even more important, however, is the fact that word-weaving as a dominant stylistic device can be found in Serbian hagiography at least a hundred years before Euthymius was appointed Patriarch of Trnovo. From the beginning of the thirteenth century onwards, this style reached a new stage in the panegyrical biographies of secular rulers which developed in connection with the cult of the Nemanja dynasty. The authors of these *Lives* even quoted verbatim from Hilarion's *Sermon on the Law and Grace,* whose style they consciously imitated.

Like late medieval Russian word-weaving, Serbian hagiography was long regarded as inferior by scholars unappreciative of what they considered "empty and redundant ethico-religious reflections, all kinds of rhetorical amplifications that are incessantly woven into the exposition, always retarding it," to quote Popović's characterisation of this literature (1912:39f.). Not surprisingly, it was by comparing Euthymius of Trnovo's writings with early Serbian hagiography that Radčenko arrived at his positive evaluation of the Bulgarian Patriarch's style. Despite all his comparisons with figures and events from the Bible and other canonical writings, Biblical reminiscences and quotations, in Radčenko's view Euthymius rises high above the Serbian hagiographers, "in whose Lives one text is added to another, although these texts have little or no relation to each other or to the story as a whole" (1898:289).

Early Serbian hagiography begins with two *Lives* of Stephen Nemanja, Grand Župan of Raška (1166–1196), and founder of the Serbian Empire of this dynasty. One of the *Lives* was written by Stephen's son Rastko, better known under his monastic name of Saint Sava, the first archbishop of Serbia (1219–1235) and founder of the autocephalous Serbian Church. The other was written by Stephen Nemanja's second son, Stephen Prvovenčani, the First Crowned, who in 1196 mounted the throne, after his father's abdication, when the latter had decided to take vows on the Holy Mountain and become the monk Symeon. Archbishop Sava succeeded in reaching a settlement of the antagonism that had prevailed between Church and state, which required neither the Church to become subordinate to the secular Prince nor the state to become subordinate to the Church: he founded the cult of his dynasty, "the race of Nemanja," who were to rule over both Church and state. Sava himself became the object of cultic glorification soon after his death, and his imprecation threatened any other race of princes that tried to usurp power in Serbia. Sava established the right of the Church to crown the king, and he himself crowned his brother with the crown that the latter had brought home with him from Rome in 1217, an act that took place with Rome's consent even though the two brothers had already decided to join Byzantium. In the future all Serbian kings were crowned by the primate of the Church, and in this way the Church gained a decisive influence on Serbian politics, as the election of the king came to depend upon the Church's blessing (Radojičić 1963). An important means for wielding the power thus acquired by the Serbian Church lay in the creation of the ruler-cult, the glorification of Serbian kings and bishops of Nemanja's race. In connection with this cult there grew up a whole literature, consisting of hymns, eulogies, and Lives, combined with a pictorial art—frescoes and panels of icons—in which the rhetorical glorification was translated into visual images (Radojičić 1963:43f.). The *Lives* of their father by the two princely hagiographers,

Sava's from 1208, and Stephen's from 1216, were followed in the middle of the thirteenth century by a *vita* of the Archbishop Sava, *Žitie svetoga Save*, and a third *Life* of Stephen Nemanja, *Žitie svetoga Simeona*, written by the monk Domentijan of the Hilandar Monastery, founded by Sava and his father. Domentijan's *Life* of Sava is dated to 1253/54, his *Life* of Symeon to 1263/64 (Trifunović 1965:557f.).

Yet another *Life of Saint Sava* was written in the second half of the thirteenth century by another Hilandar monk, Teodosije. From a purely stylistic point of view this *vita* is simpler than that of Domentijan. Therefore their works are by some scholars regarded as examples of two different stylistic trends in early Serbian hagiography: Teodosije's of a popular narrative, Domentijan's of an aristocratic rhetoric which was presumably written for a more discerning public at the royal Serbian court (Birnbaum 1972:250).

To these *Lives* are added fourteenth-century works like the *Zbornik kraljeva i arhiepiskopa srpskih*, composed by Archbishop Danilo II and his assistants. In the following century this style was further developed by such representatives of political Hesychasm as Gregory Camblak and Constantine of Kostenec, both Bulgarians active in Serbia. The former subsequently became metropolitan in Kiev. His *Life of Stephen Dečanski* shows that he had fully acquired the traditional modes of expression current in Serbian hagiography when, as abbot of the Dečani Monastery, he had the task of composing a new *Life* of its founder, Stephen Uroš III. Unlike Constantine of Kostenec, who in his *Lives* tended towards the secularised historico-biographical type of Life, Gregory Camblak's *Žitije Stefana Dečanskog* marks a continuation of the old panegyrical hagiography (see Popović 1965:436, 454).

In the Lives of the Serbian kings and bishops of the thirteenth and fourteenth centuries word-weaving reached its peak with Domentijan, Teodosije, and Danilo II and his disciples, who all lived and wrote their works before the so-called Trnovo school of the Patriarch Euthymius came into existence. In their works the whole rhetorical apparatus, usually regarded as the distinctive characteristic of the lofty style of a century later, is already in full bloom (Mulić 1963, 1965, 1968, 1971, 1975).

All the stylistic devices emphasised by Likhačev (1958, 1973) as typical of word-weaving in Russian hagiography around 1400 are represented in the works of the Serbian hagiographers: *periphrasis,* noun-compounds on Greek models, the use of Greek terms alongside the Slavonic equivalents; long chains of semantically different, phonetically similar words, or words that are phonetically different but identical in meaning; accumulations of traditional *topoi* and quotations from Orthodox canonical books, especially from the Bible, where the number of quotations from the Old Testament is noticeably higher than the number of quotations from the New Testament, and where the quotations from the

Psalms exceed by far the number of quotations from the other books of
the Bible (Mulić 1968:136, Mošin 1963:87, Stanojević and Glumac 1932).
Similarly, the application of these stylistic devices may be explained as a
reflection of the same generalising abstraction that Likhačev (1958:27)
finds underlying the use of word-weaving in Russian hagiography
during the second South Slav influence: "the tendency to an abstraction
of the world, to a deconstruction of its material concreteness."

In Serbian literature of the thirteenth and fourteenth centuries,
however, not only were the rhetorical apparatus of word-weaving and
the authors' intentional dematerialisation of reality already a fact, but
the term itself— "word-weaving"—was known to Serbian hagiographers and used by them to characterise their style (see Mulić 1965, 1968).
Far from having been invented by Epiphanius as a definition of his
individual mode of expression, the figurative use of the word *pletenie*
can be found in the earliest translations from the Greek surviving in
Kievan literature. Sreznevskij in his *Materialy* quotes the expression
"Glъ tvoikhъ pleteniï vražiju lъstъ razorilъ esi" from a copy of the
September Menaia of 1096. The metaphorical use of *ploke̅*/*pléko̅*
(*úmnon, rémata, lógous*) was, in fact, commonplace in Byzantine rhetoric and goes back to classical Greek literature. It was taken over by
Serbian and Russian writers together with the style it had referred to in
the Greek tradition.

The numerous correspondences in both style and content that Mulić
has been able to establish between Russian word-weaving during the
second South Slav influence and Serbian hagiography in the thirteenth
and first half of the fourteenth centuries seem fully to bear out his
conclusion, anticipated by Petrov (1876) almost a century earlier: that
the Serbian Lives of rulers and bishops served as models and incentives
to late medieval hagiographers in Russia.

The establishment of word-weaving in Serbian hagiography as early
as the thirteenth century makes it necessary to push back the *terminus
post quem* of this style to Domentijan's *Lives* of Symeon and Sava, that
is, at least a hundred years before Euthymius' appointment in 1374 as
Patriarch of Trnovo.

As regards the function of word-weaving in the Serbian *Lives*, which
incidentally appear above all to have been aimed at listeners, not readers,
its purpose was, to Mulić (1968), to emotionalise the exposition and
captivate the audience by its mysterious ambiguity, its alliterations and
assonances, its long sequences of parallel links and reiterations of
equivalent elements according to particular rhythmical patterns.

The ornamental style of the princely *Lives* is combined with a subject
matter that may be summed up in the concept of the glorification of the
ruler. By means of the quotation technique characteristic of word-
weaving, the accounts of Serbian kings' lives are linked with those of
Byzantine emperors and Old Testament kings. The young Serbian

dynasty is thus integrated with the course of history as it was understood by medieval historians. The regal authority of the Nemanjids received its divine legitimacy through the comparison with the Old Testament line of kings and Byzantine emperors, Christ's vicegerents on earth. The Serbian rulers, too, are depicted as the vicars of Christ in their land.

The regal ideology found its expression in the visual arts as well. This is not without interest for the debate about the character and origin of word-weaving. We recall that Likhačev has defined word-weaving in Russian hagiography around 1400, and the emotionally exalted style in Russian painting of the period, as an expression of the same mystical theology in different artistic media. As far as I know, the glorification of rulers in thirteenth-century Serbian painting has not been mentioned in this context.

Svetozar Radojčić (1969:36) has explicitly called attention to the close ideological connection between Serbian princely *Lives* of the second half of the thirteenth century and a particular trend in Serbian pictorial art of the same period. If we are to reckon Mulić's studies as sufficient proof that Serbian and Russian word-weaving are variants of one and the same style, then the parallel between pictorial and verbal art, as far as the Serbian ruler-cult is concerned, will have significance for our assessment of the ideology that may have produced word-weaving in Russia.

In the 1260s, when Domentijan wrote his *Life* of Symeon, a change took place in Serbian fresco painting. The dramatic emotionalism of the monastic tradition as we know it from Nerez and the interior of the Sopoćani Church gave way to a classicist court art, which totally predominates in the decorations of the old narthex of the Sopoćani Church. Compared with the roughly contemporaneous decorations of its interior, the narthex frescoes possess a more conservative character. In spite of all its sophistication, the style is rather monotonous (Radojčić 1969:36). The decorations differ from the conventional iconographic programme of such interiors by a number of characteristic additions: we find that Stephen Nemanja's Church assembly has been added to the succession of ecumenical councils. Inserted into the traditional Day of Judgement fresco is a panoramic representation of Queen Anne Dandolo on her deathbed. Anne Dandolo was the daughter of the Venetian Doge Enrico Dandolo and the mother of Uroš I, the founder of the Church. The artist has represented her body surrounded by mourning members of the royal family, clearly patterned on the conventional iconographic representation of the Dormition. The picture was also probably patterned on group portraits of the imperial family in Constantinople. Other members of King Uroš I's family are portrayed in the lowest register of the frescoes on the west and south walls, beneath the representation of Christ's genealogy, the Tree of Jesse, and scenes from the story of Joseph. This montage of scenes from the history of the

132                                                        VISIONS OF GLORY

Nemanja dynasty into the traditional iconographic programme creates
a pattern of parallels between dynastic portraits and events on the one
hand, and on the other, figures and events from Biblical history. The
technique corresponds exactly to the way in which Serbian
hagiographers depict their rulers, when, for instance, Teodosije calls
Stephen Nemanja "a new Joseph," or when Domentijan compares Sava
to Joseph and Nemanja to Jacob. Similarly, the hagiographers'
expression of the Nemanjids, "scions of a noble race," corresponds to the
Tree of Jesse. The juxtaposition was clearly intended to illustrate the
political power and spiritual significance of the dynasty and to glorify
the rulers with their families. The technique first occurred in literature,
then in painting, from which it soon disappeared, whereas in literature
it remained a living mode of thought (Radojčić 1969:36f.).

In painting, the style and iconography of the Sopoćani narthex gave
way to more abstract and schematic representations of the royal family
in the churches of Gračanica, Peć, and Dečani. The affectionate
portrayal of the rulers with their families in the Sopoćani frescoes has
been displaced by "genealogical diagrams" (Obolensky) patterned on
the Tree of Jesse, and in one case, in the Macedonian monastery of
Matejče, the Nemanjids are grafted onto the genealogical tree of Byzantine emperors, reflecting Dušan's claim to the political legacy of the
Empire (Obolensky 1971a:347).

Against this background we may safely conclude that the technique of
parallelism in mid-thirteenth-century hagiography found its visual
equivalent in monumental painting of the same period. The hagiographers' use of quotations and *topoi*, and the artists' juxtaposition of their
own portraits of the Nemanjids with historical figures serving as their
models, are expressions of the same principle, a reflection of a common
ideology in different media. This ideology is no longer identical with
the mystical Christocentrism of Nerez and the Sopoćani Church. This
mystical trend in Orthodox painting has its origin in the monastic idea
that through contemplation of Christ's Passion and through *imitatio
Christi,* individual Christians will attain the highest stage of inner
union in God and *theosis,* or deification. The glorification of the ruler as
Christ's vicegerent in his own realm presupposes a different relationship
between God and the individual. Here, the ruler represents the power of
God in the state of which he is the head in a way that may be compared to
the role of the bishop as head of the Church. In this context, the
emphasis is shifted from imitation to participation; each individual
member of the community shares in the power of the divine embodied in
the ruler, by being incorporated into the body of the state. Thus, the
relationship between image and spectator in mystical art is determined
by the principle of similarity and imitation, whereas in the relationship
between the audience and the royal heroes of Serbian hagiography the
principle of proximity and participation prevails. With the help of

word-weaving the hagiographers were able to emotionalise their discourse and thus create a feeling of unity and oneness with the saint among their listeners, suspending the original distance between the king and his subjects by rhetorical means.

Ideologically as well as stylistically, early Serbian princely Lives and ruler portraits have their origin in Byzantine literature and art. Although it has not been possible to trace specific textual models for the Serbian princely Lives in Byzantine literature, it is not difficult to detect Byzantine patterns for their style and general composition. The stylistic and compositional models cited by scholars are Symeon Metaphrastes' hagiographical rhetoric, Byzantine chronicles, chrysobulloi, typica, Lives of emperors, and liturgical writings—a combination of modes of expression from both secular and sacred literature, corresponding to the combination of secular and sacred elements of meaning in the ruler hagiography (see Hafner 1964, Birnbaum 1972:262ff.). The apparently exaggerated use of rhetorical effects taken over from Byzantine panegyrics of emperors, chronicles, hagiography, and liturgical texts is no more a redundant embellishment than are the parallels and quotations for the content of this literature, where it is precisely by means of these elements that its authors compose their glorifying portraits of princes and develop a Slavonic variant of the medieval cult of the Prince as *vicarius Christi*. The encomiastic representation of the life of the ruler is a genre taken over by the Slavs from Byzantine literature. In Slavonic lands the genre was cultivated both in Orthodox and Catholic areas. Bulgarian medieval literature forms an exception as it knows no such dynastic *vitae* or legends (Birnbaum 1972:266). In Russia the genre was known in early Kievan literature, as is shown by Hilarion's *Sermon on the Law and Grace* with its encomium to Prince Vladimir. In early Slavonic literature the stylistic devices of word-weaving were not confined to this genre, however, but were used more widely, just as in Byzantium. In early Kievan writing the style of word-weaving found a further development in the sermons and prayers of Kirill Turovskij, whose texts are closely related both generically and stylistically to the canonical texts of the Orthodox liturgy. This early Kievan adaptation of Greek rhetoric did not remain unknown to the authors of the *Lives* of the Nemanjids. On the contrary, Domentijan, the chief exponent of Serbian word-weaving, made active use of Hilarion's encomium to Prince Vladimir, quoting from it and expanding on it, combining it with other texts, thus making it serve his own purpose (Adrianova-Peretc 1963:8, Mulić 1968:127, Sasonova 1974:46). To Domentijan, Hilarion's encomiastic mode of expression must have been felt as the Slavonic variant of a common Greek style. Moreover, Domentijan's adaptation of Hilarion's encomium indicates that the cultural interchange between Orthodox Slavs in the Middle Ages was multidirectional, and that Bulgaria was not necessarily the centre from

VISIONS OF GLORY

which Byzantine civilisation radiated eastwards to the Serbs and northwards to the Russians (see Birnbaum 1984).

Returning to Epiphanius' *pletenie sloves,* we must ask whether
Russian word-weaving at the end of the fourteenth century should not
be regarded as a late stage in the development of the encomiastic style of
the Slavonic ruler hagiography. At any rate, it is not a *new style.* From
the beginning of the thirteenth century onwards, this style, which had
produced Hilarion's masterly praise of the first Vladimir, reached a new
stage in the panegyrical biographies of secular rulers which developed
in connection with the cult of the Nemanja dynasty. There seems thus to
be a close connection between this style and the translation of Byzantine
imperial ideology to the Orthodox Slavonic nations, where the rulers
sought to create their own states on the Byzantine model; in Kiev, in
Serbia, and finally, after the Turkish conquest of the Balkans, in
Moscow, the Third Rome.

In Muscovite literature the device of word-weaving appears first to
have come into evidence from the end of the fourteenth century onwards.
In all probability the style developed partly on the lines of Hilarion's and
Kirill Turovskij's sermons, partly on Serbian and Greek literary models
(Mošin 1963:106). Judging by the extant material, Epiphanius the Wise
was the first and at the same time the foremost representative of this style
in post-Mongolian Russia. His *Life of Saint Stephen* is generally considered to be the most important and best-preserved example of word-
weaving in Muscovite literature. While today it appears that the style
reached its peak in Russia at the beginning of its development, this may
be due to a modern misconception, as the bulk of Muscovite literature
from before the fourteenth century was lost when, in revenge for the
Russian victory on the field of Kulikovo in 1380, the Tartars two years
later ravaged Moscow under their Khan Tokhtamyš. As the Tartars
approached the city the manuscripts from the surrounding countryside
were brought into what was believed to be safe custody in churches
behind the city walls. When the enemy entered the city and set fire to it,
the whole of this literary treasure was destroyed (Mošin 1963:105).

Whatever may have been the history of word-weaving in Russian
literature in the period before Epiphanius, there seems to be no basis for
the theory that his hagiographical work represented a continuation of
the South Slav Hesychasts' Lives of saints combined with elements from
an indigenous, national tradition. Hesychast hagiography is too
different from that of Epiphanius in both form and content. First,
Hesychast Lives are not stylistically dominated by word-weaving, and
second, they are marked, to a far greater extent than Epiphanius' *Life of
Saint Stephen,* by Hesychast mystical terminology, as we have seen it in
Cyprian's *Life of Saint Peter.* Likhačev (1958:55, 1973:87) has noted both
these points, and has observed that Epiphanius' style is much closer to
the panegyric of Gregory Camblak, without, however, drawing the

obvious conclusions from his own observations. The similarity between Epiphanius' style and the style of Gregory Camblak's panegyrical *Life of Stephen Uroš III* is hardly a coincidence. From our knowledge of Serbian word-weaving we may assume that Gregory's and Epiphanius' hagiographical modes of expression are two versions of a common style. Furthermore, Gregory's style provides an important clue to the meaning of the so-called linguistic reforms at the end of the fourteenth century, without enabling us, however, to draw any conclusions about Euthymius of Trnovo's original intentions, of which nothing is known. Euthymius' alleged reform programme is a modern reconstruction based on the writings of such political Hesychasts as Gregory Camblak and his countryman Constantine of Kostenec, both of whom took refuge at the Serbian royal court after the Turkish conquest of Bulgaria. Constantine was a disciple of one of Euthymius' disciples. It is especially on the basis of the *Skazanie o pismenima*, his orthographical treatise of the 1420s, that a reconstruction of the so-called Trnovo linguistic reforms has been attempted. The treatise has long been regarded as a highly schematic formulation of Euthymius' programme (Goleniščev-Kutuzov 1973:38–54, Obolensky 1971a:336ff.). However, the research undertaken by Talev (1972) has shown that the process of emending the Church books had begun long before Euthymius was appointed Patriarch of Trnovo. The process seems to have been initiated under Ivan Asen II (1218–1241) with the aim of reconciling the Slavonic liturgy as much as possible with the norms of the first translations into Church Slavonic from the Greek. This revision must be seen in connection with the reintroduction of the Church Slavonic liturgy when the Bulgarian patriarchate of Trnovo was restored in 1235. By the late fourteenth century, the first phase of this process was virtually complete, and spelling rules as well as grammatical and lexical norms had been fairly well established (see Birnbaum 1984:15).

Judging by his treatise, Constantine of Kostenec's idea of language is marked by an idealising of the Cyrillo-Methodian tradition, of the old, unitary Church Slavonic, which is contrasted with the lack of unity in Constantine's own time. Also characteristic of Constantine's linguistic conservatism is his invocation of the absolute authority of Byzantine models, which led to his demand for a literal translation of Greek texts into the Slavonic language. For Constantine form and content are identical, so that the least deviation in orthography or writing implies dogmatic aberration and heresy. In his struggle for linguistic unity among the Slavs as a means of fighting heresy and moral decline, Constantine appeals to the secular authorities for assistance, a feature he has been thought to have in common with the Hesychasts of Euthymius' circle (Goleniščev-Kutuzov 1973:43).

Constantine's doctrine of the identity of form and content is hardly compatible with the idea of the "unspeakable", divine "first cause," which escapes all verbal representation, an idea central to mystical Hesychasm and also found in the teachings of Palamas. By the same token, Constantine's concern with any possible deviation from the "true word" is very different from the linguistic policy of Constantine the Philosopher and his brother Methodius, the founders of old Church Slavonic. In his efforts to create a liturgical language in the Slavonic vernacular, Constantine the Philosopher, this "innate linguist," was led by "his fabulous and remarkable intellectual flexibility ... repeatedly and significantly to deviate from Greek models in his innovative experiments" (Jakobson 1985). The linguistic doctrine expounded in the *Skazanie o pismenima* reflects a very different attitude. At a time when the Byzantine Commonwealth was politically in a state of dissolution, bookmen like Constantine of Kostenec fought to restore, to purify, and to preserve the Orthodox cultural heritage. However many points of similarity their activity may have with the pre-Renaissance (see Goleniščev-Kutuzov 1973:38–54), the term *restaurazione del christianesimo slavo-ortodosso* (Picchio 1958:197), in the sense of a restoration of the Cyrillo-Methodian tradition, seems best to cover their intentions and activity.

The idealising of history and glorification of the present through assimilation to a heroic past is a feature common to Euthymius, Cyprian, Gregory Camblak, and Constantine of Kostenec. In Russia as in the Balkans this glorification of the past is related to the development of an imperial ideology on the Byzantine pattern and to the struggle between the secular Princes and the Princes of the Church as to who represents the supreme power of the Lord in Heaven.

# Epic Distance and Lyric Lament: Word-weaving in Epiphanius' *Life of Saint Stephen, Bishop of Perm*

## Stages in the Study of the *Life*

Our discussion of word-weaving has centred on the view that it is a panegyrical style taken over from the Greeks by the Orthodox Slavs, who in their turn developed an indigenous version of it in their own encomiastic literature. This view, it seems to me, is historically better founded than the thesis offered by Likhačev about the origin of word-weaving in mystical Hesychasm. Returning now to Epiphanius the Wise, we shall presently see how he adapted this style to his own purpose in the *Life of Saint Stephen, Bishop of Perm*. His other main work, the *Life of Saint Sergius of Radonež*, has not been preserved in its original version and cannot be considered here. It has come down to us only in the redaction of Pachomius the Serbian, dating from the middle of the fifteenth century, and should be treated as a work by Pachomius.

The *Life of Saint Stephen* has been published twice; first by N. Kostomarov (1862) and later by V. Družinin (1897). This second edition was reprinted in 1959, this time with a foreword by Tschižewskij instead of Družinin's own. His edition is now accepted as the more satisfactory, although not on every count (Golubinskij 1900:263). Družinin based his edition on a copy of the *Life* found in a *poluustav* manuscript of a Reading Menaia presumably written in the late fifteenth or early sixteenth century. This copy, so Družinin believed, is a fairly accurate reproduction of Epiphanius' original. It is a hypothesis that has not been contested, and until new evidence is produced we shall have to accept it. But strictly speaking we are dealing with a text written about a hundred years after Epiphanius composed his *Life*.

Epiphanius' own life is poorly documented. As so often happens in early Russian literature, facts are mixed with fiction, both in the sources and in the works of the scholars. The *Life of Saint Stephen* is particularly disappointing in this respect. Ključevskij (1871:88f.) found it well-nigh useless. He was willing to consider as a fact only that Epiphanius became acquainted with Stephen in Rostov, in the Monastery of Saint Gregory the Theologian, and that this meeting took place before 1379, the year when the saint went to preach the Gospel to the pagan Zyrians, or Permians, as they are called in the *Life*. This East Finnic tribe, today known as Komi, lived in the northeastern part of European Russia, in the basin of the river Vyčegda. Ključevskij further assumed that the *vita* was written soon after the death of the saint in 1396, while the *Life of Saint Sergius* is of a later date, written probably about 1417, only a few years before the death of Epiphanius in 1422.

Other, less critical scholars have written more extensively about the life of Epiphanius, claiming to know that he travelled widely in the East, making a long journey to Constantinople, and visiting both Mount Athos and Jerusalem on his way. When the sources for this information are scrutinised, however, we find that it is based on a passage in the encomium to Saint Sergius, in which the author writes that the saint

> did not leave his place in order to go to other lands except when he had to. He did not go on a search for Constantinople, Mount Athos, or Jerusalem, like me, cursed as I am, and devoid of reason. O woe is me! I creep about here and there, swim hither and thither, and walk from one place to another. The saint did not walk around like this, but sat in praiseworthy silence and contemplation. (Epifanij Premudryj 1981a:422)

Since this passage, as Ključevskij has observed (1871:91), in all probability belongs to Pachomius the Serbian, who, incidentally was a great traveller, its source value for the biography of Epiphanius the Wise is more than dubious and would have to be supported by other evidence in order to be accepted.

In both the *Life of Saint Stephen* and that of Saint Sergius there are passages containing a clear anti-Muscovite tendency. Modern scholars have given these passages a biographical interpretation, noting that Epiphanius, like Stephen and Sergius, had close connections with Rostov, a city that was sacked by Muscovite princes in the fourteenth century. It was in Rostov that Epiphanius met Stephen, in the Grigor'ev Monastery, where the saint had received his education; and Epiphanius' other hero, Sergius, belonged to a noble Rostov family that moved to Radonež after the fall of their native city. Within the context of the *Life of Saint Stephen*, however, the attacks on Moscow are not connected with these events, but with the merciless exploitation of the Zyrians by merchants and officials from Moscow and Novgorod. And the denunciation of Muscovite colonisers in the speech of Stephen's main adversary among the pagans, the shaman Pam, does not prevent Epiphanius from representing Moscow as the spiritual and political centre of the Russian Church. It is therefore possible that Pam's accusations are meant not as expressions of the author's anti-Muscovite feelings, but should instead be seen together with a similar passage in the lament of the people of Perm at the death of their bishop, a passage which occurs towards the end of the *Life*. Here, it is the Novgorodians who are being accused of exploitation. What these passages have in common is the juxtaposition of the exploiters with the saint, who illuminates the people of Perm with the word of the Gospel, incorporating them into the Russian Church by converting them to his own Christian faith. Within the context of the *Life*, these passages may be read as representations of a struggle between good and evil forces, rather than as an expression of the author's personal resentment.

The interpretation of these passages shows how difficult it is to use the text of the *Life of Saint Stephen* as a documentary account of events and characters. This is the more disappointing in view of the fact that Epiphanius in his introduction emphasises his closeness to the saint, claiming that in composing the *Life* he has relied not only on information gathered from others, but has also based his account on his own observations and on his conversations with a man whom he knew personally and as a friend. These remarks have raised the expectations of many scholars who like Ključevskij have approached the *Life* in the hope of finding in it a detailed account of the saint's character and of his role in the colonisation of northeastern Russia. They have all been forced to conclude that Epiphanius' account of the saint's life is not what one might expect from the author's own words in the introduction.

Ključevskij was right in stating that the biographical data provided by
Epiphanius were far too general to be of any real use to the historian
(1871:96). Re-examinations of the *Life's* documentary value, such as
those of Bugoslavskij (1946) and Adrianova-Peretc (1947a) could not
change this view. Instead, the absence of biographical data was
explained as a necessary consequence of the South Slavonic influence
and Epiphanius' word-weaving, with its orientation towards the style as
such, its focusing on "the brilliant stylistic treatment of the material"
(Stender-Petersen 1952:127). There was a shift from the factual side of the
*Life* to its style, and the *Life* was reduced almost to a collection of rhetorical devices and *topoi*, while the function of these *topoi* within the
context of the *vita* as a significant whole, the *vita* as an expression of
something, was overlooked (e.g., in Tschiževskij 1960:175ff.). It was
partly in reaction to this that Likhačev put forward his thesis, trying to
understand Epiphanius' account of the saint's life as an instance of the
"abstractive psychologism" of the Middle Ages, transferring to the study
of Epiphanius' work the psychologism found in Radčenko's interpretation of late medieval Bulgarian hagiography (1898). But by emphasising the emotive function of Epiphanius' style almost to the exclusion of
other functions, Likhačev, too, fell short of interpreting the *Life* as an
aesthetic whole (see 1958, 1967, 1970, 1973).

Before such an interpretation could be made, a reassessment of the
*Life's* content was needed. This came with the publication of
Konovalova's important paper (1969) about the principle underlying
the selection of facts in the *Life of Saint Stephen*. Konovalova demonstrated how the *Life*, far from being devoid of factual information,
contains a great deal of knowledge which must be of interest not only to
local historians and geographers but to Church historians and students
of political history as well. What strikes one from a literary point of
view, however, is the way these facts have been combined with the biographical strain of the narrative in the narrower sense of the word, for
while the biographical theme is developed with the help of traditional
schemes and biographical *topoi*, the passages characterised by factual
information about the land and people of Perm take the form of cen-
trifugal digressions away from the description of Stephen's character.
The factual content of the *Life* is of a very general kind and clearly not
intended to give an individualised account of the saint's personal experience. This absence of individual detail has been explained as a consequence of word-weaving, where the biographical component is
supplanted by panegyrical and didactic elements (Trubetzkoy 1973:131),
and it has also been seen in connection with Epiphanius' own intentions
in the *Life,* which, in Likhačev's view, were to teach and preach, rather
than to relate facts (1973:75). Konovalova (1969) sees the biographical
schematism of the *Life* as a generic feature. As a *vita* the main purpose of
the *Life of Saint Stephen* was to glorify the saint, and this purpose

imposes its own restrictions on the facts allowed into the narrative. Despite their friendship and his personal knowledge of the saint, Epiphanius as the author of the *Life* is only a vehicle for the expression of the divine meaning of Stephen's life, and he therefore "consciously avoids detailed biographical information about the hero of his work" (Konovalova 1969). Viewed within the framework of the genre, this is certainly a relevant observation. But I think we can be more specific in our discussion of the *Life's* handling of biographical facts, by trying to recreate the historical context of Epiphanius' work.

In his discussion of the *Life of Saint Stephen* and its immediate historical context, Klibanov (1960:158ff.) has singled out the following lines as the key passage in Epiphanius' description of his hero:

> ...ne dobivalsja vladyčьestva, ne vertelsja, ne tščalъsja, ne naskakival, ne nakupalsja, ne nasulivalsja posuly; ne dal bo nikomu že ničtože, i ne vzjal u nego ot postavlenija niktože ničtože, ni dara, ni posula, ni mzdy; nečego bo bjaše bylo dati emu, ne stjažaniju stjažavsu emu ... (he did not seek office, nor did he ingratiate himself, or strive to get promotion, or seize office by force, or let himself be bought, or promise to give bribes; he did not give anything to anyone, either present, or bribes, or reward; for he had nothing to give away, having never acquired any acquisitions ... – Klibanov 1960:160, quoting Kostomarov's edition.)

This catalogue of virtues presents us with a highly idealised description of Stephen as the perfect bishop. At the same time the selection of verbs listed in this catalogue is hardly fortuitous. In all probability Klibanov is right in seeing this passage in relation to the accusations launched against the clergy for the covetousness and corruption of its members at a time when the Russian Church was assailed by heretical sentiments both from within its own ranks and from the laity. Anti-trinitarian and iconoclastic sects attacked the dogmas of the Church and the life of the priests. The *strigol'niki* living in the region of Pskov and Novgorod seem to have been particularly vehement in their castigation of the priests' desire for wealth and power, which from their reading of the Gospels they found to be irreconcilable with the Christian idea of the pastor. The crucial concept in this struggle is *stjažanie* (a translation of Greek *ktēsis*, acquisition, possession), which is also the conceptual nucleus of the passage focused by Klibanov. It looks therefore as if one of the main purposes of Epiphanius' portrayal of Saint Stephen must have been to represent him in the image of a *nestjažatel'*, a *non-acquirer*, or *non-possessor*. This purpose would then also explain the passages where the saint's missionary work, by which he brings the message of the Gospel to the wilderness, is seen in contrast to the material greed which has prompted the merchants and officials from Novgorod and Moscow to go to the land of Perm.

*Stjažanie,* the acquisition of property by the Church and the monasteries, led eventually to the division of the hierarchy into two factions, the *stjažateli,* led by Iosif of Volokolamsk (1439–1515), and the *nestjažateli,* who rallied around the Hesychast mystic Nil Sorskij (1433–1508). Although the problem of Church property was brought to a head only a hundred years later, the struggle had been going on for a long time. Dane (1961) claims that this struggle forms the ideological background against which we must view Epiphanius' portrait of Saint Stephen as a non-possessor, a portrait which according to Dane should be seen as an intentional alteration of Stephen as we know him from other sources, in particular from his own treatise against the *strigol'niki,* written during a visit to Novgorod. Here he emerges in his own words as a ruthless advocate of the militant Church in her campaign against the heretics, an aspect of the saint that has been suppressed in Epiphanius' representation of his life. Although we cannot accept Dane's oversimplified characterisation of the possessors as a "wealthy clique," we would agree with his view that Stephen as we encounter him in Epiphanius' *Life* is the result of a transformation of the historical material into an image of the saint which is no longer identical with the person Epiphanius actually knew. All this presupposes, however, that Epiphanius had a definite conception of the saint's role and the meaning of his mission. Our next task will be to analyse the text of his *Life* in order to reconstruct this conception and the strategies by which it was given verbal form.

## The Stylistic Dominant of the *Life*

The rhetorical devices that seem to predominate in word-weaving are alliterations and assonances, etymological figures (long sequences of words from the same root in different forms, or the same form with different roots), an accumulation of synonyms, comparisons, antitheses, periphrases, and a large number of quotations from other texts, above all from the Bible, where the Old Testament, and especially the Psalms, are quoted noticeably more often than the books of the New Testament.

Even in purely quantitative terms, the Biblical quotations form a salient feature in the style of the *Life of Saint Stephen.* F. Wigzell (see Kitch 1976:132) has identified 340 quotations from the Bible. In accordance with what is usual for the genre, Epiphanius' quotations from the Bible and other sacred scriptures have either been incorporated into his own discourse or mounted into the text in a way that marks them off from the narrative. In the latter case they are introduced with the help of stereotyped formulae that indicate the source: "as the prophet Isaiah said of old," "as the Apostle says," "and John Chrysostom said," and so forth. The quotations occur separately or in tirades. An example of the latter is the introduction to the chapter "On the Calling and Conversion of Many Nations" (64f.)[1], a tirade consisting of 46 quotations from the Psalms, 2 from Jeremiah, one from Isaiah, one from Micah, another from Isaiah, one from Zechariah, and finally 7 more from Isaiah.

Epiphanius' predilection for the Old Testament, especially for the Psalms, is striking. They account for half the number of Biblical quotations in the *Life*. This predominance of quotations from the Old Testament over those from the New, and the absolute preponderance of the Psalms over the other books of the Bible, form one of the most important characteristics that Epiphanius' writing has in common with thirteenth- and fourteenth-century word-weaving in Serbian hagiography. Historically this may be explained by the fact that the Psalms were part of the daily worship in the monasteries. The Serbian hagiographers quoted above all from the texts they knew by heart, either because these texts were obligatory reading or because they heard them read out daily during the services at different times of the day (Stanojević and Glumac 1932:XXIII).

It is easy to show that Epiphanius quotes the Bible from memory and not verbatim. Wigzell (see Kitch 1976:131ff.) has convincingly shown that he even alters the quotations to fit the meaning of the passages into which they are integrated. But this gives us no grounds for presuming that he was being unusually bold or free in his treatment of the texts. If he has changed them "despite medieval man's fear of even the least alteration of the Bible" (Kitch 1971), this merely shows that on this point Epiphanius does not differ from other medieval authors. It is, in fact, a general characteristic of these Biblical quotations that their form is not normally textual, but shaped to fit the writer's own exposition. This Erwin Panofsky (1955:124) has demonstrated in his analysis of Abbot Suger's Biblical quotations; they are not copied verbatim, but adapted to the abbot's own context: "This does not mean that Suger deliberately 'falsifies' the Bible. ... Like all medieval writers he quoted from memory and failed to make a sharp distinction between the text and his personal interpretation." The interaction between quotation and narration in the *Life of Saint Stephen* shows above all that the quotations have not been mounted mechanically into the *vita*. They have been woven into the narrative in the course of an active, creative writing process.

The extensive use of Biblical quotations by Epiphanius and the South Slavonic word-weavers indicates that these quotations must have had a particularly important function in their works. The Psalms and other

---

[1] Here and in the following, references are to pages in Družinin's edition (Epifanij Premudryj 1897).

texts from which these authors quote gave them not only a lofty vocabulary and a poetic diction but also a pattern for building up single lexical units into wider contexts. It was especially from their reading of the Psalms that the word-weavers learned to fuse individual components into a higher unity. The Psalms provided them also with a stock of expressive images and comparisons which were transmitted to the lives of their heroes.

In his characterisation of Domentijan's style, Mošin (1963:88ff.) has traced its separate devices and their combinations back to the Psalms. The quotations already contain all the images and periphrastic expressions, similes and antitheses, and semantic and morphological parallelisms that distinguish his style throughout. These stylistic devices are used to give the discourse emotional colour, the particular feature of word-weaving that Likhačev has emphasised.

The tropes and figures of psalmic poetry that give Serbian word-weaving its distinctive character are also typical of the *Life of Saint Stephen*. Repetition of the same root with different suffixes occurs frequently, either as derivation (*paregmenon*):

obyčai bo estь vdovamъ novoovdověv'šimъ plakatisę gorko vdovьstva svoego (for it is the habit of newly widowed widows to weep bitterly over their widowhood) (93);

prošu u tebe prošenia věrno prosęšču mi (I ask you to forgive me who truly asks your forgiveness) (98);

or as inflection (*polyptoton*):

napadajušče, napadakhu na nь sъ jarostiju, i sъ gněvomъ i sъ voplemъ, jako ubiti i pogubiti khotęšče (attacking, they attacked him with fury, and with anger, and with clamour, wanting to kill and destroy him. (25)

Both figures associate words that are formally similar and semantically contiguous.

The words may also be aligned on the basis of a formal similarity, a similarity on the signans level, not accompanied by a corresponding semantic similarity. The result of this alignment is a kind of pun, in which formal similarity of the components forms a contrast to their semantic difference:

ne povelě mi mučiti, no učiti... ni povelě kazniti, no nakazati (he did not order me to torture, but to teach... nor did he order to execute, but to instruct. (56)

The asymmetry between *signatum* (meaning) and *signans* (form) falls short of our expectations and creates a semantic tension in the text. This play on similarity and contrast between meaning and form also underlies Epiphanius' synonymous couplings, either in pairs:

> zělo želaše i velmi khotęše (they very much wanted and greatly wished) (8); vozdivisę zělo, i čjudisę vel'mi (they were astonished and greatly surprised) (14); bez' bojazni i bezъ užasti (without fear and without horror) (37);

or in sequences, as in the following anaphoric repetition:

> edinъ [črьnecь složi(l)]... edinъ kalogerъ, edinъ mni(kh), edinъ inokъ (one black brother composed it... one *kalogeros*, one *monachos*, one monk). (72)

Mulić (1968) is inclined to trace this particular sequence back to a similar tirade in Domentijan's *Life of Saint Symeon* (= Stephen Nemanja).

A special variant of Epiphanius' synonymous couplings is his explanatory juxtaposition of Greek and Russian words (*homoioptoton*):

> kherotonisanie, rekše rukopoloženie sščeństva (cheirotonia, that is, ordination) (17);
> dev'toronomia, rek'še vo v'torozakonii (Deuteronomy, that is, in the Second Law) (46);
> anafema da budetь, rek'še da budetь proklętъ (anathema be he, that is, be he condemned). (84)

Antithesis, the juxtaposition of two components in a pair, where the one negates the other, is also one of Epiphanius' characteristic figures:

> ne bo o(t) m(d)rosti, no o(t) grubosti (and not from prudence, but from ignorance) (4);
> i nestь mira v nikhъ, no raz'glasie (and there is no peace among them, but discord). (30)

The antithesis, too, may be concatenated, as in the following example, clearly modelled on Psalm 115, where Epiphanius goes on to weave and couple the antitheses to form anaphoric sequences in a rhetorical arabesque:

> Kumiri vaši, drevo sušče bezdušno, děla rukъ člčeskъ,
> usta imu(t), i ne glju(t):
> uši imu(t), i ne slyšatь,

oči imu(t), i ne uzrę(t),
noz(d)ri imu(t), i ne obonęjutь,
rucě imu(t), i ne osęzaju(t),
nozě imutь, i ne poidu(t), i ne khodę(t), i ne stupajutь ni s města,
i ne voz'glasę(t), gor'tan'mi svoimi,
i ne njukhaju(t) noz(d)ręmi svoimi,
ni žer'tvъ prinosimy(kh) priimajutь,
ni pijutъ ni jadu(t)
(your idols are lifeless wood, the work of men's hands, they have
mouths, and speak not, they have ears, and hear not, they have eyes,
and see not, they have nostrils, and smell not, they have hands, and
feel not, they have feet, and walk not; and cannot move, and leave
not their place, and do not speak through their throats, and do not
smell through their nostrils, nor do they receive the offerings
brought to them, nor do they eat or drink). (28f.)

In this tirade the semantic contiguity between the components is combined with a formal equivalence between their verbal predicates in the
first part of each line, whereas in the second part of the line it is the
anaphoric repetition of the conjunction *i* "and" that creates formal
equivalence between the components, while semantic contiguity is
retained.

The interchange of figures gives the discourse a varying rhythm, the
tempo increases or decreases, rises towards a climax, or prepares the
transition to a fresh theme. The main device is to create rhythm in the
syntactic similarity between the individual components of the tirade, the
*isocola,* which are linked up anaphorically, through repetition of the
same initial word; epiphorically, through repetition of the same word at
the end, or by the aid of flectional rhyme *(homoioteleuton).*

At the same time, the above tirade is an example of *distributio,* the
breaking down of a composite concept or object into its component
parts. Here it is the idols of the Zyrians that are itemised. This figure of
speech is one of the most important in the *Life of Saint Stephen.* It may
have either a concretionary function, as in the passage cited, where the
concretised object is subsequently negated and thereby annihilated, or it
may serve a dematerialising, abstractive objective. In each case the figure
is based on the principle of contiguity.

Another instance of concretionary *distributio* is Epiphanius' manner
of describing land and people, for example, in the paragraph about the
land of the Zyrians:

A se imena městomъ i stranamь, i zemlę(m) i inojazyčnikomъ,
živuščimь vъkrugъ okolo Per'mi: Dvinęne. Ustьjužane. Viležane.
Vyčežane. Pěnežane. Južane. Syrьęne. Galičęne. Vęt'čane. Lopь.
Korěla. Jugra. Pečera. Goguliči. Samoědь. Per'tasy. Permь Velikaa,

glemaa Čjusovaa. Rěka edina, eiže imę Vy(m) si obьkhodęščię, vsju zemlju Per'mьskuju i vnide v' Vyčegdu. Rěka že drugaa imenemь Vyčegda: si iskhodęščia iz' zemlę Permьskia i šestvujušči kъ sěvernĕi stranĕ, i svoi(m) ustiemъ vnide vъ Dvinu, [niže] grada Ustjuga za m̃. popriščь. /Rěka(ž) tretiaę naricaemaa Vę(t')ka. jaže tečеtь sъ druguju stranu Per'mi i ... (And these are the names of the places and countries and lands and barbarians living around Perm: the Dvina people, the Ustjug people, the Vilija people, the Vyčegda people, the Pinega people, the Jug people, the Syrians, the people of Galič, the Vjatka people, the Lapps, the Carelians, the Obugians, the Pečora people, the Gogulič people, the Samoyeds, the Pertasians, the Great Perm, called Čusovaja. A river, whose name is Vym, it encircles the entire Permian land and flows into the Vyčegda. For Vyčegda is another river: it flows from the Permian land towards the north and into the Dvina forty miles below the city of Ustjug. A third river is called Vjatka, which flows on the other side of Perm, and...). (9)

Further we have the enumeration of various methods the Permians used in their attempts to kill the saint:

... sъ drekolmi, i s posokhy, i oslopy, i s velikimi urazy, inogda že s' sokyrami, inogda že strělami strělęjušče, ovogda že solomu okolo tebe zapalęjušče, i simъ sъžešči tę khotęšče, i mnogymi obrazy umrĭviti tę myslęšče. No Gь Bgъ Spsъ spse tę svoimi sudbami... (with cudgels, and with poles, and sticks, and with big clubs, and sometimes with axes, sometimes shooting with arrows, at other times putting fire around you, wishing to burn you to death, and they sought to kill you in many ways. But the Lord, God the Saviour, saved you through his will....) (103)

An example of abstractive segmentation, or *distributio*, is the periphrastic description of Stephen in the concluding encomium. The figure of the saint is detached from the action of the story, and his deeds are transformed into timeless and generalised ideas of what he is—a nominal characterisation in which a whole string of predicates are invoked and made to stand synecdochically for the man. Gradually, however, the totality of the figure is lost in this segmentation, until it finally defies all decription. The tirade opens with a *dubitatio* of a traditional kind— *quo te domine dicam, nescio* (Hafner 1964:98)— and weaves the saint's qualities together in a catalogue of virtues that forms a stylistic climax of the *Life*:

No čto tę nareku, o ep(s̃)pe,
ili čto tę imenuju,

ili čim' tę prizovu,
i kako tę prověščaju,
ili čim' tę měnju,
ili čto ti priglašu,
kako pokhvalju,
kako počtu,
kako ublīžju,
kako razložu,
i kako khvalu ti sъpletu?
těm že, čto tę nareku pr(ō)ka li,
jako pr(ō)rčeskaa prorečenia protolkovalъ esi,
i gadania pr(ō)rkъ ujęsnilъ esi
i posredě ljudii nevěrnykhъ i nevěgl(s̄)nykhъ jako pr(ō)rkъ imъ
bylъ esi;
ap(s̄)la li tę imenuju, jako ap(s̄)lkoe dělo sъtvorilъ esi,
i ravno ap(s̄)lo(m) ravno obrazujęsę podvizasę, stopamъ ap(s̄)lkymъ
poslěduję;
zakonodavca li tę prizovu ili zakonopoložnika,
imže ljudemъ bezakonnymъ zakonъ dalъ esi,
i ne byvšu u nikhъ zakonu, věru i(m) ustavilъ esi,
i zakonъ položilъ esi;
kr(s̄)tlę li tę prověščaju, jako kr(s̄)tilъ esi ljudi mnogy,
gręduščaa k tebě na krs̄čenie,
propovědnika li tę proglašu, pone(ž), jako biričь na torgu kliča,
tako i ty vъ języcěkhъ velegl(s̄)no propovědalъ esi slovo bžie;
ēvalista li tę nareku ili blgověstnika, im'že blgověstilъ esi v'
miře sīoe ēva(g)lie khvō, i dělo blgověstnika sotvorilъ esi;
sīlę li tę imenuju, el'ma že bol'šii arkhierei, i starēišii sīlъ,
ssčenniky postavlęa vъ svoei zemli, na(d) pročimi ssčenniky bylъ
esi; učīlę li tę prozovu, jako učitelьsky naučilъ esi jazykъ
zabluždьšii, ili nevěrnyę v' věru privede,
i člky nevěglasy sušča;
da čto tę pročee nazovu str(s̄)toterp'ca li ili mčika,
jako mčičesky voleju vdalsę esi v ruky ljudemъ, svěrěpějuščimъ na
muku,
i,
jako ovca posrědě vol'kъ, der'znulъ esi na str(s̄)ti,
i na terpěnie,
i na mučenie...
(But what shall I call you, O bishop,
or how shall I name you,
or how shall I address you,
and how shall I announce you,
or how shall I mention you,
or how shall I invoke you,

how do I praise,
how do I honour,
how do I argue,
and how do I weave your praise?
By calling you a prophet?
—for you have interpreted the prophecies of the Prophets,
and explained the forecasts of the Prophets,
and among infidel and ignorant people you weie like a prophet to
them;
shall I call you an apostle?
—for you have done an apostle's work,
and struggling to imitate the Apostles you have been formed like the
Apostles, following in their footsteps;
shall I invoke you as legislator or as the founder of the law?
—for you have given the law to lawless people,
and because they had no law,
you set up a creed for them and founded their law;
shall I announce you as the baptist?
—for you have baptised many people, who came to you for baptism;
shall I proclaim you as a preacher?
—since like a herald shouting in the marketplace you have loudly
preached the word of God among the heathens;
shall I call you an evangelist or a bringer of good news?
—for you have brought them the Holy Gospel of Christ in peace,
and done the work of an evangelist;
shall I call you a prelate?
—insofar as you are a great *archiereus* and senior priest,
ordaining priests in your land, you were above other priests;
shall I address you as a teacher?
—for you have taught a bewildered people like a true teacher,
brought the ignorant infidels to the faith; and I could further call
you a sufferer or a martyr, for with a martyr's will you gave yourself
into the hands of people who in their fury wanted to torture you,
and like a sheep among wolves you had the courage to face suffering
and martyrdom...). (102f.)

This encomiastic catalogue is built on the same scheme as the eulogy of
Stephen Nemanja in the *Life* that Stephen Prvovenčani wrote of his
father; it also has, as pointed out by A. V. Solov'ev (1961), another
parallel in the *Slovo o žitii i o prestavlenii velikago knjazja Dmitrija
Ivanoviča, carja Rusьskago.* A shorter variant is found in Saint Sava's
*Life* of his father (Ćorović 1928:5-16, 160). In early Russian literature
there is an example of the same scheme used by Kirill Turovskij in his
*Slovo o sьnjatii tela Khristova s kresta.* It occurs here in his eulogy to
Joseph of Arimathea. The variants differ in their degree of embellish-

ment. Those of Sava and Kirill are plainer than those of Epiphanius and Stephen. But there can be no doubt that they all have a common basic scheme.

The abstractive *distributio* in the example above dissolves Stephen's character into an indefinite series of qualities, each of which will warrant inclusion in a particular heroic category. In this way enumeration approaches comparison, as a kind of similarity is presupposed between Stephen and the various heroic ideals he is seen in relation to. Nevertheless, this figure of speech is predominantly metonymic, primarily analysing the totality into its component synecdochic parts.

However, direct comparison is not an alien feature in the *Life of Saint Stephen*. Epiphanius employs both quite brief comparisons of individual components and elaborate allegories and examples. On the other hand, pure metaphors, in which the conjunction of comparison is left out and one component represents the other, are rare.

The second component in Epiphanius' comparisons is usually a quotation from the Bible, especially from the Psalms. The few metaphors to be found are also traceable to the Bible, and like the comparisons they belong to the traditional stock of hagiographical tropes. Life on earth is in its transience "like the river's flood, like the flower of the grass," an allusion to Psalm 90 (89):4-6, which is subsequently combined with a direct quotation from 1 Pet. 1:24, a variation of the same flower image, introduced by "as the apostle says." The attempts by the heathens to kill Stephen are represented in direct parallel to Psalm 117 (118):12, through the introductory formula "as the word of David says," which leads from narration to quotation:

> vsi jazyci ob'šedše, obidoša mę jako p'čely so(t),
> i razgorěšasę jako ognь v ternii
> (All nations compassed me about,
> they compassed me about like a swarm of bees and
> burned like the fire of thorns). (20)

Even in his rendering of the shaman Pam's speech, Epiphanius paraphrases the Psalms in comparisons such as the following:

> pre(d) lice(m) moi(m) priiti ne ster'pę(t), no jako voskъ protivu plameni veliku približivsę i istae(t), neželi slovesy sъprětisę so mnoju smēju(t) (They dare not appear before me, but as wax melteth when it comes near a great fire, nor do they dare to dispute with me). (44, cf. Psalm 67 (68):2.)

When Stephen lets the shaman go, the latter runs off "jako elenь" (like a deer) (cf. Isa. 35:6).

The comparisons may be extended, the second component acquiring the character of an image, as in the account of Saint Stephen's life in the monastery, where it becomes a variation on Psalm 1:3:

> i by(st) jako drevo plodovito nasaženo pri iskhodišči(kh) vo(d), i často napaęemo razumomъ bž(s̄)tveny(kh) pisanii, i o(t)tudu prorastaa gresnъ dobrodĕteli, i procvĕtaa vidy blḡovolenia, tĕmъ i plo(d) svoi dastь vъ vremę svoe. Kyja že plody,plody dkhōvnyę, iže Pavelъ ap̄(s)lъ isčitaetъ, glę: bratie, plo(d) dkḣovnyi estь: ljuby, radostь, mirъ, dol'goter'pĕnie, vĕra, krotostь, vъzderžanie i pročaa (And he was like a tree full of fruit that is planted by the rivers of ~~water, and is often drenched by the knowledge of the Divine~~ Scriptures and thus brings forth the grapes of virtue and the flowers of divine delight and also bears fruit in due time. And what fruits, the spiritual fruits which the Apostle Paul enumerates, saying, brethren, the spiritual fruit is: love, joy, peace, longsuffering, faith, meekness, temperance, etc....). (101)

Interpretation of metaphor, as in this case, is characteristic of the *Life of Saint Stephen*. The tendency is in the direction of the combined metaphor, where the two components are juxtaposed:

> Sego radi ubo vъzljublen'ne, prepoęši istinoju čresla svoę krĕpko, aky khrabryi voinъ Khv̄ъ, vobronisę vъ vse oružie bž(s)tvenoe, obui nozĕ na ugotovanie blḡovĕstovania vĕry, oblecysę vъ bronę pravdy, priimi že i šči(t) vĕry, i šlemъ sps̄enia, i mečь dkḣovnyi, eže estь glъ̄ Bž̄ii (Therefore, my beloved ones, gird your loins fast with the truth, like the bold soldier of Christ, don the divine armour and shoe many with the preparation of the gospel of faith, take on the breastplates of righteousness, receive the shield of faith, and the helmet of salvation, and the spiritual sword, which is the word of God).(15)

The combined metaphors—"the breastplates of righteousness"; "the shield of faith"; "the helmet of salvation"—equate the two terms by the help of a genitive relationship, in which the meaning of one component is transferred to the other, or the metaphors are created by means of an adjective and explained in a relative clause: "the spiritual sword, which is the word of God."

The passage is taken from Bishop Gerasimus' exhortation to Saint Stephen before his departure for Perm, and elucidates an inner spiritual reality by means of traditional imagery. The individual metaphors are strung together loosely and may be viewed separately or as a whole. The principle is the same as in the previous passage, where the saint's intellectual growth is conveyed through a comparison with the image of the growing tree, taken from the Psalms. Another instance of this

allegorical representation of a spiritual situation is the author's
description of his own sinfulness, at the end of the *vita:*

Uvyi mně
kto mi plamenь ugasitъ
kto mi tmu prosvětitъ,
se bo v' bezakonii začatъ esmь
i bezakonia moa umnožišasę zělo,
i bezakonia moę volnakhъ prilagaju mor'skykhъ,
pomyšlenia že vъ jalicakhъ protivnykh' mi větr;
uvy(i) mně,
kako skončaju moe žitie,
kako preplovu se more velikoe i prostrannoe, šir'šeesę, [pečalnoe,
mnogomutnoe, nestoęšče, smętuščesę];
kako preprovožu dševnuju mi lodiju promežu volnami sverěpymi,
kako izbudu trevolnenia strastei, ljutě pogružajusę vъ glubině zolъ,
i zělo potoplęęsę v' bez'dně grěkhovněi;
uvyi mně, volnuęsę posrědě pučiny žitiiskago morę,
i kako postignu v' tišinu umilenia,
i kako doidu vъ pristanišče pokaania...
(Woe iš me,
who will extinguish the flame for me,
who will illuminate the darkness for me?
—for I am conceived in sin
and my sins have greatly increased,
and I compare my sins to the waves of the sea
and my good intentions to small boats against the headwind.
Woe is me,
how shall I end my life,
how shall I cross this great and extensive sea?
—wide, gloomy, troubled, unstable, unruly;
how shall I steer the ship of my spirit through the furious waves,
how shall I be saved from the storm of the passions?
—grievously I sink into the deep of evil,
vehemently drowning in the abyss of sinfulness,
woe is me,
storm-tossed in the middle of the ocean of terrestrial life,
how shall I reach the calm of humility,
and how shall I arrive at the heaven of repentance...).(101)

The hagiographer's equation of his own life with a voyage, in this extended ship metaphor, varies a *topos* that is not ultimately traceable to
the Bible, but to classical rhetoric. In the *Life of Saint Stephen* it must be
seen in connection with the distribution in the Middle Ages of this

*topos*, not as an indication of Epiphanius' familiarity with classical rhetoric, as has been suggested.

To the category of expanded comparison belongs also the drawing of parallels between Stephen's mission and Biblical examples, in order to bring out its historical significance. The device is used even from the beginning of the *vita*. Epiphanius here describes the situation of the Permians at the time when the saint started his mission, comparing them to the hired workers in the Biblical parable, whom their master employed "at the eleventh hour." This parable is at the same time a key to understanding Epiphanius' use of parallels:

> podobno estъ cr(s̄)tvo nb(s̄)noe čĺku domovitu, iže izide rano izoutra naimovatъ dělatelę v' vinogra(d) svoi. I smol'vi s nimi po srebreniku na dn͠ъ. I iše(d) vъ g̅ časъ vidě drugyę stoęšča praz(d)ny, i tě(m) reče: idite i vy v' vinogra(d) moi, i šedše dělaite, i eže bude(t) vъ pravdu, damъ vamъ. Oni že idoša. Paky že vъ šestuju i devętuju godinu sъtvori takož(d)e. Vъ edinu že na desę(t) godinu obrěte drugya stoęšča praz(d)ny, i reče i(m): čto zdě stoite vesь dn͠ь praz(d)ny, per'męne, nikto(ž) li va(s) ne najalъ? Oniže o(t)věščavše, glaša emu: jako nikto že nasъ ne najalъ, rekše nikto(ž) na(s) ne naučilъ věrě kr(s̄)tienьstěi, nikto(ž) nasъ ne prosvětilъ sīymъ krĭščeniemъ, nikto že na(s) ne v'velъ v razumnyi vinogradъ, rekše v zakonъ Gn͠ь (The kingdom of Heaven is like unto a man that is a householder, who went out early in the morning to hire labourers into his vineyard. And he agreed with them for a penny a day. And he went out about the third hour, and saw others standing idle, and he said unto them: Go ye also into my vineyard, and whatsoever is right I will give you. And they went. Again he went out about the sixth and ninth hour, and did likewise. And about the eleventh hour he found others standing idle, and said unto them: Why stand you there all day idle, Permians, has no one hired you? And they answered, saying unto him: Because no man has hired us, meaning no one has taught us the Christian faith, no one has illuminated us through the holy baptism, no one has led us into the vineyard of knowledge, that is the Law of the Lord).(12)

Analysis of the most characteristic features of the *vita* shows that Epiphanius builds up his text by means of various kinds of parallel constructions which activate its language with regard to sounds, morphological and syntactical categories and classes of words, as well as larger thematic entities. The correspondences between word-weaving and the poetry of the Bible make it natural to link the historical growth of this style with the development of an Orthodox Slav liturgical poetry based on Greek models. Epiphanius' style has even been thought to derive directly from the *akathistos*-hymns of the fourteenth-century Hesychast patriarchs Isidoros, Callistos, and Philotheos (Mathiesen 1965). The similarities between Epiphanius' word-weaving and the word-weaving of early Serbian hagiography, however, point in another direction. They indicate that Epiphanius' style represents a late phase in the development of an original panegyrical hagiography in Slavonic literature, modelled on the encomiastic style of Byzantine literature. As early as the eleventh and twelfth centuries this style had displaced the older, narrative *vita* in Byzantine hagiography. The Lives of saints now became a sublime genre, the anecdotal narrative was replaced by a more objective account. The hagiographer no longer addressed a circle of initiates, or a closed monastic community, but the common reader and listener (Poljakova 1972:266ff.). The lofty style that evolved in Byzantine hagiography represents a combination of stylistic devices of the Bible, especially those of the Old Testament, with the encomiastic style of Hellenistic rhetoric (Hunger 1965).

As we have observed already, the heroes of the Serbian princely *vitae* are juxtaposed with the heroes of Biblical and Byzantine history. The principle of parallelism is used to integrate them into a wider historical context. That it has the same function in the *Life of Saint Stephen* is shown in the parallel created by Epiphanius between the Zyrians and the hired workers of the Biblical parable. Epiphanius' account of the heathens of Perm is at this point woven into the Biblical quotation, so that they are equated with the last unit in the sequence of parallel components: the workers who came "at the eleventh hour." Characteristically, the relations of equivalence, based on the principle of similarity, are not in themselves the dominant feature in this passage; they are merely a prerequisite for the allegorical representation of the Permian people as a link in a chronological chain, as part of a larger whole. Epiphanius' use of quotations from the Bible is determined by his endeavours to create a significant context for his hero. The concatenation of parallel links in a series of sequences is part of a process in which the contiguity principle is preponderant. The enumeration of lands and peoples surrounding the Zyrians, and the breaking down of objects and concepts into synecdochic details, also form part of this process. That is to say, the text is dominated by figures of speech based on metonymic correspondences between the components. This kind of alignment has traditionally been considered a mere accumulation of elements and thus of limited poetic value. It was difficult to see in it any integrative function. But it is not quite as simple as this. I shall try to show how Epiphanius' metonymic sequences contribute to the creation of a holy universe around his protagonist.

## External Form in the *Life*

With respect to external form—that is, the division into separate sections—the *Life of Saint Stephen* follows, on the whole, the con-

ventions of the genre. First is an exordium, where the hagiographer
introduces himself and his hero to the audience by means of traditional
*topoi*. Then follows the *Life* proper, which starts with the portrayal of
the saint's childhood and adolescence in his hometown of Ustjug. The
next phase in the *Life* is the account of the years Stephen spent absorbed
in studies, after having taken vows at the Grigor'ev Monastery in Rostov.
This phase is concluded by his departure for Moscow, where Bishop
Gerasimus of Kolomna, deputy metropolitan after the death of Alexis,
gives him the blessing of the Church to evangelise the Zyrians. The story
of Stephen's journey to Perm, and his work among the heathens, is the
central part of the *vita*. It moves from the description of their resistance
to the saint and his preaching, on to his victory through the power of the
word and through his gentle character. The apex of this section is the
account of Stephen's disputation with the shaman Pam, who tries to stir
up the people by urging his compatriots to stick to the faith of their
fathers, at the same time reminding them of their brutal exploitation at
the hands of the Muscovites:

O(t)čьsky(kh) bogo(v) ne ostavlivaite, a žer'tvъ i trebъ ikhъ ne
zabyvaite,
a staryi pošliny ne pokidyvaite,
davnyi věry ne pometaite,
iže tvoriša o(t)čy naši, tako tvorite,
mene slušaite, a ne slušaite Stefana, iže novoprišedšago o(t)
Mos'kvy;
[o(t) Moskvy bo] možet li čto dobro byti namъ?
ne o(t)tudu li namъ tęžesti byšę,
i dani tęž'kyę i nasilьstvo,
i tivuni i dovo(d)ščici i pristavnicy?
sego radi, ne slušaite ego,
no mene pače poslušaite, dobra vamъ khotęščago.
Az' bo esmь rodъ vašъ i edinoę zemlę s vami,
i edinъ rodъ i edinoplemenъ,
i edino kolěno,
edinъ językъ…
(Do not abandon the gods of your fathers and do not forget their
sacrifices and offerings, and do not give up the old customs, and do
not throw away the old faith, but do as your fathers did, and listen to
me and not to Stephen, this newcomer from Moscow; for what good
can there come from Moscow? Have we not had enough of their
oppression, and heavy tributes and outrages, and commissioners,
and collectors and inspectors? Therefore, do not listen to him, but
listen rather to me, who wish you well. I am of your kin and we are
one country, and one kin and one tribe, and one clan, one
tongue…).(40)

However, Epiphanius' description of Stephen's mission belies the shaman's words that nothing good can come from Moscow. The saint is seen in contrast to the secular officials. He is coming to Perm with the Gospel, they to levy taxes. The disputation between the shaman and the saint ends with Stephen challenging his opponent to a trial of strength. They are to walk through the burning fire and to let themselves be carried by the current under the frozen river, from one hole in the ice to another, to prove whose faith is the stronger. The shaman backs out and retreats from the area that Stephen has christianised. Stephen builds a church for his new community, and translates Greek as well as Russian liturgical books into the written version of the Permian language that he has worked out, so that the Zyrians can, in accordance with Orthodox tradition, worship in their mother tongue. This central section of the *Life* is followed by the account of the saint's return to Moscow and his appointment as bishop of Perm. He dies in Moscow, having first foretold his death and given a valedictory speech to his disciples, in accordance with the conventions of the genre.

The story of the saint is enlarged with a number of prayers, instructions, and lamentations, which Epiphanius has inserted into the narrative in the form of static monologues, to use a term suggested by Zubov (1953). Although he also uses dialogue, it is the static monologues that characterise the *Life of Saint Stephen*. It follows that the character drawing is not predominantly dramatic. The characters are described mostly through strings of epithets.

The most original feature of the external form is the conclusion of the *vita*, where the author deviates quite radically from the conventional scheme, which requires the hagiographer to go on from the saint's death to describe his posthumous miracles, ending with a *conclusio* that links up with the exordium. Instead of this traditional ending, the *Life of Saint Stephen* has a coda consisting of three lamentations (*threnoi* or *plači*): *Plač' perm'skykh ljudej*; *Plac' cerkvi perm'skia* (where Stephen's Church emerges in the allegorical guise of a mourning widow), and, finally, *Plačeve i pokhvala inoka spisajušča*. In these lyric outbursts, sorrow over the departed saint is expressed in forms that derive from both the indigenous Russian *plač'* and from the eulogies and lamentations of the Orthodox Church (Adrianova-Peretc 1947a, Holthusen 1967). Nor were similar lamentations unknown to the Serbian word-weavers, although they used them differently. The close of our *vita* thus differs radically from the combination of eulogy and accounts of posthumous miracles that conventionally concludes a saint's Life, and that emphasises the mystical or, rather, magical presence of the saint among the living. To explain this departure from the conventions of the genre, attention has been called to the fact that Stephen had not yet been canonised when the *vita* was written (canonisation did not take place until the Council of 1549, under

Makarij) and had not performed any posthumous miracles (Kitch 1976:50). It would seem natural also to see a link here with early Russian princely *vitae*, which even from the eleventh century have glorifying *threnoi* of this kind. The authors of these *vitae* occasionally developed their lamentations on the basis of the laconic mention accorded by the chronicles to the grief of bereaved relatives (Adrianova-Peretc 1947b). In the Lives of the saints, however, such *threnoi* are rare, and Epiphanius' use of them is a fresh and original feature in the history of the genre, according to Ključevskij (1871:84):

> This original form of eulogy is exclusively Epiphanius' invention: in not a single translated Greek *vita* would he have been able to find anything similar, and not one of the later Russian *vitae* that borrowed a few isolated passages from Epiphanius' eulogy had the courage to reproduce its literary form.

Adrianova-Peretc (1947b) has subsequently demonstrated that the use of *threnoi* for the purpose of glorification is not wholly unknown to Greek hagiography. At all events, *threnoi* may be found in Russian Lives of saints after Epiphanius. She has thus modified Ključevskij's enthusiastic contention. Nevertheless, Epiphanius' *conclusio* in the form of three *threnoi* must be regarded as an innovation in Russian hagiography.

## Time and Space in the *Life of Saint Stephen*

This survey of its external form shows that the *vita* generally follows the rules of the genre, while the deviations from the conventional scheme in the shaping of its conclusion are clear proof that we are not here faced with a mechanical imitation. The question will thus be whether Epiphanius' deviation from the scheme has also an intrinsic function in the *vita*, and is not, albeit an historical necessity, merely a poetic contingency. I shall therefore analyse the *vita* with a view to defining its structure and try to find a systematic coherence between its component parts, including the lamentations.

A basic feature of the *Life of Saint Stephen* is the juxtaposition of Epiphanius' own narrative with quotations from other texts. Historical facts and dates are generally rendered in the form of an enumeration of contemporary events, which are subsequently, by means of the quotations, related to events in an historical past. For example, Stephen's work in creating an alphabet for the people of Perm is compared with similar events in the history of the Greek and Slavic languages. Thus the events of the narrative are incorporated in a diachronic sequence.

Accordingly, an analysis of time and space in the *vita* may be divided into two stages: first, an examination of the narrative to find the principle for selection and combination of historical facts and dates, geographical information, and similar synchronic elements in the *Life* proper; and second, an examination of the function of the quotations to determine the principles for their selection and combination with the narrative.

In Epiphanius' story, the combination of facts and dates into a syntagmatic sequence may be shown in an example taken from the very first section of the *Life* proper:

> Sii prp(d)bnyi o(t)c̃ъ našь Stefanъ bě ubo rodomъ rusinъ, o(t) języka slovenьska, o(t) strany polunoščnyę, glemyę Dvinьskia, o(t) grada, naricaemago Ustьjuga, o(t) roditelju naročitu, sñъ někoego khōljubca, muža věrna khȓ(s)tiana, imenemъ Simeona, edinago o(t) klirikъ velikyę sъbornyę cȓkvi sīyę Bc̃a, iže na Ustьjuzě, i o(t) mȋre, tako(ž) khȓ(s)tiany, naricaemyę Mȓia (And this our holy father Stephen was Russian by origin, of the Slavonic people, of a Northern land, called the land of Dvina, of a city called Ustjug, of distinguished parents, the son of a lover of Christ, a true Christian man called Symeon, one of the clergy of the Great Cathedral of the Holy Mother of God in Ustjug, and of a mother who was also a Christian, called Maria).(4)

Through the information given about the saint's origin, his birthplace, and the names and status of his parents, his figure is placed in an historical, geographical, and social context. The exposition is dominated by the referential or denotative function of language and is focused on the third person.

A more comprehensive example of a presentation focused on the context is the portrayal of Stephen being tonsured and his stay in the Grigor'ev Monastery in Rostov. The example shows how the factuality in the portrayal of the saint's surroundings is combined with a purely conventional description of his figure by means of hagiographical *topoi*:

> Semu pride Bz̃ia ljuby, eže ostaviti o(t)c̃ьstvo i vsę suščaa iměnia, i prosto rešči, vsěmi dobroděanii ukrašenъ bě otro(k) toi, pospěvaa vъzrastomь vъ strakhъ Bz̃ii, i strakho(m) Bz̃iimъ umilivsę, i ešče mla(d), sę Bg̃u da vъ unosti, otrokъ syi ver'stoju, postrižesę v' černьci vъ gradě Rostově, u sīgo Grigoria Bgoslova v' manastyri, naricaemě(m) v' Zatvorě, blizъ ep(s)kpьi, jako knigy mnogy běkhu tu dovolny sušča emu na potrebu, počitania radi, pri ep(s)pě

rostov'stěmь Par'fenii, o(t̲) ruku že ostrižesę někoe(g) starca, prozvitera sušča, sanomъ sščeńnika, imene(m) Mak'sima igumena, prozvišč̌o Kalina... (Unto him came the love of God, which is to leave the house of one's father and all one's property, and in simple words, this youth was adorned with all virtues, he advanced in age, in the fear of God, and was seized by fear of God, and still being young, giving himself to God in his youth, he was, yet only a boy in years, shorn a monk in the city of Rostov, in the Monastery of the Holy Gregory the Theologian, called "in the Hermitage," near the bishop's residence; for there were many books, enough of what he needed for his reading, under Bishop Parthenius of Rostov, and the boy was tonsured by a certain *starec*, a presbyter, of rank a priest, the abbot Maximus, called Kalin...).(5f.).

The theme of the above paragraph is Stephen's tonsuring, an event accurately defined in time and space. The event is locally defined through the relationship between the monastery, the abbot's domain, and the episcopal residence. It is temporally defined in relation both to the man who was abbot of the monastery and the man who was bishop of Rostov at the time of the event, that is, in relation to the highest ranks of the city's ecclesiastical hierarchy. This means that, first, the event is defined through a relationship of local contiguity. Second, the historical persons are combined in a hierarchical proximity (between the abbot and the bishop) and distance (between Stephen and the other two). The elements related to each other here belong to a different class. But the principle for the combination of elements is the same: the alignment on the *signans* level corresponds to a semantic contiguity between the components.

The principle of contiguity also dominates the further account of Stephen's life. The story moves on through the depiction of his gradual rise in the hierarchy: the abbot having received his monastic vows, it is the bishop of Rostov who ordains him as a deacon, and the deputy metropolitan, Gerasimus of Kolomna, who installs him in his priestly office. In this way, the saint's promotion is expressed through the rising ecclesiastical status of his immediate superior. At the same time his preferment is also expressed through a shift in location: the removals from Ustjug to Rostov, from Rostov to Moscow. Thus parallels are established between the ecclesiastical hierarchy and the hierarchy of the cities: metropolitan Moscow ranks higher than diocesan Rostov.

In the paragraph quoted, the combination of the *signantia* corresponds to the relations between the *signata:* hierarchical relations within the Church, between the cities, and between the buildings. We might call this a diagrammatical representation of reality, a representation in which the similarity between *signans* and *signatum* appears "only in respect to the relations of their parts," according to the definition given by Charles S. Peirce and cited in Jakobson (1971:350). To the extent that Epiphanius is representing an historical reality in the *Life of Saint Stephen*, his mimesis, his representation of reality, is predominantly an "icon of relation."

As soon as we have become aware of the significance of this principle for the structure of the *Life*, we shall find that it determines Epiphanius' story throughout. Even in sections that are thematically very different from those already quoted, the narrative is similarly oriented towards the context, giving expression to an event in the saint's life by combining components from the same semantic field, so that they form contiguous parts of a larger whole. The description of Stephen's linguistic studies is one example. The components are here the saint's three languages. In addition to Russian, he has a command of Greek and also of the language of the Zyrians. The progress of his studies is illustrated by linking these components in a sequence:

Želaa(ž) bolšago razuma, jako obrazomъ ljubomudria izučisę i grečeskoi gramotě, i knigy grečeskia izvyče, i dobrě počitaše ę, i pr̄(s)no imęše ę u sebe. I bęše umĕę glati tremi jazyki; tako že i gramoty tri umĕaše, ja(ž) estь ru(s)skyi i grečesky, per'mьskyi, jako zbytisę o se(m) slovesi onomu, gljušču, iže rečesę: jako jazyky vъzgljutь novy; i paky: inĕmi jazyky glati ustroi. I dobrě obderžaše i pomyslь, eže iti vъ Per'mьskuju zemlju i učiti ę: togo bo radi i jazykъ per'mьskyi pokušašesę izučiti, i togo radi i gramotu per'mьskuju sotvori, poneže... (In his desire for more knowledge he also learned Greek as the prototype of wisdom, and studied Greek books, and he read them thoroughly and always kept them with him. And he could speak three languages, and also read and write them, they are Russian, and Greek, and Permian, so that in him the word was fulfilled which says that they shall speak with new tongues, and again: he let them speak with other tongues. And he was strongly seized by the thought of going to the land of Perm and to teach it, and therefore he undertook to learn the Permian language, and therefore he created a Permian alphabet, because...).(8)

In the latter as in the former examples, the linking up of elements from the same semantic field leads to their semantic and/or grammatical similarity being subordinated to their contiguity relation, so that together they represent extensions in space and time.

The representation of Stephen's life as a number of removals within a geographically limited space lends to the narrative the character of a travelogue. The saint moves, in the first part of the *vita*, from his hometown of Ustjug, on the periphery, to Moscow, which is the centre, via Rostov as an intermediary stage. The story of his journey to Perm takes us back to the periphery and beyond it. Stephen crosses the boundary of the Christian *oikoumene* on his mission to the heathens, who are converted and grafted onto the Russian Church. His mission describes an expansion of boundaries in the universe of the *vita* and forms a climax in the story of his life. After this the story takes us back to Moscow, where Stephen's career culminates in his appointment as bishop. The final section of the narrative gives an account of his departure from this world.

The accounts of Stephen's journeys are at the same time the story of his gradual perfection and his rise in the hierarchy of the Church. The story of his rise is combined with a description of his itinerary, so that its individual stages correspond to the individual stages in his career and ethical progress. Time and geographical space thus acquire an ethical and religious significance. The hagiographer's system of moral and religious values is projected into Stephen's surroundings according to the principle of contiguity which underlies the narrative. The first stages of his life represent, all of them, positive values in the ethico-religious system of the *vita*. Heathen Perm stands for the negative pole of this system. The transformation of the landscape into a reflection of moral and religious values is reinforced by the introduction of conventional symbols. Heathen Perm, the negative pole, is experienced as the equivalent of darkness; Stephen, who represents the positive pole, illuminates the people of Perm, bringing them the light. The ultimate source of Epiphanius' light symbolism is the quotation from Isa. 9:2: "The people that walked in darkness have seen a great light: they that dwell in the land of the shadow of death, upon them hath the light shined"(67).

The horizontalised space axis of the *Life of Saint Stephen* thus becomes an indication of Epiphanius' ideology. Likhačev's (1958, 1962, 1973) and Dane's (1961) attempts to interpret the *vita* as an expression of Hesychast mysticism and of the saintly ideal of the Trans-Volga monks are not confirmed by an analysis of its structure. Epiphanius' representation of the saint's perfection as a progress in the hierarchy of the Church, combined with the story of his journeys, is almost the opposite of the teachings of the Trans-Volga monks about withdrawal from the world, and spiritual perfection in mystical contemplation.

It is the horizontal character of the time and space axes in the *vita* and the transmission of the *vita's* ethico-religious values to this system of coordinates that determine the representation of Stephen's sanctity. The opposition of good and evil, of holiness and the ungodly, is in the *Life of Saint Stephen* equated with the opposition of "we" and "the others," of the Orthodox Russian Church and the heathens. Saint Stephen's mission does not bring about any fusion of the opposites in a higher unity. It leads to strife among the Zyrians, who split up in two

1. Giotto.
*Lamentation over the
body of Christ.* 1306.

. *Lamentation over
he body of Christ* in St
anteleimon at Nerez.
164.

3. Detail of *Lamentation*
in St Panteleimon.

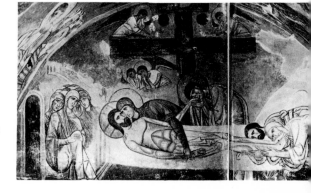

4. *Lamentation over
the body of Christ* in
the Spaso-Mirožskij
Monastery at Pskov.
About 1150.

5. Detail from the Trinity Church in Sopoćani. 1262.

5. Detail from the Trinity Church in Sopoćani. 1262.

7. Theophanes the Greek. *Christ the All-Ruler.* 1378.

8. Theophanes the Greek. *The Old Testament Trinity.* 1378.

9. Theophanes the Greek. *Stylite.* 1378.

). Theophanes the reek. *Saint Macarius.* 378.

11. *The Raising of Lazarus* in the Volotovo Church of the Dormition. 1363

12. Andrej Rublev. *The Raising of Lazarus.* 1405.

13. School of Theophanes the Greek. *The Transfiguration.* End of fourteenth century.

14. Andrej Rublev. *The Transfiguration.* 1405.

15. Andrej Rublev. *The Old Testament Trinity*. 1411.

irreconcilable groups: those who have taken Stephen's creed, and those who, like the shaman Pam, stick to their old religion:

Oni že ubo, slyšavše propovědь věry kȓ(s)tianьskia, ovii khotękhu věrovati i kȓ(s)titisę, a druzii(ž) ne khotękhu no i khotęščimь vozbranękhu věrovati. Elikož pervěe malo někto o(t) ni(kh) věrovaša i krešćeni byša o(t) nego, tii često prikhoždakhu k nemu i presědękhu pȓ(s)no emu, sьbesědujušče i sьvьprašajuščesę s nimь, i povsegda deržakhusę ego, i zělo ego ljublękhu; a iže ne věrovaša, tii ne ljubętь ego i o(t)běgajutь, i ubiti pomyšlęju(t) (But they, hearing the preaching of the Christian faith, some wished to believe and be baptised, whereas others did not want to, and prevented those who wanted to believe. Though at first only a few of them believed and were baptised, these often came to him and sat next to him and he talked and discussed with them, and they always kept to him and loved him gently, whereas those who did not believe, love him not and run away and plan to kill him).(19)

The discord among the Zyrians culminates in the story of how the heathens tried to kill Stephen. The conflict between the two groups is resolved in Stephen's disputation with the shaman. Three times Stephen exhorts the other to follow him into the crackling fire to see who has the stronger faith. Frightened by the flames, the heathen priest flinches, and loses. He has revealed his impotence face to face with the new—in the presence of the whole tribe, who hand him over to Stephen, their new leader, demanding that he pronounce the death sentence on the shaman:

vozmi sego i kazni i, jako povinenь estь kazni, i po našei pošlině dolženь estь umreti, poneže... (Take him and execute him, for he is guilty of death, and according to our custom he must die, for...).(55)

Stephen refuses to comply with their demands. The pagan law has been superseded by his Christian mercy:

O(t)veščav' že Stefanь i reče imь: ni ubo da ne bude(t) tako, i ne budi ruka naša na naše(m) vrazě, ne skoro ruky moea ne vozložu na nь, ni kaznę pokaznju ego, i sm̄rti ne predamь ego. Ne posla bo mene Kȟs biti, bo blḡověstiti... (Then Stephen answered and said: No, this must not be, and that our hand never be against our enemy, and I will not hastily lay my hand on him, nor execute him, nor deliver him unto death. For Christ has not sent me to punish, but to preach the Gospel...).(56)

The shaman is permitted to leave in peace, on condition that he will never more appear in Stephen's congregation. The old leader is ejected from the community where Stephen, the victor, has now taken over his role:

> da něstъ emu ni časti, ni žrebia s novokŕščenymi, ni jasti ni piti s nimi nigdě že, nikogda že, ni v' čem' že sovokupľętisę s nimi. Koe bo pričęstie světu ko t'mě, ili kaę ob'ščina věrnu s nevěrny(m)? (And let him have neither lot nor share with the newly baptised, and let him never either eat or drink with them, nor join them in anything. For what part has light in darkness, or what common cause has the faithful with the infidel?).(57)

The conflict of the *vita* is thus resolved through a shift of boundaries between good and evil forces, between the positive and negative fields, without effecting any change in the values themselves. By Stephen's work, the positive field in the ethico-religious space of the *vita* is extended to include Perm, which becomes part of the Orthodox *oikoumene*. In close conformity with the horizontal space-coordinates in the *Life*, Stephen's sanctification is represented through the account of his work to extend the territory of the Russian Church. Through contiguity and expansion, Stephen's new community has been incorporated into a larger totality.

It is interesting to compare the structure of our *vita* with the different types of "cultural codes" discussed by Lotman (1970b). In this context Epiphanius' *Life of Saint Stephen* would have to be defined as a realisation of the "syntactical code" typical of periods in Russian history characterised by strong centralist tendencies. In contrast to the symbolic structure of early Kievan culture, in which the relationship between parts and wholes is based on the principle of analogy and every single part may represent the whole, the syntactical code defines the parts in their interrelationship with other parts belonging to the same whole, or in contrast to parts from different systems. To be part of a larger whole becomes a sign of cultural significance, and the whole is valuable in itself, as State or Church, not as symbols of another world, a higher reality. An element that is not incorporated into the whole of the State or of the Church, on the other hand, has no value whatsoever, and is rejected. An example of this would be the expulsion of the shaman from Stephen's community in the *Life*.

## Historicism in the *Life of Saint Stephen*

Another feature that connects the *Life of Saint Stephen* with Lotman's syntactical type of culture is its historicism. Texts belonging to this type form parts of a system in which the addition of new texts is seen as a stage in an historical development. In this development, there is an opposition between the "old" and the "new" in which the former is regarded as worthless, the latter as important. In Epiphanius' *Life* this opposition is manifest in the confrontation between the shaman and the old faith of the Zyrians, on the one hand, and on the other, Stephen with the new Gospel. In addition to this, however, the historical development is conceived in terms of a constant progress, in which every new element forms part of a process of perfection, surpassing everything that has gone before. Again, we shall find a realisation of this conception in the *Life of Saint Stephen*.

By way of introduction, Epiphanius states his task as a eulogy of "the preacher of the faith, Perm's teacher and the successor of the Apostles" (3). His aim is to praise the saint's mission as an historical continuation of the Apostles' work in spreading Christianity. Epiphanius sees his protagonist in a diachronic perspective even from the beginning, a perspective that opens up the frame of references in the narrative and sets Stephen in a wider historical context. How, then, is this idea of the apostolic successor realised? The question brings us back to the amplifying digressions that are mounted into the narrative, in particular to the quotations from the history of the Church dealing with events similar to those in Epiphanius' own story. A clear instance is the account of Stephen's journey to Perm, in which Epiphanius' narration is juxtaposed with a description of the itineraries of the first Apostles to spread the word of God. In a long and elaborate excursus, Epiphanius enumerates the various journeys that, according to Orthodox tradition, the Apostles made to many countries. The whole excursus is divided into parallel components, one for each Apostle, which are also paralleled with his own account of Stephen's itinerary. The connection beween narrative and quotations is further emphasised by an almost refrain-like repetition of the words "to Perm they never came," and similar phrases, in the survey of the itineraries of the Apostles:

> ne zakhodili sutь ap̄(s)li v' Per'mьskuju zemlju; ašče v Permi ne byli su(t); a v' Per'mi(ž) ne bylъ; Ašče i v' Permi ne uspěša byti... (The Apostles had never visited the Permian land; although they had not been in Perm; but he never was in Perm; Although they never got as far as Perm...).(10f.)

The repetitions refer back from the quotations to Epiphanius' own narrative, where we find a corresponding enumeration of geographical and ethnographical terms as in the quotations. In the interplay between narration and quotations, these terms acquire a poetic function in addition to their denotative reference. However, the similarity between the saint and the Apostles, whose successor the saint is, is subordinate to contiguity, their work being inscribed in an historical process of redemption. Stephen's mission to the Zyrians and their incorporation into the Christian *oikoumene* acquire hagiographical significance only when, through the quotations, Epiphanius' narrative is set in this historical perspective. The work that the Apostles began Stephen helps to complete through his Christianisation of the Zyrians "at the eleventh hour." The process of redemption of which Stephen's mission is a part is first introduced through the retelling of the parable of the workers in the vineyard, and this follows immediately on the excursus about the journeys of the Apostles. The parable is, like Epiphanius' version of world history, formed as a sequence of parallel events in time. Its allegorical function in the *vita* is laid bare in Epiphanius' retelling of the last component, where he substitutes the Zyrians for the workers hired "at the eleventh hour." Stephen's preaching among the Permians enters history at a point corresponding to the "eleventh hour" in the parable of the hired workers, that is, at a time immediately before the consummation of the ages:

> v' poslědnęa dňi, vъ skon'čanie lě(t), vo ostatočnaę vremena, na iskho(d) čisla sed'myę tysęšča lětъ... (In the last days, at the end of time, in the years that remained, at the wane of the seventh millennium).(13)

Epiphanius dates the conversion of the Permians from the eschatological concept of time of the Middle Ages, which reckoned that the Last Judgement would take place at the end of the seventh millennium, in 1492 A.D., that is, barely a hundred years after Stephen's death.

Analysis of the function of the excursus gradually reveals the model of world history that Epiphanius, by means of the quotations, reflects in his narrative. The central passage for the decoding of the historical system of the *vita* is the description of the Church's memorial feasts in the excursus on the month of March:

> Jako se estь mar'tъ m(s̄)cь načalo vsěmъ m(s̄)cemъ, iže pervyi narečetsę vъ m(s̄)cekhъ, emu(ž) svidětelьstvue(t) Moisii zakonodavecь, glē: m(s̄)cь že vamъ pervy vъ m(s̄)cěkhъ da budetь mar'tъ. Da jakože učimi esmy, iže i naučaem'sę javě načalo bytiju: mar'ta bo m(s̄)ca načalo bytia; vsę tvarь Bḡomъ sotvorena bystь o(t) nebytia v' bytie; mar'ta bo načalo zdaniju bystь, mar'ta že m(s̄)ca vъ k̄a' dňь i pervozdan'ny čl̄kъ rodonačalnikъ Adamъ rukoju bžieju sъzdanъ bystь. Mar'ta že [m(s̄)ca] někogda Iil̄ьtestii lju(d)e drevle, jakože i Grigorii Bḡoslovъ věšča, o(t) zemlę Egipe(t)skia, i o(t) raboty faraonit'sky izbyša, i morę Čer'mnago pučinu ne mokrymi stopami, jako po sukhu, pěši šestvovaša. Mar'ta že m(s̄)ca paky Iil̄ьtęne v'

zemlju obětovan'nuju vnidoša, Ier(s̄)lmъ sostaviša; marta že m(s̄)ca paky Iiĺьtomъ paskhu pra(d̄)novati po vsę že lěta uder'žasę byvati. Marta(ž) m(s̄)ca i blḡověščenie bystь st̄yę Bc̄a, eže arkhagglъ Gavriilъ blḡověsti ei, egda Sn̄ъ bz̄ii za naše spsenie s nbše snide i vselisę vъ prečistuju utrobu vest̄yę Vl(d̄)čca našeę B(d̄)ca i pr(s̄)nodv̄yę Mr̄ia, i bez' sěmeni plotь o(t) nea vъspriimъ. Marta(ž) m(s̄)ca i raspętie Khs̄ voleju preter'pě, i smr̄tь za nasъ postrada, i vъskrsenie bḡolěpno namъ praz(d)novati ustavi. Marta že m(s̄)ca paky čaemъ vъskr̄šenia mr̄tvy(m), i vtorago prišestvia Kh(s̄)va i strašna(ḡ) groznago trepetnago gor'dago, pritranago, ne obumen'nago, besposulnago vsemirnago suda, egda priidetь sъ slavoju, khotę suditi živymъ i mr̄vy(m), i vъzdati komuždo po dělomъ ego; emu(ž) slava vъ věky (For the month of March is the beginning of all the months, which is called the first among months, to which Moses the lawgiver bears witness, saying: let March be the first of the months. And as we have been taught, let us teach ourselves boldly about the beginning of Creation: for the month of March is the beginning of Creation; all things created by God were made out of nothing into something; for the month of March was the beginning of Creation, and on the 21st of March the first created man and progenitor of mankind, Adam, was created by the hand of God. In the month of March the people of Israel some time long ago, as Gregory the Theologian said, were rescued from the land of Egypt and from the slavery of the Pharaohs, and walked dry-shod through the depths of the Red Sea as if over land. And again in the month of March the Israelites entered the Promised Land and founded Jerusalem; and again in the month of March the Passover began to be celebrated every year by the Israelites. In the month of March was also the Annunciation of the Holy Mother of God, which the Archangel Gabriel announced to her, when the Son of God for our Salvation came down from the heavens and dwelt in the pure womb of Our Holy Lady, the Mother of God and the eternal Virgin Mary, and received flesh from her without seed. In the month of March Christ voluntarily underwent Crucifixion and suffered death for our sake, and commanded us to celebrate the Resurrection to the glory of God. Again in the month of March we expect the Raising of the Dead, and the Second Coming of Christ, and the fearful, terrible, awesome, trembling, vehement, unwarned, irredeemable Judgement of the world, when He shall come with glory and judge the living and the dead, and reward every man according to his works; glory to him in all eternity).(23f.)

In the *Life of Saint Stephen,* the birth of Christ, His death and resurrection form links in a chronological chain of events that the Church commemorates for their historical significance. The sacramental aspect of the feasts, however, the ritual revelation of the eternal mystery of the divine—*večněj taině javlenie*—in perceptible images, is absent from Epiphanius' discourse, which refers to it, but never represents it.

Within the historical system of the *Life of Saint Stephen,* the sacrificial death of Christ has its function as an historical event which is, as such, unique. This event marks the decisive turning point in the teleological movement, which progresses from the Creation of the World and of Adam, the progenitor of mankind, towards the close of the ages and the resurrection on the Day of Judgement. Both at its beginning and at its end, this movement transcends history, while in the interim a transcendent Godhead rules its course through His providence. In the interim between the beginning and the end of the world, God acts through His Prophets, His Son, the Apostles, and their successors.

This idea of history is not unique to the *Life of Saint Stephen.* It is central to the teaching of the Christian Church. In early Russian literature we find a similar view of history in the thirteenth-century *Life of Alexander Nevsky.* Here "the mystical truths upon which the Christian dogma is founded, the Incarnation and Resurrection of Christ are simply included in the chain of historical facts" (Fedotov 1960:383). What makes this linear idea of history special in Epiphanius is its function as the structural dominant of the *Life.* With its linear structure, the *Life of Saint Stephen* is very different from early Kievan saints' Lives. The *Life of Saint Theodosius* and the Boris and Gleb legend are based on the idea of the life of the saint as an imitation of the life of Christ. The saints become *imitatores Christi.*

In the *Life of Saint Stephen,* it is the linear idea of history that determines the selection of quotations and their combination with Epiphanius' narrative. The time-space between beginning, middle, and end in the course of history is replete with quotations by and about the Prophets of the Old Testament, the Apostles, and their successors. In this connection, the monk Khrabr's tract on the evolution of languages acquires its full significance in the structure of the *vita.* The tract was written pseudonymously by a Bulgarian monk at the end of the ninth or the beginning of the tenth century. It was originally an apologia for the written language of the Slavs against those who claimed that Greek ought also to be the language of the Slavonic Churches. The author of the tract justifies his stand by pointing out that the other languages had been created by heathens over many generations, whereas the Slavonic language had been moulded by one individual, Constantine the Philosopher, who was also a Christian saint. Epiphanius links his story of Stephen's work on a written language for the Zyrians to this sequence of languages, so that the relationship between narration and quotation becomes the same here as in the story of Stephen's itinerary. Through the parallels between Stephen's work and events and characters referred to in the quotations, Epiphanius assimilates his protagonist to the historical heroes of the Church. Stephen is "in truth the New Philosopher" (69), equal to Saint Cyril in goodness and wisdom. But as has been observed by Obolensky (1971b:X,64) and Ševčenko (1982:IV,225), Epiphanius goes one step further: Stephen's merit is greater than Cyril's. For whereas the Apostle of the Slavs was assisted by his brother Methodius, Stephen had no helper but God. The dominant function of the parallel is not to create an equality relation between Stephen and Constantine-Cyril, but to show how Stephen's mission forms part of the history of the Christian Church, seen as a process of progressive expansion and perfection. As a new chain in this development, Stephen's mission surpasses all similar missions in the past, according to the "syntactical code" underlying the *Life*.

This integration into the historical development of the Church is, however, only an intermediate stage in Epiphanius' story of Stephen's sanctification. The final aim of the *vita* is to transcend history, to overcome the distance between Stephen and the Wholly Other. When Epiphanius tells us about the death of Stephen, the saint's life has become a link in an historical time sequence that is perfective in relation to the author of the frame and his audience. The departure of the saint creates an insuperable cleft between the "I" of the narrator and his audience in the frame, on the one side, and Stephen, on the other. In his *threnos* the hagiographer laments:

> uže bo mežju nami meža velika sotvorisę, uže mežju nami propastь velika utverdisę... (Already a great division has been created between us, already a great abyss has been set between us).(101)

At the moment when Epiphanius is about to leave the story of past events for his representation of the present, it becomes clear that the glorification of Stephen has created a distance between his figure and its frame.

Epiphanius and those to whom he addresses his story are outside the *perfectum* of the quotations, into the context of which the saint has been incorporated through Epiphanius' technique of montage, while both he and his audience, the recipients of the message of the *vita*, are left in the transient *nunc* of the frame. The absolute distance between the narrator-situation in the frame and the *Life* proper is a feature that, together with Epiphanius' orientation towards the historical context and the third person, points in the direction of the epic. The epic past is absolute, precisely because it represents a time plane totally different from the time of the narrator and his audience:

> The singer and his audience, both immanent in the epic qua genre, are on the same time plane and on the same level of meaning (hierarchical level), but the represented world of the heroes is on a

> totally different, unattainable level, in respect of time as well as
> significance, separated by epic distance. (Bakhtin 1975:457)

Unlike an author of the folk epic—that is, epic poetry dealing with a
people's or a nation's traditions about heroes and events from a distant
past, as they appear to the poet at his epic distance—Epiphanius
glorifies a hero of his own times. Whereas in the exordium the writer
emphasises his own contemporaneity with Stephen, the *conclusio*
consists of a sequence of *threnoi* which, as we have seen, stress the
distance that has arisen between the glorified figure of the saint and the
mourners in the frame. In the course of the biography, the figure of
Stephen has been shifted from the transient, contemporaneous time of
the hagiographer onto a heroic, everlasting past, through a representation of his life that both in form and meaning imitates the
canonical writings Epiphanius has woven into his own story. This kind
of mimesis has the character of stylisation. The author adapts his own
narrative to the authoritative texts of the past in a way that seeks to
abolish the difference between them. The projection of certain figures
and events of the present onto an epic past—that is, onto a past that has
no connection with the present as part of the continuous flow of time—
is typical of "classicist" art and literature, which seek permanence in an
idealised past seen in opposition to both the formless transience of the
present and to the future, perceived either as a pure continuation of the
present or as an impending catastrophe and destruction (Bakhtin
1975:462f.). In the *Life of Saint Stephen* this impending catastrophe is
represented by the concept of the Last Judgement. This projection of
figures from the author's own time into an epically perceived, idealised
past is characteristic of the *Kunstepos*. In a strongly hierarchical society,
representatives of the law and power are already, by virtue of their high
position in the hierarchy, shown to be separated from others in a way
that recalls epic distance, representing as they do tradition handed down
from their forebears. In the poet's own time, it is only elevated figures of
this kind, and their actions, that can be represented by means of the epic
form. With the aid of various intermediary links and connections, the
poet weaves them into the epic tradition of the heroic past.

Against this background one may define the *Life of Saint Stephen* as
an epic representation of a church prince of the hagiographer's own
time, determined by a "classicist" view of the history of the Orthodox
Church. This in turn is interpreted as a divine process of redemption.
The intermediary link is the use of the quotations, by which Epiphanius
integrates Stephen into the glorified past. The absolute distance created
between this heroic past and the author's own time shows that history
seen as a God-ordained process from Genesis to the Last Judgement
constitutes a self-contained, closed universe in the *vita*. The series of
figures and events in this closed universe is distanced from the

hagiographer and his audience: it has its own beginning, middle, and end. The figure of the saint acquires its significance precisely in its separation from the author and his audience, in the establishment of this absolute epic distance between the frame and the *Life* proper.

## Lyricism in the *Life of Saint Stephen*

The absolute division between narrator-situation and narrative in epic poetry implies a particular epic author-attitude inherent in the genre. This author-attitude, which characterises Epiphanius' representation of the life of his hero, is defined by Bakhtin (1975:457) as "the stance of a person speaking about a past unattainable to him, the reverential stance of a descendant." But in the three concluding *threnoi*, the point of view is no longer that of the epic narrator. In his final lament, Epiphanius takes an admiring upward-looking view towards his hero from the transient here and now of the frame.

The first of the concluding *threnoi*, in which Epiphanius describes the grief of the Zyrians over the loss of their bishop, takes the form of the lamentation of the "flock" over its "shepherd" and is distinctive—compared with the next two—for its factual content. It sketches Stephen's significance for the people of Perm, whom he had helped against both Russian colonisers and neighbouring enemy tribes. This survey is interspersed with rhetorical elements which according to Adrianova-Peretc (1947a:164) are traditional in early Russian eulogies of holy educators such as, for example, Saint Vladimir, Leontij Rostov-skij, and Constantine Muromskij. "The lamentation of the Permians goes together with the type of eulogy addressed to the 'illuminator,' created as early as in the eleventh century by Metropolitan Hilarion and by the author of the *Life of Vladimir I*." The admixture of an oral Russian *plač'* tradition is noticeable in the lamentation of the Permian Church, which is, as Holthusen has shown (1967), an amplified version of Gregory of Nyssa's Funeral Oration to Bishop Meletios of Antioch. The oral elements have been integrated into the typical word-weaving style, where the discourse is dominated by Biblical phraseology and allusions to Biblical prototypes for the Church's lament, to Rachel's, Joseph's, and King David's laments, and to those of other Biblical figures. The oral discourse is discernible only in a few formulaic phrases, such as the recurrent *Uvy mne* ("Woe is me").

In the third and final *threnos*, Epiphanius' own lament and eulogy, the author no longer cites the laments of others, but bursts into lamentations of his own. This lament, like that of the Zyrians, gradually becomes a eulogy. Adrianova-Peretc (1947a:164) has called attention to an essential feature in the construction of this *threnos:* Epiphanius moves away from the traditional motifs of oral lamentation for the dead at the same time as the discourse is noticeably shifted in the direction of the author: "the talk is not so much about the deceased as about the sinful author's helplessness."

The opening of the lament, like the opening of the *Life* proper, is a remembrance of the time when Stephen was still alive. This recollection of their time together is seen by the author in contrast to the unbridgeable gulf that separates them now. The opposition between the author's here and now and the saint's existence beyond time and space is then developed in the form of an extended comparison, in which the relationship between author and saint is equated with that of the rich man and Lazarus in the parable:

> ty ubo, jako onъ dobryi Lazarь niščii, počivaeši nně, jako v loněkhъ Avraamlikhъ, az že okaan'nyi, aky bogatyi onъ plamenemь pekomъ syi... (For you, like the good poor Lazarus, now rest in Abraham's bosom, whereas I, wretched man, am consumed by the flame like the rich man) (101).

Epiphanius uses the parable of the rich man's adversities to elucidate his own spiritual misery. Through the comparison he abases himself and elevates the saint, so that the distance between them is already maximal when he starts his eulogy. From the lowly standpoint he has taken, he addresses the transcendent saint *de profundis.*

A comparison of the three *threnoi* shows that despite some differences, they are composed on the same scheme and form variants of the same structure. With their vertical viewpoint *de sotto in su,* they are in clear contrast to the epic structure of the third-person narrative describing Stephen's work in the context-oriented *Life* proper. The laments are represented in the first person and addressed to the saint in the second person as exclamations of woe on his departure. Gradually they become encomiastic invocations of his absent figure:

> Ašče(ž)i umršu ti, aky k' živu k tebě glju... (Even if you are dead, I speak to you as to a living man).(102)

The shift in orientation from the third to the first person in the final *threnoi* means that the discourse has now acquired another structural dominant, different from the third-person narrative with its epic thrust. With its focus on the lamenting subject, the series of *threnoi* becomes finally an expression of the feelings of the lamenters when faced with the reality of the saint's absence.

The summaries of Stephen's deeds no longer refer primarily to the historical context of the *vita.* Their main function is to generate the emotional outbursts of the bereaved. Stylistically they are dominated by such interjections as *O, Uvy mne*—words belonging to that part of speech in which the purely emotive stratum is most clearly felt. The involvement of the emotive function marks the *threnoi* as belonging to the lyric genre. However, one factor that complicates the lyric structure of the laments is their panegyric passages, in which the lamenters address their words to the absent saint and call him by a *you* that seems to run counter to the lamentations on his departure. The panegyric invocations of Stephen in the *threnoi* culminate in the author's own concluding eulogy, addressed directly to the glorified figure of the saint, as if Epiphanius wants to bring him back to the level of the frame and overcome the distance between them. Through this shift in point of view, the saint becomes the addressee, the recipient of the message: "But what shall I call you, O Bishop, or how shall I name you, or how shall I address you ...?" After this sequence of invocations follow the "decomposition" passage and the metonymic portrayal of Stephen's character through personification of his individual qualities, in an attempt to make him present in the frame. The passage shows how Epiphanius uses language also in its magic, incantatory function, a function which is "chiefly some kind of conversion of an absent or inanimate 'third person' into an addressee of a conative message" (Jakobson 1960:355). In the laments of the *vita* this magic use of language is, however, subordinate to its emotive function. Starting from the historical life-work of the saint, the hagiographer abstracts and "decomposes" his figure, so that it dissolves and disappears behind the words, in which the referential function is no longer predominant. The main function is now to connote the grief of the lyric first person. The words refer to one another and are woven into ornamental sequences based on lexical proximity and phonemic similarity. Finally, in the discourse the saint is present merely in the lyric outbursts of the hagiographer grieving at his absence, present in his absence.

Thus Stephen emerges finally in his *vita* as a sign, a symbol of something other. But this other is not the presence of the divine prototype in the image of the saint, as we know it from the *Life of Saint Theodosius*. The saintly figure of the *Life of Saint Stephen* is transformed through the laments and eulogies into an expression of a state of mind. This state of mind belongs to a first person faced with the omnipresent absence of the Wholly Other. The concluding transformation of Stephen through a series of rhetorical attempts to determine the essence of his character describes a lyric withdrawal from what is the true theme of this *vita*, namely, the story of Stephen's glorification, until it is no longer the saint's figure that is represented in the words of the hagiographer, but the withdrawal itself, through a sequence of metonymic decomposition. The *you* at which the eulogy is directed transcends all that Epiphanius is capable of expressing. The Wholly Other can only be expressed in terms

172                                                    VISIONS OF GLORY

of absence, the rapture of the lyric subject in its enthusiasm before the
ineffable. The set towards the saint's *you* and the withdrawal in the
direction of the lamenters' state of mind seem to have created a situation
in which the audience of the frame have been excluded from the
exposition. But this is only apparently so. In the capacity of a lyric
subject, the lamenter at the end of the *vita* is no longer identical only
with the author, but rather with any auditor or reader of the *vita* who
makes Epiphanius' words an expression of his own feeling and is carried
away by the author's enthusiasm. The emotional integration of his
audience into the lyric subject, which takes place through the
concluding *threnoi* of the *vita*, implies that Epiphanius' function is no
longer that of the epic narrator, but rather that of the *koruphaios* whose
"I" not only represents his own person but also the others, when he
directs his eulogy towards the Wholly Other. The reason why
Epiphanius in his final gesture again turns towards the audience, is
precisely that he wants to integrate them into his encomium, with an
exhortation to take part in a concluding prayer to the *you* that is the
infinite Godhead itself, for whom Stephen was once a missionary to the
Zyrians, and with whom he has now become reunited:

> ...i molju sprosta vse(kh)' va(s)' o(t) mala i do velika, jako da
> sotvorite o mně mĺtvu kъ Bg̃u, jako da mĺvami vašimi okon'čavaa
> slovo vozmogu rešči: slava ti G̃i sъtvorivšemu vsę; slava ti sъveršitelju
> Bg̃u, slava davšemu na(m) Stefana, i paky vzem'šemu... (And now I
> simply ask you, great and small, to pray with me to God, so that I
> may finish my account with your prayers, saying: glory to Thee, O
> Lord, who have created everything, glory to Thee, O God, who have
> accomplished everything, glory to Thee, who gave us Stephen
> and took him back again) (111)

## Epiphanius' Word-Weaving
## and its Russian Context

It is in the lyric laments at the end of the *Life of Saint Stephen* that the
emotional exaltation of Epiphanius' word-weaving, so strongly
emphasised by Likhačev, is brought out most clearly. Likhačev did, in
fact, base his theory of word-weaving solely on its expressive, or emotive,
function. Epiphanius' use of word-weaving as a means of appealing to
his audience, what we would call its conative function, is barely mentioned, whereas its referential and poetic functions are simply overlooked.

Likhačev's focusing on the emotive function of word-weaving is a natural consequence of the role allocated to it in his schema of early Russian literary history. According to this schema, Epiphanius' "abstract psychologism" replaced the "monumentalism" of early Kievan literature. As the verbal expression of this "abstract psychologism," word-weaving designates the stage when early Russian writers for the first time became conscious of the inner world of man and discovered the psychological life of their characters:

> From the end of the fourteenth century and throughout the fifteenth, it was as if the writers for the first time looked into the inner world of their heroes. And it was as if they were blinded by the inner light of feeling. They do not distinguish halftones. They are unable to understand the coordination of the emotions. The writer sees the inner world of man for the first time. But for the time being he still sees it "with the eyes of a child," to whom the colours of an enormous world are laid bare, but for whom these colours have not as yet been united into objects, into objectively existing realities. (Likhačev 1970:74)

Word-weaving is here seen as a necessary stage towards a unitary character-drawing based on the idea of man's complex and composite self. It is a view not supported by textual evidence. The distinction between the hero's public appearance and his true, inner self is a characteristic feature of Russian hagiography even in Kievan times. Moreover, the theory about the "abstract psychologism" of word-weaving fails to distinguish between psychological character-drawing and the emotive use of language. In the *Life of Saint Stephen* the representation of the saint is contextual and extrovert. His inner self, on the other hand, remains a closed world. On no level does Epiphanius' representation seem to be focused on the "inner man" in any other way than in the allegorical depiction of his intellectual progress. The inner life of the saint, which Nestor illustrated in the portrayal of Theodosius' ritual-like initiation and in the visions of his mystical glorification, is inaccessible to the author of the *Life of Saint Stephen*.

There is a connection between the inaccessible mystery of holiness and the representation of the protagonist in the *Life of Saint Stephen*. In order to bring out the "inner man" in his portrayal of the saint, the hagiographer needs a divine prototype, whose features are reflected in the character of the holy man in the form of a likeness. But if, as in the *Life of Saint Stephen*, the Godhead is to remain beyond all human experience, and the absolute distance between the human and the divine is to be maintained, the saint's "inner man" must remain hidden also.

In the *Life of Saint Stephen*, where metonymical relationships not only serve to link the elements together in a linear course of events, but where the principle of contiguity is employed in order to emphasise the relational and hierarchical character of the presented world, the protagonist's activity becomes an integral part of the divine economy of salvation. The idea of sanctification as the restitution of man's original God-likeness, presupposing Christ as the mediator and prototype for man's imaging of God in his soul, is incompatible with the structure of Epiphanius' *Life*.

In its extreme metonymity the *Life of Saint Stephen* differs also from the Serbian princely Lives. Both in Sava's and Stephen Prvovenčani's *Lives* of their father, and in Domentijan, the protagonists are represented as *vicarii Christi* in this world. This motif is absent from Epiphanius' *Life of Saint Stephen*. On this point Cyprian's representation of himself and his predecessor as vicegerents of the Heavenly All-Ruler and High Priest comes closer to the rulers portrayed by the Serbian hagiographers.

Cyprian's predominantly metaphorical representation of himself in his capacity of vicegerent of the All-Ruler becomes indirectly a testimony to his political intentions as head of the Russian Church. The *Life of Saint Peter* is evidence that not only *jure ecclesiastico* did Cyprian place the metropolitan of Moscow above the other bishops of the Russian Church, but he wanted also to state his reasons for the metropolitan's suzerainty *jure divino*.

In the *Life of Saint Stephen* the *imitatio*-motif does not even enter the portrayal of the Russian Church's primate, despite the subordination of Stephen and his new community to the authority of the metropolitan through Epiphanius' diagrammatic representation of the Moscow-centred hierarchy of the Russian Church. The author of the *Life of Saint Stephen* has concentrated on depicting the Church in her historical aspect: the process of redemption which will cease on the day when Christ returns to judge the living and the dead. This eschatological perspective marks Epiphanius' account both of Stephen's life and of his own grief at Stephen's death. It underlies the parallel drawn between the saint's evangelisation of the Zyrians "at the end of the seventh millennium"(13) and the employment of the labourers in the vineyard "about the eleventh hour." Another reflection of it in the *vita* proper is Epiphanius' brief reference to Muscovite criticism of Stephen for wishing to give the Zyrians a written language of their own "120 years before the close of the ages" (70). In the life story of the saint, however, the idea that history is coming to an end remains a secondary theme, subordinate to the absolute, epic past of the quotations and to the narrative's retrospective point of view.

It is when Epiphanius at the end of the *Life* reverts to his own situation that the eschatological point of view takes control over his discourse. Contemplating his own death and the impending Judgement, he invokes the saint to intercede for him before God. In his lyric self-abasement towards the end, Epiphanius strikes one of the favourite themes of his time. Although an eschatological dimension is never absent from Christian thought, we know that it was particularly strong in Russia from the end of the fourteenth century onwards, when it left its mark on icon-painting and hagiography, as well as on the chronicles. It is reflected in Cyprian's meditations on his impending death and the "terrible judgement of the Saviour," and it later becomes a main motif in the pastoral letters and sermons of his successor, the Greek Photius, who, as Plugin (1974:30ff.) has observed, in his writings constantly preaches the imminent end of the world.

This strengthening of the eschatological theme in the teaching of the Church cannot be explained merely by referring to the idea that the world was soon coming to an end. More important is the function of this idea in the anti-heretical struggle of the time. The heretics combined their criticism of the iniquitous covetousness of the clergy with the teaching of a judgement without punishment and with full absolution for all sins on the Last Day. Plugin (1974:36f.) is undoubtedly right in pointing out that this heresy implies a negation of the Church's official dogma of the judgement passed on the living and the dead by a just Godhead, in the fullness of time, and of the status of the clergy as representatives in history of this divine Judge and His Law. Furthermore, it should be remembered that the support given by the dignitaries of the Church to the centralist endeavours of the Muscovite princes had led paradoxically to a tension between the Church and the Prince, who gradually threatened to intervene in the independence of the Church and its sovereign control of all its property, and to restrict its judiciary power. This policy was based on the conception of the divine origin of Tsardom, an ideology that the Church herself had been instrumental in translating from Byzantium to the Balkans and to Moscow.

The antagonism between Church and State is still only alluded to in the *Life of Saint Stephen.* The struggle against the heretics, on the other hand, is one of its major themes. It breaks through, for instance, in the saint's valedictory speech from his deathbed—an ardent admonition to fight heresy, adhere to the traditional faith, and never try to alter the Law of God:

> Furthermore, brethren, stand firm in the faith. Be steadfast. Observe the tradition which I have handed over to you, and the faith which you have received from me. Do not add or detract from the Law that has been laid down. Obey the Law of God and everything that God has decreed in the whole of His Law (83).

This emphasis on the tradition and the Law is in complete conformity with the glorification the *Life of Saint Stephen* accords to the historical Church and its leaders, and with the hagiographer's concluding eulogy of the one, triune Godhead. The whole of this thematic syndrome has sprung from the main idea of the *vita*, that God, until the Second Coming on the Last Day, works through His historical Church, whose hierarchy takes care of the true dogma and upholds the Law in God's absence, having been invested with divine authority.

Against the background of spiritual life in Russia at the turn of the fourteenth century it is natural to interpret the *Life of Saint Stephen* as a reflection of the official Church's campaign to defend her authority. By accepting this authority and identifying the laws of the Church with the Law of God, to which he humbly submits, the author of the *Life* found an ideological basis for his epic version of the *vita* genre. This ideology, underlying Epiphanius' account of Saint Stephen's mission and the hierarchical structure of the *Life,* is hardly compatible with the *theologia* of mystical Hesychasm. As we have seen in our discussion of Cyprian's writings, however, fourteenth-century Hesychasm cannot be defined exclusively in terms of mystical theology. In the context of four-teenth-century "political Hesychasm" the mystical theology of inward-ness with God has been combined with an active, outward life in the service of the Church. Far from being contradictory, these two aspects of political Hesychasm are complementary. The systematic justification of this duality is to be found in the works of Dionysius the Areopagite, one of the Greek Fathers translated into Church Slavonic by Cyprian. In the writings of the Areopagite individual contemplation of the mystery of God and active participation in the ecclesiastical hierarchy are different modes of union with God, one belonging to the sphere of personal holiness, the other to the institutional sphere of the Church. But although the two modes are different, they do not exclude one another. They are two different aspects of the same search for divine knowledge. The Church in its hierarchical order as a legal and social institution is only the other side of an inner, spiritual theology, realised in the mystical illumination of the individual (Roques 1954:282).

Looking at Epiphanius' *Life of Saint Stephen* from this angle, it would be difficult to exclude the idea of a connection between the *Life* and the division into the threefold ministry of bishops, priests, and deacons found in the writings of the Areopagite. The threefold scheme is, in fact, repeated in Epiphanius' representation of Saint Stephen's career. In view of this structural coincidence it might be tempting to interpret the *Life* as a literary manifestation of the ideology of Hesychasm in its outward, "political" aspect.

A disciple of Saint Sergius of Radonež, who spent more than thirty years as a monk in Sergius' Monastery of the Holy Trinity, Epiphanius would most certainly have been familiar with Hesychasm both in its mystical and its hierarchical aspects. But why did he so one-sidedly emphasise the latter in the *Life of Saint Stephen?* The obvious answer to that question would, of course, be that Stephen was not a mystic. To this we might respond, however, that the work of a hagiographer is not necessarily based on historical facts only. Another, more plausible explanation is the requirements of the genre: in writing the Life of a hierarch, Epiphanius would highlight the stages of Saint Stephen's external career and focus on the elements that fit into this pattern. This is all the more likely since his accentuation of the saint's activity as a member of the hierarchy would be the best way to bring out the didactic significance of his life.

Our functional analysis of Epiphanius' word-weaving again raises the question of its affinity with contemporary icon-painting. According to Likhačev (1958:58f., 1962:163f., 1973:114f.) the hagiographer Epiphanius and the icon-painter Andrej Rublev, despite their individual differences, have in common that they were both Russian and that both worked within a national Russian tradition. In his description of their art, Likhačev therefore sees them in contradistinction to foreigners such as Theophanes the Greek and Pachomius the Serbian, who, although they received impulses from local schools, brought their own traditions to their Russian works.

However, it is questionable whether it is at all possible to single out a clearly distinguishable *national* factor, as opposed to local and individual elements, in early Muscovite art and literature. Epiphanius and Rublev both produced their works in the supranational idiom of the Orthodox Church at a time when the Church was particularly intent on working out a common mode of expression for artists and hagiographers in the Orthodox world. On the other hand, local patrons were always able to a certain extent to influence the artist; even immigrants like Theophanes and Pachomius modified their styles in accordance with local traditions. Theophanes, for instance, changed his style when he moved from Novgorod to Moscow. Instead of looking for national elements in the art of Epiphanius and Andrej Rublev, one should therefore try to define the specific character of their art irrespective of their nationality, as the result of an interplay of local tradition and impulses from abroad. They managed to combine the different elements into new entities, and in this creative activity Epiphanius' manner is closer to Theophanes' than to the manner of Andrej Rublev, with whom Epiphanius has very little in common. There is in fact a remarkable affinity between Epiphanius and Theophanes the Greek, an affinity manifest not only in their art, but in their personal relationship as well.

Our main source for this relationship is a letter written by Epiphanius to his friend Cyril of Tver and preserved in a single copy from the seventeenth century (Epifanij Premudryj 1981b). From this letter we learn that Epiphanius met the Greek painter while he was decorating the Church of the Annunciation in the Kremlin, which according to the Chronicle of the Monastery of the Holy Trinity, took place in 1405. The other masters engaged in the work were the monks Prokhor from

Gorodec and Andrej Rublev. Epiphanius' letter makes no mention of the other two; he seems to have been wholly absorbed in the art of Theophanes, giving a detailed account of how the latter went about his painting:

> in the stone church of the Holy Annunciation he also painted the "Tree of Jesse" and the "Apocalypse." When he drew or painted all this, no one saw that he ever looked at standard patterns, as certain of our own iconographers do, who in their bewilderment constantly stare at them, looking hither and thither, and do not so much paint with colours as they look at standard patterns. But he seemed to be painting the picture with his hands while at the same time walking around, always in motion, talking to visitors, and in his mind pondering wise and lofty thoughts, seeing the beauty of the spirit with the sensitive eyes of his inner vision. This divine and famous man took a great liking for my insignificance, and I, of no account to him and stupid, took courage many times and went often to converse with him, for I always loved to talk with him. (1981b:444)

For a comparison of Epiphanius' style with the style of Theophanes, the most illuminating passage of the letter is that in which Epiphanius tells of his request to the painter to produce for him a picture of the Hagia Sophia in Constantinople and the account of the answer given by Theophanes:

> I beg of your philosophy with your colours to make a depiction for me of that great church of Holy Wisdom in Constantinople, erected by Justinian, who in his endeavour made himself equal to the wise Solomon. Some people have said that her character and magnitude are like the Moscow Kremlin within the walls and its circumference and its foundations when you walk around her. And if some stranger enters her, wanting to walk around without a guide, he will not be able to get out again without losing his way, however clever he might seem, because of the multitude of colonnades and peristyles, descents and ascents, passages and crossings, and various courts, and churches, and staircases, and storehouses, and sepulchres, and chancels and side-altars of various names, and windows, and gangways, and doors, entrances and exits, and pillars of stone as well. ... But he, the wise man, answered me wisely: "It isn't possible for you to have, or for me to paint this—he said—I will, however, because of your persistence, paint a little something as from a part for you, and even that will not be from a part, but from the hundredth of a part, a little of much, but so that from this little pictorial representation, painted by us, you will be able to know and understand the remaining larger parts." Having said

this, boldly taking a brush and a sheet, he quickly painted a church-
like representation in imitation of the church in Constantinople
and gave it to me. (1981b:446)

Epiphanius' description of Justinian's edifice as he imagines it to
himself bears a striking structural similarity to his *Life of Saint Stephen:*
starting from a traditional interpretation of Justinian as the new Solomon, an interpretation based on the principle of metaphor, Epiphanius
soon develops his imaginary description of the church into an *ecphrasis,*
employing his favourite device of *distributio* in order to dissolve the
whole of the building into its smallest components. The result of this
process is a text that is essentially metonymic in nature, based on the
same principle of contiguity that also dominates the structure of the *vita.*

The same principle is at work in Theophanes' answer. If Epiphanius'
quotation of the Greek painter's words is actually an account of how
Theophanes himself described his working method, and not only a
reflection of Epiphanius' own method, there is really a remarkable
correspondence between the iconographer's synecdochic representation
of the whole through one of its smallest parts and Epiphanius'
decomposition of the whole into its constituent components. In each
case the mimetic operation is determined by the principle of contiguity;
individual details are selected and recombined according to reciprocal
and total proximity.

Epiphanius' characterisation of Theophanes' method has at any rate
emphasised a typical feature of his painting, what Alpatov (1972:198)
calls his "elliptical mode of expression."

For Theophanes the metonymic principle, the synecdochic detail, has
nevertheless another function than it has for Epiphanius. Theophanes
metaphorises it, so that the detail not only refers to the totality of which
it is a component, but also acquires a symbolic significance. In consequence, the meaning of his paintings is more complex than the meaning
of Epiphanius' verbal art. Still, I think we are right to ask whether Theophanes' emphasis on the antinomy of spirit and body, as well as his portrayal of the Pantocrator in the guise of the severe Judge, in Novgorod,
does not form a certain ideological parallel to the hierarchical structure
of the *Life of Saint Stephen.*

This impression of a common ideological background for Epiphanius' and Theophanes' art is reinforced by the latter's Moscow
paintings, both the lost "Tree of Jesse" and "Apocalypse" mentioned in
Epiphanius' letter, and the extant Pantocrator, Mother of God, John the
Baptist, and Basil the Great, all of them from the iconostasis of the
Church of the Annunciation. These life-size icons form part of what is
now commonly referred to as the Intercession- or *deesis*-group, a term
introduced by the Russian art historian Kirpičnikov at the end of the last
century (Lazarev 1970:128–139). As part of the Russian iconostasis, the

*deesis* represents the saints interceding before Christ the Pantocrator, seated on the throne of Judgement, led by the Prodromos and the Mother of God.

The iconography of the *deesis* and the development of the iconostasis in medieval Russia seem to have a certain significance in connection with the question of a common ideological background for the art of Epiphanius and Theophanes the Greek.

According to Lazarev (1970:128–139), the concentric group of life-size figures around Christ Enthroned developed from the Byzantine *deesis*-icon depicting Christ between Mary and Saint John the Baptist, which was probably originally placed centrally on the architrave, above the columns between the sanctuary and the central part of the church, above the Holy Door. Beneath the architrave, between the columns on either side of the Holy Door, a second register of icons developed, fixed in place and usually including an icon of the holy person or event to which the church was dedicated. Lazarev's theory is that the Russian iconostasis in its classical form represents a fusion of these tiers into a whole, which was subsequently enlarged to include in the upper tier Christ's ancestors centred around the Holy Trinity, followed by the Mother of God of the sign (*Znamenie,* after Isa. 7:14), surrounded by the prophets who predicted the coming of Christ, and by the icons of the *dodekaortion* and its derivations, immediately above the *deesis* range.

When this multitiered iconostasis reached its full development we do not know. The oldest surviving iconostases date back no further than to the seventeenth century. Written sources show a noticeable increase in the number of iconostases in the fifteenth and sixteenth centuries. But as Il'in (1966) has observed, multitiered iconostases had been spreading in Russia even in the thirteenth and fourteenth centuries.

A decisive phase in the development of the iconostasis appears to have been the time around 1400. Il'in (1966) has tried to reconstruct the iconostasis of a stone church from this period, that is, an iconostasis of the type Theophanes helped to build in the Church of the Annunciation. His reconstruction shows that the sanctuary was separated from the rest of the interior by a stone wall between the eastern pillars, where an opening was left for the Holy Door. On the side of the wall, facing the central part of the church, there was usually a fresco of frontal representations of the Church Fathers. In lieu of frescoes the wall might be covered by costly fabrics, which occasionally replaced the entire partition wall. On each side of the Holy Door, between it and the eastern pillars, were two ciboria containing icons of the Mother of God, Christ, or a patron saint. Beneath the icons were hung cloths, embroidered or studded with precious stones.

Above the partition was the iconostasis. Most likely it consisted of two tiers: the festival icons and the *deesis* register. The latter appears to have comprised life-size portraits of Christ Enthroned, surrounded by Mary,

Saint John the Baptist, apostles, and saints, such as we know from Theophanes' *deesis*. The tier of festival icons was composed of small icons depicting scenes from Christ's life on earth, which can hardly have been visible from the congregation's point of view.

In this way a horizontal partition was created between the chancel, that is, the sanctuary, and the rest of the interior, between clergy and congregation. At the same time a vertical opposition was established between the lower half of the partition wall and the iconostasis proper. But here the relationship is more complex. The ciboria and the Holy Door show that the lower part of the partition wall was an imitation of the Imperial Palace, where the God-Emperor appeared to the supplicants as the curtains were drawn apart like "clouds hiding the heavenly light," according to the court poets of Byzantium (L'Orange 1958:86). As an imitation of this glorification pediment the Holy Door corresponds symbolically to the throne of the heavenly Pantocrator in the middle of the *deesis*-range. The celestial hierarchy represented in the iconostasis is reflected in the hierarchy of the Church. The priest as he appears in the Holy Door during the liturgy is glorified as the representative of Christ in the historical Church. In this way, the iconostasis "not only acted as a physical barrier between the clergy and the laity. It was also an ideological frontier" (Walter 1977:III, 261).

Among the many factors contributing to the development of the Russian iconostasis at the turn of the fourteenth century, Il'in (1966) mentions the influence coming from Hesychast mysticism. He sees the closure of the inner sanctum of the chancel as an expression of the Hesychast idea that sanctification required complete isolation from the world and its temptations. Behind the partition the priests could devote themselves entirely to the divine service. Il'in's theory provides one important factor, but is too narrow, overlooking as it does the active function of the partition vis-à-vis the congregation: while excluding the uninitiated from the holy mystery, it illustrates, in the relationship between glorification pediment and *deesis*-register, the relationship between the historical Church and its transcendental prototype. In this dual function of a veiling of the inner sanctum and a symbolic illustration of the Church's authority, the screen, or partition wall, becomes a monument not only to esoteric, introvert Hesychast theology, but equally to Hesychasm in its extrovert, political aspect.

The message of the *Life of Saint Stephen* may be seen as a parallel to the message expressed in the iconostasis in its relation to the Holy Door. In Epiphanius' *vita*, too, the mystery of the inner sanctum remains hidden. The devotion and awesome enthusiasm that once filled his audience must have been similar to the experience of the congregation when beholding Theophanes' white Pantocrator surrounded by saints interceding for sinful humanity, in the half-light of the Church of the Annunciation. The intercession motif of the *deesis* corresponds to the hagiographer's cry to the saint to intercede before the heavenly throne for his community on earth. This "theology of intercessory prayer" (Walter 1977:I, 318) is nothing new in the Orthodox tradition, but is an idea developed in analogy to the intercession of high officials at the Imperial court, where petitions were brought to the notice of the Emperor through their mediation. What seems to be new in thirteenth-century Moscow, however, is the function of the *deesis*-motif in the iconography of the fully developed iconostasis, where the image of the saints interceding before the throne of the All-Ruler is symbolically reflected in the liturgy. In the *deesis*-icons the saints are not represented in individual prayer. Their attitude and the inclination of their heads show, according to Alpatov (1932:314), that it is "a communal act, in which each individual being is rather like a link of a larger chain."

As regards the relationship between Epiphanius and Pachomius the Serbian, Epiphanius' heir and successor as Russia's most distinguished hagiographer, it is of a kind quite different from the relationship between Epiphanius and the icon-painters of the time. Although Epiphanius and Theophanes the Greek knew each other personally and were active in the same milieu, they worked after all in different media, which led necessarily to a differentiation also in content, despite ideological correspondences in their art.

However, not only did Epiphanius and Pachomius work within the same genre, but Pachomius took up and rewrote at least one of Epiphanius' texts, the *Life of Saint Sergius of Radonež*, the founder of the Monastery of the Holy Trinity, the Troice-Sergieva Lavra, outside Moscow, now Zagorsk. Epiphanius wrote this *Life* probably some time immediately before 1420. Pachomius revised it, apparently, first in the years 1438–1443, and again in 1449–1459, according to Ključevskij (1871:118f.).

Epiphanius' *Life of Saint Sergius* and Pachomius' first redaction of it have been preserved merely as "incrustations" in later redactions of the *Life*. In the following I shall use the text of the *Life* published by the Archimandrite Leonid in the *Pamjatniki drevnej pis'mennosti i iskusstva*, vol. 58 (Pachomius 1885) and the revised version of Leonid's edition (Pachomius 1981). Leonid's edition represents a sixteenth-century compilation in which different manuscripts of the *Life* have been brought together. Nevertheless, the *Life of Saint Sergius* as we know it from the manuscript published by Leonid is essentially that of Pachomius' second version, according to Zubov (1953). Although the examination of the manuscripts has not yet reached a stage where it is possible to determine with any certainty the respective contributions of Epiphanius and Pachomius, Zubov (1953) has attempted to identify them through a stylistic comparison of the *Life of Saint Sergius* with the *Life of Saint Stephen*. In so doing, Zubov has been able to establish a number of features common to the two *vitae*, typical of Epiphanius' word-weaving, such as the accumulation of rhetorical figures, personal names, and topographical designations, tracing back to Epiphanius the passages in which these elements predominate. On the other hand, Zubov has enumerated a number of characteristic differences between the two *Lives*, in style as well as in content. These differences have presumably resulted from Pachomius' revisions, and Zubov finds corroboration of this in other writings of Pachomius, in which the same features occur.

The crucial difference between Epiphanius and Pachomius is that the latter does not copy Epiphanius' word-weaving. As Jablonskij has shown (1908:218ff.), Pachomius knows the individual stylistic devices of word-weaving, but does not string them together in ornamental sequences in the way Epiphanius does. The same is true of his scriptural quotations. In addition, Pachomius' discourse is marked by a tendency to dramatise events, as opposed to the long monologues and static characters of Epiphanius.

However, the most important difference between Epiphanius' and Pachomius' art of hagiography is not of a stylistic, but of a thematic nature. In Pachomius, light mysticism has entered the account as a formative element, while in the *Life of Saint Stephen* it plays no part at all. Both in the *Life of Saint Sergius* and in Pachomius' *Life of Saint Cyril of Belozersk* light visions play an important part in the portrayal of the saint.

The light visions of the *Life of Saint Sergius* form part of its miracle tales. Now it is the saint himself who has a nightly vision: "a bright light appeared in the sky, chasing away the darkness of the night" (Pachomius 1981:364), now it is the Hesychast Isaac who sees an angel standing beside the saint "in great brightness, and shining in appearance, and with glistering garments" (1981:384). A third instance is that of the monk Micah who witnesses the appearance to the saint of the Mother of God together with the Apostles Saint Peter and Saint John, in an ecstatic light vision that transfigures his face: "and lo, a great light overshadowed him, shining more brightly than the sun" (1981:394). Finally, there is the tale of the ecclesiarch Symeon about the "divine fire" he once saw poised above the saint during the service, which gathered itself into a ball before plunging into the chalice from which the saint was going to drink. The significance of this vision is explained to the saint by Symeon in the following words: "Lord, I have seen a wonderful vision, how the Grace of the Holy Spirit worked together with you" (1981:402).

In this series of miraculous visions the sanctification of Sergius is expressed in the "language of fire and light" (Fedotov 1931:136), the language of mystical Hesychasm. The mystical light shining forth in the *vita* is the divine Light of Tabor, God's visible energy, according to Hesychast theology, emanating from His invisible essence, transfiguring that which it illuminates by its rays. Through this representation of the visible presence of the invisible Godhead, the *Life of Saint Sergius* has been invested with a symbolic meaning of which there is no trace in the *Life of Saint Stephen*. Nor is this light symbolism identifiable with Theophanes' synecdochic highlights, reflecting a supernatural light in the ecstatic physiognomies of the ascetics. In the *Life of Saint Sergius* the light visions are depicted to show a gradual glorification of the figure of the saint, until the Spirit in the shape of light makes its dwelling in his heart and illuminates him from within. In the mystical imagery of the Hesychast fathers this is a sign of the saint's *theosis*: "God unites with gods (= godlike men) and appears to them; this happens when the Holy Spirit in person enlightens the heart," to quote the words of Gregory Nazianzus as they are reproduced in the late fourteenth-century handbook of Hesychast mysticism compiled by the monks Callistus and Ignatius (Ammann 1938:91).

The light visions form the climax in the process of sanctification as it is represented in the *Life of Saint Sergius*. The tales of Sergius' glorification occur in the concluding part of the *vita* and are arranged to make the most significant one of them, the account of how the Spirit took up His abode in the saint, come at the end of the sequence. This concluding glorification is the objective of the story of Saint Sergius' life, the account of his birth, adolescence, ascetic exercises, and his work for the brethren of his Monastery of the Holy Trinity. This pattern is very different from the pattern underlying the account of Saint Stephen's career.

In the expanded version of the *Life of Saint Sergius* published by Leonid, the motif of the mystical light appears in combination with the motif of the saint's imitation of Christ. This aspect of Sergius' life is explicitly emphasised in the hagiographer's account of his death, in which he sums up his own task by saying that the subject of his praise is one "who in everything has devoted himself to the imitation of Christ, the first martyr" (Pachomius 1981:406).

The *imitatio-Christi* motif is signalled also elsewhere in the *Life*, by means of similar commentaries. When asked to become the Father Superior of the monastery, he first declined: "For he had much meekness and great, true humility in him, in everything always imitating his master, Our Lord, Jesus Christ, He who has given Himself in imitation to those wishing to imitate Him and to follow Him" (1981:320) After he has let himself be persuaded to let other monks come and live with him, the saint becomes himself an example to his brethren: "And each of them built a cell for himself and lived in God, watching the life of the Holy Sergius and trying to become like his figure, each according to his ability" (1981:318). Not only does the individual monk in this way imitate the example of Christ by following the saint, but the whole of the community that grows up around Sergius in the wilderness is depicted in imitation of Christ and the twelve Apostles:

> At the beginning of his abbacy the number of the brethren amounted to twelve monks, not counting the abbot himself, the thirteenth. And behold the number: twelve monks turned up and lived in this way for two years, and for three, without becoming either more or fewer than this. And when it happened that one of them died or went away from the cloister, another brother would come in his place, in order that the number should not be reduced. And they were always living together, always in this number, so that some people talked about it thus: "But what shall come of this? Are there really going to be twelve monks in this place always, after the number of the twelve Apostles, as it is written: 'Our Lord called unto him his disciples; and of them he chose twelve, whom also he named Apostles...' " (1981:334)

The idea of an analogy between Christ surrounded by His Apostles and the abbot with his monks is typical of Hesychast monasticism. Phrases very similar to those emphasising this analogy in the *Life of Saint Sergius* are quoted by Plugin (1974:72) from the sermons of the Bulgarian Hesychast Romil to his monks.

Traditionally, the figure of Saint Sergius has been seen as moulded on Nestor's Saint Theodosius. In the words of Fedotov (1931:133), "The image of Saint Theodosius shows through in him very clearly." The correspondence between the two saintly heroes emerges in the stories of Sergius' manual work, his gentleness towards the brethren, and his uncouth garb, beneath which he hides his saintliness, to appear to the eyes of the world in the guise of a beggar: "I came to see a prophet and you showed me an orphan" (Pachomius 1981:354), says the pilgrim to the monks when they show him Sergius at work in the kitchen garden of the monastery. To Fedotov, the spirituality expressed in the figure of Saint Sergius is the same "kenotic ideal" of Russian monasticism for which Theodosius first provided the pattern. According to Fedotov (1952:50f.), however, the kenotic ideal of Saint Theodosius underwent a "mystical deepening" in Saint Sergius: "in his interior life, in the quality of his prayer, Sergius belongs to another epoch than does Theodosius; he is the first Russian saint in whom mysticism is observed." Tracing this mystical element back to Hesychast mysticism, Fedotov sees a reflection of it in the light visions of the *vita*: "Sergius is the earliest saint in Russian hagiography to be favored by heavenly visions in his contemplations" (1952:52).

There can be little doubt that Nestor's *Life of Saint Theodosius* at one stage or another served as both model and source for the *Life of Saint*

*Sergius*, such are the many points of similarity between the two *vitae*. But the light mysticism found in the *Life of Saint Sergius* is nothing new. The function of the light visions is the same in the glorification and *theosis* of both saints. Whereas Fedotov was fully aware of their importance in Sergius' biography, he showed no interest in the light visions illuminating the figure of Saint Theodosius. Morover, the mystical element should not be viewed out of the context of the saints' gradual assimilation to their divine prototype. In the last resort, the correspondences between the two saints have their origin in the common prototype, both being conceived by their biographers as imitators of Christ. By the same token, the differences between them are traceable to a single principle, as Sergius' imitation presupposes an idea of the exemplary significance of Christ that is somewhat different from the idea underlying Nestor's representation of the saint's *imitatio*: in the *Life of Saint Theodosius* we have seen how the life of the saint is transformed into a re-enactment of the Incarnation, Passion, and Resurrection of Christ.

In the *Life of Saint Sergius* the accent shifts from the Christ of the Passion sequence to Christ as he is portrayed in the Gospels, in the company of His apostles. The climax in Sergius' imitation is the transformation of his appearance in the presence of the brethren, described in the light vision modelled on the Transfiguration of Christ, when His face did shine as the sun and His raiment was white as the light, and the three disciples who were with Him were vouchsafed the vision of His glory. In Sergius' imitation of Christ nothing remains of tenth- and eleventh-century Passion mysticism. The re-enactment comes to a halt before the Passion sequence. This development in the direction of emphasising the exemplary significance of the Transfiguration to the displacement of the Passion is a feature characteristic of the Palamite version of Hesychasm. It differs from earlier Hesychast mysticism in its teaching of the mystic's real, not merely symbolic, vision of God as light, modelled precisely on the story of the Transfiguration of Christ, when the triune Godhead appeared before the eyes of the disciples. The Church prayer in commemoration of this event reads: "In Thy light, which has today appeared on Tabor, we have beheld the Father as light and the Spirit as light."

It follows from our discussion that it is not mysticism as such that distinguishes the *Life of Saint Sergius* from the *Life of Saint Theodosius*, but Hesychast mysticism in its Palamite version. Zubov's analysis (1953) lends support to the view that it was Pachomius who incorporated the light visions and thereby the motif of an *imitatio Christi* into Epiphanius' *Life of Saint Sergius*. This gives us reason to believe that the element of Palamite mysticism was introduced into the *Life* by the Serbian hagiographer. The absence of Hesychast motifs in the *Life of Saint Stephen* would indirectly confirm this view. Pachomius' rewriting of the *Life* thus seems to have played a decisive role for the development of the light mysticism of the *Life of Saint Sergius*, and his work on Epiphanius' text can no longer be reduced to an abridgement of it, or to stylistic alterations and the addition of the stories of Sergius' posthumous miracles, as has usually been maintained, after Ključevskij (1871:115f.).

On the other hand, it appears that the second major theme of the *vita*, the Trinity theme, is traceable to Epiphanius' version, although not even this can be proved. According to Klibanov (1971), Pachomius overlooked the Trinitarian ideology of Epiphanius in his emphasis on the mystical light of the Hesychasts. The peculiar cult of the Holy Trinity that is reflected in the *Life of Saint Sergius*, especially in the first chapter, has always been associated with the saint. Tradition has it that Sergius' Monastery of the Holy Trinity became the centre of a characteristic cult of the triune Godhead even towards the end of the fourteenth century, a cult that in the fifteenth century found expression in icon-painting, in the celebration of Pentecost as the feast of the Holy Trinity, and in the building of churches dedicated to the triune Godhead (Florenskij 1919).

It is not possible from the surviving material, however, to document that the fifteenth-century Russian cult of the Holy Trinity goes back to Saint Sergius (c.1314–1392). No writings by Sergius have been preserved, and there is much to indicate that his forte was for practical matters. Theological problems seem to have engaged his mind to a lesser degree. Even if the Trinity passages of the *vita* were most probably composed by Epiphanius, it cannot simply be assumed that they reflect Sergius' own teachings. Be this as it may, our task must be to try to find an historical reason for this interest in the doctrine of the Holy Trinity.

In the *Life of Saint Sergius*, the key passage about the Holy Trinity occurs in the story of the saint's childhood, where it is first established that he was the "disciple of the Holy Trinity," and that the number three is revered more than all other numbers, being "everywhere the origin of all good things" (Pachomius 1981:272). After this follows a selection of examples from the Old and the New Testaments of the significance of the number three, and the whole paragraph is rounded off with a tirade, where the dogma of the Holy Trinity is couched in the characteristic idiom of word-weaving:

But how can I speak of the number three without mentioning the greatest and most awesome, which is the triune Godhead in three sanctities, in three figures, in three hypostases; in three persons the one Godhead of the Holy Trinity, both the Father, and the Son, and the Holy Ghost; the thrice-hypostasised Godhead, one power, one authority, one dominion? (1981:274)

Lazarev (1966b:35) ascribes this "almost maniacal reference to triadism" to Epiphanius, seeing a connection between this obsession with Trinitarianism and the struggle of the Russian Church against heretical sects with a strong anti-Trinitarian tendency. According to Lazarev (1970:279ff., 292ff.), this struggle also found expression in icon-painting, where new, Trinitarian motifs were introduced, in which Christ is depicted as one of the hypostases of the transcendent triune Godhead, and no longer represented as a simple human being. This emphasis on the divine nature of Christ has led Lazarev to assume with scholars like Konrad Onasch that the dogma of the Holy Trinity is set against the heretics' view of Christ as the Son of Man and their accentuation of His human nature.

The ideological passages in the *Life of Saint Sergius* that may be assumed to go back to Epiphanius' original text thus form part of the same struggle against the heretics as does the *Life of Saint Stephen*. Epiphanius' hagiographical writings appear to have been part of a larger campaign with a view to strengthening the position of the official Church in her fight against heretical ideas that threatened her authority.

Accordingly, as far as we can judge, Pachomius has modified Epiphanius' original version by transforming the story of Sergius' life into an exposition of the Palamite idea of the *theosis* of chosen individuals, of the saints, after the example of Christ's Transfiguration on Mount Tabor.

The foremost representative of this aristocratic light mysticism in Russian art in fifteenth-century Russia was not a hagiographer but an icon painter. The prototype reflected in Saint Sergius' imitation of Christ is also the one we meet in the icons of Andrej Rublev.

Despite mutual differences in both motif and execution, the icons today attributed to Andrej Rublev possess a number of common features and may be regarded as representing a special trend in early fifteenth-century Russian icon-painting (Lazarev 1966b, Alpatov 1971). Rublev's icons differ quite distinctly from those of Theophanes the Greek. Although according to the chronicle Rublev worked with Theophanes in the Annunciation Cathedral, his art shows no sign of influence from the senior master. Rublev's icons link up directly with Constantinopolitan painting in Palaeologan times. The resemblance is so close that Gervase Mathew, the distinguished connoisseur of Byzantine icon-painting, (1963:39, n.2) considered Rublev's Old Testament Trinity to be "most probably" a Constantinopolitan work of about the year 1400.

Rublev's icons are distinguishable by almost unnoticeable but significant departures from the traditional iconographical schemata. Slight alterations and shifts in the formal patterns have produced crucial shifts on the semantic level. These semantic shifts are particularly distinct in Rublev's depictions of the Transfiguration and in the Raising of Lazarus, both from the iconostasis of the Church of the Annunciation, and in his Old Testament Trinity.

The motif of the Transfiguration icon is the story in Matthew 17 about the transfiguration of Jesus in the presence of Peter, James, and John, whom he had taken with him to the mountain which in the Orthodox tradition has been identified as Tabor: "And [he] was transfigured before them: and his face did shine as the sun, and his raiment was white as the light. And, behold, there appeared unto them Moses and Elias talking with him."

The traditional schema for this icon catches the dramatic moment when the frightened disciples fall on their faces and a bright cloud has overshadowed them while a voice out of the cloud says: "This is my beloved Son, in whom I am well pleased; hear ye him."

A comparison between Rublev's Transfiguration icon and a roughly contemporary depiction of the same motif in an icon from Pereslavl-Zalesskij, today attributed to the school of Theophanes the Greek, shows how the common schema may be varied and imbued with a different ideological content. The Pereslavl-Zalesskij icon depicts the dazzlingly white figure of Christ set in an equally dazzling radiance of white light emanating from a circular background of shimmering blue in the upper half of the picture. On each side of Christ, but outside the circle of light, we find Moses and Elias in conversation with Christ, while the Apostles in the lower half of the picture are represented as hiding their faces in terror at the blinding blue light beams radiating from the circular source of light behind Christ. This light signals the invisible divine presence in the same way as do the highlights in Theophanes' Novgorod frescoes. It represents the Godhead as absolutely transcendent and inscrutable in its relation to mankind. This is not in accordance with the Palamite idea of Christ's transfigured body as "source of the light of grace" (Meyendorff 1964:151). The figure of Christ of the Pereslavl icon emerges in the space between God and men, and the figure itself has no intermediary function between the two planes.

In Rublev's icon, on the other hand, there is no antinomy between light and darkness, no psychological drama. The light does not emanate from a hidden source, but infuses the whole picture, which receives its light from the transfigured Christ, whose body is represented against an almost black, star-like background and inscribed in a dark green, mandorla-like circle, so that Christ no longer reflects the light, but is light. Rublev's Christocentrism is also conveyed in the portrayal of Moses and Elias, the representatives of the Law and the prophets. In this painting they are not outside the circle, but inscribed in its upper half, bending towards its centre. They are thus connected with the central figure of Christ and combined into a rhythmic whole overarching the Apostles. The opposition between the divine and the human planes has been resolved in a harmonious totality, where light and darkness are no longer contradictory forces, but where darkness yields to the radiance suffusing the Apostles at the foot of the mountain.

The icon of the Transfiguration does not represent the only case where Rublev emphasises the Christocentric aspect of the traditional motifs through a discreet alteration of the schemata. His depiction of the Raising of Lazarus perhaps conveys an even better idea of how he transformed his prototypes and of the significance of this transformation for the spiritual content of the picture.

In the traditional schema, the infidel Jews are centrally placed in the raising of Lazarus. The latter appears in the entrance to the grave, on the right-hand side of the picture, Christ is to the left, with Martha and Mary at his feet and the disciples behind him. One or two minor figures remove the stone from the grave. Occasionally, the Jews may be pushed away from the centre, or they may be absent, as on the Vasilevskij doors in Novgorod (1336), where a single figure with his nose covered by a cloth represents the whole group of infidels (see Onasch 1961:365, n.40).

Rublev in his depiction of this motif regrouped the figures, so that Christ is to be found in the centre of the picture, with the Apostles placed between Him and Lazarus, the traditional place for the Jews, who are now to be found behind the figure of Christ. Rublev's execution of the Raising of Lazarus has often been praised for its rhythmic arrangement of the figures around Christ as the centre of the whole composition (e.g., Lazarev 1966b:20, Alpatov 1971:33). The iconological significance of the regrouping was, however, realised only in Plugin's analysis of the picture (1974:61ff.). By placing Christ in the middle and the Apostles in the space between Him and Lazarus, and by pushing the unbelievers into the periphery, the artist has shifted the accent from the miracle towards the significance of the event for the Apostles. The central motif is no longer the effect of the miracle on the unbelievers. It now refers to the answer given by Jesus earlier on in the story, when he says to the Apostles: "Lazarus is dead. And I am glad for your sakes that I was not there, to the intent ye may believe." The idea that the raising of Lazarus took place for the sake of the Apostles is not elaborated in the Gospel. In the Orthodox tradition, however, as observed by Plugin (1974:64), there existed an interpretation of the event as Christ's own forewarning to the Apostles of His impending death and resurrection. As an example of this reading of the story, Plugin cites the following commentary from Clement of Okhrid: "With this miracle He wished to confirm His disciples, more than the people, in the faith, thus announcing His own resurrection." Rublev's icon gives expression to the same idea. The story of Lazarus is seen as a prefiguration of the death and resurrection of Christ.

The rearrangement of Jews and Apostles in relation to Christ is not the only departure from the conventional iconographic schema which has relevance for the semantic content of Rublev's icon. An equally radical breach with the schema is to be found in the representation of Lazarus.

His white grave-clothes are not outlined against the black entrance to the grave, as in older icons and, indeed, in later copies of Rublev's picture. In the icon from the Church of the Annunciation he is depicted in a radiance hiding the darkness of the grave and suffusing his whiteclad figure. The "Glory of God," by which "the Son of God might be glorified"—those are the words of Jesus in the story—shines in Rublev's icon around the resurrected Lazarus and not around Christ himself, who is the centre of the picture and its source of light. Lazarus emerges as a *figura Christi* and an image of the deification of man after the example of Christ. In this way Rublev has given form to the meaning of Christ's impending death. His figure is the compositional centre of the picture. It is to Him, and not to Lazarus, that the Apostles turn, when through His miracle He has revealed to them the meaning of His Passion.

The climax of Rublev's Christocentric symbolism is his Old-Testament Trinity, which Lazarev (1966b:135f.) has dated to 1411, relating it to the building of the wooden church above the grave of Saint Sergius, and other scholars have dated to the 1420s, when a stone church was built in the same place. Both churches were consecrated to the Holy Trinity, and the icon is believed to have been a festival icon fixed in place in the lowest register of the iconostasis. The motif is the so-called Old-Testament Trinity, which goes back to the story of the three angels visiting Abraham and Sarah in the plains of Mamre (Genesis 18). This story was early construed as a prefiguration of the coming of Christ, and even in Byzantine times became part of the Church's iconographic programme. One of the earliest extant depictions of the motif is in a mosaic in San Vitale in Ravenna, dating from the first half of the sixth century. The earliest version of the icon is known as "Philoxenia." It depicts the hospitality of Abraham. The narrative element is predominant. The picture recapitulates the course of events in the Biblical story about the three angels appearing to Abraham. Besides this narrative version another variant of the icon developed, where the emphasis is on the dogma of the Holy Trinity. A pre-Rublevian example of this variant in Russian art is Theophanes the Greek's Trinity fresco in Novgorod. The figures of Abraham and Sarah are here still part of the picture, although Abraham has since been obliterated. But in Theophanes' strictly hierarchic composition they have become minor figures in the lower part of the picture. Attention is focused on the three angels, who in turn are portrayed in hierarchic order: the largest angel is enthroned in the middle, high above the other two, who are placed underneath his powerful wingspan. In accordance with the whole of Theophanes' pictorial theology, his Trinity group is an illustration of the antinomy between high divinity and low humanity.

Rublev has departed even farther from the original Philoxenia motif than did Theophanes. All the narrative elements have disappeared:

Abraham and Sarah waiting on the visitors, the tableware, the exquisite dishes and similar paraphernalia have become superfluous. The artist has kept only the elements that possess symbolic significance: the three heavenly guests, each with a halo and a sceptre, the chalice on the table, and in the background a rock, a tree, and a church. According to Lazarev (1966b:35), Rublev's Trinity icon is modelled on a Panhagia icon, in which the three figures are inscribed in the circular shape of the Panhagia. In Rublev, however, the figures are no longer mechanically subordinate to the circular form. The circle is invisibly present as a dynamic principle behind the representation of the angels. Alpatov (1971:114) refers to the circle as the "basic theme" of the picture. By letting the purple tunic and the azure mantle of the middle angel be reflected in the pink, sky-blue, and shimmering green colouring in the clothing of his companions, Rublev has subtly expressed the dogma that the three are one in essence and in nature, united in divine love. Together they form a hypostatisation of the force which moves the universe, and which is present in the picture in the form of the invisible circle, the integrative principle of the icon:

> l'amor che move il sole e l'altre stelle
> (Dante, Paradiso XXXIII:145)

The symbolism in Rublev's Trinity icon in many ways corresponds to the symbolism in Dante's *Divine Comedy*. Demina (1963:44) has suggested a common source in Christian Neo-Platonism. Like Dante's work, Rublev's icon is polysemous, and may be read in a way similar to the one we have applied to Nestor's *Life of Saint Theodosius* (see Alpatov 1967:119-126, Børtnes 1970).

On the literal semantic level Rublev's icon is a representation of the Biblical story of the three angels appearing to Abraham in the plains of Mamre. This level is subordinate to the others. On the anagogical level the icon is an image of the eternal *synousia* and perfect harmony of the triune Godhead in its heavenly glory. This transcendent being is shown symbolically by having the circular movement set in an octagon, outlined in the contours of the footstools, the rock, and the church. This geometric figure is traditionally a symbol of eternity and the new aeon. The centre of the circular movement is the chalice on the table between the angels. The four semantic levels of the picture meet in this centre. On the historical or literal level the chalice represents the festival meal set before the visitors by Abraham and Sarah. On the figural, mythical level of meaning, the chalice is a prefiguration of Christ's sacrificial death, the cup of Suffering; tropologically it is the cup of Grace and a symbol of the Eucharist, when the Christian shares in the divine nature of Christ. Thus it becomes also the cup of Life and an anagogical symbol of eternal life. Between the chalice and the central angel the artist has established a compositional relationship, repeating the shape of the chalice in the contours of the table, as they are outlined in the space between the lateral figures. By the same token this enlarged chalice becomes a reflection of the central angel.

Which of the three hypostases of the Holy Trinity does the central angel represent? Lazarev (1959) contends that he is Christ, the second person of the Godhead, wearing as he does the golden *clavus*, the Christ symbol, over his right shoulder. Demina (1963:52) has identified the central angel with the Father, on a comparison with the so-called Zyrian Trinity that Stephen of Perm, according to tradition, brought to the Zyrians in the 1370s, and where the initials of the individual persons have been added above the angels.

Alpatov (1967:121) has with some justification maintained that these attempts to identify the individual persons of the Holy Trinity run counter to the artist's intentions, which were not primarily aimed at defining the differences between them, but which on the contrary intended to show that they constitute an inseparable, indivisible unity.

Against the background of the Christocentrism which is expressed in Rublev's other icons, the question is still not without its significance for our understanding of the picture. It seems to me that Lazarev's argument is based on the safest criterion. The golden *clavus* is a codified symbol of Christ. Demina's comparison can be interpreted both ways from what we know about Rublev's independent attitude to the traditional schemes in his other pictures. The comparison may equally well be used to show how Rublev has departed from the schema, whereas the Zyrian Trinity icon represents the figures traditionally, with the Father in the middle, the Son on His right, and the Holy Spirit on His left. This is also how the figures have been depicted in a Greek Trinity icon, probably from the end of the fourteenth century, now in the Hermitage (Bank 1965:276–277). Here the golden *clavus* is not worn by the central angel, but by the angel on his right, by the Son.

The transference of the golden *clavus* to the central angel must be construed as one of Rublev's intentional departures from traditional schemes. It makes Christ, the second of the three hypostases, the compositional and semantic centre of the icon.

At the same time, the other two hypostases of the Trinity are present in His figure, in conformity with Orthodox teaching about unity without confusion, between the three hypostases of one and the same Godhead, about their reciprocal being in one another without any change or loss of identity (see Pelikan 1974:77). The two angels flanking the central angel reflect the colours of his clothing and form different variations of the same circular theme. The expressive gestures of the angels converge on the centre of the chalice, as if we were witnessing a *sacra conversazione* between the Father, the Son, and the Holy Ghost about the eternal mystery of the Incarnation, when "God became man in order that we should be deified," in the words of Saint Athanasius.

# Sainthood and Subversion:
# The *Life* of the Archpriest Avvakum and
# Russian Literature in the
# Seventeenth Century

## Russian Literature in the Seventeenth Century:
## A Historiographical Problem

One of the most confusing periods in the history of Russian literature is the period of transition in the seventeenth century, when the Muscovite tradition gave way to a literature modelled on Western European genres.

It was all fairly simple as long as the reforms of Peter the Great were regarded as the dividing line between two different cultures, and the transition might be defined through the opposition of pre- and post-Petrine: on the one hand the Middle Ages and "Byzantinism," on the other hand "Enlightenment," "Europeanism," and literary "Classicism." But historians have long since demonstrated that Peter's reforms did not occur spontaneously. They were prepared for by a long process, stretching throughout the seventeenth century. From being a medieval "feudal" society, the state of Muscovy was turned into an autocratic, multinational Russian empire. According to some scholars, this process started as early as with Ivan IV's *opričnina*, which was not merely an instrument of political terror, but a kind of scale model of the state, in which he tested the problems of a transition to a modern autocracy (Onasch 1967:49). In the time of upheavals that followed, up to Peter the Great, the period which Ključevskij (1956:33f.) called *Rus' Velikaja, Moskovskaja, carsko-bojarskaja, voenno-zemlevladel'českaja*, was transformed into *period vserossijskij, imperatorskij, period krepostnogo khozjajstva, zemledel'českogo i fabrično-zavodskogo*.

In accordance with this view of a gradual transition and not a rupture, Stender-Petersen tried to redefine the concepts of Byzantinism and Europeanism, by regarding seventeenth-century literature as the result of an ideological struggle, in which this conceptual pair symbolises a profound historical divide between earlier and later literature:

> The ideological struggle between Byzantium and Western Europe, whose eventual outcome was only clearly acknowledged by the leading Russian intellectuals of the eighteenth century, in actual fact took place even in the seventeenth century. This was primarily reflected in the fact that the Western European genres, based on the classical Roman heritage, gained a foothold in Russia, and that drama, poetry, and prose, seen as separate aesthetic concepts, displaced the early Russian and Byzantine homiletic, hagiographical, and annalistic genres. The age of the liberal arts was at hand. (1952:229)

Stender-Petersen's scheme might have become a useful point of departure for a revaluation of the history of Russian literature in the seventeenth century. Already in the above quotation we see, however, how the divide between Western European and early Russian genres, between the classical and the Byzantine legacy, is regarded as absolute: one system superseded another. All attention is drawn to the final outcome of the ideological conflicts of the seventeenth century, to Russian classicism, romanticism, and realism (see Stender-Petersen 1952:VI). Seventeenth-century literature itself, on the other hand, remains "a colourful play, not without suspense, but devoid of any consciously leading idea and hence to some degree unsystematic and chaotic" (Stender-Petersen 1952:228).

If we exchange Stender-Petersen's diachronic point of view on extant seventeenth-century literature for a synchronic one, we shall see that the struggle between the opposing ideologies of the time led not only to a final victory for the European genres, but also that the struggle above all manifested itself in a literary activity marked by tensions, insoluble antinomies, breaches with tradition, extreme conservatism, desperation at the loss of any fixed values, a confusion of genres, and a predilection for hybrid forms.

The earlier homiletic, hagiographical, and annalistic genres coexist with the first syllabic verse poetry on Polish models, with translated novels of chivalry, with translations from Polish of medieval Latin stories in such popular anthologies as the *Gesta romanorum* and the *Speculum magnum,* with the first Russian plays, modelled on the Jesuit school drama, with the first records of Russian folklore, with the first extant parodies and satires on the official ideology and its literary forms. In the seventeenth century a literature of religious protest comes into being among the Old Believers, the schismatics (*raskol'niki*) who broke away from the official Church after the decrees issued by the Patriarch Nikon early in 1653.

This rich variety will seem unsystematic and chaotic on the theory of an opposition between early Russian literature and a literature that follows classical models. In the first place such a scheme takes no account of the transformation of early Russian genres that went on at this period, and second, it leads to an underrating of the fact that Western European literature of the time reached Russia mainly via Poland, the Ukraine, and White Russia, and through the intermediary of the Jesuit school system.

In connection with the Catholic reconquest of Poland and the attempts to gain a foothold in the West Russian lands under Polish suzerainty at the end of the sixteenth and the beginning of the seventeenth centuries, the Jesuits founded a number of schools and academies in these areas. Gradually the new learning spread to the Orthodox clergy as well. In the beginning they had reacted with bitter opposition, but subsequently adapted the Jesuit curriculum in their own schools, which enabled them to continue to fight the Roman Church with the weapons of the enemy.

From a literary point of view, the most remarkable event in the first phase of this process is the polemic between the Ukrainian Athonite, Ivan Vyšens'kyj, and the first head of the Jesuit Academy at Vilnius, Peter Skarga, about the year 1600. The second phase culminated in the founding of the Mogilian Academy in Kiev in 1630 or 1631, named after its founder, the Metropolitan Petr Mogila. The Academy became a centre for the propagation of a new, slavicised version of the cultural programme of the Counter-Reformation, to which the Muscovites later turned for teaching staff when, around the middle of the century, they realised that they too could not dispense with the new culture. The Western European genres thus reached Moscow in the form they had received during the Counter-Reformation.

Against this historical background several attempts have been made to define seventeenth-century Russian literature as a version of a Slavonic, and in a wider context European, Baroque.

Although the theory about a Russian seventeenth-century Baroque was put forward as early as the 1930s, it is still much disputed. The theory has, however, proved useful in the works of scholars like Angyal, Tschiževskij, and Morozov, who by defining the Baroque as an *Epochenstil*—the style of an epoch—have tried to show how this style became manifest on all levels of cultural life within the given period, and how in literature the Baroque is not merely a formal concept, but a concept referring to content as well. Historically, the Baroque, as these scholars see it, constitutes a synthesis of the Renaissance and the Middle Ages (see Tschiževskij 1952:57).

Although this definition of the Baroque may easily cause history to be perceived as a predetermined sequence of changing stylistic epochs—it has accordingly been heavily criticised for its schematism (Likhačev 1967:68ff.)—the theory has proved useful in establishing points of similarity between Russian literature and other Slavonic, as well as Western European, literatures in the transitional period between the

Middle Ages and modern times. Such a definition, based on analogies, has proved less useful in defining the *differentia specifica* of individual works and national literatures. Tschižewskij (1956b:312) ends up by characterising Russian literature in the seventeenth century as an offshoot of the Ukrainian.

Angyal (1961) tries to differentiate by means of dual concepts such as "Gothic Baroque," "Humanist Baroque," etc. For the Muscovite Baroque, Morozov (1962) has tried to demonstrate how the Jesuit Baroque in its *Drang nach Osten* underwent continual change as the result of its confrontation with Greek-Orthodox and old Muscovite traditions. This approach has enabled Morozov to establish a certain coherence in seventeenth-century Russian literature, not only in relation to Polish and West Russian prototypes, but also in relation to Russian literature in the following century.

The West Russian influence in Moscow reached its greatest extent under Tsar Alexis Romanov (reigned 1645–1676), when the Ukraine and White Russia were separated from Poland and came under Moscow.

Concurrently with the creation of a new East Slav empire went the work of removing the differences between Moscow and Kiev in the liturgy and church books of the Orthodox Church. While Moscow had by the middle of the fifteenth century broken away from Byzantium and developed its own Orthodox tradition in "splendid isolation" from the other Church communities within the Orthodox *oikoumene*, the Orthodox Church in Lithuania had kept up its link with the Greek tradition, even after the creation of its own metropolitanate in Kiev, about the time when Muscovite isolation commenced. Ukrainian Orthodoxy had also received important stimuli from Western European Protestantism and Catholicism.

The initiator in the effort to bring the Muscovite Church out of its isolation was the Patriarch Nikon, who in 1652 was elected head of the Russian Church. His career was a remarkable one. He came of peasant stock from the Nižnij Novgorod region, born and bred not far from the home village of his later adversary, the Archpriest Avvakum.

In Russia, Nikon is the Baroque church prince *par excellence*. Alexis was only sixteen when he succeeded his father on the throne. With the tsar so young, Nikon acquired almost unlimited power during the first few years of the reign. This was especially so because he gained the tsar's trust, and at the end of the 1640s, after having first been abbot of the Romanov family's Novospasskij Monastery, he was appointed Metropolitan of Novgorod.

At the beginning of 1653 Nikon issued his decrees ordering a number of changes in liturgy and ritual. These changes formed part of his attempt to bring Muscovite liturgy into line with West Russian traditions. It was, for instance, decreed that the Muscovites were now to make the sign of the cross with three fingers, instead of two, as before.

This was soon to become the object of a bitter conflict between the official Church and the leaders of the *Raskol*, who refused to comply with Nikon's orders and chose instead to adhere to their "old belief" in open opposition to Nikon and his representatives.

As patriarch, Nikon also immediately went ahead with the task of consolidating the Church's position of power *vis-à-vis* the service nobility, which, in the course of the first half of the century, had become the leading stratum of Muscovite society. With Tsar Alexis' Code of 1649—the *Uloženie*-the service nobility had acquired a new weapon in their endeavours to secularise the property of the Church and make an end to her legal independence. In this situation Nikon took up the idea that it is the Church's supreme shepherd and not the Tsar who is God's vicegerent in this earthly life, and he fought under the watchword *svjaščenstvo vyše carstva* (Kapterev 1912:545f.). Nikon had thus modelled his church policy on that of Joseph of Volokolamsk and the Metropolitan Cyprian in a way which might indicate that his ultimate objective was to transform the Moscow Patriarchate into a power centre on the pattern of the Papacy in Rome. This policy failed. When in 1658 he demonstrated against the Tsar by leaving the Patriarchate, contrary to his expectations he was not recalled. This was a triumph for the absolute monarchy and for the service nobility. From then on the Tsar was *de facto* head of the Church. With the abolition of the Patriarchate under Peter the Great, the Russian Church also formally became subordinate to the state.

In the 1650s, and still in the early 60s, Nikon was an energetic builder, founding a number of churches and monasteries as visible signs of the power of the Church. One instance of Nikon's building activity was his own residence, the Monastery of the New Jerusalem, on the river Istra. With the Church of the Holy Sepulchre as its centre, and places like Gethsemane and the Plains of Mamre nearby, the whole layout was meant as a topographical *figura*, an image of Jerusalem, and doubtless also a prefiguration of the eternal Jerusalem. Nikon regarded himself as the vicar of Christ on earth and, as Russian Patriarch, head of Orthodox Christendom (Kapterev 1912:546).

Nikon's church, built by West Russian craftsmen, is, however, no direct copy of the twelfth-century Church of the Holy Sepulchre in Jerusalem, but a combination of Russo-Byzantine and West Russian sacred architecture, even though Nikon had received a scale model of the church in Jerusalem from its patriarch, Paisios, when abbot of the Novospasskij Monastery, and had probably also seen a reproduction of it in Bernardino Amico's book, which was well known in Moscow at the time (Il'in 1959:167ff.). Nikon let his idea of the patriarchal residence as an image of the Heavenly Jerusalem materialise in an architecture distinguished by the admixture of elements from the new West Russian Baroque.

In Nikon's monastery the Vulgate was read in a Polish translation, and the Psalms of David in a free Polish rendering. Poetry was written, too, on Polish models, and with the aid of Jesuit handbooks. A particular hymnodic poetry was developed, Baroque in form as well as in content, with a predilection for allegory and *carmina curiosa* (Pozdneev 1961).

The centre of this Russian Baroque poetry based on Western models in the second half of the seventeenth century was not, however, Nikon's monastery, but the court of the Tsars, where the new style reached its peak after Nikon's defeat at the hands of the secular powers.

The adaptation of Polish and West Russian Baroque poetry as an ideological medium for the new absolutist empire is clearly to be seen in the works of Simeon Polockij (1629–1680), Alexis' court poet and the most important representative of the Baroque "imperial style" in seventeenth-century Russian literature.

An instance of Simeon's panegyric style is his *Orel Rossijskij—The Russian Eagle*—presented to the Tsar and his son Alexis on the occasion when the tsarevitch was proclaimed heir to the throne.

*Orel Rossijskij* is one of the five great occasional poems composed by Simeon as court poet. The poem, which still awaits publication, has been described by Smirnov (1915) and by Eremin (1966:211–233).

In the magnificent manuscript presented to the Tsar, Simeon bursts the framework of the pure verbal artifice. The poem is there to be seen as well as heard. Some passages take the form of geometric figures, the verbal imagery is supplemented by polychrome illustrations, and the manuscript as such acquires the character of a "verbal-architectonic composition" (Eremin 1966:214).

Its centre is a representation of the starry sky with the sun in its middle, radiating forty-eight beams of light. Each beam inscribes one of the Tsar's virtues. In the foreground we see the crowned two-headed eagle with sceptre and orb in its claws. The sign of the zodiac encompasses these emblems, adding illuminations to the text. A columnar ode praising the Tsar carries the whole structure (Eremin 1966:214).

Among the most frequent verbal images in Simeon's panegyric poetry are the sun and the eagle. Both emblems have a long tradition, in Western European as well as in Russo-Byzantine imperial iconography. In general, Simeon has taken over the whole stock of conventional metaphors and similes from the official panegyric, and his poetry becomes a veritable museum of allegorical animals, stones, and plants, well-known from the encyclopedias, Bestiaries, and Lapidaries of the Middle Ages.

This variety of conventional rhetorical tropes leads to an imagery where on the one hand the same image may have different meanings, depending on the context, whereas on the other hand a number of different images may have the same meaning. Instances of the former are the sun—now designating Tsar Alexis and Christ, now the tsarevitch Alexis and Tsar Fedor; the moon—in one passage referring to the Tsarina, in another to the arch-enemy the Turks; and the stars—now representing the daughters of the Tsar, now the Russian cities. Instances of the latter method are seen in the Christ-metaphors such as vessel, sea, mirror, stone, vine, lion, and the bird Phoenix, all of which may denote Christ.

Eremin (1966:211–233) explains this metaphorisation as "an analogy on the similarity between secondary, coincidental features." A word denoting an animal may for instance come to designate a property closely related to the *denotatum* (semantic contiguity). The result is a synecdochic figure: "lion" may thus signify one of the qualities of a lion, for example, "courage." In its turn, this synecdoche may function as a metaphorical paraphrase of another being, provided with a similar quality. In its extreme form this technique is typical of the Baroque *concetto*, as when Simeon says that Christ "may also be called an herb because of the purity of his flesh."

What is new in Simeon's similes and metaphors is the fact that ornamental Russian rhetoric and Russo-Byzantine imperial ideology are combined with syllabic verses on Polish models, with the Ukrainian, rather Baroque version of Church Slavonic, and with tropes and figures taken over from ancient and contemporary Western European rhetoric. Traditional Russian glorification formulae are amplified by means of elements taken from Baroque ruler-iconography: a whole repository of ancient gods, muses, heroes, authors, and philosophers make their entry into Russian literature. In the *Orel Rossijskij* they all occur—Apollo and the Muses, Greek and Roman authors—but in a lamentably non-classical context: Thalia quotes the Song of Solomon; in a monologue Apollo expresses his doubts as to the ability of the Muses to compose a eulogy worthy of the tsarevitch, a task that even Athena, Homer, Vergil, Ovid, Cicero, and Aristotle would have been unable to fulfil. Only "celestial singers" would be able to describe the effulgence of this new "sun" in the Russian sky.

The gods and authors of Antiquity have been torn out of their historical context and given a purely ornamental function. The mythological representation of reality by means of classical and Biblical symbols in apparent but uneasy harmony is a distinctive feature of the Baroque. However, in Simeon the symbols have lost their humanist connotations and become subordinate to the allegorical glorification of the Russian Tsar.

By adapting the West Russian school Baroque into a medium for absolutist ruler-ideology, Simeon has laid the foundation for an occasional poetry that was continued in the works of his pupil, Silvester Medvedev, and further developed by Theophanes Prokopovič, Peter the Great's court poet. It culminated in the odes of Lomonosov. The concept of the Baroque thus enables us to uncover a connection between pre- and post-Petrine literature. This literary development from Kievo-Mogilian to Petersburg Baroque has a parallel in architecture: from Muscovite Baroque on Polish and Ukrainian models in the second half of the seventeenth century to the masterpieces of Rastrelli the Younger, a contemporary of Lomonosov. It is the new imperial style of Russia that manifests itself in two different media.

The concept of the Baroque has proved more useful than that of classicism for the understanding of the literature that grew up in the second half of the seventeenth century, when the victorious absolutist ideology was shaped. The question is, however, whether the concept of the Baroque is applicable to the study of genres other than the panegyric, for example to the literature of the Time of Troubles (*smuta*), to the satires, parodies, and novellas from the second half of the century, and to the *Life of Avvakum*.

In the debate about the Russian Baroque we have here struck a sensitive nerve. Angyal sees the whole of the seventeenth century in the light of the Baroque. He emphasises (1961:61ff.) the affinity between Avvakum's *Life,* Comenius' *Labyrinth,* Grimmelshausen's picaresque *Simplicissimus,* and Descartes' *Dream.* Without applying the concept of the Baroque, Gudzij (1966:422) has connected the predominance of the demonological element in seventeenth-century Russian hagiography to influence from *Speculum magnum* and similar works. According to Morozov (1967:116) this Western influence has affected the creation of works as different as Simeon Polockij's *Vertograd Mnogocvetnyj* and the *Life of Avvakum.* Tschiževskij (1970:13) maintains that the tales of Frol Skobeev and Savva Grudcyn "in their kind correspond to the Western novella literature of the Baroque."

The dangers of this kind of comparison are that although it can establish similarities, it cannot explain the differences. If Russian Baroque is to include Simeon Polockij's panegyric as well as Avvakum's *Life,* it will be necessary to work out differentiating criteria. The adherents of the Baroque theory are here faced with the same dilemma as Stender-Petersen: how to explain the antinomies in seventeenth-century Russian literature.

Morozov (1962) tried to solve the problem through the definition of the Baroque as a style in which apparent dichotomies are polar oppositions within the same system, due to the clash between West Russian and Byzanto-Muscovite traditions. In his conception Simeon and Avvakum represent "opposite poles in Russian seventeenth-century Baroque literature, but not fundamentally different phenomena." This polar definition of Russian Baroque is Morozov's most important theoretical contribution to our understanding of seventeenth-century literary life in Russia. He does not, however, seem to be fully aware of its implications. When it comes to the point, the two versions of the

Baroque—works "closely related to West Slav (especially Polish) and Ukrainian Baroque tradition" on the one hand, and on the other a "Baroque on Russian, national soil"—are characterised independently of each other, despite the suggestions of a common stylistic system.

The reasons for this shortcoming must be sought in Morozov's comparative method, which moves along the surface of a work, hunting for typically Baroque features. This method takes it for granted that similarities between works of art and national literatures within a given epoch are due to the same spiritual and stylistic trends and influences. The danger of this method is seen in the endless accumulations of typical characteristics, detached from the context, to which it leads. It is too easily forgotten that these characteristics may have different functions in different literatures. Eventually it may turn out that they are not even exclusively typical of the Baroque. Occasionally, they may, without difficulty, be traced in works of other periods as well.

We may take as an example the features in the *Life of Avvakum* that Morozov (1967:121) has stressed as being Baroque: the allegoric representation of reality, the painterly quality of the portraiture, the combination of everyday, naturalist details with the fantastic, an incipient feeling for landscape, and the admixture of vulgarisms in the written language. Apart from the depiction of scenery, all these features are quite common in both Russian and Western literature of the Middle Ages, and Likhačev (1973:210) has no difficulty in refuting Morozov's attempt to define the *Life of Avvakum* as a work of the Baroque by means of these criteria.

In this way Morozov's idea of the Baroque may be criticised on the grounds of methodological shortcomings, without his critics ever having to enter into the essence of his definition of Russian Baroque literature as two polar variants within the same system.

The bipolar character of Russian Baroque is further developed by Svetla Mathauserová (1968) in an attempt that abandons any comparison of isolated stylistic features. She takes instead her point of departure in the "ontological problematic of the Baroque":

> The prevailing social conditions played a major part in the growth of the Baroque style, where the general atmosphere of the time, what may be called its *crisis-atmosphere*, became manifest. Although the historical roots were different, the excited atmosphere in Russia was not unlike that in Western Europe. Even the beginning of the seventeenth century arrived with unheard-of upheavals. A runaway monk mounted the throne of the Tsars, the old boyar aristocracy gave way to the lower nobility, the people rebelled in both the towns and in the country, the Poles tried to grasp the Russian throne, Orthodoxy was threatened through the candidacy of the Polish Prince, and the country was now defended by a peasant army and

heroes sprung from the people, instead of those of myth. Faced with the new reality, where nothing—throne, property, social classes, moral and social values—remained static, the old dogmas came to seem meaningless and were ground between the millstones of the new reality. A new epoch appears where the medieval world view is annihilated and many a legend comes to an end: the one of Moscow as the Third Rome and the definitive centre of Christianity in the world, the legend of a self-redeeming Orthodoxy, and of the perpetual division into masters and servants, of the infallibility and suzerainty of the Church. That world fell apart, and all the truths of yesterday turned out to have been mere assumptions. The meaningful divine hierarchy collapsed and faith in it was shaken in its foundations, with the consequence that all social values were relativised, the dichotomy of the society revealed. (1968:253)

The theory that the Time of Troubles forms not only a social and ideological divide in Russian history, but that the crisis also led to a distortion and shattering of the fifteenth- and sixteenth-century hagiographical and annalistic genres, and thereby to a Baroque end phase in early Russian literature, differs from the traditional view of this epoch.

The paucity of historical facts, and an exaggerated use of traditional rhetorical devices, are the common features usually emphasised in the literature of the *smuta*. This literature comprises works like the *Inoe skazanie*, Ivan Timofeev's *Vremennik*, the *Russkij khronograf* in its second redaction, Katyrev-Rostovskij's *Povest'*, Avraamij Palicyn's *Skazanie*, and the *Povest'* of Prince Šakhovskoj, all, with the exception of the *Inoe skazanie* (1606), written under Tsar Mikhail Fedorovič in the time following the long interregnum. A few new elements have been singled out at random, for example the influence in Katyrev-Rostovskij of Guido de Columna's Trojan novel, or an admixture of secular prose lyricism in Prince Šakhovskoj's "defunct theological rhetoric" (Stender-Petersen 1952:165). But generally scholars have been content to note that these works essentially continued the literary tradition that had found its final form by the middle of the sixteenth century (see Gudzij 1966:386).

The distortion of the traditional genres has admittedly been noted, but only in the negative:

One marvels at the art with which the writers spin their stylistic cobwebs around futilities merely in order to avoid having to say the important things which they may want to conceal; sometimes they are quite unable to render the content, this having to be moulded into the strict formulas firmly laid down by tradition. Except for these formulas there is nothing else. (Tschiževskij 1960:311)

This discrepancy between form and content is, according to Mathause-rová, a symptom of that crisis in early Russian culture which, in the middle of the century, led to a desperate struggle to restore totality, a struggle that resulted only in a deepening of the existing ideological antagonisms, and in the final analysis in the Schism of 1666, the division between the Old Believers and the supporters of a "window-opening towards Europe":

> Despite the great distance between Avvakum's clamour for the old Russia, and the definitive breach with it, the "opening of the window on Europe," *a common cultural basis* for both trends had to exist. If both these poles were thus able mutually to threaten each other, this might be evidence of the special style of the epoch called "the Baroque," which penetrated all aspects of culture, and dis-tinguished itself precisely in that it united what was contradictory and irreconcilable. (Mathauserová 1968:254)

With this approach we might have expected a presentation of seven-teenth-century Russian Baroque as a dialectical process, where con-tradictions mutually determine each other. Instead, Mathauserová, like Morozov, has chosen to put forward a hypothesis of "two Baroques," sprung from different traditions:

> 1. the indigenous, spontaneous one, which decomposes and questions the indigenous forms, which is destructive, created under a strong social pressure, contradictory, irrational, with a pre-dilection for myth, which expresses the loss of a fixed point, but which at the same time searches for another basis; 2. is rather derivatory, concluded, complete, and based on the textbooks of poetics, rationalistic, and inclined to mannerism. Thus in one and the same trend we find both elements prevalent in the German Baroque and the rationalist features of the French, classicist trend. (Mathauserová 1968:256)

An essential difference between Mathauserová's and Morozov's con-ceptions lies in the fact that while Morozov defines the relationship between the two versions of seventeenth-century Russian Baroque as a polarisation within the same system, Mathauserová aligns them in a diachronic sequence: one phase supersedes another. "Early Russian art ends in a 'Baroque' of its own, and in this transitional situation it be-comes open to an influence from mature forms of Baroque" (1968:259), that is, to the influence of the international Baroque. The national Baroque is defined as a transitional style between literature before the *smuta* and the poetry of Simeon Polockij. In other words, we might say that it fills the interval between the sixteenth-century Muscovite imperial style and the style of the new empire in the second half of the seventeenth century. The schema does not quite fit, for Mathauserová like Morozov regards Avvakum's *Life* as the highwater mark of the national Russian Baroque, although it was written as late as the 1670s, at the same time as Simeon Polockij composed his occasional poems to glorify the new tsardom.

Compared with Morozov's conception, Mathauserová's schema gains its significance primarily by drawing attention to the difference between early Russian literature before and after the *smuta*. In thus becomes possible to characterise the end phase of the early Russian genres in contrast to the official panegyric prevalent in Muscovite literature, as this had evolved from word-weaving. This official literature was deformed and burst from within, as the authors of the *smuta* literature changed to first-person narrative, to what Mathauserová calls a "monological mode of expression". The difference between the literature before and after the *smuta* is no longer defined purely stylistically, but more as a trans-formation of the old genre system. With this opposition between the older, heroic "epicism" and the new, non-epic forms, the whole concept of the Baroque is called in question. Likhačev (1970) has taken a further step in this direction and categorically rejected the use of the Baroque in connection with the end phase in early Russian literature, reserving this term for the trend represented by Simeon Polockij (1973:165–214). At the same time, Likhačev has given us a new reading of the literature of the *smuta*, a reinterpretation of its historical and aesthetic value that differs sharply from the negative assessment of traditional scholarship.

Likhačev (1970:6–24) starts by reminding us of the role of this literature in the works of Russian historians, from Karamzin to Solov'ev, Ključevskij and Platonov. It was in this literature that they found the material for their portrayals of Ivan the Terrible, Boris Godunov, the False Demetrius, the Patriarch Hermogen, and other "strong characters" from the Time of Troubles. Karamzin, who with his romantic view of history was primarily preoccupied with precisely "the character of our old heroes," held the chapter on Ivan the Terrible to be the summit of his history, while the period before appeared to him as an "African sand steppe" (see Likhačev 1970:6). A similar view, cited by Likhačev (1970:6f.), was expressed by Ključevskij (1957:49):

The historical documents from the fourteenth and fifteenth centu-ries offer no possibility of reproducing the physiognomies of the individual Grand Princes in a lifelike way. The Muscovite Grand Princes emerge in these documents as rather pale figures. One fol-lows the other on the throne under the names of Ivan, Simeon, another Ivan, Dimitri, Basil, another Basil. On closer scrutiny it is easy to see that these are not distinctive individuals who are here filing past, but tiresome repetitions of one and the same family type.

> All Muscovite princes up to Ivan III resemble one another like two
> drops of water, so that the observer occasionally has difficulty in
> determining which of them is Ivan and which Basil.

Both Karamzin and Ključevskij begin their account of the "strong
characters" of Russian history with Ivan the Terrible. Karamzin's
portrayal of Groznyj became a model for a number of romantic Groznyj
portraits. Poets, musicians, and pictorial artists of the last century found
in the figures from the Time of Troubles a Russian parallel to
Shakespearean characters.

From a psychological as well as an historical point of view, this
sudden emergence of "strong characters" around 1600 is a puzzling
phenomenon. Could it really be true that the contrast between the
monotonous repetition of one and the same ruler-type of previous texts,
and the complex characters like, for instance, the *smuta* literature's
representation of Boris Godunov, was historically based? The question
does not seem to have engaged scholars until Deržavina (1946) put
forward the theory that Russian authors at the beginning of the
seventeenth century for the first time began to ponder the contradictions
of human character, whereas the writers of previous centuries represented the individual either as a vehicle of God's will or as a tool of
the devil. Against this theory, and starting from the accounts undertaken
by Russian historians, Likhačev (1970) offered his reinterpretation of the
*smuta* literature, on the hypothesis that the strong characters emerging
in Russian history about the year 1600 were primarily a literary
phenomenon and a problem belonging to the theory of literature.

In their accounts of the *smuta*, Russian historians followed the
descriptions given in sixteenth-century literature of the men of the
period, paraphrasing the ruler-portraits found in memoir literature.
Thus nineteenth-century historians reproduced in their works the
image of man they found in their sources. This image differs from the
abstract idealisation of preceding epochs. But like this, the new complex
image of man cannot be explained solely with reference to those
historical persons on whom it was based. These ruler-portraits, too,
must be understood with the help of the literary method and ideological
presuppositions of their authors.

The memoir writers of the Time of Troubles discovered the possibility
of representing historical personalities as *complex characters*. The fundamental feature of this new image of man is the abolition of the absolute contrast between good and evil, between the sinners and the
righteous, typical of the epic hero worship of earlier Muscovite
chronicles and hagiography.

The new trends appear first to have come into evidence in the second
redaction of the *Russkij khronograf* (1617). This version contains a
number of significant differences from the earlier redaction of 1512. Its

author no longer interprets historical events by means of references to Holy Scripture. Western European history has been brought in, along with Biblical history, and that of Byzantium. Knowledge about Western Europe has typically been gleaned from Polish chronicles recently translated into Russian, a fact that incidentally shows the Western influence to be well under way at the beginning of the seventeenth century.

The secular trend is brought out also in the portrayal of contemporary leaders like Ivan the Terrible and Boris Godunov. In the picture of Groznyj the contradictions are still explained diachronically. The author relies on descriptions given by others, in particular on that of Prince Kurbskij. The change, or turn, in Groznyj's character is marked by an event that according to Kurbskij radically altered the Tsar's behaviour: the early death of the Tsarina Anastasia. Prior to this event he is represented as a wise and brave ruler, only to be changed after it into a cruel tyrant who finally murders his own son. The psychological interpretation of the Tsar's character marks, as it were, the transition from the ideal of the epically detached, sublime ruler of earlier Muscovite literature to the ruler-portraits of the *smuta*, whose authors try to represent the characters as their contemporaries and explain their actions as products of an internalised struggle between good and evil.

The contrasting technique is fully developed in the accounts of Boris Godunov. As the author of the *Russkij khronograf* turns to Boris, he also passes on to a character-drawing where good and bad qualities no longer mutually exclude each other, but form a syndrome, modifying each other and creating a dramatic conflict. This conflict between the forces of good and evil in the contemporary picture of Boris was discovered by the poets of the nineteenth century and further developed on the analogy of Shakespearean character-drawing.

The degradation of the Tsar and the ensuing complication of the ruler-portrait were carried out also in other contemporary works about the Time of Troubles. Ivan Timofeev's characterisation of Groznyj was achieved by rhetorical panegyric combined with passionate denunciation. The Tsar has become a sinful human being like all others. It is better, according to Timofeev, "to cover the Tsar's unseemly life with silence as with a cloak, like Noah, our ancestor, whose nakedness was covered by his quick-witted sons. For as the one got drunk on wine, so the other disgraced himself by sin, of which we all have our share" (Platonov 1891:278).

The old Muscovite image of the divine ruler, God's vicegerent on earth, has yielded to a humiliating comparison between sinful Groznyj and drunken Noah. Timofeev's "amazingly quaint and elaborate style," described by Mirsky (1949) as "the *reductio ad absurdum* of Muscovite rhetoric," obscures his revelations, but not to the extent that the truth does not emerge. His portrayal of the epoch is consistently composed by means of a *pro et contra* argument.

This contrasting technique is also used by Timofeev in his depiction of Boris, where it forms part of his endeavours to create a truthful picture. For, as he says. "if we were to speak about evil things only, and suppress the good ones, leaving it to others to relate them, this would clearly reveal that the author was not telling the truth. But if both good and evil are told without any addition, all mouths will be shut" (Deržavina 1951:63).

This ambivalence shows that Timofeev and his contemporaries put another interpretation on the concept of truth than did the writers of the preceding century. Truth, too, has become secularised. Timofeev sees it from a human point of view. Under this perspective not even the Tsar's apotheosis in death is certain. Of Boris Godunov's death he says laconically: "But nobody knows what prevailed at the hour of his death and which scale tipped the balance of his deeds, the good or the evil one" (Deržavina 1951:64).

Boris Godunov's character is explained as an interplay of many factors: human "nature," "free will," striving after fame, the influence of other men. The good qualities are explained as a result of being in the company of his brother-in-law, Tsar Fedor Ivanovič, whose role in relation to Boris is similar to that of Anastasia in relation to Groznyj.

The portrayal of Boris Godunov as a complex, paradoxical character may be traced to the *Russkij khronograf,* for while lacking in previous *smuta* literature, such as the *Inoe skazanie,* and Palicyn's *Skazanie* in its principal redaction, it occurs in several later works. We find it in both Ivan Khvorostinin's *Slovesa dnej i carej i svjatitelej moskovskikh* and in the *Povest'* of Katyrev-Rostovskij (Likhačev 1970:17f.).

In the *Russkij khronograf* we see also the rudiments of a paradox where good may cause evil, and evil good: "There are occasions when the bitterest harshness is clothed in praiseworthy words for the healing of illnesses, and, similarly, goodness came out of this evil" (Popov 1869:193, Likhačev 1970:19).

This paradox is further developed in the literature that in the second half of the seventeenth century grew up in opposition to the official genres and the new autocratic ideology.

With the analyses of the ruler-portraits of the *smuta,* Likhačev (1970:6–24) has convincingly shown that the "strong characters" of early seventeenth-century literature do not have their cause in a fundamental change in the nature of the Russian rulers of that time, but are due to a new literary technique and a fresh image of man. We have to agree with Likhačev that strong and complex characters must always have existed in Russian history, but that the representation of man as a psychological *coincidentia oppositorum* became a literary problem only with the writers of the *smuta.* In this way Likhačev has succeeded in demonstrating that this literature of transition has its own distinctive qualities, which mark it off from the preceding literature and enable us to define its place in the development of early Russian literature.

In the official historiography, however, the paradoxical image of man had no future. Here the traditions of sixteenth-century annalistic writing soon prevailed. This was a form that, like traditional hagiography, was based on fifteenth-century word-weaving and had long since become stereotyped and incapable of rejuvenation. A final attempt to create a monumental historical work on old models is Fedor Griboedov's *Istorija o carjakh i velikikh knjaz'jakh zemli Russkoj* (1669). Although the author makes use of Western European sources, his idea of history is determined by the notion of Moscow as the Third Rome. The same is the case with the so-called *Latukhinskaja Stepennaja kniga,* compiled in 1670 by the monk Tikhon of the Monastery of Makarij Želtovodskij. In its traditional form this ideology was, however, defeated by the new vision of the Russian empire, expressed in Simeon Polockij's poetry.

We have seen that the literature of the Time of Troubles reflects the critical period when the old ideology of national Muscovite absolutism was dissolved, and that of the new, multinational Russian empire had not yet found its form. The paradoxical image of man we meet with in this literature was incompatible with the official ideologies and their literary modes of expression. With the consolidation of a new absolutist ideology, the ambivalence of the *smuta* literature was displaced by Simeon Polockij's moralising allegories and emblematic representation of order restored.

Also, from the second half of the seventeenth century traces have been preserved of an unofficial, at times directly subversive literature. In Soviet literary history it usually passes by the name of seventeenth-century "plebeian" literature (Demokratičeskaja literatura XVII veka) on the grounds that judging by the surviving manuscripts it seems to have been read particularly among the lower orders, by artisans, small tradesmen, the lower clergy, by court and chancellery scribes. We should bear in mind, however, that these manuscripts date mostly from the end of the seventeenth and the beginning of the eighteenth centuries, and thus give no complete picture of the diffusion of this literature in the early seventeenth century.

From a sociological point of view, the growth of an unofficial literature in the lower strata of society has been explained as the result of deteriorating material conditions for the "plebeian" part of the town population in the time following the *smuta*. The landowning service nobility emerged as the most powerful social class. With its help the new dynasty built up a centralised state bureaucracy and carried through a state monopoly of trade. This led to an impoverishment of the "bourgeoisie" (*posadskie ljudi*), who in the time before and during the *smuta* had been prosperous, since both Boris and Demetrius had founded their authority on the service nobility as well as on the bourgeoisie (Vernadsky 1969:230).

According to Gudzij (1966:449) the impoverished bourgeoisie, in its opposition to the official policy, had to make common cause with the mass of people. Gudzij finds support for this theory in the strong admixture of colloquial elements in the "plebeian" seventeenth-century literature, in its stylistic and linguistic connection with oral folklore, with popular humour, with the puns and proverbs of everyday speech.

The main texts of the seventeenth-century "plebeian" literature have been edited and annotated by Adrianova-Peretc (1937, 1954), under the common designation of *Demokratičeskaja satira XVII veka*. Most of these texts have survived in manuscripts dating from the early eighteenth century and later. They must be regarded as examples, preserved by chance, of an unofficial literature flourishing in the seventeenth century, which has since been lost because the authorities did everything in their power to suppress it. This literature comprises works like the *Povest' o Šemjakinom sude*, the *Azbuka o golom i nebogatom čeloveke*, the *Poslanie dvoritel'noe nedrugu*, the *Skazanie o roskošnom žitii i veselii*, the *Povest' o Fome i Ereme*, the *Služba kabaku*, the *Kaljazinskaja čelobitnaja*, the *Skazanie o pope Save*, the *Skazanie o kure i lisice*, the *Lečebnik na inozemcev*, the *Rospis' o pridanom*, the *Slovo o mužakh revnivykh*, and the *Povest' o Karpe Sutulove*.

Seventeenth-century "plebeian" literature also includes texts of a different character, such as *Povest' o Savve Grudcyne*, which has been described as the first Russian novel, *Povest' o Gore i Zločastii*, one of the most peculiar works in early Russian literature, and the autobiographical *Lives* of the two martyrs for the Old Belief, Avvakum and Epiphanius. It is precisely these two "subversive *Lives*" that make unofficial seventeenth-century literature so important for the study of Russian hagiography. In what follows I shall try to demonstrate the importance of the "plebeian satire" for the *Life of Avvakum*, written by himself in the early 1670s.

The sociological approach used by Soviet scholars has uncovered the significance of the "plebeian satire" for the understanding of the contradictions of Russian society in the last decades before Peter the Great. On the other hand, the method threatens to lead to a rather one-sided view of satire as the weapon of the "plebeians" in their fight against the "feudal" lords, secular as well as clerical (Gudzij 1966, Adrianova-Peretc 1974:120ff., Robinson 1974).

A definition of seventeenth-century unofficial literature as an expression of the anti-feudal and anti-clerical opposition of the "plebeian" strata of society, as we find it in Adrianova-Peretc (1974:120), that is, as a literary weapon in the class struggle, assumes that the contradictions of Russian society in this period can be explained on a purely horizontal stratification. But this leads to an oversimplification of the evidence. The most important ideological conflict in the second half of

the seventeenth century, the Church schism, is a conflict that ran vertically through Russian society. Opposition to Tsar Alexis and Patriarch
Nikon's official policy sprang from court circles, from the conservative
boyar nobility and the circle of zealots who gathered round the Tsar's
confessor, Stefan Vonifat'ev, at the end of the 1640s, that had originally
included both the later Patriarch Nikon and the man who was to
become his most fanatical adversary, the court preacher Avvakum.

Where Soviet literary scholarship has been shackled by official theories of literature as a direct reflection of society and the class struggle, it
has either had to split up seventeenth-century unofficial literature into
what is today called "plebeian satire" on the one hand, and the writings
of the Old Believers (Adrianova-Peretc 1937) on the other, or it has had to
make the *raskol* into a "plebeian" movement (Likhačev 1970:136; Robinson 1974:194f.) by referring to its quantitative composition and ignoring
the connection between its active literary leaders and the old boyar
aristocracy.

The combination of Marxist-Leninist class theory and literary sociology with its view of literature as a direct reflection of society, a
combination that has greatly influenced Soviet literary scholarship, has
in practice worked to perpetuate the nineteenth-century "bourgeois"
view of the relationship between the subversive literature of the Old
Believers and the other seventeenth-century satirical writings. What is
today called "plebeian satire," Tikhonravov (1898:3f.) called the "new
satire." Because these texts could be traced back to Western European,
especially Polish sources, they were seen to represent something new and
progressive in early Russian literature, in contrast to the Old Believers'
social satire, which in the eyes of Tikhonravov was an expression of
intellectual and religious backwardness, a satire with its roots in the
Russian tradition, "doomed to boorishness of form and emptiness of
content."

We are here faced with an aspect of seventeenth-century "plebeian"
literature that has been intentionally played down by official Soviet
literary scholarship: its international character. Instead, all elements
indicating a genetic connection between the satires and native oral
folklore are emphasised (Adrianova-Peretc 1974:120ff.). Nineteenth-
century Russian literary historians, on the other hand, were drawn to
this kind of literature precisely because of its obvious links with Indian
fairy tales—as early as 1859 the German scholar Theodor Benfey had
drawn attention to the similarity between the Russian Tale about
Šemjaka's Judgement and one of the fables of the *Panchatantra*—and
with the *fabliaux* and *Schwänke* of French and German literature.
Scholars like Pypin, Buslaev, and Tikhonravov had studied the Russian
versions of such tales from a comparative point of view, and their work
was continued by the investigations of A. N. Veselovskij into the age-old
repertoire of international storytelling. By his distinction between

motifs—small narrative units that may travel freely from one literature
into another—and plots, or action patterns underlying the individual
tales, Veselovskij was able to deal more systematically with the problem
of foreign elements in seventeenth-century Russian literature, confining
Western European influence to works that may be traced back to
concrete prototypes.

The Russian version of a story also known from Western European
literature is found in the *Povest' o Karpe Sutulove*. It describes how a
friend of the family, a priest, and an archbishop, all in turn try to seduce
a wife while her husband is away, but are themselves revealed and
ridiculed by wily Tat'jana, the wife. The *Skazanie o roskošnom žitii i
veselii* varies the Cockaigne-motif, the *Skazanie o kure i lisice* contains a
theme known from the European animal fable, the *Povest' o bražnike*
translates into Russian the story of the man who is barred from Heaven
until he has shown that he is not inferior to the patriarchs and
evangelists with whom he gets into discussion. Veselovskij rediscovered
the theme in a German *Schwank*, which, in turn, he traced back to the
French fabliau of *Le Vilain qui conquist Paradis*.

On the basis of such analogies, Veselovskij concluded that the "droll
histories" (*smekhotvornye povesti*) of seventeenth-century Russian
literature had come from the West and had their origins in the Western
European animal fable, the French *fabliau*, the German *Schwank*, and
Italian Renaissance novellas. They came to Russia first and foremost
through Polish collections of *facetiae* and form the humouristic
counterpart to the remnants of the Western European novel of chivalry
which came to Russia at the same time, but which unlike the *facetiae*
was unproductive in seventeenth-century Russian literature. It was the
"droll histories" that were absorbed and transformed in the Russian
environment (Veselovskij 1880:496, 502).

The salient question in Veselovskij's exposition is this: what made
such an absorption possible? The solution lies implicit in his characterisation of the *fabliau* as a "bourgeois answer to the fantasies of bygone
days" (1880:500):

> A playful, brief story with features from real life, with an everyday
> theme and characters we all know; a story imbued with a healthy
> naive laughter, now good-natured and ironic, now brazenly satiri-
> cal—such is the nature of the fabliau and the novella created in
> a medieval bourgeois environment. (1880:496)

The view of the *fabliau* as an exponent of the "spirit" of the bourgeoisie,
in contrast to the idealist literature and courtly poetry of the aristocracy,
was systematically developed in Joseph Bédier's study of the *fabliaux*
(1893) and subsequently became prevalent in the history of European
literature throughout the first half of our century. The contrast between

high and low genres is explained against the background of social contradictions:

> Il y a d'un bourgeois de XIIIᵉ siècle à un baron précisément la même distance que d'un fabliau à une noble légende avantureuse...: ici la poésie des châteaux, là celle des carrefours. (Bédier 1893:371)

Today, Bédier's theory has come in for heavy criticism. Per Nykrog (1957) went back to the texts used by Bédier and subjected his theses to a scrupulous revaluation, showing that Bédier's sociological definition of the relationship between aristocratic poetry and the *fabliaux*, as well as his view that historically the former was succeeded by the latter, was unfounded. As Nykrog has demonstrated, the *fabliaux* and the *poésie courtoise*, far from being mutually exclusive, in actual fact presuppose each other, the comic "low" genre being a caricature of the sublime. The courtly public in their tastes ranged from the subtlest refinement to the coarsest platitudes. The *fabliaux* "may be regarded as a conscious, burlesque parody of the main forms of courtly literature," according to Nykrog (1957:281).

The rejection of Bédier's theory of a causal link between the bourgeoisie and genres like the *fabliau* renders invalid the attempts made by Soviet scholars to trace the origins of seventeenth-century Russian satirical literature back to the lowest strata of the *posad*-population (Gudzij 1966:448ff., Adrianova-Peretc 1974:137). Instead of regarding this literature as a direct reflection of social conditions, and "explaining the better known through the less known, literature through class consciousness," to quote V. I. Jarkho's poignant characterisation of this brand of literary sociology (Gasparov 1969:513), we have to start from the fact that the so-called plebeian literature in seventeenth-century Russia consisted mainly of parodies of the official genres. We shall have to analyse the relationship between the parodies and the texts parodied. Social criticism and the satirical attack contained in the texts will have to take second place in our analysis.

A characteristic trend of seventeenth-century Russian literature is that it starts by exploiting the traditional genres for purposes of parody, at the same time as official and private letters and documents are made use of for pure entertainment, either through parody or through stylisation. In Polish and Ukrainian literature this trend came into evidence as early as the sixteenth century. These fictitious documents were long taken by scholars to be genuine. Well-known examples are the Ukrainian version of the *Letter written by the Cossacks to the Sultan,* known in the West from Repin's famous picture, and the fictitious White Russian *Ivan Meleško's Speech in the Polish Parliament,* which even an expert like N. Kostomarov published in a collection of official documents (Tschiżewskij 1956a:316). From the 1670s we know a Russian translation of the

letter to the Sultan, but a fictitious correspondence between Ivan the
Terrible and the Sultan has been preserved even from the beginning of
the century. In the second half of the century a collection of fictitious
documents from the Sultan to the European princes was written. The
genre must have been popular throughout the seventeenth century
(Kagan 1955, 1957, 1958). The same is the case with fictitious diplomatic
correspondence. From the beginning of the seventeenth century we
know the *Povest' o dvukh posol'stvakh*, where the official epistolary
form is made use of for pure entertainment. The court parodies in the
stories about Erš Eršovič and Šemjaka's trial, the liturgical parody in the
*Služba kabaku* and in the *Skazanie o pope Save*, the parody of an official
petition in the *Kaljazinskaja čelobitnaja* and of travelogues and medical
books, must all be seen in this context.

Even if parody and stylisation are highly different modes of expression, they have one feature in common: in both cases another text (or
texts) underlies the representation. In respect of stylisation, however, the
writer takes over another's mode of expression, his system of devices,
without changing or distorting either the form or the other's viewpoints.
In parody, on the other hand, the writer's own intentions and the
intentions of the other texts are at odds, contending for the meaning of
the words.

This collision of meaning is easily discernible in a text like *Služba
kabaku*, which is a parody of the "little" and the "great" Vesper and of a
traditional saint's Life. The parody comes about as the story of the
drunkard who ruins himself in the tavern. The author must have had a
thorough knowledge of the liturgical texts. In most cases the parodied
passages are easily recognisable, even if they are distorted and combined
with typical elements from oral poetry, proverbs, alliterations, and
rhyme. The parody culminates in the account of the drunkard's life as a
travesty of the traditional *vita*. The saint's pious deeds are replaced by the
shameless conduct of the drunkard. The conventional depiction of the
saint's birth, the devout piety of his parents, the protagonist's youthful
struggle against the temptations of the world, until he renounces all
worldly possessions and begins his ascetic life behind the walls of the
monastery, the whole of this schema underlies the biography of the
drunkard, where it has been inverted. The parents are no longer pious
but "unseemly and out of their minds." Unlike the saints, the hero is not
an obedient child: "but it pleased him to go his own ways"; when he
leaves his parents, it is not to enter a monastery, but, on the contrary to
indulge in feasting and carousing. Instead of giving all his possessions
to the poor, he wastes everything in the tavern.

The distortion of conventional hagiographical *topoi* is sustained, up
to and including the drunkard's end. Whereas the saints in death leave
the monastic life for the kingdom to come, the drunkard is first to land in
prison and thereafter to be led "to evil death" (*Služba kabaku*, in

Adrianova-Peretc 1954:64).

Through the parodies the glorified heroes of the official genres acquire a set of critical doubles. The idealisation of reality receives its corrective in the parodic *monde à l'envers*. The heroic modes of expression and their comic inversions cannot therefore be set up as absolute contrasts. It is the same vision of reality that underlies both the parodies and the texts parodied.

The relationship between traditional hagiography and its parody in the *Služba kabaku* in several ways resembles that between courtly poetry and its grotesque inversion in the *fabliau*. Just as the *fabliau* presupposes a public familiar with courtly poetry, seventeenth-century parodic literature in Russia assumes a public well-versed in liturgical texts and sublime genres. Both authors and public must in their taste have been able to run the gamut from high seriousness to coarse ridicule.

The study of seventeenth-century Russian literature from this point of view has been obscured by research that has, in accordance with the theory of reflection, equated parodic, "low" style with the "lower" orders. Likhačev (1969, 1970) has, however, touched on the problem in his interpretation of the image of man in this literature.

By viewing the extant texts collectively, Likhačev has indirectly shown that the various heroes of seventeenth-century "plebeian literature" were represented according to a common pattern. In relation to the heroes of early Russian literature as they appeared in the official genres, this type of hero is better described as an anti-hero: a young man who clashes with his environment, acts against the will of his parents, wastes his patrimony in the company of the dregs of society, and finally ends up as an outcast, devoid of any social status. The inns and taverns of the slums are the *loci* of his debasement, accompanied as it is by feasting and carousing.

We recognise the anti-hero not only in the *Služba kabaku,* a mock mass and travesty of the heroic ideals of the saint's Life. He also emerges in the parodic *Azbuka o golom i nebogatom čeloveke* (Adrianova-Peretc 1954:30–36), and we meet him as a merchant's son in the figure of Savva Grudcyn, who, like Faustus, trades his soul to the devil for the gratification of sinful desire, and who gains glory and honour by the aid of the devil (Skripil' 1947). The type is further varied in the figure of the anonymous youth in the *Povest' o Gore i Zločastii* (Simoni 1907), and in my opinion we have here one of the prototypes for Avvakum's representation of his own life story.

The last three variants are, however, more complex than the parodic doubles found in the *Služba kabaku* and the *Azbuka*. The ambivalence of the parodic genres here points in the direction of a new disambiguation which in the story about Savva Grudcyn and the tale of Woe-Misfortune is expressed in the heroes' final conversion before entering a monastery, whereas in the *Life of Avvakum* the monastery has been replaced by the notion that death means a release from the prison of this earthly life and from the evil of the world, and Avvakum's final rebirth into a new life.

A striking feature in the portrayal of the seventeenth-century Russian anti-hero is the ambivalent attitude of the anonymous authors to his breach with the established order. Whereas the official literature would have condemned any such breach, and identified with society and its norms, the unofficial literature and its authors take sides with the anti-hero, showing how in his misery he still has in him a potential for good. The first-person narrator in the *Azbuka* depicts his own abasement with an ironic smile, as if through his humiliation he has broken away from the transitory values of this world. The stories about Savva Grudcyn and the youth who is pursued by Woe-Misfortune end with the heroes, at the low point of their moral degradation and physical misery, undergoing a moral and spiritual conversion, while they are liberated from the forces of evil that caused their downfall. The narrator regards their lives as they appear from his own standpoint at the monastery gates where their aberrations end. From this viewpoint their abasement becomes a transitional stage between the world with all its evil, and their new life in the monastery. The parody has come to an end, and so, therefore, has the distortion of the world. Characteristically, the *Povest' o Gore i Zločastii* had originally a somewhat different title from the one we usually find in modern textbooks. Its full title was given as *Povest' o Gore i Zločastii, kak Gore-Zločastie dovelo molodca vo inočeskij čin (The Tale of Woe and Misfortune, How Woe-Misfortune Brought the Young Man to the Monastic Order)* (Simoni 1907). The anti-hero is a symbolic representation of sinful man, which becomes explicit in the opening verses of *Povest' o Gore i Zločastii*, where poverty and misery are interpreted as the wrath and judgement of God, a means to bring fallen man back to the road of salvation:

> And because of this great transgression
> God Our Lord grew angry with them
> and expelled Adam and Eve
> from Eden, the holy Paradise
> ...
> And lo,the generations to come were frail
> and they turned to madness
> and began to live in vanity and untruth
> in great discord
> and rejected true humility
> And for this God grew angry with them
> he put them to great misfortunes
> he sent great sorrows unto them
> and shameful disgraces without end

wretched misery, Satan's assaults
wretched nakedness and deprivations without end
and infinite poverty, and lack of everything
all to humiliate us, to punish
and conduct us on to the road of salvation.

In the end it turns out that his humiliation has brought the young man all the way to his moral destination. By choosing salvation in the monastery, he breaks away from Woe-Misfortune, thus anticipating the transition to eternal life, by renouncing the world and becoming a monk:

The youth remembered the road of salvation
and therefore he entered a monastery to be shorn
but Misfortune remained at the holy gates
no longer leaning on the youth
And we have no doubts about the end of his life.
Deliver us, o Lord, from eternal torment
And give us, o Lord, radiant Paradise
In all eternity, Amen.

With this shift of perspective the narrator finally undertakes a complete reshuffle of his account. Whereas the universe of the story has previously been defined by means of the contrast between the established order and the underworld in which the protagonist lands when he breaks the laws of society, the angle is finally shifted so that this contrast is replaced by another and fundamental split between the transience of this world and the kingdom to come. At the same time there is an inversion of meaning: the youth's transition from the world to the monastery signals a transition from death to life. His misery and humiliation have been a symbolic death which is succeeded by the rebirth that occurs when he is taking monastic vows. The tavern and his drinking companions are no longer seen in absolute contradiction to the society that condemns the anti-hero, but have become an allegorical representation of this society, of a world contrasted with life behind the monastic walls.

Through the negation of a reality where the fundamental message of the old genres has lost its function and become a mere cliché, the authors of the anonymous, unofficial literature have invested this message with a new meaning, by setting it forth as another reality, as the Wholly Other, the reality that opens up before the anti-hero at the end of the road of his sinful life.

If this is social satire, it is of a kind different from the social satire of our own time. As represented in these texts, life's evil does not directly reflect social, political, or economic iniquities in seventeenth-century Russia. At the root of this satire lies a tragic vision of a world in which evil has got the upper hand, and the conception that those who govern society no longer represent the will of God, but have become a vehicle for the power of evil. This vision of reality governs the *Life of Avvakum*, where the Patriarch Nikon and Tsar Alexis are both represented as precursors of the Anti-Christ. Equally, it lies at the root of the story of Savva Grudcyn and the story of the young man and Woe-Misfortune, in which the evil of this world is described from a tragic angle by an author who, like the hero, has escaped from its misery.

Is this interpretation of seventeenth-century unofficial literature compatible with its alleged "realism" as a reflection of contemporary social conditions in Russia?

The reflection theory has dominated Soviet scholarship to the extent that problems of form seem not to exist. It is forgotten that even "realism" designates a literary mode of expression. The concept "reality" is seen in contrast to the conventions of official literature, as if the unofficial literature of the time were more real. The sympathy felt by their authors for a type of hero "who from an ecclesiastical point of view could not avoid being reckoned as a 'sinner,' " was, according to Likhačev (1970:141), a remarkable phenomenon of this literature, a sign that the normative ideal of the Middle Ages was waning, and that in literature there was a shift to an inductive generalisation based on reality.

This tendency to apprehend literature as more real when it represents a life story as an abasement than when it idealises it seems to be a general aesthetic phenomenon. In an analytical study of literary forms this view is highly questionable. The representation of abasement has its own conventions and *topoi*, its own generic models. The portrayal of the anti-hero and of the stages he has to pass through in his abasement is generically conditioned. We find ourselves historically within the genres which in Late Antiquity came under the heading of the serio-comic (*spoudogéleion*). These genres were forgotten by the scholars of a later age, although they have had a continuous development from Late Antiquity down to our own times. They have been rediscovered only recently, not least thanks to the works of Bakhtin (1963, 1965).

Within the group of serio-comic genres one of the most important is the "Menippean satire," or *menippea,* to use Bakhtin's term (1963). It is characteristic of the *menippea* that the action is located in prisons, madhouses, marketplaces, inns, taverns, brothels, galleys, and suchlike "low" places. What, with a phrase from Bakhtin, may be called "slum naturalism" in seventeenth-century unofficial Russian literature— because of its portrayal of suburban misery, of life among the outcasts of society, on the highroads, in taverns and prisons—is a version of this Menippean topography. In the same way as Menippean satire traditionally humiliates its heroes in order to reveal the Truth—not the truth about the hero, but a philosophical, religious, or ideological truth, according to Bakhtin (1963:150ff.)—so do the authors of texts such as the *Služba kabaku* depict their vision of Truth in the form of a tragic farce, in which the demons play their tricks on men in a godforsaken world ruled by Satan, the Anti-Christ, or their henchmen. This again leads to the inversion and travesty of liturgical symbols that play such an important part in the *Life of Avvakum*.

The ontological dualism of this literature, its antinomy between an evil world and the divine reality beyond it, becomes manifest on the psychological level as a split in the protagonist's personality. Both Savva Grudcyn and the young man in the story of Woe-Misfortune are obsessed by sinful desire which is expressed in dreams and fantasies, and materialises in the guise of the protagonist's demonic double, his *alter ego*, a negative counterpart of his real self. This double emerges beside Savva Grudcyn as his brother and companion. By giving his soul in return, Savva has all his wishes and desires fulfilled through this demon's help. Together they journey to his brother's country to visit his father, who is Satan himself. Later, Savva wins honour and fame in the Russian campaign against Poland and is introduced to the Tsar. Only on his deathbed, as he is about to fulfil his part of the contract, is he released from his obsession, at the intervention of the Mother of God, who destroys the pact with the devil. In *Povest' o Gore i Zločastii* the double is represented in the guise of the protagonist's familiar, an incarnation of death, appearing as Woe-Misfortune. When the hero changes into a falcon, Woe-Misfortune is over him as a white vulture. If he becomes a dove, Woe-Misfortune descends on him as a hawk, if he tries to hide by becoming grass on the steppe, Woe-Misfortune is there with a scythe, if he throws himself into the sea as a fish, Woe-Misfortune throws his net out for him.

The fantastic element in the "slum naturalism" of these stories is, as Bakhtin has pointed out, generically in accordance with the *menippea* and its later varieties. In their attempts to arrive at the truth about existence, the authors of the *menippea* take their heroes both to hell and to the gates of Paradise (1963:150ff.).

Also generically determined is the split in the protagonist's personality. The Menippean hero is not identical with himself in the sense that the epic hero is, not unambiguous and finished, but in a state of development, with the potentiality to transcend himself and become another, a travesty or a demonic parody of himself, or an incarnation of the divine and Wholly Other.

The anti-hero becomes unambiguous and complete only when in the conversion he is rid of the demons and finally begins a new life. On the threshold of eternity the divine order is restored in the stories of Savva Grudcyn and the youth pursued by Woe-Misfortune, on the psychological as well as on the ontological level.

If we regard these texts as variants of the *menippea*, their endings

become generic variations on the utopia-motif. The protagonist's liberation from his aberrations, and the restoration of the divine world order,
form a common motif in texts that combine a Christian vision of reality
with Menippean modes of expression.

New life is identical with the restoration of divine truth, the conquest
of temporary chaos and of the demonic inversion governing the
fictitious worlds of Savva Grudcyn and the young hero in the story of
Woe-Misfortune.

How are we to explain the sudden emergence of these parodies in
seventeenth-century Russia, when their origin can be described neither
as a reflection of social reality nor as a borrowing from Western sources?

There is a third possibility: unofficial seventeenth-century literature
in Russia may go back to an oral tradition. The transition from oral to
written forms was, after all, a characteristic feature of the period. It is
from this century that we have the first records of Russian folk songs,
undertaken on the initiative of Richard James, who brought these texts
back with him to England in 1620.

That there is a strong element of oral poetry in works like the *Povest'*
*o Gore i Zločastii* has always been emphasised (see Fennell and Stokes
1974:253ff., Jakobson 1966b). In more general terms, Šambinago
(1948:42) and Adrianova-Peretc (1948:152, 205) have suggested a link
between seventeenth-century "plebeian satire" and the jokes and
buffoonery of the *skomorokhi*, the wandering jesters of pre-Petrine
Russia. More recently, this idea has been taken up by Børtnes (1975), and
by Likhačev, Pančenko, and Ponyrko (see Likhačev 1984), all of whom
have approached the so-called plebeian satires in seventeenth-century
Russian literature from the point of view of Bakhtin's theory of a
medieval "laughter culture."

"Medieval laughter" had its own idiom, its *code*, closely connected
with the archaic symbolism of regeneration rites and carnival festivities.
Moreover, it was continually infiltrated by new folkloric elements,
creating a strange hybrid of Christian and pagan forms. Medieval
parody and satire grew up as literary expressions of this carnivalesque
symbolism, whose meaning we have to relearn in order to understand
the deeper significance of its pranks and buffoonery. According to
Bakhtin (1965:6), "the scope and importance of this culture were
immense in the Renaissance and the Middle Ages":

> A boundless world of humorous forms and manifestations opposed
> the official and serious tone of medieval feudal culture and the
> culture of the Church.In spite of their variety, folk festivities of the
> carnival type, comic rites and cults, clowns and fools, giants,
> dwarfs, and jugglers, the vast and manifold literature of parody—all
> these forms had one style in common: they belonged to the culture
> of popular carnival humour.

Bakhtin's theory of laughter implies a radical revaluation of all the various forms of *parodia sacra* that flourished throughout Europe in the Middle Ages, until they were denounced by the Reformation and no longer understood in their ritual and poetic ambiguity, but seen as impious expressions of irreverence to the Church. In spite of the work done by scholars like Chambers (1903), Lehmann (1922), Speirs (1951), and Jakobson (1958) there are still many students of medieval literature who are scandalised by the seeming blasphemy of the innumerable parodies and travesties of the Bible, of the liturgy, and of individual liturgical genres, official documents, and formulae of every kind. From a modern point of view, *parodia sacra* is usually seen as a certain sign of moral decline. Studies like the ones referred to above have shown, however, that in the Middle Ages the attitude towards parody was essentially different from our modern pattern and these parodies were not experienced as offensive irreverence. In their medieval context, the sacred parodies had an edifying, recreational function. An idea of their popularity may be gathered from the fate of one of the oldest sacred parodies known to us today, the *Cena Cypriani*. This is a parodic transformation of the Bible into a cheerful symposium, composed in the fifth or sixth century. It was still appreciated by Carolingian scholars in the second half of the ninth century, when it was recast by a Roman deacon named John, who dedicated his version to Pope John VIII (Curtius 1954:471).

*Parodia sacra* evolved without effective hindrance in connection with the great feasts of the Church's year. Mock liturgies like the Feast of Fools, *festum stultorum,* and the Feast of Asses, *asinaria festa,* were celebrated by the subdeacons and the secular clergy of the lower orders during Christmastide and especially on the Feast of the Circumcision. The solemn service of Easter week found its carnivalesque counterpart in the *risus pascalis,* in which life's victory over death was celebrated according to the ancient pattern of regeneration rites.

As already observed by Chambers (1903:I,278), the keynote of the mock festivals is to be found in the words of Luke 1:52, quoted in the *Magnificat,* the canticle sung at Vespers: "Deposuit potentes de sede,/ Et exultavit humiles." All the grotesque symbolism of the mock liturgies was destined to affirm the truth of these words: the braying of the ass replacing the words of the liturgy, or the subdeacons throwing dice before the altar and censing with the stinking smoke from the soles of old shoes, such seemingly blasphemous gestures were destined to represent the merry inversion of the status of the hierarchy, and to ensure the exaltation of the humble and the meek. As the carnivalesque counterpart of the official liturgy, mock festivals like the Feast of Fools and the *asinaria* demonstrated that the representatives of the Church were not identical with the divine truth they represented. Parody and inversion revealed the arbitrariness of symbolic representation, brought out the discrepancy between human forms and divine meaning. In this way, medieval *parodia sacra* had a critical function, preventing those elected to represent the truth of the Word of God from regarding themselves as identical with its message. Through parody and laughter, the Word of God was reaffirmed as something other than and different from the transitory forms of symbolic representation. It is a "dissimilar" representation of the divine, reminding us of the negative symbolism of the Areopagite and the holy madness of the nun at Tabennisi. From this point of view, we can more easily understand Bakhtin's insistence on the *dialogic* character of medieval *parodia sacra*. It should be seen in relation both to the official formalism, which it ridicules, and to the divine truth, which it reaffirms.

Medieval *parodia sacra* was not confined to the Catholic Church in Western Europe. The sources quoted by Chambers (1903:I,327f.) show that mock festivals had a long tradition and were just as popular in the Orthodox East. In Russia there are few traces of sacred parodies. Perhaps the most interesting is the liturgical play about the Three Youths in the Fiery Furnace (Daniel 3), described both by Fletcher and Olearius (Ponyrko 1984:157ff.). This play was performed in the churches a week before Christmas in merry prefiguration of the solemn celebration of the birth of Christ, and, according to Fletcher, always in the presence of the Tsar and the Tsarina. In these performances those who played the roles of the evil Chaldeans were dressed like mummers, carrying torches in their hands. During Christmas, the "Chaldeans" were allowed to run about in the streets with burning torches, setting fire to hayloads and to the beards of passers-by. We can only agree with Ponyrko that these pranks must be part of a Russian "carnival culture," a symbolic representation of life's victory over death, expressed in the ambivalent imagery of light and fire.

In Byzantine literature, parodistic imitation of liturgical and para-liturgical forms was a much-favoured device, practised by such eminent writers as Michael Psellos, the eleventh-century court philosopher. Parodies imitating the form of Orthodox hymns seem to have been particularly popular. A well-known example is the anonymous treatise *On Urine (Peri ourōn)*. The most notorious work of *parodia sacra* in Byzantine literature, however, is the *Mass of the Beardless Man: Akolouthia tou anosiou tragogenē spanou tou ouriou kai exouriou, mēni tō autō, perusi en etei efeto (The sequence of the Unholy, Buckbegotten, Fairwinded (?), Watermaking (?) beardless Man, the Same Month, Last Year in This Year)*. Written in the metre of Byzantine liturgical verse probably in the thirteenth or fourteenth century, according to Krumbacher (1897:809f.), it follows the pattern of a church service. In spite of its unrestrained ribaldry, it is regarded as a major work in middle Byzantine literature.

There is, of course, nothing like the obscenities of the *Mass of the Beardless Man* in early Russian literature. The traces of Byzantine parody found here are of a much more innocent nature, such as the *Beseda trekh svjatitelej (The Conversation of the Three Bishops)*, going back to a Byzantine catechismal parody from the sixth or seventh century, known in Western Europe as the *joca monachorum* (Veselovskij 1875, Ždanov 1892). The *joca monachorum* is a "frivolous catechism with a number of questions on Biblical themes," but more restrained than the *Cena Cypriani*, according to Bakhtin (1965:95). Parodic elements of this recreational kind are found in compilations like the *Istoričeskaja paleja (The Historical Paleja)*, translated from a Greek ninth-century original that reached the Eastern Slavs through South Slavonic literature, and the *Tolkovaja paleja (The Interpretative Paleja)*, a thirteenth-century Russian collection, containing apocryphal motifs and legends of a parodic nature, many of which subsequently found their way into Russian folklore, where they were rediscovered by scholars more interested in these secularised versions than in their monastic sources. In our context, however, these elements are important as evidence of a monastic "laughter culture" in pre-Petrine Russia.

In the past, the paucity of literary texts has been regarded as sufficient evidence for rejecting the possibility of a parodic-satirical tradition in early Russian culture. Precisely the penury of such texts from before the year 1600 is the reason why late seventeenth-century satire has been described as a trend of its own, as the first civic poetry in early Russian literature, in contradistinction to a more random admixture of parody and satire in earlier texts (Adrianova-Peretc 1954, Likhačev 1969:321).

Such manifestations acquire a fresh significance against the background depicted by Bakhtin (1965). He has convincingly demonstrated that the carnivalesque symbolism of the Middle Ages was not limited to written modes of expression, where it is secondary, but expressed itself primarily in gestures, ritualistic scenes, and oral poetry.

The reason why this laughter culture is so scarcely represented in early Russian literature is that the written language was reserved for the official culture of Church and State. This, incidentally, was the explanation given already by Zabelin (1872), who, in his work on the daily life of Russian Tsarinas in the sixteenth and seventeenth centuries, devoted the fifth chapter to manifestations of what he calls "pre-Petrine laughter" (*dopetrovskij smekh*).

Soviet scholarship has until recently either overlooked or reduced to the absurd Zabelin's investigations into the pre-Petrine laughter tradition (see, for example, Adrianova-Peretc 1974:121). Nonetheless, Zabelin's attempt to define early Russian buffoonery by seeing it in contrast to the asceticism of official culture is a clear anticipation of Bakhtin's theories.

In old Russia, the written word was a tool closely guarded by State and Church. Any irregular or unwarranted use of it was looked upon as heresy and punished accordingly. The prohibition applied not only to writings of a parodic or satirical nature, but to fairy tales, songs, and secular stories as well. A temporary breach with this attitude did not occur until the seventeenth century.

However, the ban on parody and satire, on droll stories and secular songs, was not absolute. But the presentation was oral and reserved for particular groups of professional performers, fools, jugglers, dwarfs, and suchlike figures. The fool, to use this designation as a general term, had become an institution in old Russia, the house jester at least from the beginning of the sixteenth century (Zabelin 1872:419), the jugglers even from Kievan times. Nestor mentions them in the *Life of Saint Theodosius.*

Old Russian buffoonery survived even the reforms of Peter the Great. The reforming Tsar himself had a complete mock court of fools and used carnivalisation as a weapon in his fight against old institutions. In this way he resembled his predecessor, Ivan the Terrible, who with his *opričnina* created a travesty of the Muscovite state in order to crush the power of the boyars (Bakhtin 1965:294ff., Likhačev 1984). The accounts of the predilection of Russian Tsars for jesters and buffoonery are in fact our most important source for the study of early Russian laughter tradition.

Besides the secular fools, old Russia had also the holy fools, the *jurodivye*—holy fools in Christ, corresponding to the Greek *saloi.* The portrayal of their lives in early Russian hagiography is regrettably so etiolated, and so adapted to the official idiom, that through it we get to know little or nothing about *jurodstvo.* Western European travellers in Muscovite Russia frequently emphasise the holy fools as a peculiar feature of city life and their social significance as a critical institution. The *jurodivye* expressed the will of God in inverted and comical forms, hurling their cynical accusations against the Tsar and the Church's official representatives (Kovalevskij 1900, Fedotov 1931, Pančenko 1973, 1984).

Sporadic evidence about early Russian buffoonery again shows that a carnivalesque idiom must have existed long before the seventeenth century. Otherwise the symbolism of the fools and the *jurodivye* would not have been understood. In seventeenth-century unofficial literature we may see an attempt to seek a meaning to existence by the aid of this old idiom at a time when the official modes of expression had lost their credibility.

That old Russian buffoonery suddenly becomes manifest in writing in the seventeenth century has already been pointed out by Zabelin (1872). Whereas the authorities both before and after this time did their utmost to prevent a written distribution of satire, in the seventeenth century it was virtually mass-produced in the form of the *lubočnye kartiny,* woodprints containing both texts and illustrations, wherein "popular literature," according to Zabelin (1872:428), "of itself discovered the printed word.'' A case could be made for replacing this explanation with he question of who was behind this mass-produced unofficial literature, but the problem cannot be discussed here.

While the seventeenth-century *lubočnye kartiny* are usually described as popular art and reading, they were, in fact, common in all layers of society, decorating the walls in both the homes of ordinary people and in the mansions of the nobility. Printed freely in large impressions in Kiev as well as in Moscow, they were sold openly and cheaply in the streets throughout the century. The original seventeenth-century *lubki* are now rare. Even under Patriarch Joachim, at the end of the century, the authorities started to intervene with censorship, and after him they tried to destroy the prints as soon as they could lay hands on them. In the second half of the nineteenth century, the last wood blocks were still being destroyed by order of the civilian authorities. Zabelin and other scholars, who had in the meantime discovered their historical value, were unable to prevent this destruction.

The seventeenth-century *lubok* prints mark a clear break with contemporary rules for decorum and decency, in respect of themes as well as in style. In them it was permissible to mock and distort everything sublime and holy. Zabelin's examples of this profanation are precisely those texts that in modern Soviet scholarship are known as "plebeian satire": the *Kaljazinskaja čelobitnaja*, the *Skazanie o pope Save*, the *Skazanie o kure i lisice*, and others.

With the reconstruction of a pre-Petrine laughter tradition, these texts can no longer be lumped together in a single category. We shall have to distinguish between those taken over from Western European *fabliaux* and *facetiae*, which may be defined as an extension of the traditional repertoire of droll stories, and those going back to an indigenous oral laughter culture, either in its secular or in its monastic variant. A piece like the *Kaljazinskaja čelobitnaja*, for example, with its monastic *monde à l'envers* and its parody of the official petition, clearly belongs to the second group. It is the jolly recreational self-parodying of a monastic community, in which the solemn forms of the daily ritual are transcended in anticipation of a higher reality.

If, on the other hand, the profanation breaks the bond between this higher reality and the symbols in which it is represented, these symbols are emptied of their divine meaning, and the merriment disappears. The result is a *reduced laughter,* and the seriocomic emerges in a form where seriousness prevails. When this happens in art or literature, the world appears as a tragic farce and the principle of evil reigns supreme. God has withdrawn from the world and becomes manifest as pure absence, as *deus absconditus.*

It is this tragicomic carnivalisation of reality that we encounter in the *Povest' o Savve Grudcyne* and the tale of Woe-Misfortune. In addition to elements deriving from oral storytelling, these texts have also absorbed others from Byzantine and Slavonic apocryphal literature, which, however, had long circulated in oral form. On the other hand, apocryphal literature belongs precisely to those early Christian genres that were shaped under the influence of the *menippea*. Therefore, no generic contradiction exists. On the contrary, both the story of Savva Grudcyn and the one about Woe-Misfortune may be viewed as examples of Russian apocryphal literature.

The figure of Woe-Misfortune goes back to representations found in the Slavonic apocrypha of the hop (*humulus lupulus*) as an animate creature and the devil's helper (instead of the grape, which we find in South Slavonic texts) (Veselovskij 1880:471f.). In the oral tradition there existed a number of synonyms for this figure, *Zlaja dolja, Zlydnja, Okh,* all describing versions of the *Khmel'*-figure. This figure may be a product of the Church's fight against drink, but equally probable is Veselovskij's conjecture that it may have a connection with heretical writings produced by the South Slav Bogomils. In them the wine is depicted as the work of the devil, and thus belongs to his domain, which accords with the Bogomils' strictly dualistic world picture, where God's elder son, Satanail, has his realm, and Christ, God's second son, has his. This dualism without doubt recalls the structure of both the *Povest' o Savve Grudcyne* and of the *Povest' o Gore i Zločastii.* (Bogomil literature is incidentally strongly influenced by Menippean genres, demonstrated by a work such as *The Dispute between God and the Devil.*)

As regards the pact with the devil in the story of Savva Grudcyn, this motif may be traced back to early Christian literature, where we know it from the apocryphal *Story about Adam,* and from the popular medieval tale of Theophilus where, however, sinful desire is lacking as a motif. The motif does occur, in the early Christian legend of Euladios, who makes a bargain with the devil to obtain Kerasia, because her parents had promised her to a monastery as a child. It was probably from this legend that the motif came to medieval German literature. The Faustus-motif and the story of the Russian merchant's son, Savva Grudcyn, go back to the same literature of the transition period between Late Antiquity and the Middle Ages.

If, on the basis of this examination of unofficial seventeenth-century Russian literature and its generic roots, we are to form a picture of the environment in which it evolved, and of its anonymous authors, it can be defined neither as an expression of the fight of the "plebeian" strata of society against the "feudal" aristocracy, nor as a reflection of atheism and anti-religious feelings, as has been done, for example by Adrianova-Peretc (1954:141 *et passim*). On the contrary, it seems to me that this literature gives expression to a genuine spirituality, even if this be in the form of merry and self-critical parodies of the type of the *Kaljazinskaja čelobitnaja,* or in hilarotragic satires like the *Služba kabaku* and the *Azbuka.* For the latter work the anonymous authors should, in my opinion, be sought among those Russian churchmen who in the seventeenth century tried to bring the Church out of its moral and spiritual decline after the Time of Troubles.

This reformist movement among the Russian clergy began as early as the first half of the seventeenth century. One of its first leaders was Ivan Neronov, who later became Avvakum's teacher and collaborator. Its spiritual centre was the Makarij Želtovodskij Monastery in the Nižnij Novgorod area, which both Avvakum and the later Patriarch Nikon and a number of other prominent churchmen of the seventeenth century visited in their youth (see Borozdin 1898).

After Alexis Romanov's ascension to the throne in 1645, Moscow became the centre of this reformist movement. Its leader was the Tsar's teacher and father confessor, Stefan Vonifat'ev. In the late 1640s he gathered about him the so-called circle of zealots. Ivan Neronov, Nikon, and Avvakum all belonged to this circle, in whose activity even interested laymen took part. One of them was the young nobleman Fedor Rtiščev, a close friend of the Tsar and one of the few men of the time who tried to arrive at a synthesis between Orthodox belief and Western European culture.

The reformist activity of the zealots took a tragic turn, however, when in 1652 Nikon succeeded Joseph as Patriarch and began his own reform policy. With him the Graecophile party gained the ascendancy in the Russian Church, and those of the zealots who had worked with Stefan Vonifat'ev to restore the spiritual ideals of old Muscovy, as they had been formulated in the *Stoglav* in 1551, came into opposition to the new Patriarch. Several of them broke away from the official Church and continued their reformist work as leaders of the *raskol*. Among these we find both Neronov and Avvakum, who in their writings started to attack Nikon and the Tsar for having betrayed the true Church and joined the Anti-Christ. With the mordant satires of the Old Believers against the official Church and its representatives, unofficial literature in Russia had become in earnest a literature of subversion. Given the lack of concrete information about other literary opposition in Russian spiritual life in the second half of the seventeenth century, it is tenable to see the emergence of an unofficial literature as connected with those religious reformist movements that eventually turned against the official Church and the new absolutist empire.

# The Life of Avvakum

## Introduction

Since it was first published by Tikhonravov in 1861, Avvakum's autobiography—*Žitie Protopopa Avvakuma, im samim napisannoe*—has held a unique position among the surviving texts of early Russian literature. Quite apart from the historical value of the *vita*, its topical character has always fascinated readers, stylistically as well as thematically. It made a particularly profound impression on such writers as Tolstoy, Dostoevsky, Leskov, and Turgenev, who were suddenly faced with a two-hundred-year-old text whose author had succeeded in solving what they themselves regarded as a principal stylistic problem: how to integrate spoken Russian with the written language of literature. In Avvakum they found a synthesis of his own oral idiom and the traditional written Church Slavonic, a synthesis that seemed like an anticipation of their own stylistic experiments. The same topical character obtained thematically. After Avvakum had put himself at the head of the Old Believers' opposition to the Church policy of Patriarch Nikon and Tsar Alexis, he was tortured in the dungeons of the Patriarch and then, in 1653, deported with the whole of his family to Siberia. After a relatively tranquil period in Tobolsk, he was forced in 1655, together with his wife and children, to join the expeditionary force of the Voivode Afanasij Paškov on his campaign to the east, which brought them all the way to the river Amur under conditions of inhuman toil, constantly exposed to Paškov's cruelty. In 1662 Paškov was recalled to Russia, and Avvakum, too, was ordered to return. However, the voivode abandoned him to his fate, and Avvakum and his family took two years to complete the return journey. In Moscow, the Tsar and Avvakum's former friends of the circle of zealots, who pursued a fairly moderate line towards Nikon, had hoped that Avvakum would now adopt a more conciliatory attitude. As this did not come to pass he was deported again, this time to Mezen, northeast of Archangel, and finally, after the denunciation of the Old Believers at the Ecumenical Council of 1666–1667, to the arctic fortress of Pustozersk at the mouth of the Pečora river, this time without his family, who were detained in Mezen. Avvakum was kept at Pustozersk until 1682, when he was burnt at the stake as a heretic together with three followers and fellow prisoners, the monk Epiphanius, the priest Lazarus, and the deacon Fedor. It was at Pustozersk, in the early 1670s, that he wrote his *Life*, in close co-operation with Epiphanius, who also recorded the tale of his own sufferings.

Avvakum's account of his tribulations seemed to have a strange topicality for its readers, published as it was at the same time as Dostoevsky's *The House of the Dead*, the account of his deportation to a Siberian prison camp. In this context Avvakum's *Life* appeared as a forerunner of a new genre, and not as the final stage in early Russian hagiography, a view of the *vita* which is still relevant today (see Mandel'štam 1970), and which indicates that it is difficult to draw an absolute divide between early and modern Russian literature. The history of its reception has, however, become a field of research in its own right and can be referred to only very briefly in our context. We are first and foremost interested in the connection between the *Life* and the old hagiographical tradition.

Scholars have never denied that Avvakum's *Life* contains hagiographical components. But from the very beginning their significance has been played down. Borozdin (1898:327, 332) maintained that the hagiographical character of the *Life* is manifest mainly "in certain external features," as opposed to what he calls its "factual aspect." A survey of Avvakum scholarship would demonstrate that it is this factual aspect, the documentary value of the *Life*, that has had first priority. Pascal (Avvakum 1938:49) criticises Borozdin for having exaggerated the hagiographical character of the *Life*, and thinks that Avvakum borrowed only superficially from the traditional framework of hagiography to relate his own memoirs. The *Life* "must be regarded as a source of primary importance not only for the biography of its author and his companions, and for the history of the *raskol*, but for the whole history of the reign of Alexis" (Avvakum 1938:51).

Today it is still the autobiographical aspect of the *Life* that seems to interest most scholars. In reference books it is described as the first genuine autobiography in Russian literature (Stokes 1969:677). Avvakum's first-person narrative signals his victory over the "fear of individualism" in traditional hagiography. In Avvakum's *Life* "individualism celebrated veritable orgies" (Stender-Petersen 1952:174).

These quotations, representative as they are of the prevalent view of Avvakum's *Life*, reflect an axiological norm where modern autobiography and documentary literature, psychological and historico-factual information rank higher than the hagiographical vision.

This reading cannot, however, uncover the structure of Avvakum's *vita*. It is precisely the interplay between hagiographical components and facts selected from the history of Avvakum's life that determines the composition of the work. What is new in his autobiography is not that Avvakum made the traditional hagiographical elements redundant, a purely negative definition which in the last resort rebounds on the *vita* itself, reducing its aesthetic value. The innovative character of the *Life* must be sought in the combination of these elements, the bringing together of traditional elements with components which are both new and hitherto uncommon in hagiographical texts.

## The Genesis of the *Life*

The *Life of Avvakum* has long been known in three different redactions, today usually referred to as A, B, and C, in accordance with their order in the Avvakum edition issued by Barskov and Smirnov (Avvakum 1927). The first of these redactions, the A-redaction, is based on the holograph in the so-called *Pustozerskij Sbornik*, which includes also the holograph of the autobiography written by the monk Epiphanius, Avvakum's father confessor and critical interlocutor. The holograph of Avvakum's *Life* has preserved Epiphanius' corrections to Avvakum's text, so that we have here, in fact, the concrete traces of a dialogue between author and audience in the manuscript itself. The B-redaction is based on a copy that belonged to the Metropolitan Macarius, with variants from a copy in the library of A. I. Khludov and from another in A. N. Popov's collection. Although this redaction is much shorter than the A-redaction it contains some episodes not found in A. The third, the C-redaction, was published on the basis of a copy that belonged to the Kazanskaja Dukhovnaja Akademija and on another that belonged to V. G. Družinin. This last redaction is far more comprehensive than either the A or the B. A holograph of it was, incidentally, found by I. N. Zavoloko (see Demkova 1974:12ff.).

The ordering of the redactions in the Academy edition was based on Barskov's dating (Avvakum 1927:X). According to Barskov, Avvakum first recorded the version known as the A-redaction, which was later much shortened and reworked to become the B, whereas the C-redaction came finally as a new expansion. All three versions are dated to between 27 July 1672 and 19 April 1673.

The frequent revisions may have resulted from the author's wish to improve his exposition, or they may have been connected with the fact that Avvakum's *vita* was intended for distribution among his followers and had to be rewritten several times.

Barskov's datings have been taken over by a number of other scholars (Pascal 1938, Gusev 1960, Robinson 1963). Following Barskov, they have explained the differences between the redactions as a result of Avvakum's endeavour to improve his work, so that the ordering of the manuscripts as A, B, and C implies a value judgement.

However, they made no textual analyses to establish what these improvements, if any, consisted in. Descriptions of qualitative differences between the redactions were limited to rather general terms. In Pascal (Avvakum 1938:34) we find, for instance, the following account of how the French scholar imagined Avvakum at work:

> Ce qu'on sent dans B, et plus encore dans C, c'est la réflexion s'exerçant sur un texte de premier jet. L'auteur veut rendre son texte

> plus clair, supprimer des redites, améliorer la composition, de
> même que pour le contenu il élague ou étend ou ajoute ou modifie
> la présentation.

The trouble with this explanation is that B and C cannot always be said
to reflect any improvement on A. Already to Pascal (Avvakum 1938:34)
this was a problem:

> B mutile le dialogue épique entre l'archiprêtre et sa femme... C
> nous fatigue par ses réflexions pieuses interminables; tous deux
> affaiblisent, banalisent parfois le texte primitif.

Pascal tries to find an explanation in the fact that Avvakum's literary
taste was different from ours. At the same time he maintains that
Avvakum had no literary aspirations in writing his *vita*. The first of
these arguments is a trivial one. The second is not very clear and
probably wrong.

V. I. Malyšev in 1949 discovered a copy of a then unknown version of
the *vita* in a manuscript belonging to G. M. Prjanišnikov (Avvakum
1960:305–343, 445ff.). The history of the work's genesis again came into
focus. It became necessary to find a place for the Prjanišnikov version in
the development of the *Life*. After a meticulous examination of the four
redactions in a number of variants, Demkova (1974) arrived at a totally
new dating of them and put forward her own theory of their genesis and
relative chronology. As there is not space here to go into all the details of
Demkova's argument in this connection, I will confine myself to those
factors that have direct relevance for my own study.

Demkova (1974:140) defines the B-redaction as the earliest of the three
redactions contained in the Academy edition and dates it to the first half
of 1672. It is followed by A, dated to the first half of 1673, based on a
version of the B-redaction other than the one we know from Barskov's
edition, a version more closely related to both A and C. As regards the C-
redaction, the longest of the three, it is dated as late as 1675, but it must
have been written down before the death of the boyarina Morozova on 2
November, since Avvakum does not mention her death, an event that
strongly grieved him, as we know from other sources. The reason for the
previous dating of all three redactions to between 27 July 1672 and 19
April 1673 is that Avvakum sometimes simply accumulates events, without adjusting his approximate datings. By restricting himself to the
datings that recur from one redaction to another, Barskov (Avvakum
1927:X) arrived at his chronology, while Demkova reaches hers by
emphasising the datings that differ in the respective redactions.

The B-redaction, accordingly, is not a shortened version of A, as has
been maintained in the past. The passages it lacks were inserted at a later
stage in the writing process.

The passages of the C-redaction that are not entirely new come close to both A and B, so it constitutes a combination of them. In the C-redaction occur a number of episodes that are otherwise only to be found in A: the story of Avvakum's encounter with the natives on the river Irtyš; the detailed account of his life in Moscow after the return from Siberia, of how he was offered a position at the Pečatnyj Dvor, and of how the boyars showered gifts on him; the tale of the holy fool Fedor of the Pafnutij Monastery, and others. At the same time the C-redaction tallies with B in lacking the A-redaction's passages about the torturing of Old Believers in Mezen and in Moscow, together with the attack on the Nikonians. In B and C, Avvakum proceeds directly from an account of the mutilations at Pustozersk on 14 April 1670 to an appeal to all true believers to forgive him for having made bold to write his own *Life*. For this he seeks justification by referring to the Acts of the Apostles and to the Epistles of Saint Paul.

As regards the Prjanišnikov version, Demkova (1974:107ff.) assumes that it can be traced to an even earlier redaction. The account has a marked factual character when compared with that of the other redactions. It is to a far greater extent oriented towards the historical context, and lacks the wider spectrum of meaning that is to be found in the later redactions. There is a clear connection here between the *Life* and the autobiographical passages that may be found in Avvakum's letters and petitions, and which Demkova (1974:134) takes to represent the first stage in the genesis of the *vita*. The account given by the Prjanišnikov version of the incarceration in the Pafnutij Monastery, for instance, is identical with the description of the same event in Avvakum's first petition (1664) to the Tsar. The Prjanišnikov version is dated to 1669–1672 and forms an intermediate stage between the autobiographical notes contained in Avvakum's writings from before this period and the shortest of the versions of his *Life* contained in the Academy edition, namely the B-redaction.

Demkova's reconstruction of the history of the *vita* becomes decisive for its generic definition, because she succeeds in disproving the theory that Avvakum gradually discarded his hagiographical models. In fact, she has shown that the opposite is the case. The hagiographical element acquires an increasingly predominant function in the structure of the *vita* (Demkova 1974:97ff.).

A comparison of the redactions in the order B–A–C demonstrates how Avvakum in the last two enlarged and amplified his own story by means of a growing number of quotations from Holy Scripture, from theological writings, and from hagiography. By juxtaposing or contrasting these quotations with his own account, he places it in a new context, transforming his literary self-portrait into a saintly figure by the help of this hagiographical stylisation. The process reflects the author's increasing awareness that his life on earth will end in martyrdom. When writing the C-redaction Avvakum foresaw his own death and that of his followers, and in the light of this foresight he represents himself and his disciples as Christ's saints. Christ "elected us and you before the creation of the world, in order that we shall be holy and pure before Him," he wrote in a letter to the boyarina Morozova and her two fellow prisoners in the Borovsk prison, the Princess Urusova and the officer's wife Narija Danilova (Avvakum 1927:405ff.). In the C-redaction the *vita* is called "*kniga života večnogo*", another evidence that Avvakum and his party intended the writing down of the *vita* as a work to perpetuate themselves and their fight for God's cause, for "*delo Božie*," as it is named in the *Life*.

The gradual tranformation of Avvakum's life story on hagiographical models leads also to a stylisation of his antagonists, of the Tsar, the Patriarch Nikon, and their representatives: these historical figures increasingly emerge as embodiments of anti-holy forces. A clear instance is the portrayal of Paškov. In the Prjanišnikov redaction Avvakum not only included the negative traits of Paškov's character, but also mentioned such redeeming features as the information that Paškov furnished Avvakum and his family with provisions prior to their return journey from Siberia. In later versions this information was suppressed, and Avvakum even gives a totally different account of the incident. In both the A- and the C-redactions we may, to quote Demkova (1974:113), "observe a distinct tendency to accentuate the evil features of Paškov's character, an increasingly 'hagiographical' stylisation of it."

By reading the *Life* on the basis of Demkova's reconstruction of its genesis, we form an image of its author as he has shown his hand in his choice of material, his interpretation of it, and his attitude towards it. The comparison of the redactions shows that Avvakum intentionally represented his life in the way a hagiographer would choose to do it. Demkova's reconstruction lends substance to the theory that the *Life* was composed as a work of hagiography.

## The Structure

### Abolition of Epic Distance

In its basic scheme the *Life of Avvakum* follows an entirely traditional hagiographical pattern: an *exordium* and a *conclusio* constitute the framework around the life story and miracles of the protagonist. It is, however, possible to see even here how the autobiographical form modifies the traditional scheme. It has to exclude, of course, tales of posthumous miracles. The miracles Avvakum reports have been experienced by him, and form part of the exposition of his life story as it is seen from the point of view of the narrative situation depicted in the frame.

In a Life where narrator and protagonist are identical, the *epic distance* between them can no longer be absolute. Consequently, the boundary line between frame story and life story is abolished. Avvakum's *vita*, like unofficial literature in seventeenth-century Russia generally, breaks with the epic heroicisation of the official literature.

The coincidence of narrating and narrated first person creates a direct contact between frame story and *Life* proper. From the narrative situation of the frame, the narrator Avvakum represents his life story in retrospect, looking back on an uncompleted sequence of events, of which the telling of the *vita* forms the last link. But this event will soon be succeeded by another, which is anticipated in Avvakum's concluding exhortation to his interlocutor Epiphanius to take up the narrator's part and proceed with his life story: "You have enjoyed listening to me, so don't be shy, tell at least a little!" (82).[1]

In Avvakum's autobiographical *vita*, the epic opposition between a narrative situation present in relation to narrator and audience, and a narrated story, which is perfective in relation to the narrative situation, has been resolved in an uncompleted, imperfective flow of events, comprising both the past of the narrative and the *nunc* of the act of narration. The first-person narrator concludes his exordium with the words "Thus do I, the Archpriest Avvakum, believe, thus do I confess, and with this do I live and die." He then immediately proceeds with his life story, starting according to the traditional pattern with his origins, parents, and birth, but with the difference that narrator and protagonist are one: "I was born in the Nižnij Novgorod region, beyond the Kudma river, in the village of Grigorovo. My father was the priest Peter, my mother Maria, as a nun Martha" (8). The autobiographical form was not in itself entirely new in seventeenth-century Russian literature. It has a long tradition in early Russian literature, where it occurs even in Kievan times, in works such as Vladimir Monomakh's *Instruction* and *The Pilgrimage* of Abbot Daniil. As we have seen in our examination of Cyprian's *Life of Saint Peter,* the autobiographical element was known also in early Russian hagiography. Autobiographical records are, in fact, known even from the Prologues and Paterica of Byzantine literature. Robinson (1963:60) is probably right in assuming that these works were the models for Avvakum's and Epiphanius' autobiographies. In his introduction to the C-redaction Avvakum quotes the Palestinian Abbot Dorotheus' *Instructions* from the sixth century, a work on which the author has set an autobiographical stamp by including in it examples and anecdotes from his own life.

---

[1] The numbers in parentheses after the quotations refer here and in the following to the columns of the Academy edition (Avvakum 1927).

The autobiographical *vita* thus in no way represents a break with hagiographical tradition. It must rather be regarded as a variant, in which the distance between the narrator and audience on the one hand, and the narrative on the other, no longer exists. The narrative is tied to the narrator's point of view, as opposed to the epic mode of representation, where the narration now takes place in the third person, now is seen through one of the characters, but where the boundary line between narrator and narrative is absolute. In the frame of the first-person story the fictitious narrative situation is on the threshold of the story proper, so that the exposition is based on the point of view contained in this threshold situation.

If the first-person narrator goes beyond this point of view, he departs from the autobiographical discourse. The narrator transports himself to previous stages of his own self, removing himself from the *nunc* of the frame, renouncing his function as mediator between author and representation. In the *Life* this happens when Avvakum abandons his retrospective angle and proceeds to give a direct representation of dialogues between himself and others in a remote past, and of his own thoughts and emotions at earlier stages of his life. This tendency to restore epic distance runs counter to the autobiographical discourse and is linked with Avvakum's endeavours to transform his historical figure into a hagiographical protagonist. These endeavours collide with the restrictions imposed by the first-person narrative, and this tension between hagiography and autobiography makes Avvakum's *vita* different from the other hagiographical texts we have examined.

The tendency to restore epic distance in the *Life* will, however, have to be kept within certain bounds, if the first-person form is not to lose one of its main functions, which is to give the narrative its special documentary value, a function that Lidija Ginzburg (1970) has defined as the "set towards genuineness" (*ustanovka na podlinnost'*) found in memoir literature. This set, or orientation, should not be confused with historical factuality. It is a structural element, which causes us to read the *Life* as an autobiographical document, in the same way as its hagiographical elements induce us to read it as a *vita*.

## The Function of the First-person Narrator

In order to bring about this transition from autobiography to hagiography, the identity between protagonist and author must be broken. Avvakum has to be annihilated in order to re-emerge as the glorified hero of his own saint's Life. But this *stirb und werde* can only be a transcendent objective, for were it realised, it would render the continuation of the autobiographical tale impossible. Avvakum's account becomes a balancing act between breaking down and restoring the epic distance, between negating and affirming the first person as an exponent of himself and of the Wholly Other.

The identity between narrator and protagonist is thus merely the starting point for the differentiating process that takes place in the course of the narration. The relationship between protagonist and narrator becomes a dialectical one: they are identical, and also different. The same is true of the relationship of the narrator-protagonist to the "implied author" of the *Life* as he is reflected in the text and as the text reflects his relationship to the reality that is represented and to the audience at whom this representation is aimed. Accordingly, the "implied author," a term taken over from Booth (1968:67ff.), refers not to Avvakum's historical personality, but to the basic attitude determining the world vision found in the *vita*. The concept may in this definition be said to equate what Robert Weimann (1977:234ff.) has called the author's "narrative standpoint" versus his "technical point of view", which determines his optical, linguistic, or narratological position.

Whereas the author's *technical point of view* is a category of fiction and becomes manifest in the mode of representation, in Avvakum's *vita*, through the first-person narrator as he emerges in the narrative situation of the frame, the author's *narrative standpoint* is a category of non-fictional reality, whose spiritual and social presuppositions may be sought in the historical and biographical context. But because it functions merely as a represented system of values in the text, a definition of the author's standpoint can be reached only through an examination of it in its represented, that is, aesthetically objectified form.

This theoretical definition of the author's narrative standpoint and technical point of view shows that the frame story of the *vita* must be regarded as a fiction, while its implied author refers, if not to the multifaceted personality of the real Avvakum, at any rate to the world vision that is expressed in the *Life*.

The author's narrative standpoint and technical point of view are correlative concepts, and in their interaction or synthesis they form the "narrative perspective" (Weimann 1977:241f.).

The *narrative perspective* of the *Life*, then, is produced in the interaction between (1) Avvakum's *narrative standpoint*, his attitude to life, and (2) his *narrative strategy*, or technical point of view, the ways in which he chooses to tell his life story, the use of first-person narrator, the narrative tone, etc.

The relationship between these two aspects of the narrative perspective may be unambiguous, but sometimes forms tensions of a satirical, ironical, or naive kind. At all events, the technical point of view constitutes the paradigmatic aspect of the narrative perspective and belongs to the code. The author's narrative standpoint, his world vision, is, on the other hand, the decisive factor in his choice of literary codes and determines the variation of the invariant meaning of the code found in an individual, concrete work. It relates the work to its context. The specific meaning of the work may therefore be defined as a product of narrative standpoint and technical point of view, of world vision and literary conventions.

## The Narrative Situation in the *Life of Avvakum*

The definition of narrative perspective as an interplay between the technical point of view and a represented system of values may contribute to shedding new light on the narrative situation of Avvakum's *vita*, where the representation of Avvakum's life story takes the form of a dialogue between himself and the monk Epiphanius.

We shall regard this dialogue as a version of the traditional hagiographical frame story and not as a documentary account of the oral stage prior to the writing of the *Life*, as has been the usual interpretation.

The view of the frame story as an historical document was put forward without reservation by Pascal (1938:484), in his description of life at Pustozersk: "Naturellement, dans ses longs entretiens avec le moine Épiphane, il lui était arrivé bien des fois de conter tel ou tel épisode de ses innombrable aventures..." This view was subsequently taken up by, among others, Robinson (1963:48), who in his account of the Old Believers' prison life at Pustozerk dates this oral stage in the genesis of the *vita* to the period before 1669, which seems to have been a relatively easy time for the prisoners but not so fruitful from a literary point of view.

The last circumstance led Robinson to conclude that in this period the prisoners were busy getting to know each other and establishing mutual contacts. This was thus primarily a stage of conversation. Avvakum and Epiphanius became close friends at this time, evidence of which Robinson finds both in the *Life of Avvakum* and in an unpublished biography of Epiphanius, dating from the early 1730s, which he quotes. It says there that the two prisoners, "the fellow sufferers, often had spiritual conversations together, strengthening each other in the faith and encouraging each other for the sufferings to come." Against this background, Robinson (1963:43) tries to render plausible Pascal's theory about an initial oral stage in the genesis of the *Life*:

> There is little doubt that, apart from questions concerning the "true faith," Avvakum in these conversations told Epiphanius about his life, so full of adventures and incarcerations. Such autobiographical conversations, embellished by the imagination, on the whole quite natural in the conditions of severe banishment, were particularly appropriate in this group of ideologists of the *raskol*, who regarded

themselves as martyrs for the "true" faith. When Epiphanius afterwards "urged" Avvakum to write down his autobiography, it was because he had already clearly realised how important this work would be for their common cause.

Not only is the origin of the *vita* here traced back to the talks between the two fellow prisoners at Pustozersk, but the frame story, too, is interpreted as a literary reproduction of these conversations, without regard to the conventional, generic aspect of the narrative situation.

The matter is not quite as simple as that. First, Demkova (1974) has demonstrated that the extant redactions of Avvakum's *vita* are based on autobiographical passages in his previous writings, and thus cannot be traced back to the conversations at Pustozersk as a kind of oral proto-stage prior to the written form of the *Life*. Avvakum's writing down of his life story must have started long before the talks with Epiphanius. Second, through a juxtaposition of the chronological sequence of events in the *vita* with the sequence of external, historical events, it is possible to demonstrate that Avvakum's picture of the narrative situation in the form of a conversation between Epiphanius and himself cannot possibly refer to any concrete situation from the Pustozersk period. If this were the case, the frame story would have to refer to conversations from the time after the mutilations at Pustozersk, on 14 April 1670, when Avvakum's fellow sufferers had their hands chopped off and their tongues cut out, and all prisoners were kept in solitary confinement in subterranean dungeons, since the depiction of these punishments forms the last segment in the first-person narrator's account of his life from birth and adolescence down to the dungeon on the Arctic Ocean, and its numerous sufferings—as his life story appears to him from the retrospective angle of the frame. Thus, the account moves continually in the direction of the narrative situation, which, had it referred to a concrete historical situation, would have to date from the time after these punishments, when, however, it was no longer possible for the two fellow sufferers to sit and converse together. The prisoners were now isolated and could meet only in a hurry, and in danger of severe reprisals, by crawling out through the peep-holes of their subterranean dungeons at night (Robinson 1963:49). Their most important means of communication was no longer the spoken, but the written word. Sympathetic guards acted as messengers.

Against this background we shall have to radically revise Pascal's and Robinson's view of the frame story and its genesis. The narrative situation of the frame story is, rather, an attempt to recreate in writing a situation which no longer had any correlation in the daily life of the prisoners. Its fictitious character lies precisely in this fact.

The narrative situation is not primarily oriented towards the historical context. It has its most important function in connection with the first-person narrator's account of his life story in the *vita* proper. As he is drawing near to the point where narrative time and narrated time will coincide, he approaches also the point where protagonist and narrator converge. But this point is never reached in the *vita*. Gradually, as the narrative approaches the frame plane, a distance arises between the temporal planes of the narrative and of the frame respectively, so that the narrator and protagonist will never become identical. Before the events have reached the narrative situation, the chronological sequence is interrupted by a number of miracle tales, where the first-person narrator diverges from his chronological principle, at the same time as Avvakum is here no longer identical with himself, but becomes a vehicle for God's will. In this way the *vita* ends by representing Avvakum as an embodiment of the Wholly Other. Thus the protagonist becomes different from the narrator. When in the conclusion the latter turns to his interlocutor with the behest that he now take the narrator's part, this is a gesture that does not simply refer to the situation experienced by the two fellow prisoners at Pustozersk, but is rather to be regarded as part of the fictitious frame.

From the point of view of genre history the most important distinctive feature of Avvakum's frame story is that it takes the form of a dialogue between narrator and audience.

Throughout the *Life* we are frequently reminded of the dialogic form of the frame story through the lines spoken by the first-person narrator. He interrupts his discourse with apostrophes such as "listen why" (34), "you see, how kind they were!" (45), "Once, Father, in the land of Dauria, if you and the other servant of Christ won't be tired of listening, I'll tell you" (47), *passim.*

The narrator gives the impression of taking note of the reactions of the audience, turning to them with questions, apologies, and spontaneous self-criticism: "I, Sir, forgive me, lied" (39), "But I, forgive me for God's sake, lied then" (39), "Father, will you forgive me with the other servant of Christ, that I lied then. What do you think, was it a great sin?" (39).

The narrator here refuses to continue until his interlocutor has had his say. At this moment the fiction of an orally told story is broken: "And now, for God's sake, consider carefully: if I committed a sin, then you must forgive me; but if it was not against the tradition of the Church, then everything is all right as it is. Here I have left an empty space for you: write out in your hand for me, my wife, and my daughter, either absolution or penalty" (39).

The illusion of free and easy conversation hides the fact that the communication between Avvakum and his audience, be it Epiphanius or "the servant of Christ" to whom the manuscript is addressed, could not in the circumstances take place in the form of conversations, but only by written messages.

In the Pustozerskij Sbornik holograph this translation of an oral dialogue into writing has received its graphic mark: Avvakum left an open space in his manuscript for his interlocutor and confessor Epiphanius to fill in his answer, which he duly did. Equally, it was Epiphanius who wrote the opening lines to the exordium:

> The Archpriest Avvakum has been charged to write his life by the monk Epiphanius, as this monk is his spiritual father, so that the works of God shall not pass into oblivion. And to this end has he been charged by his spiritual father, to the glory of Christ our God. Amen. (1)

This behest from his interlocutor is inverted in the conclusion of the *vita* when Avvakum rounds off by asking Epiphanius to continue with his life story. Along with the narrator's frequent interruptions throughout the account, the interlocutor's participation in the dialogue manifests itself in the form of the corrections Epiphanius made in the original, corrections that are not purely orthographical, but reflect real differences of opinion between Avvakum and Epiphanius, of a stylistic as well as an exegetic nature. This does not, however, ever clash with the picture of the narrative situation as a dialogue between close friends.

Literally and graphically the *Pustozerskij Sbornik* holograph shows how the *Life of Avvakum*, like a number of seventeenth-century unofficial texts, forms a link between the spoken and the written word.

The portrayal of the narrative situation in the form of a confession shows also that Avvakum understood how to exploit this transitional phase for an aesthetic purpose. The recording of the *vita* is justified because Epiphanius in his capacity of father confessor urges Avvakum to do it, "so that the works of God shall not pass into oblivion."

In the representation of Avvakum's *Life* as a confession, the use of this well-known *topos* acquires a particular function, suggesting as it does a duality characteristic of the structure of this *Life*: in the frame Avvakum is shown in the guise of a repentant sinner, while his confessions bear witness to the works of God, the *delo Božie*, in the father confessor's words. Already at this point the difference between Avvakum the narrator and Avvakum the protagonist is anticipated.

With his frame story Avvakum established also a difference between his roles as author of the *vita* and its narrator. The illusion of an oral dialogue conceals the process of writing. The author Avvakum hides behind Avvakum the narrator, whose *vjakan'e*, or "babble," is a verbal mask.

What function or functions do the frequent interruptions of the narrator have in the *Life* proper? The question is one that has previously been raised by, among others, Vinogradov (1923) and Likhačev (1967:303ff.).

Likhačev is particularly interested in the way Avvakum uses interruptions to bring the past into the present. He lays the main emphasis on the use of temporal adverbs which relate the narrated time of the *vita* to the narrator's time, the life story to the frame, on interruptions such as: "Without shearing me they took me to the Siberian chancellery and handed me over to the secretary Tret'jak Bašmak, who now suffers in Christ as Father Savatej and sits in the Novospasskij, also a dungeon pit. Save him, o Lord, already then he was good to me" (18); "Neronov had then announced to the Tsar many times and repeatedly told him of the three misfortunes that would be the punishment for the schism in the Church: plague, war, and inner strife; this has now come to pass in our time" (20) (see Likhačev 1967:305ff.)

According to Likhačev (1967:303ff.) it is characteristic of Avvakum that he sees his past in relation to the present, trying as he does to explain the present in the light of his past. Avvakum represents his life story as it appears to him in the *nunc* of the narrative situation. This angle causes his account not only to become a tale of past times, but also to imbue with meaning Avvakum's situation in his arctic dungeon. *The time perspective* of the *Life*, as Likhačev calls its technical point of view, becomes in his interpretation a sign of its connection with new trends in seventeenth-century Russian literature, with a more subjective perception of time, and with the individualised author. The time perspective, of the *Life* is compared to the linear perspective in painting, which is likewise deduced from the requirement to portray reality as seen from an individual observer's angle, that is, from the artist's *nunc*. In Russia this demand first came into evidence in the seventeenth century (Likhačev 1967:305).

Likhačev is primarily interested in seeing Avvakum's *Life* in connection with modern Russian literature. He says explicitly (1967:310) of the way in which Avvakum's own times are introduced into the account that it recalls analogous phenomena in modern literature. Equally, it appears that the narrative situation, identified by Likhačev with the author's existential situation, is not the only correlate to the events of Avvakum's past. His past is not even primarily oriented towards the *nunc* of the narrative situation, but towards the point when time will cease. Events, even the most commonplace of them, acquire their significance only "*sub specie aeterni*" (1967:310).

This eschatological perspective of the *vita*, its "eternity-aspect," to use Likhačev's designation, abolishes the narrator's time perspective, so that the narrative situation becomes not the final goal towards which the chronological sequence of events moves, but a coordination point between a past that has gone by and a future immortality. And in this connection the past, too, is immortalised.

However, the relationship between time and eternity in the *vita* becomes undefinable, if, like Likhačev, we identify the narrator Avvakum with Avvakum the author. The frame-story narrator exists in a threshold situation on the boundary between time and eternity. At the same time he is on the threshold between Avvakum, the author of the *Life*, and Avvakum, its protagonist. The time perspective of the narrative is subordinate to the eternity perspective that Avvakum, from his narrative standpoint, has chosen to apply to his life story. This eternity perspective calls for a hagiographical representation. The alleged modernity of the *Life* is illusory, and results from inadequate analysis of the relationship between the author's technical point of view and his narrative standpoint. In the last resort, Likhačev (1967:303ff.) is compelled to negate his own thesis about the significance of present-time perspective in the *Life*, as regards both its immanent time perception and its time structure seen as a sign that Avvakum anticipates a modern development.

Vinogradov's (1923) examination of the narrator's interruptions is very different from Likhačev's, in both his point of departure and in his professed aim. His Avvakum treatise was written at a time when he was strongly oriented towards a functional stylistic, and his classification of narrative interruptions forms part of the attempt to define the stylistic system of the *Life*.

Basing his work on the stylistic nuances of the narrative interruptions, Vinogradov arranges them in two main groups. In the first group he includes lines of the type we started by quoting, where the narrator interrupts his account to emphasise his own shortcomings, either as narrator or as protagonist. To this group belong also the lines connecting the individual episodes of his account, lines marking the transition from one to the other, for audience and readers: "Enough of this. I have gone too far as it is" (40), "Forgive me, I have sinned, it's none of my business ... I said it just in passing" (57), "Once I've got a talking, I'll tell you another story" (76).

Vinogradov (1923:209) assigns this type of narrative interruption to the stylistic level where the narrator "in the form of an oral, naive improvisation" has one event follow another: it is a style identified with what Avvakum himself calls *beseda* (conversation) and *vjakan'e* (babble). According to Vinogradov (1923:209), this style constitutes the keynote of the *Life*, "the basic tone, in which Archpriest Avvakum conducts the story of his life,—the deeply personal tone of a naive, trusting narrator, whose swarm of memoirs is rushing past in a rapid flow of verbal associations, creating the lyrical digressions and the unsystematic, emotional concatenation of its compositional parts." On this level the *Life* may be defined stylistically as "an intimate, friendly 'conversation' about remarkable events in the life of the narrator." It is, however, worth noting that Vinogradov (1923:209n.) makes a reservation about the credibility of this narrative tone, even if he does not broach the question of its fictional character.

In clear contrast to this group of interruptions are those lines in which the narrator no longer addresses the interlocutor inherent in the narrative situation, but apostrophises an audience beyond the fictitious situation: Avvakum's real adherents and antagonists, Old Believers and Nikonians alike. Here, the naive stance must give way to lofty preaching. Vinogradov offers the following quotations as intances of this style: "Forgive me, please, Nikonians, for blistering you. Live as you like" (41); "You see, dear listener, our misfortune is necessary. We can't get away from it" (52); "Woe unto you, poor Nikonians! you are doomed to ruin, owing to your wicked and contumacious behaviour!" (60); "So then, you who are an Orthodox Christian, proclaim the name of Christ, stand right in the middle of Moscow, cross yourself with the sign of Christ our Saviour, with five fingers" (65f.).

By thus ordering the narrative interruptions in two stylistically contrasting sequences, Vinogradov has found a key to the *Life's* narrative structure: the alternation between stylised *vjakan'e* and the exhortative pathos of *propoved'* (sermon). The narrator speaks, as it were, with two voices, each with a different stylistic tone.

The question is, whether Vinogradov's grouping may be used as a basis for an analysis of the functions of the narrative interruptions. Common to both groups of interruptions is their *phatic* function: they establish a contact with the audience in and beyond the frame. But in addition to this, the two groups also serve different functions.

In the *vjakan'e* group the interruptions are marked by the narrator's attitude to himself and his own past. As a confessing sinner in conversation with his spiritual father, he emphasises his own inadequacy and asks forgiveness both for the actions he recounts and for the way in which he relates his story. The stylistic dominant of these lines is the narrator's self-accusatory eruptions, which express in the narrative situation his emotional involvement with the story of his own life. This set towards the narrator's attitude to his subject gives the *vjakan'e* group a marked *emotive* function.

In the other, contrasting group, where *vjakan'e* is replaced by a lofty, exhortative preaching, the interruptions are not oriented towards the narrator, nor are they addressed to his interlocutor. These interruptions apostrophise an audience beyond the fiction of the frame, Nikonians or Old Believers forming a collective third person beyond the text. With this set towards the addressee the lines acquire a distinctly *conative* function, expressed grammatically by the frequent use of vocatives and imperatives. Since the narrator here addresses an audience beyond the frame, the conative function of the interruptions acquires a magic touch; the author diverges from the narrative fiction and apostrophises friends and foes in an attempt to transform them into recipients of his message. Behind the fiction of the narrative situation we discern the outlines of Avvakum's situation as the author of his *Life*: incarcerated in his subterranean dungeon, he tries to interfere in the struggle outside, through the written word.

## The *Life* as *skaz*

In the preceding pages we have seen how Avvakum's *vjakan'e* and *propoved'* serve different functions in the narrative situation, constituting an asymmetric relationship: the lines predominated by the emotive function form an integral part of the fictitioūs frame, while the other group of lines through its magic-conative function goes beyond and breaks with the narrative fiction.

The opposition between *vjakan'e* and *propoved'* is not confined to the narrative situation. The *vjakan'e* determines also the keynote of the account of Avvakum's life story. But the oral tone is here interrupted by quotations from the Bible and from theological literature, which form a stylistic stratum of their own, where we recognise the rhetorical tone of the *propoved'* lines. The question will be, therefore, what functions the *vjakan'e* group and the *propoved'* group acquire when translated from the narrative situation to the narrative itself, when their functions are no longer definable on the basis of the set towards narrator or interlocutor, as in the narrative situation, but where the predominant factor is the set towards the narrative itself.

Vinogradov (1923:209, 210, 216, 285, *et passim*) has several times substituted *skaz* for *vjakan'e*, defining it as the "colloquial speech element." This colloquial *skaz* element is seen by him in opposition to the quotations, which constitute the literary, rhetorical element of the text.

The introduction of the *skaz* concept to characterise this colloquial style, Avvakum's attempt to create an illusion of *beseda*, of free-and-easy conversation, in his written narrative, implies a connection between Vinogradov's examination of the *vita* and the prose theory developed by the Russian Formalists in the 1920s. In their theoretical work, *skaz* had become a key term.

According to Ejkhenbaum (1969a, b, c) *skaz* is a device used by some authors (Gogol, Leskov, Remizov, Bely) to recreate in writing an oral mode of expression, by breaking the norms of the written language and approximating it to oral speech as far as possible, both phonetically, grammatically, and lexically, thereby creating the illusion of an oral discourse. In this connection Ejkhenbaum (1969b:166) mentions Avvakum, both as an example of the struggle between the literary language and the spoken word in early Russian literature, and as a stylistic model for Leskov, the modern master of *skaz*. In his treatise *Leskov i sovremennaja proza* (1925), Eikhenbaum amplified his *skaz* concept, in a definition that has won general acclaim:

> What is important is not the *skaz* in itself, but *the set towards the word (ustanovka na slovo), towards the intonation, the voice*, albeit in their written transformation. (1969c:240)

The set towards the spoken word, towards the voice, underlies also Vinogradov's definition of Avvakum's *vjakan'e* as *skaz*. Like Eikhenbaum, but far more systematically, he places the *skaz* elements of the *vita* in opposition to the scriptural quotations, and attempts to describe its composition on the basis of the interaction between these two levels.

Vinogradov's identification of *skaz* with *vjakan'e* causes the text to split up into two different strata, *vjakan'e* and *propoved'*. In Vinogradov's view this is a defect in the *vita* itself: Avvakum did not succeed in creating a coherent whole. This view became established in Vinogradov's writings. On the basis of his demand for unity, he gave, as late as 1959, a purely negative evaluation of Avvakum's style:

> Archpriest Avvakum's attempt in his "Life" to combine a colloquial, everyday style, with the literary conventions of Church Slavonic and traditional hagiography, did not produce either artistic unity or a complete image of the protagonist. Dynamically changing units of everyday *skaz* are intersected by a unifying sermonising in which the bright colours of colloquial speech are blurred in the pale halo of the "true Christianity," of the holy martyr (1959:468)

Vinogradov's definition of Avvakum's *vjakan'e* as an intimate, friendly *beseda* and *prostodušno-delovoj skaz* has subsequently been taken up by other scholars, but the *skaz* concept has been severed from the Formalist prose theory on the grounds that Eikhenbaum's attempt to see Avvakum's colloquial discourse as a device, as a means of creating the illusion of *skaz*, is without an adequate foundation (Robinson 1963:46). The prevailing view in Avvakum scholarship is that the colloquial style of the *vita* has the character of a "naive improvisation," and cannot therefore be placed on a par with the use of *skaz* as a conscious device. Avvakum's work is assessed on the basis of an attitude that recalls Schiller's distinction between the naive and the sentimental.

If we accept the definiton of the frame story as a fictitious narrative situation into which the author Avvakum introduces a first-person narrator as the intermediary between himself and his audience, the objections to the use of the Formalist *skaz* concept in connection with the *vita* will no longer apply. The narrative situation serves precisely to create the illusion of a colloquial narrative.

Criticism of Vinogradov's *skaz* concept should not, therefore, be levelled against his use of it in connection with Avvakum's *vita*. It is the concept itself as it was defined by Eikhenbaum and used by Vinogradov that must come under scrutiny.

The narrow definition of *skaz* as "a set towards oral speech" leads in Vinogradov (1923) to the *skaz* element of the *vita* being left in unmediated opposition to its scriptural quotations, even though these, too, have been integrated with the narrative discourse. We must therefore see whether *skaz* cannot be defined as a superordinate concept for both *vjakan'e* and *propoved'*.

Before proceeding we shall have to take a closer look at a passage from the text to see whether Avvakum's *vjakan'e* is really as colloquial and improvised as has been alleged. The passage is taken from the first part of the *Life* and should be typical of Avvakum's narrative style:

> When I was still a priest, a young woman came to me for confession, burdened with many sins, guilty of fornication and all kinds of self-abuse. Weeping, she began to tell me about it all in detail, in the church, standing before the Gospel. But I, thrice-accursed healer, was afflicted myself, inwardly kindled by a lecherous fire. And it was a bitter moment for me. I lighted three candles, and fixed them to the lectern, and placed my right hand on the flame, and held it there, until the evil blaze had been extinguished. Then, having dismissed the young woman, I took off my vestments, prayed, and went home in great distress. It was about midnight, and back at my own house I wept before the holy image of Our Lord until my eyes were swollen, praying fervently that God must separate me from my spiritual children. For the burden was too heavy and too difficult to bear. And I fell to the ground on my face, sobbing bitterly. And lying there I lost consciousness. I forgot that I was weeping, and with the eyes of my heart I was on the Volga. I saw two golden ships sailing loftily, and their oars were golden, and the masts golden, and everything was golden. There was one helmsman in each. And I asked: "Whose ships are these?" And they answered: "Luka's and Lavrentij's." These had been my spiritual children, who had set me and my house on the path of salvation and died in a manner pleasing to God. And lo, then I saw a third ship, not decorated with gold, but with many different colours: red, and white, and blue, and black, and ashen. No one can imagine its beauty and excellence. A radiant youth was sitting at the helm steering. He came rushing towards me from the Volga as if he wanted to swallow me. And I cried: "Whose ship?" And he who was sitting in it answered: "The ship is yours! Here it is! Sail in it with wife and children, if such is your prayer!" And I woke up trembling. And sitting up I wondered: "What have I seen? And how will the sailing be?" (9f.)

The text differs to an equal extent from the old word-weaving style and from the late seventeenth-century rhetoric. Avvakum was quite consciously opposed to the latter, and expressed it through his own idiom. This emerges especially clearly in his introduction to the C-redaction of his *Life*:

do not despise our vulgar speech, for I love my Russian mother tongue. And I am not in the habit of embellishing my speech with philosophical rhymes, since God does not listen to our beautiful words, but wants our deeds. (151)

What is linguistically striking in the passage about the girl's confession is the mixture of Russian and Church Slavonic elements, of speech and written language: *az* alternates with *ja*, the old literary aorist and imperfect tense with the more usual *l*-preterite of the type *prelepil*, *vozložil*, *vskričal*. The syntax is a simple one, without any rhetorical embellishment. The sentences are constructed around a finite verb, extended with a few adverbs, while the subject is frequently omitted. Parataxis predominates over hypotaxis, or the latter is sometimes confused with the former, so that we get, for instance, the gerund *plakavsja* for the aorist *plakakhsja*: "i prišed vo svoju izbu, plakavsja pred obrazom Gospodnim, jako i oči opukhli" (see Černykh 1954:285 for this "free use" of the gerund in the seventeenth century).

This parataxis forms the basis of what is stylistically the most prominent feature of the text. There is a distinct tendency to combine components that are juxtaposed in sequences on the basis of similarities and differences of a grammatical, phonological, lexical, or semantic nature, for instance by verbs:

| | |
|---|---|
| zažeg tri svešči | I lighted three candles |
| i prilepil ... | and fixed ... |
| i vozložil ... | and placed ... |
| i deržal ... | and held ... |
| i ...pošel ... | and ...went ... |

or by noun phrases

| | |
|---|---|
| dva korablja zlaty, | two golden ships |
| i vesla na nikh zlaty, | and their oars were golden |
| i šesty zlaty, | and the masts golden |
| i vse zlato | and everything was golden |

This anaphoric sequence is interrupted by a negative parallel, before going on to a new string of anaphora:

| | |
|---|---|
| tretej korabl' | a third ship, |
| ne zlatom ukrašen, | not decorated with gold, |
| no raznymi pestrotami, | but with many different colours, |
| krasno, | red, |
| i belo, | and white, |

i sine,                                  and blue,
i černo,                                 and black,
i pepeleso.                              and ashen.

The components are no longer combined only through parataxis and contiguity, but on the principle of similarity as well. This projection of similarity onto contiguity marks an incipient poetic use of language in the text.

The same principle of *parallelismus membrorum* underlies the description of Avvakum's "fall," the central point in the passage quoted:

> Az že, treokajannyj vrač, sam razbolelsja, vnutr' žgom ognem bludnym, i gorko mne byst' v toj čas; zažeg tri svešči, i prilepil k naloju, i vozložil ruku pravuju na plamja, i deržal dondeže vo mne ugaslo zloe ražženie. ...

The two events that have here been combined in a time sequence form a parallelism, in which the two links take place in different planes, an outer and an inner one, and are related to each other as visible to invisible, as active to passive. The verbal expression is chosen to give the two links a number of similarities, semantically, because the lexemes are taken from the same semantic field—"žeč'" and "ogn'" are the cues— and phonetically by repetition of the same phonemic combinations: AZ ŽE ... ŽGOM ...ZAŽOG ... vOZlOŽIl ...dondEŽE ... rAZŽEnie. ... When in this way the similarity is, in Roman Jakobson's (1960) terms, projected "from the axis of selection to the axis of combination," the chronological sequence is transformed into an equation, in which the first component functions as the *signatum* (meaning) and is expressed through the other, which acquires a metaphorical function: Avvakum's external, visible gesture illustrates the psychological state he finds himself in, according to the account. In this way the use of parallels becomes a means of abolishing "disambiguation" and creating a connotative level of meaning in the texts, in addition to its denotative level.

At present we know too little about the nature of this ambiguity to be ready to return to the question of the extent of improvisation and colloquialism in Avvakum's discourse. We have not yet discussed the function of the quotations in the passage under review. They are difficult for a modern reader of the *Life* to discern, because we have lost contact with the texts that constituted Avvakum's literary repository. Readers well versed in the Bible will be able to identify the quotation from the Epistle of Saint Paul to the Ephesians, "oči serdečnii," (see Eph. 1:18, "the eyes of your understanding being enlightened"), a phrase that forms part of the hagiographical stock of commonplaces in early Russian literature. We know it even from Nestor's *Life of Saint*

*Theodosius.* Another recurrent *topos* in early Russian hagiography is "life as a voyage," a *topos* mentioned in connection with our analysis of Epiphanius' *Life of Saint Stephen.*

A closer examination of the text shows, however, that the quotations play a far more important part in its structure than this sporadic identification of them seems to indicate. Avvakum's description of the confession bears a distinct mark of the stereotyped formulae of the Prayer-Book (*Trebnik*), and some of the phrases in his text may easily be traced to the chapter on the Confession, *Čin ispovedaniju (The Order of Confession)*, in the Prayer-Book issued in Moscow in 1651, the last one accepted by the Old Believers. Robinson (Avvakum 1963:218) has shown how a number of elements in the passage about the young girl's confession are traceable to this text. We recognise the Greek word *malakia*: "Sogrešikh malakiju i bludom vsjakim"; the "nača mne, plakavšesja, podrobnu vozveščati" of the *Life* corresponds to the Prayer-Book's "Egda voprošaeši kajuščegosja o rastlenii i mnogorazličnykh krovosmešeniikh i o padeniikh ... togda voprošaj podrobnu"; Avvakum in tears before the icon, "jako i oči opukhli," recalls the "no real repentance without tears"—" ...slezy eže plakatisja grekhov svoikh, bez plača bo nevozmožno pokajatisja"—of the Prayer-Book; and his phrase "poneže bremja tjaško, neudob' nosimo" varies its "bremena ne udob' nosima."

Most surprising of all to the modern reader, perhaps, is the fact that even the description of Avvakum's "fall" is a quotation, taken from the early Russian Prologue. In the Moscow edition of 1641, we find under 27 December a novella with the heading "Slovo o černorizce, ego že bludnica neprel'stivši umre i voskresi ju, pomolivsja Bogu," which relates how a notorious whore once tried to seduce an Egyptian hermit. He let her into his cell, and the devil at once started his play:

> The devil began to inflame him towards her. But he kindled a lamp, and afire with lust ... put his fingers on the lamp and burnt them. And he did not feel the flame, because of the conflagration of the flesh. (quoted by Robinson in Avvakum 1963:218)

The quotations create a network of connotations in addition to the historial, denotative meaning of Avvakum's life story. Elements taken from other texts are mounted into the context of the *vita*, redistributed, absorbed, and transformed, while Avvakum' story, too, is transformed in the interplay between the historical narrative and the quotations.

The main characteristic of Avvakum's *vjakan'e* thus is not the oral, colloquial element as such, as opposed to the literary, rhetorical element represented by the quotations, nor is it the set towards the voice, towards the spoken word, but rather the mixture of colloquial and literary elements and their interaction. If this narrative mode is to be designated as *skaz*, the term will have to be redefined.

A drawback of the Formalist *skaz* concept is that in actual fact it became synonymous with "colloquial speech." It was not the *skaz* *structure* that was analysed, but only its "phonetics." In his 1925 paper *Problema skaza v stilistike*, Vinogradov (1969) clearly recognised the importance of translating the *skaz* problem to the systematic level, that is, of analysing the invariant *skaz* structure, and formulated a *skaz* definition that we may apply to Avvakum's *vjakan'e*, even if Vinogradov himself never seems to have used it in his Avvakum studies.

Vinogradov (1969:188) sees *skaz* as a transitional phase between speech, which is dominated by dialogic relations, and so-called monologic discourse, in which the dialogic elements have been to some extent suppressed. *Skaz* in this sense is characteristic of the *byvalye ljudi*, a term used of professional storytellers, whose discourse is marked by its mixture of popular speech elements and the argot of various trades, all interspersed with a literary residue, and interrupted by the narrator's interjections, emotional comments, and apostrophes of his audience. This mode moves away from the dialogic forms of colloquial speech in the direction of an artificial, monologic discourse, a "narrative monologue." *Skaz* is created in the space between these two extremes, where the movement has reached a stage in which the dialogue still determines the mode, but where the repartees have disappeared, and where the style alternates between the norms of the written language and various forms of popular dialects and argot, both oral and written, including, for instance, the language of the clergy.

This definition of *skaz* takes us back to the seventeenth-century unofficial literature, already defined above as a transitional phenomenon between oral folk poetry and the written word. It is also clear that Avvakum's *vjakan'e* may be defined as a version of *skaz*, not by excluding the quotations, but on the basis of the interaction taking place between the heterogeneous elements of the text, from its vernacular components to its clerical jargon and scriptural quotations.

What is especially problematic in Vinogradov's 1925 paper is his use of the concepts "dialogue" and "monologue," and his predilection for the latter. The development of monologic modes of expression is given priority over the dialogic elements of *skaz*, the possibility of a synthesis over the heterogeneity of the transitional forms (1969:204ff.). This may explain the negative view he always took of Avvakum's "polyglossia."

Vinogradov's analyses of the dialogic character of the *skaz* were, however, taken up and further developed by Bakhtin (1963:242ff.). In his definition of the *skaz*, speech interference, the "dual voice," or even "polyphony" represents its basic feature.

Bakhtin (1963:256), too, develops his *skaz* concept from Ejkhenbaum's definition of *skaz* as the set towards the voice and the spoken word. But he criticises this definition, contending that the oral aspect of *skaz* is of secondary importance, and this is a consequence of what is in his view the crucial feature of the *skaz* structure: *the set towards the voice of the other, the word of the other (čužoj golos, čužoe slovo).*

Historically, *skaz* as defined by Bakhtin (1963), belongs to periods marked by a transition between different ideological systems, different world-views, and different styles, periods in which old authorities and established norms and values are in the process of losing their significance, without new ones' having been formed in their place. In such stylistically undetermined periods, authors either have to use the styles of others, that is, to stylise their own expression, or must have recourse to modes of expression previously not included in the canon. In these cases the author's ideas are not directly expressed in his own words, but refracted through those of another.

The author's set towards the word of the other determines the double-voiced structure of the *skaz*: two different voices, two different accents cross each other in the same discourse. The variation in the relationship between the crossing voices produces different versions of *skaz*, corresponding to the main types of dialogic representation found in seventeenth-century unofficial literature and ranging from stylisation and analogous forms, where the discourse tends to abolish the opposition between the voices, to forms where the voices collide, where the author exploits the style of another, investing it with semantic intentions directly opposed to those of the original, a device characteristic of parody and related phenomena.

If the word of the other resists direct parody, thereby forcing the author to take a polemic stance, the result will be a version of *skaz* in which the other despite his absence actively influences the author's discourse. The possibility of a different, competing representation of the same events forces the author to argue for his own views. In such cases the parody ceases to be passive, and the voice of the other becomes an active interference. A hidden polemic becomes a predominant feature of these texts.

This possibility of active interference is latent in all literature, in so far as an author always orients his discourse towards a reader or an audience, tries to influence their reactions, to anticipate their objections and criticisms, to reject the styles of others in hidden polemics against texts within as well as outside the same genre. Whereas in "monologic discourse" the author reigns supreme, in a dialogised discourse the author will constantly find himself in a field of tension.

A similar tension characterises a hidden dialogue, a discourse that may be compared to a dialogue in which the repartees of the other have disappeared, leaving their traces in the set towards the absent interlocutor's unspoken words. This orientation leads to an internal dialogisation of the text, a distinctive feature of autobiography and first-person stories of the confessional type, a feature we should therefore expect to find precisely in the *Life of Avvakum.*

When we proceed to examine a particular text such as Avvakum's *vita*, we cannot, however, expect to find the various types of *skaz* in their abstract, schematic form. In practice there will be an infiltration of different variants. The set towards the word of the other will always shift and change in a dynamic relationship, ranging from uni-directional stylisation to a vario-directional, open or hidden parody. The interrelationship of the voices may be active or passive, and the degree of internal dialogisation will vary in intensity.

After Bakhtin's redefinition of the *skaz* concept, it can no longer be used to identify an isolated textual component, an individual voice, as for instance that of the first-person narrator in the *Life of Avvakum.* Its *skaz* structure becomes a product of the interplay between the different textual elements as these elements are being oriented towards each other, instead of being dominated by the set towards the narrator, the interlocutor, or the historical context. In the interchange between the different "voices" of the text—the narrator's discourse, the comments of the implied author, the whole sequence of quotations, and the implied or realised repartees of the audience—the predominant function becomes the poetic funtion of language, "the set toward the message as such" (Jakobson 1960:356).

It is in this juxtaposition of narrative, commentary, and quotations that Avvakum's story is transformed into a *vita*, as the account of his life becomes subordinate to compositional principles other than the chronological ordering of events. The flow of events is interrupted, the historical account is deformed, and so is the historical figure of Avvakum, who has to die in order to be reborn as saint.

What makes this transformation so complex in Avvakum is the dialogic character of the *skaz*-structure, the projection into each other of elements put together according to a number of different rules and patterns.

## Passion through Parody: The Story of Avvakum's Metamorphosis

Read in the simplest way, the chronological account of Avvakum's life story takes the form of a sequence of travels, starting from the moment he leaves his native village in order to become a priest in the neighbourhood. It goes on to relate how he was forced to flee to Moscow, where he became a member of the circle around Stefan Vonifat'ev. Then follows the tale of his exile to Siberia after the breach with Nikon, of his participation in Paškov's expeditionary force, and of the long return journey to Moscow, a journey that he and his family had to undertake on their own. The last part of the life story deals with the deportations after the denunciation of the Old Believers at the Ecumenical Council of 1667, when Avvakum was first sent to Mezen, and finally to Pustozersk.

The travelogue represents a well-known compositional pattern in early Russian, especially Muscovite hagiography, with its tales of itinerant saints leaving for the wilderness to evangelise the pagans and conquer new land for the Russian Church. *The Life of Saint Stephen* is composed according to this pattern. Avvakum, however, applies the conventional pattern in a way that differs radically from its traditional use. His travelogues do not portray the hero as the Church's representative at work in propagating its official teaching; he stands in opposition to the ideology of the official Church and its leaders. Avvakum's travels take the form of escapes, deportation, and exile, which are negative variants of the travel motif. Moscow is no longer the centre of Orthodoxy, but has herself fallen into the hands of the infidels, led by the Patriarch Nikon and Tsar Alexis. Unlike Saint Stephen of Perm, Avvakum is not the saviour of the pagans. He himself becomes a prisoner, who is first tortured in Nikon's monasteries and finally incarcerated in a subterranean dungeon on the Arctic Ocean, where he sits waiting for his death, "buried alive," to quote his own words.

The distortion and negation of the travel pattern begin in the account of Avvakum's situation after his father's death: "My mother then became a widow; still young, I was now an orphan, and we were driven into exile, away from our kin" (8).

The portrayal of Avvakum as a poor and homeless outsider is further developed in the story of how, after his mother's death, he has to leave his home together with Anastasia, his wife, like himself a poor orphan. Her father was a well-to-do blacksmith whose fortune was squandered after his death. Rejected by his own relations, Avvakum moves to another place—"ot izgnanija pereselikhsja vo ino mesto" (8)—where as a young priest he incurs the wrath of his congregation and is very nearly killed by the excited crowd. To save his life he flees to Moscow. In the stories about his deportation after the breach with Nikon, the deportation motif is varied and emerges in new contexts. Thus the selection of events from Avvakum's life story forms a sequence of degradations. The reason for this must be sought in the principle that underlies this selection, a principle we have already touched on in connection with the travesty of official genres in works like the *Povest' o Gore i Zločastii*, the *Služba kabaku*, and the *Azbuka o golom i nebogatom čeloveke*.

A comparison with these texts will show that their similarity with the *vita* cannot be a coincidence, but reflects structural correspondences. And these correspondences are evidently a result of Avvakum's work on the text. If we compare the account given in the Prjanišnikov version of the orphaned Avvakum's childhood and adolescence up to the moment he leaves his home together with Anastasia, with the corresponding passages in the A-, B-, and C-redactions, we perceive a distinct movement away from historico-biographical details towards a representation that follows the pattern underlying the conflict of the anti-hero with his surroundings in late seventeenth-century unofficial literature:

|  The Prjanišnikov version | The A-, B-, and C-redactions |
| --- | --- |
| I lost my father when still a boy. At seventeen my mother wanted to have me married and brought me a wife of fourteen... And when I became a priest we moved to another place, Lopatišča. (Avvakum 1960:310f.) | Then my mother became a widow and I an early orphan, and we were driven into exile, away from our relatives... And in the same village there was a young girl, also an orphan... Her father was a blacksmith... quite rich ... but when he died, everything was squandered. So she lived in poverty...Then my mother departed to God in great glory. And I was driven out and moved to another place. (8) |

In the earliest version, the precise age of the protagonists, the reason why they leave their home—Avvakum's calling to a neighbouring village— and the name of this village: all these particulars are stated. In the later redactions all this factual information has disappeared. Avvakum and Anastasia emerge as impoverished orphans, rejected by their own relations, who take to the road into the great unknown. This is a pattern we recognise from the *Povest' o Gore i Zločastii* and the *Azbuka*. Like the youth in the tale of Woe-Misfortune and the first-person narrator of the *Azbuka*, Avvakum emerges as a variant of the seventeenth-century anti-hero, an inverted image of the idealised saint of official hagiography.

In the *Life of Avvakum*, however, the relationship between traditional hagiography and parodic distortion is more complex than in the other seventeenth-century texts we have mentioned. Avvakum combines the two modes of expression, idealisation and parody, within the context of his *vita,* with the result that his use of parody is more subtle than the merry inversion of official genres in the *Azbuka* or the *Služba kabaku.*

The combination of the modes of expression found in official hagiography with their parodic inversions marks the *Life of Avvakum* even from the passage about his parents: "My father was the priest Peter, my mother Maria, as a nun Martha. My father was given to drink; my mother fasted and prayed, instructing me always in the fear of God" (8). To a reader set on interpreting the *vita* as an historico-biographical document, the striking deviation from a conventional portrayal of the saint's childhood will be an evidence of Avvakum's truthful recording of historical facts. Such a reader will use the above passage as an instance of Avvakum's undiluted representation of facts. In contrast to early Russian hagiographers, he makes no attempt to embellish the picture of his father, who is, on the contrary, characterised through an emphasis on his vice, seen in even sharper relief against the piety of his wife. Thus Pascal (1938:74ff.) perceives Avvakum's parents, as they are depicted in the *vita*, as typical representatives of his age, and reads the figure of his father as an expression of the moral decline among the Russian clergy in the first half of the seventeenth century, the mother as an expression of the existence at the time of a religious elite among the laity, who took care of religious ideals in this period of decline.

Whatever the truth about Avvakum's father, from a literary point of view Avvakum's representation of him is a variant of the drunken priest found in seventeenth-century parody. By picking on this particular negative feature of his father's character, Avvakum has diverged from hagiographical convention and instead portrayed his father as an inversion of the pious parents of the traditional *vita*. The figure of the mother, on the other hand, is portrayed in conformity with the heroic women we know from late sixteenth-century and early seventeenth-century hagiography in Russia, works like Kalistrat Družina-Osor'in's *Life* of his mother, *Žitie Ulijanii Osor'inoj* and the *Povest' o Marfe i Marii*. In these works the ascetic life pattern of Russian monasticism is projected onto the representation of a woman's life outside the monastic walls. Sainthood is expressed in the way she realises this pattern in daily life.

This feminine ideal is, furthermore, characteristic of Avvakum's writings. In the *Life* it is reflected in the figures of his mother and of Anastasia, and in his glorification of the boyarina Morozova and her sister after their martyrdom in 1675.

By representing his father as the negative counterpart of his mother, Avvakum inverts the traditional relationship between the holy and the profane: his mother, a laywoman, represents the former, which is profaned and degraded in the drunken figure of the priest, his father. In Avvakum's self-portrait, this opposition has become internalised, and the negative features of the seventeenth-century anti-hero are combined with the positive features of the ascetic ideal of hagiography. Avvakum is a sinner, who in the story of the young girl's confession is seized by sexual lust, and overcomes this lust by exposing himself to physical pain, all in accordance with the heroes of traditional hagiography. This combination of elements from two contrasting codes into a novel, composite whole makes the *Life* essentially different from the stories about the anti-hero, despite the similarities. Avvakum emerges both as a negation of the idealised heroic figures of conventional hagiography

and as an affirmation of the ascetic ideal that these heroes were originally meant to embody. This sets him apart from other versions of the anti-
hero, in whom the glorified figures of official hagiography are parodied
and distorted, in the awareness that they have lost their content and become mere stereotypes. In the tale of Savva Grudcyn, as in that of Woe-
Misfortune, it is only at the end of the story that the possibility of a
reaffirmation of the word is suggested, as a means of expressing this
ideal, divine reality beyond the world of the senses. In the *Azbuka* this
possibility is implied in the first-person narrator's retrospective account
of his own abasement, as it appears to him after the conversion. The
narrator of Avvakum's *Life* takes a further step in the same direction.
Avvakum not only sees his own abasement in the light of a divine reality
from the retrospective point ov view of the narrative situation, but has
also projected this illumination onto himself as the hero of his own
story:

> I once saw a dead cow at a neighbour's, and that night I rose, and
> wept much over my soul before the icon, thinking of death, and how
> I, too, must die; and from that time I grew accustomed to praying
> every night. (8)

This is Avvakum's first encounter with death, a central event in the story
of his childhood, which occurs in all the redactions. The carcase of the
cow becomes metonymically an expression of the presence of death in
human life, while the icon, on the other hand, is a metaphor of a divine
reality, present in Avvakum only as an absence, as the transcendent aim
of his striving. This absence, the divine reality beyond death, becomes,
unlike the semblance of reality in this earthly life, the true reality in
Avvakum's *Life*. The antinomy of life and death is resolved in the
antinomy of mortality and immortality, as this is expressed in the
contrast between the carcase as a symbol of death's presence in life, and
the icon, a symbol of immortality as something other than and
different from both life and death.

   The relationship between immanence and transcendence thereby becomes a different one in Avvakum from that of the *Azbuka* and the
stories of Savva Grudcyn and the youth chased by Woe-Misfortune, even
if the goal of the protagonist's life story remains the same: the transcending movement saving him from degradation and the power of
death. In the stories about the anti-hero this movement represents the
final stage of the action pattern and forms an antithesis to his original
breach with his surroundings and the corresponding distortion of
reality. The transcending movement takes the form of a conversion,
where the protagonist regains his original innocence. The typical anti-
hero is a passive victim of life's negative forces, which in various in-
carnations get him in their power and let him go only at the end of the

road. At this point of *desengaño*, from his illusion of reality, the true meaning of the story is revealed.

From the first moment Avvakum interprets his life in the light of a transcendent reality beyond death, illuminating the story of his "fall" with a vision of his future life in the image of a voyage, in which his own multicoloured ship is seen in striking contrast to the golden vessels symbolising the glorification of his departed friends.

Throughout the *Life* the allegorical interpretation of life as a voyage is projected onto the historical account, so that implicitly or explicitly it acquires the character of a fulfilment of this vision. The boat journey on the East Siberian rivers is depicted in this allegory when, for instance, Avvakum refers to the ship of his vision in the tale of his onward journey from Tobolsk: "Again I sat up in my vessel, the one that had appeared to me, which I have already spoken of ..." (20). The voyage motif is combined with a number of other, related motifs in a complex allegory. One of them is the storm in the picture of Avvakum's struggle with the elements:

> My barge was completely swamped by the storm; in the middle of the river it became full of water, the sail torn to shreds, and only the deck was above water, everything else had disappeared into the water. My wife, her head uncovered, managed somehow to drag the children out of the water onto the deck. But I shout, looking to Heaven: "Lord, save us! Lord, help us!" And by God's will we were thrown ashore. (21)

The voyage and the storm motifs are in turn linked with winter and darkness, torture and other forms of physical suffering in a picture of Avvakum's life on the threshold between life and death. After having been tortured by Paškov, bound hand and foot, Avvakum is tossed into one of the open boats, where he is abandoned, half-dead, all night long:

> It was autumn, the rain was falling on me, all night I lay in the downpour... And it was then that my bones began to ache and my veins grew taut. And my heart failed. I felt that I was dying... In the morning they threw me into a boat and carried me onwards ... The rain and snow were pouring down, and I had only a thin kaftan over my shoulders. The water was pouring down my belly and my back. ... (23f.)

The hardship and the misery in the winter quarters on Lake Irgen is similarly depicted:

> I was lying under some birch bark, naked on the stove. And my wife was in the stove, and the children here and there. It was raining.

> There were no clothes, and the winter quarters were leaking. We
> wrapped up in what we could find. (33)

Fire and heat, like water and cold, are means of torture in this universe,
where the rays of the sun do not penetrate, where the only light is the
flickering flame in Paškov's torture chamber:

> One day he had a torture chamber built and a great fire erected. He
> wanted to torture me. I prepared myself, saying the prayers of the
> dying, knowing his treatment. There aren't many who come out of
> that fire of his alive. (37)

The nautical vision at the beginning of the *Life* is the first clue to an interpretation of Avvakum's life as a voyage on a wintry sea. Throughout
the story there follow a number of such anticipatory clues to the
allegorical meaning of the *vita*. The winter metaphors, for instance, are
anticipated in the commentary on the breach with Nikon: "we see that
winter is approaching, my heart froze and my feet began to shake" (15).
The systematic concatenation of semantically related motifs into a
coherent allegory of life as a wintry voyage clearly demonstrates an
intention behind all allegorisations. The metaphorical element of the
text cannot be explained on the theory of a mental background un-
consciously influencing Avvakum's narrative and neutralising his
realistic account of his life story, as maintained by Vinogradov
(1923:212, 233). The metaphorisation of Avvakum's life story becomes
part of an active process in which the story of his life is transformed into
something more than and different from an historical account.

The allegorical interpretation of Avvakum's life story follows a
definite pattern, which we recognise from a number of *raskol* texts of the
seventeenth century, representing the Old Believers as shipwrecked sea-
farers on a wintry sea. It is in this image that for instance the brothers
Pleščeev described the sufferings of the Old Believers in a letter to their
confessor, Ivan Neronov, quoted by Vinogradov (1923:232):

> For truly our winter is harsh and our drowning bitter. ... The waves
> are now gathering around the Church: therefore many zealots of
> Christ's Church are lying in the bottom of the ship, crying and
> suffering.

And in a variant from *Otrazitel'noe pisanie* (Vinogradov 1923:232): "a
storm blew up and the whirling wind roared ... and there was great fear
among the drowning."

Closely linked with the *Life's* voyage theme and its storm allegory are
the episodes in which Avvakum's struggle takes the form of conflict
situations: the officers threatening to kill him early on in the story, the

excited mob that beat him up and force him to abandon his village community, his arrest in Moscow on the Patriarch's orders, the confrontations with Paškov in Siberia, and with the members of the Ecumenical Council, back in Moscow, to mention some of the most striking clashes in the *Life*.

Despite this multiplicity of enemies, who appear now individually, now together, the theme of these various episodes is constant. Avvakum's historical adversaries, however different in real life, are transformed in his memory into agents of the universal power of evil. They represent all that is anti-holy and negative in the *Life* and are profoundly similar in spite of their superficial dissimilarity.

The conflict situations are described in the awareness that behind Avvakum's clash with society is hidden another struggle, a conflict of worldwide significance. The others, his adversaries, act at the instigation of the devil: "naučil ego d'javol," (the devil taught him) (10), "d'javol naučil popov i mužikov i bab" (the devil taught the priests, and the menfolk, and the women) (13), "d'javol likh do menja, a čeloveki do menja dobry" (the devil is wicked to me, but people are good to me) (45), etc.

Avvakum here applies conventional hagiographical expressions in the portrayal of his antagonists; we know them from Nestor's *Life of Saint Theodosius*. From the same repository of early Russian hagiography he has taken the traditional comparison of the saint's enemies with wild animals as a sign of their demonic possession: "biv menja, i u ruki ogryz persty, jako pes, zubami" (he beat me, and gnawed the fingers of my hand with his teeth like a dog) (10) is how one of the officers is described, and the *Life* says of Paškov that he "ryknul jako divyj zver'" (roared like a wild beast) (22), "Nikon vol" k so d'javolom predali trema perstami krestica" (Nikon the wolf and the devil commanded us to make the sign of the cross with three fingers) (58), "I patriar"si zadumalisja; a naši, čto vol"čonki vskoča, zavyli" (And the patriarchs pondered my words, but our people leapt up and howled like wolfcubs) (59), etc. (see Nestor's description of the murderers of Boris and Gleb in the *Čtenie:* "rykajušče aki zverie divii" — roaring like wild beasts.)

By means of these hagiographical comparisons, Avvakum's enemies are transformed into actors in a drama in which they all play the same role in different variations, a drama in which Avvakum is the protagonist, whose part also remains the same from episode to episode.

Avvakum's conception of this struggle between good and evil marks an inversion of the traditional early Russian representation of it, where it is the Tsar and the higher clergy that embody the divine will on earth, and who in their capacity of his superiors side with the saint in his struggle with the evil forces. To find a distribution of roles that corresponds to that of our *vita*, we must go back to early Christian *martyria* and their portrayal of the saints' struggle against the Roman

Emperor, the ruler of this world, and his representatives.

This similarity is a structural one and may become a point of departure for a positive redefinition of the function of the hagiographical elements in Avvakum's *vita*. Seen in the hagiographical tradition, the *vita* is not merely a negation of the Muscovite saint's Life, but also a rejuvenation of an earlier form, where the juxtaposition of such different textual types as the traditional early Russian saint's Life and seventeenth-century unofficial parodies becomes possible because they are subordinated to a higher structural principle. In it abasement and elevation, hero and anti-hero, do not exclude each other, but designate complementary oppositions in a dialectic process of sanctification.

In order to define this principle, we shall have to work out the structural invariant of the individual episodes.

Early on in his account, Avvakum relates a series of episodes about his confrontation with three different officers, all of whom have it in for him. The first and shortest of these episodes reads as follows:

> An officer carried off a widow's daughter. And I begged him to bring the orphan back to her mother. But he had only contempt for our plea and raised a storm against me. And at the church, where the mob had gathered, they trampled me to death. And I, lying dead for half an hour and more, came back to life at God's command. And terrified he surrendered the young woman to me. (10)

The action pattern, or plot, consists of a beginning: "U vdovy naćal'nik otnjal dočer' " (an officer took away a widow's daughter) and Avvakum's response: "i az molikh ego, da že sirotinu vozvratit k materi" (and I implored him to give the orphan back to her mother), which triggers the wrath of his adversary and leads to Avvakum's abasement and suffering, a suffering unto death: "do smerti menja zadavili. I az leža mertv polčasa i bolši" (they trampled me to death. And I lay dead for half an hour and more). This is followed by a reversal, a peripety: "i paki ožive Božiim manoveniem" (and I was brought back to life by the will of God) a change that prepares the ground for Avvakum's final triumph over his enemy: "I on, ustrašasja, otstupilsja mne devitsy" (and he, seized with fear, gave up the girl to me).

The second episode represents a shortened version of the same pattern: "Then at the devil's instigation he came to the church, beat me and dragged me by the feet on the ground, still in my vestments, I praying all the time" (10). Then follows the third episode, which differs from the preceding ones in that God's will manifests itself from the beginning: twice the pistols do not go off in the officer's attempt on Avvakum's life. The moment of pathos and the peripety are omitted, and the miracle is succeeded by Avvakum's triumph: "Az ze priležno, iduči, moljus' Bogu, edinoju rukoju osenil evo i pokloniljsa emu" (And I, walking on, praying fervently to God, blessed him with my hand and bowed to him).

The other episodes of the *vita* are constructed on the same pattern, in the stories of Nikon's persecution of the Old Believers, as in those of Avvakum's sufferings under Paškov and of the denunciation of him and his followers by the Ecumenical Council, and finally, in the stories from the prison camp at Pustozersk. The string of individual episodes may be regarded throughout as variants of a constant scheme. The conflict between the representatives of the devil and Avvakum takes the form of an *agon*, succeeded by Avvakum's abasement, suffering, and symbolic death. This symbolic death at the same time marks a turning point, where he is brought back to life by God's will, in which he himself has now become an active participant. It manifests itself in the form of a vision, a miracle, in the victory over Avvakum's enemies, and in the awareness that his abasement in this life anticipates glorification and immortality in the next, through negative analogy.

The symbolic death which marks the turning point between abasement and triumph is represented in a number of different ways: Avvakum is beaten unconscious; is bound hand and foot and abandoned lying in the autumnal rain throughout the night; is thrown into prison, where he lies on the straw, his "back rotting"; now he lies naked and exhausted in the winter quarters on Lake Irgen, with only birch bark to cover his shame, now he is buried alive at Pustozersk in his subterranean prison hole.

Paradigmatically, these different variants equate each other. Despite surface differences, they take the same place and serve the same function in the action pattern. They all represent the transitional stage between life and death, in the form of a threshold situation, in which Avvakum is neither alive nor dead; neither outside nor within; neither naked nor clothed, and so forth.

The individual episodes of the *vita* usually represent exceptional situations, in which Avvakum's historical figure is symbolically annihilated through his humiliation and suffering, and in which he comes back to life as a sign of a divine will and of the truth of the old faith.

Abasement and suffering thus play a highly ambivalent part in Avvakum's *vita*. His torture is negative because it tears his body apart, but at the same time affirmative, because it provokes the Wholly Other, an otherness which manifests itself in Avvakum's life and causes him to conquer death.

Avvakum's enemies and the negative power they represent perform a positive task, because God's will becomes present in him through their attempt to destroy his body. The paradoxical role of the devil is to torture Avvakum to death in order that God's will may become manifest in him. The greater the torture, the closer Avvakum comes to his real death, the closer he also comes to immortality beyond death and deification.

Through this interpretation of evil and of his own abasement Avvakum has represented himself as invincible. Through his tortures he is liberated from the transience of the body. The true Avvakum is he who in his abasement arises again as an exponent of the Wholly Other.

If we compare this complex figure with the Avvakum we encounter in the narrative situation as the first-person narrator of his *Life*, we shall see that in his abasement he corresponds to the confessing Avvakum in confidential conversation with his spiritual father, that is, to the fictitious mask representing the emotive function of the narrative. On the other hand, the triumphant Avvakum of his life story corresponds to the Avvakum who in the narrative situation is discernible behind his narrator's mask when the fiction is lifted and the narrative is oriented towards the real, extratextual recipients of his message, and the conative function becomes the predominant one.

In the life story proper, this dichotomous figure, in which the preaching author is discernible behind the confessing narrator, is transformed into the complex and ambivalent hero of the *vita*. The two variants of the Avvakum figure contained in the narrative situation are projected into each other by means of the poetic function of language, the set towards the text itself, towards the message of the *Life* as such.

The representation of Avvakum's abasement, and of his triumph in a world where God's will is provoked and brought to expression through Avvakum's victory over his enemies, but where God himself is perpetually absent and the negative powers rule, moves throughout in the direction of a new disambiguation, but the contradiction is never resolved: in the *vita* Avvakum has to remain in the contradiction.

The common pattern underlying the individual episodes of the *vita* reflects a *dialogisation* of reality. The *Life of Avvakum* is generically a *dialogised vita*, where life is represented as a transitional stage between the old and the new world order, a chaotic stage between a Russia that once was the true image of a higher, divine world order, and this divine order in its transcendent reality, which always is.

The structure of the individual episodes of the *Life* and the structure of its world vision are identical: the symbolic death and resurrection on the threshold between abasement and triumph prefigure Avvakum's real death, the divide which will mark his transition from the sufferings of the world to glorification beyond death.

The dialogisation, the absence of a superordinate principle in the *skaz* structure, becomes manifest in different ways on different levels, ranging from Avvakum's dialogic orientation towards his own self and his ambivalence in the assessment of the events, to the "heteroglossia" of his discourse, where Church Slavonic and Russian elements are mixed, in conscious opposition to the stylistic stratification of the new, official Baroque.

From the immanent point of view, the question of whether Paškov

tormented Avvakum or was tormented by him must remain un-
answered, and can be resolved only when disambiguation has been re-
established beyond Avvakum's life story: "Ten years he tortured me, or I
him, I don't know. God will decide on the last day" (38). Similarly, dialogisation is expressed when the borderline between the tragic and the
comic is erased in the narrator's serio-comic attitude to events: "I gore i
smekh" (28), "I plaču i radujusja" (46).

   The dialogisation of reality in Avvakum's *vita* is also a demonisation
of it, a demonisation which is in itself ambivalent. The devil forms part
of God's universe as a negative manifestation of his will in a world that
God has left to the devil, in order that the chosen, under the devil's
torture, may come forward as blood witnesses for the divine truth:

> God permits these breaches in order to bring forth the elect, that
> they shall be burned, that they shall be purified, that those who have
> stood the test shall become manifest among us. Satan has obtained
> our shining Russia from God to make her turn purple with the
> blood of her martyrs. (52)

The persecution of the Old Believers is reinterpreted into a negative
expression of God's will, which is positively manifested in Avvakum's
miracles and shows that Avvakum participates in the transcendent
reality of the absent Godhead. In this transitional situation God is both
present and absent. It is a situation that will cease only after death, when
the stormy voyage of the Old Believers through wintry darkness is over,
and when from this darkness they reach light, and glorification from
suffering.

> Let them be tortured, the dear ones, they will gain the Heavenly
> Bridegroom. God will guide them in every possible way through
> this earthly life and the Heavenly Bridegroom will lead them
> towards Him in His mansions, the Sun of Justice, Our Light and
> Hope. (53)

The light from Christ, the transcendent Sun of the *Life*, does not
penetrate down to the sailors in its allegorical representation of life as a
dark and stormy voyage on a wintry sea. The realm of God, harmony,
and unity are reached only through a negation of the negation, in
absolute renunciation of this world.

   "L'Unité gît en Dieu, en Satan le binaire," wrote the Huguenot
Baroque poet Du Bartas (1544–1590). In Avvakum's *vita* dialogisation
expresses a similar notion: with his decrees, Nikon split Russian society
and made the Church into a tool of the devil's, in a state where the Tsar

no longer appears as God's vicegerent in a social order imaging the realm of God, a state of chaos and conflict.

This world-view has sprung from an ideology which might be called "un mysticisme pour temps troublés," to borrow a term from Baroque scholarship (Dubois 1973:97). In the context of European Baroque, Avvakum's *vita* corresponds to the literature and pictorial art that have their origins in Protestantism and are marked by the Calvinist doctrine of God's absolute transcendence. From this point of view, the *Life of Avvakum* relates to the triumphant Russian Baroque art of Simeon Polockij as the art of Rembrandt to that of Rubens, as the teachings of Jansenius to those of the Jesuits. In Western Baroque the two opposites relate to each other dialectically, and this is also true of the relationship between Avvakum's *vita* and the new Russian Baroque poetry, a poetry Avvakum attacks in the introduction to his *vita*.

The demonisation of reality is not an objective in itself for Avvakum. If the transformation of his life story had stopped here, his *Life* could hardly have been called a *vita*, which it becomes only through a recoding of the life story by means of Biblical quotations. Through the juxtaposition with scriptural quotations Avvakum transforms the story of his life into a hagiographical work:

> In the process of their artistic representation the "scenes from real life" are apperceived by being assimilated to a great variety of Biblical plot patterns and stylistic formulae and embellished with rhetorical colours from liturgical and hagiographical sources. (Vinogradov 1923:211)

The Biblical quotations of the *Life* may be grouped under two headings. One comprises quotations that form part of a parallelism, where they are related to events in the narrative through similarity or contrast. Narrative and quotation here form an inner, metaphorical relationship. The second group consists of quotations that are hidden in the dialogue of the *dramatis personae*. In certain situations Avvakum has his contemporaries speak the same lines as those of the Biblical heroes, so that the result is a substitution of the latter for the former. This group of quotations should be seen in connection with the change of names, another of Avvakum's devices: he occasionally exchanges the names of his contemporaries for the names of Biblical figures. In both cases it is a question of metonymical relationships, where Biblical elements are mounted into the narrative on the basis of the similarity that has been established between the two levels.

The quotations are usually easy to identify in the parallelisms, because what we have are explicit juxtapositions with Biblical analogies. When Avvakum saves his former enemy from the Cossacks by hiding him in his boat, and denying that he is there, a comparison is immediately drawn with a passage in the Bible:

> Like the harlot Rahab in Jericho hid the people of Joshua, the son of Nun, I hid him in the bottom of the boat. ... And I lied then and said: "He is not here with me." ... Father and servant of Christ, forgive me for lying then. What do you think? Was it a great sin? In the time of Rahab the harlot, she seems to have done the same thing. And the Scriptures praise her for it. (39)

While Avvakum's own narrative, which has not been included in the above passage, goes into detail in the description of events, the second component of the comparison is introduced in the form of a synecdochic allusion to something the audience are supposed to know already. This is a recurrent pattern in the *Life*. It underlies, for instance, the story of Avvakum's flight to Moscow with his wife and newborn son, whom they baptised on the way "jako že Filipp kaženika drevle," the allusion being to the Apostle Philip and the Ethiopian courtier in the Acts of the Apostles (8:26–39). The same is true of the allusion to the sons of Zebedee who wanted to command fire to come down from heaven and consume the Samaritans, when Avvakum invokes the wrath of God on Paškov's son and his men, who in defiance of his advice have followed the auguries of a Siberian shaman. The comparison is here used to emphasise the contrast and express Avvakum's repentance, whereas it is the similarity between the components that dominates in the description of how Avvakum was forced out into the wilderness "so zvermi i so zmijami i so pticami vitat'" (to live with the beasts and the snakes and the birds), (22), a periphrasis of the eleventh Psalm: "Flee as a bird to your mountain."

The "epiphany" of the *Life*, in which the meaning of Avvakum's collage becomes evident, is the story of Avvakum's confrontations with the Church Princes at the 1667 Council, when the Old Believers were officially denounced as heretics and excommunicated.

The story forms one of the last segments in the *Life's* course of events. It is the point where the reader is given the final clue to the hidden meaning of Avvakum's narrative, equating as it does the story of the Old Believers and their sufferings with the Passion of Christ:

> And they took me to the Sparrow Hills. The priest Lazarus and the monk Epiphanius the elder were already there, shorn and mocked. ... But let them suffer! Why pity them? Christ was better than they are, and He too, our Light, had to endure from their forefathers, Annas and Caiaphas. So there is no reason why the present ones should surprise us: they do it on a pattern! (60)

It emerges from this passage that the function of the parallels is to transform Avvakum's sufferings and those of the other Old Believers into a re-enactment of the sufferings of Christ. Avvakum's life story is no mere reproduction of historical events, nor is it a passive reflection of historical contradictions, but rather an attempt to overcome the contradictions through a recoding of history on Biblical patterns. At the end of his *Life,* Avvakum emerges as a *figura Christi.* In the Tsar's farewell to Avvakum before his deportation to Pustozersk, this is made explicit: "protopop, vedaju-de ja tvoe čistoe i neporočnoe i bogopodražatel'noe žitie" (archpriest, I know your innocent, spotless life in imitation of Christ) (60).

In the concluding part of the *Life* the Passion of Christ is clearly outlined in the portrayal of Avvakum and his fellow sufferers. When Avvakum's sons deny the faith of their father, they are compared to Peter in the forecourt of the high priest. The mutilations at Pustozersk on 14 April 1670 mark the next stage. Ivan Elagin, sent by the Tsar to organise the mutilations, is referred to metonymically as Pilate, which in the context is sufficient to suggest the correspondence between the events of the Passion and those of Avvakum's story.

The analogy between the narration and the quotations makes the parallel components permutable. They may replace each other as equivalent representations of a common invariant, which is the mythical pattern underlying both sequences. This is the structural explanation for the exchange of names and the transference of quoted speech from the Bible into Avvakum's narrative, where his contemporaries are made to speak in the words of Biblical figures. One of the officers, who is out to kill him but repents, cries out to Avvakum in the words of the prodigal son: "prosti, gosudar', sogrešil pred Bogom i pred toboju," (forgive me, my lord, I have sinned before God and before you) (cf. Luke 15:18: "Otče, sogrešikh na nebo i pred toboju" - Father, I have sinned against heaven, before thee) and the phrase is repeated by others in similar situations. Paškov explains at the hour of repentance: "Sogrešikh, predav krov' nepovinnu" (I have sinned in that I have betrayed the innocent blood) (36), thereby quoting the repentant Judas of Matt. 27:4 "Sogrešikh, predav krov' nepovinnu."

This transformation of Avvakum's life story into a re-enactment of the Passion is anticipated in the exordium, in the long and difficult passage where Avvakum attacks Nikon. He interprets the solar eclipse of 1654 as a sign of the wrath of God and a parallel to the eclipse that Dionysius the Areopagite is said to have witnessed at Heliopolis during the Crucifixion of Christ. In the early Russian translation of Saint Dionysius, quoted by Avvakum, the saint on this occasion exclaimed: "ili končina veku priide, ili Bog Slovo plotiju straždet" ("either the end of the world has arrived, or God Logos suffers in the flesh") (3). Then it was the latter possibility that was realised, now it is the former. Avvakum sees the

eclipse of the sun in 1654 as a sign that Nikon has with his heresy called
down the wrath of God on Russia: "Nikon otstupnik veru kazil i zakony
cerkovnyja, i sego radi Bog izlijal fial gneva jarosti Svoeja na Russkuju
zemlju" ("Nikon the apostate was subverting the faith and the laws of
the Church, and for this God poured forth the vial of the fury of His
wrath") (4).

The figural interpretation of Avvakum's life has to be seen against the
background of this eschatological view of history, which is realised in
the demonisation of the historical reality, and in the transcending movement towards a goal beyond the *Life*. The bold parallelisation with the
suffering of Christ at the end of the *vita* points beyond the life story, in
the direction of that event which is always the goal of the narrative, but
which the autobiographical form makes it impossible to depict:
Avvakum's death, the moment in time when his sufferings will cease,
when he shall win the martyr's crown, and no longer remain a figure of
the abased Son of Man, but become united with his prototype in death's
rebirth to immortality.

This future moment, which also signifies the end of time and the
transition from time to eternity, is superordinate to the narrative
situation. It is the point in which the different strands of the *vita*
converge and the difference between author, narrator, and protagonist is
resolved. At this future point, Avvakum' historical figure will become
identical with Avvakum the hero of the *Life*. The victory over death in
death is the teleological principle that generates the structure of the *vita*.
This victory is anticipated symbolically in the stories of Avvakum's
humiliation and triumph. Represented in words, his life becomes an
unending repetition of this pattern: an annihilation of the self in the
word, and an annihilation of the self as word, in order that it may rise in
the Word, and as the Word.

The transformation of Avvakum into a *figura Christi* and a mediator
between life and death demonstrates that the *Life* is a variant of the
model also underlying Nestor's representation of the saint as an *imago
Christi* in his *Life of Saint Theodosius*.

And yet the two *Lives* are wholly different. In the *Life of Saint
Theodosius* the saint's humiliation in the struggle with his mother is a
reflection of the abasement suffered by the Holy Spirit in his figure, and
a preparation for Theodosius' symbolic death and rebirth when taking
the vows. His abasement is succeeded by an opposite, upward movement, described in the story of Theodosius' life as an abbot and builder
of monasteries. His new monastic society in the Caves Monastery is interpreted anagogically as a reflection of the heavenly abode of the Holy
Spirit, the aim of Nestor's visionary description of the saint's gradual
ascent and glorification. Abasement and elevation are, in the *Life of
Saint Theodosius* inscribed in a Neo-Platonic movement.

In the *Life of Avvakum* the heavenly glory is beyond all anagogical re-

presentation in sensible images. In its dialogic universe, figural interpretation is possible only as a continuous re-enactment of the transitional situation itself. The *vita* takes the form of a sequence of episodes
in which humiliation and triumph follow each other in a seesaw
movement. Throughout his life Avvakum must remain on the threshold
between mortality and immortality.

A divide is drawn here between the medieval, Neo-Platonic universe of
Nestor's *vita* and the dichotomous world-view of the Baroque that
underlies the *Life of Avvakum*. As in the official, triumphant Baroque
in seventeenth-century Russia, the old, medieval commonplaces are in
Avvakum combined according to a different system, dominated by new
factors. But it is particularly as a dialectic, or dialogic, negation of the
official Russian Baroque of the time that Avvakum's *Life* reveals its own
Baroque character.

Our analysis thus lends support to Morozov's and Mathauserová's
interpretation of the contradictory universe of the *vita* as a manifestation
of the dichotomous *weltanschauung* of the Baroque. It has demonstrated that the "national," "domestic" seventeenth-century Baroque in
Russia cannot be isolated from the "international" Baroque, but should
be seen in dialectic oppositon to its official forms.

It has furthermore become clear that the structure of the *vita* cannot be
deduced from Avvakum's historical epoch by means of a theory that sees
literature as a mere reflection of society. On the contrary, the *Life* marks
Avvakum's attempt to negate his times. It expresses his struggle to overcome the contradictions of his own time and to beat his enemies by interpreting his own abasement and impotence on a mythical model. In this
struggle to master a chaotic reality, Avvakum moulded his own life
according to the pattern of the martyr passion, combining this pattern
with other schemes, so that the form of figural interpretation we finally
have in Avvakum's *vita* constitutes an individual, idiosyncratic variant
of the abstract model.

The main weakness of modern, profanatory interpretations of Avvakum's biography is revealed precisely in that the basic structure of the
work remains hidden through such a reading. By interpreting the *vita* as
an instance of the breakthrough for a new conception of man in seventeenth-century "plebeian literature," a conception of man created
through an inductive interpretation of the historical reality, as opposed
to the normative ideal of earlier epochs, Likhačev (1970:141ff.) has dis-
regarded Avvakum's intentional transformation of himself into a *figura
Christi*. It is also questionable whether Avvakum's literary form represents a simplified version of the literary tradition. Likhačev's view of
Avvakum's colloquial style as the expression of an "emotional simpli-
fication of man" is rather the result of a simplified reading of the *Life*.

In actual fact, the opposite is the case. The *skaz* structure with its multiplicity of heterogeneous elements marks, like the literature of the *smuta*,

a complication compared to the traditional idealisation, both formally and in the conception of man contained in it. Only on its surface will Avvakum's *Life* appear simple to a modern reader. The complexity is uncovered in the process of deciphering its different levels of meaning.

The superordinate function of the figural interpretation in Avvakum's *Life* shows that Avvakum's self-portrait, far from being the result of an inductive method, emerges as a projection onto the narrative of the archetypal pattern implicit in the quotations.

Avvakum's interpretation, through prototypical Biblical images, of his own humiliation and misery in a lifelong fight against the power of the new autocratic state and its persecution and suppression of all opposition is not in itself an exclusive phenomenon. This method of interpretation became the answer to the triumphant Baroque in the subversive Protestant or sectarian art of the West as well. An illustration of this is found in Dutch painting at the turn of the sixteenth century: a painting such as Peter Brueghel the Younger's *Slaughter of the Innocents* depicts the punitive expedition of the Spaniards against the rebellious Dutch on the model of the old iconographic pattern, so that the peasant women begging for mercy and crying to the soldiers to spare the lives of their children emerge in the image of the desperate mothers depicted in the Biblical story.

A highwater mark in the Protestant Baroque is Rembrandt's contemporary Christ. This figure is not the beautiful athlete of the triumphant Baroque, painted on classical models, but a suffering human being, hiding the frailties of the body under his mantle. He is depicted from live models in the artist's milieu, now his own son Titus, now one of his friends from the Jewish quarter of Amsterdam.

As regards the literary manifestations of the counter-Baroque, there is a striking similarity between Avvakum's *vita* and the picaresque novel. Although the relationship between the picaresque novel and the religious reform- and counter-movements in the sixteenth and seventeenth centuries has only recently attracted scholarly attention, it has been shown that the picaresque novel in Spain at the end of the sixteenth century had its origins in a religious counter-literature. In this literature the authors satirised the moral and religious hypocrisy of their time, invoking the word of the Gospel in their fight against the powerful of this world. In this fight they attacked the idealising modes of expression characteristic of the official genres (Parker 1967:20ff., Castro 1969, Rötzer 1972).

Our examination of Avvakum's *vita* and its connection with the literature that had developed in opposition to the new imperial Baroque in seventeenth-century Russia has tried to demonstrate that we are here faced with a similar phenomenon. It should therefore be possible to see this literature as a variant of a European counter-Baroque, thereby modifying Morozov's and Mathauserová's emphasis on its "domestic" and "spontaneous" character, which isolates the unofficial literature in seventeenth-century Russia from analogous movements elsewhere in Europe.

# Avvakum's Figural Interpretation in a Russian Context

The concept of a counter-Baroque in dialectic opposition to the official, triumphant Baroque appears to be a better basis for the study of the relationship between Avvakum's *vita* and the official art and literature of contemporary Russia than is provided by a chronological sequence of a "domestic" and an "international" Russian Baroque in the seventeenth century. A dialectic definition of the Baroque makes it easier to understand the picture of Avvakum's *vita* as an answer to the endeavours of his adversary, Nikon, to transform his monastery into an image of the Heavenly Jerusalem, and himself into the representative of the Pantocrator in the Orthodox *oikoumene*. Avvakum's representation of his own abasement after the example of Christ, as a prefiguration of the glory awaiting him after death, negates the self-glorification of the Patriarch in this life. It is as if the *imitatio Christi* contained in the *Life of Saint Theodosius*, an imitation leading from humiliation to glory, had been split up, and the segments juxtaposed in a bipolar system of two mutually antagonistic ideologies (see Børtnes 1979). On the one hand is Nikon, the representative of the militant Orthodox tradition, who has realised the necessity of reforming the Church in order to turn Moscow into the religious centre of the new, multinational empire. On the other is Avvakum, whose reformist zeal had as its aim to realise the idea of the Stoglav about a Muscovite national state and bring the Russian Church out of the decline in which it found itself after the *smuta*. Typologically, this opposition has, despite all differences, characteristic points of similarity with the opposition between Reformation and Counter-Reformation in the West. These similarities acquire an increased historical significance when we take into account the opposition between Counter-Reformation and Orthodox nationalism in Lithuania around 1600.

The connection between the *raskol* literature and the one which arose among Orthodox nationalists in the Ukraine and Byelorussia awaits further research, and may for the time being only be outlined.

In our context, however, it is important to remember that the Old Believers argued for their opposition to Nikon on the basis of literature

printed in Moscow before his Patriarchate, books which were generally
adaptations and translations of works published in Kiev earlier in the
century. Thus, a number of the most important sources for their argu-
mentation against the official Church were works written by Orthodox
monks and priests in the Ukraine and in Lithuania as weapons in their
fight against Catholicism and Counter-Reformation. Without being
fully aware of it, the Old Believers thereby came to base their arguments
on the West Russians, in a way corresponding to the method the West
Russian clergy had used in their dispute with the Polish Jesuits. They
had based their arguments on the anti-Catholic literature of the
Protestants (see Robinson 1974:336ff.)

In Kiev the arguments taken from the religious counter-literature in
Western Europe were combined with elements from the patristic tradition of the Orthodox Church, especially from the writings of Saint
John Chrysostom, from mystical Hesychasm, and from the Christocentric spirituality of Orthodox monasticism. The polemical writings
of the Athonite monk Ivan Vyšens'kyj against the Jesuit Peter Skarga
became exemplary for this combination of Orthodox and Protestant
arguments in the fight against the powerful of this world. In Avvakum's
writings the arguments of the Ukrainians were taken up, and combined
with the domestic, Muscovite heritage of the Trans-Volga monks. The
books that the secular and clerical authorities had had printed in
Moscow prior to Nikon became, paradoxically, a source of strength for
the Old Believers in their fight against Church and State after the breach.
The Ukrainian influence appears to have been particularly in evidence
in their formulation of an eschatological ideology.

In Lithuania, Prince K. V. Ostrožskij (1526–1608), who supported the
Orthodox in their struggle with the Catholics, had commissioned a
former Protestant named Motovila to write an anti-Catholic tract from
an Orthodox point of view. The tract was later submitted to Prince
Kurbskij for approval, but rejected as heretical and never published. In it
the Pope was represented as the Antichrist, in accordance with Protestant propaganda (Robinson 1974:317). This notion was repeated
in Stefan Zizanij's commentary on Saint Cyril of Jerusalem's homily on
the Antichrist, published in Vilnius in 1596 and sponsored by the same
Prince Ostrožskij. This commentary argues that the Antichrist, the
representative of Satan, is already on the march towards Russia from the
West in the guise of the Pope, extending his realm by the sword and not
by the word. Wishing to subdue the whole world, he sends his false
prophets, the Jesuits and the Uniates, as his harbingers, to seduce the
Orthodox by means of their pagan science into joining the ranks of the
heretics, and to torture those who are unwilling to abjure the true faith.
Zizanij's edition and his commentaries were included in the so-called
*Kirillova kniga*, published in Moscow in 1644. The book is a polemical
encyclopedia and a weapon in the Muscovite Church's fight against

both Catholicism and Protestantism. Together with the *Kniga o vere* (Moscow, 1648), originally a Ukrainian anthology of polemical writings directed against the Uniates, the *Kirillova kniga* was an important source for the eschatological teaching of the Old Believers that their age was the last one, and that the Antichrist was coming from the West, via Rome, Poland, and the Ukraine.

In their writings, however, the Old Believers adapted Ukrainian ideas to suit their own polemic situation. Tsar Alexis and the Patriarch Nikon are substituted for the Pope in the role of harbinger of the Antichrist. Ironically, it is the spiritual successors of the West Russian polemicists, the learned collegians from Kiev who were called to Moscow early in Tsar Alexis' reign, who take the Jesuits' place as the false prophets in the Old Believers' version of the Antichrist myth.

In this way the myth moves eastwards, constantly changing, but with the same basic scheme. The cast varies, while the roles and the relations between them remain the same. It is not only in the depiction of their antagonists that the Old Believers follow West Russian models—the parallels are equally striking in the description of their own situation. The allegory used by the Old Believers, of themselves as "sailors" and "wanderers" through life, corresponds to the portrayal of life as a pilgrimage found in the writings of the West Russian polemicists. In Ivan Vyšens'kyj's self-portrait in the guise of a "naked wanderer" ("goljak i strannik," in *Obličenie dijavola miroderžca*; see Tschiževskij 1956b:238) we recognise the characteristic features of the anti-hero in the tales and satires of the unofficial literature.

The resemblance between Vyšens'kyj's struggle against Catholicism and Avvakum's lifelong fight against Nikonian heresy has been underlined both by Eremin (1953) and Robinson (1974). The basic attitude behind their arguments is the same: they attack the new philosophy and rhetoric, defending their own unembellished style against an artificial eloquence. In their opposition to the high-flown style of the school Baroque they both strove to combine the vernacular with the Church Slavonic of the Bible. Although their linguistic basis differed, their intention was the same: to preserve the stylistic ideal of the Gospels, in which the sublime and the low appear side by side, and where a subtle content is revealed in a simple and colloquial form. They both defend this mixture of styles against the graduated levels of styles found in the school Baroque.

Neither for Vyšens'kyj nor for Avvakum is the defence of the simple, of *prostota* and *prostorečie* a purely aesthetic matter. Their defence of the style of the Gospels is a defence of the humiliated God Incarnate and of the image of man found in the Gospels. Furthermore, it is a defence of the relationship between God and man represented in the New Testament. They both contended that whoever wishes to understand and share in the mystery of the Incarnation must follow Saint Paul and reject all worldly wisdom and learning to interpret the meaning of Christ in the simple words of the Gospels:

> Saint Paul himself, illuminated by the spiritual understanding of Christ, rejected the understanding and wisdom of the world and consigned them to oblivion. (Eremin 1955:179, Robinson 1974:324)

Vyšens'kyj refutes the new scholastic learning by referring to Christ as his teacher, "moj daskal prostak," who in his simple wisdom surpasses them all:

> My teacher is a simple man, but wiser than all others, he enlightens the illiterate. My teacher is a simple man who transforms fishermen into fishers of men. My teacher, who ridicules the philosophers with his simplicity ... (Eremin 1955:10, Robinson 1974:321)

In relation to the Biblical examples Avvakum goes a step further than Vyšens'kyj. He identifies himself in his abasement with the Apostles, when finally he invokes their example, that they too "o sebe vozveščali že, egda čto Bog sodelaet v nikh" (they made public statements about themselves whenever God was at work within them) (67). In himself he is nothing, but when annihilated he emerges as a sign of the divine glory:

> Not to us but our God be our glory. For I am nothing. I have said and say again: I am a sinful man, a whoremonger and a robber, a thief and a murderer, a friend to publicans and sinners and an accursed hypocrite to all men. (67)

Avvakum's hypertrophied abasement of the self implies a complementary hypertrophy of the non-ego, of God's will, in which he becomes a participator through suffering. In the account of his life Avvakum transforms himself into an expression, a medium of "razum Khristov," of the "sensus Christi" in 1 Cor. 2:

> But although I am ignorant in words, I am not in understanding. I am ignorant of dialectic, rhetoric, and philosophy, but I have the understanding of Christ in me, as the Apostle also says: Though I be rude in speech, but not in understanding. (67)

In spite of the similarities, Avvakum's Muscovite "prostorečie" is very different from Vyšens'kyj's conception of the simple style of Church Slavonic. The Athonite is wholly within the Graeco-Slavonic tradition and argues against the "Latins" on the authority of the Greek Church Fathers. Avvakum, on the other hand, is a Graecophobe, despite his quotations from the writings of the Greek Fathers, which he knows only in translation. Avvakum has no Greek, and repeatedly sees his Russian mother tongue in opposition to Greek, as in the following address to the Tsar in the *Kniga tolkovanij i nravoučenij:*

> Sigh heavily, in the old way, as it used to be in the days of Stephen, and say in Russian: O Lord, have mercy upon me sinner! And leave the Kyrie eleison. That is how the Greeks speak, scorn them. For you, Mikhajlovič, are a Russian, you are not a Greek, are you? Speak your own mother tongue, do not disgrace her either in church or at home or in your statements. As Christ has taught us, so it is right for us to speak. God loves us no less than he loves the Greeks ... (475)

This opposition between a Muscovite and a Graeco-Slavonic background makes the similarity between them even more important for the definition of a counter-Baroque. In their protest against the triumphant, imperial Baroque, they represent themselves and their own situation on the model of the humbled Christ of the Gospels, in the same way as did the Protestants in Western Europe. The common code is hidden in the New Testament, in the patristic heritage, and in the literature and the pictorial art of the Middle Ages.

The *Life of Avvakum* still presents a problem in this connection. There are no immediate literary models for its mixture of vulgarisms and Biblical language, even if we can find a similar mixture of styles in parodies like the *Služba kabaku.*

However, the question is whether we have to presuppose only written models for Avvakum's style. Is it not a possibility that his idiosyncratic combination of *vjakan'e* and *propoved'* might have a background in the oral tradition? Let us in conclusion discuss this theory, starting from Avvakum's account of his dispute with the Orthodox patriarchs at the 1667 Council in Moscow.

This episode follows the traditional scheme: first an *agon* between the parties in the form of a verbal duel, where Avvakum accuses his adversaries of being in league with the Antichrist. This accusation sparks off the *pathos.* In the scuffle that follows, Avvakum is almost beaten to death. This disaster is averted, and instead Avvakum triumphs over the Church princes:

> So they were seated. And I walked over to the door and fell down on my side: "You sit there and I lie here," I said to them. So they laughed: "Our archpriest is a fool! and he does not revere the patriarchs!" And I said: "We are all fools for Christ's sake! You are glorious, we are dishonoured! You are strong, we are powerless!" (59)

The incident occurs immediately before the "epiphany," when the Council is compared to the high priests in the history of the Passion.

Armed with a quotation from Saint Paul, Avvakum rides in triumph over the members of the Council, and shows that in his abasement he is the true representative of the Word.

As a variant of the basic scheme, this incident has a special significance, Avvakum being quite obviously represented in the guise of a *jurodivyj*, a holy fool. The moment of triumph, when Avvakum in a gesture of self-abasement lies down at the exit, from where he hurls his accusatory speech at the others, is a literary scenario which has its model in the one-man shows of the holy fools. They used precisely such eloquent gestures to underline their words when they wished to "rugat'sja miru," to accuse and to expose the powerful of this world and their worldly wisdom. In the representation of Avvakum's figure and his fight against the authorities, their nonverbal mode has been translated into the written word. The final quotation from Saint Paul is the key to this *jurodstvo:* "We are fools for Christ's sake" ("stulti propter Christum"—"mōroi dia Christon," 1 Cor. 4:10).

In monasticism the *jurodstvo* was not a regular ascetic exercise, but belonged to the so-called *opera supererogatoria.* Its aim was to follow the example of Christ and to realise the advice of Saint Paul to him that thinks he is wise in this world, to become a fool in order to become wise (1 Cor. 3:18).

Through heart-searchings, confessions, and penitential exercises, the *jurodivyj* had to annihilate his own self, in order to rise again as an expression of the divine truth. The holy fools had their own language, which in addition to their improper, often indecent speech consisted of scandalous gestures, and was expressed in the whole of their appearance and conduct, which was also a stumbling block to their surroundings. The *jurodivyj* had become a sign, and the significance of his figure depended first and foremost on the glaring contrast between the *signans* and the *signatum:* in accordance with the Pauline "folly of what we preach," the humility of the *signans* is seen as an antithesis to the sublime *signatum* of the message, the divine Truth which becomes manifest in the foolish figure of the *jurodivyj.*

This semiotic character distinguishes the holy fool in principle from all forms of "natural" imbecility and madness. From a purely "scientific" and irreligious angle, this is difficult to accept. It is interesting to note that the only existing special study of the phenomenon in Soviet scholarship contends that the *jurodivye* were "mentally ill, who suffered from both persecution mania and other fixed ideas" (I. U. Budnovič, quoted in Pančenko 1984).

An interesting contemporary insight into *jurodstvo* is found in the writings of Dimitrij Tuptalo, the Ukrainian who became Bishop of Rostov. He revised the old Russian *Čet'i Minei* on the model of Peter Skarga's hagiographical works and the Bollandists' *Acta Sanctorum.* His revision marks the transition to the new Russian hagiography.

From his thorough knowledge of the holy fools, he defined *jurodstvo* as a "voluntary martyrdom."

*Jurodstvo* appears to have been a familiar way of preaching for active Old Believers. Under the cover of their folly, they might express criticism of both State and Church. Thematically, *jurodstvo* has a prominent place in Avvakum's *vita*, from which it emerges that several of Avvakum's closest followers appeared as holy fools. One of them was the holy fool Afanasij, later known as the monk Avramij, who in 1672 suffered a martyr's death when he was burnt at the stake in Moscow.

According to Pančenko (1984), an active *jurodstvo* was irreconcilable with writing, although this did not apply absolutely. Afanasij, however, had to renounce his *jurodstvo* and become a monk in order to write.

The ban on writing for the *jurodivye* is a characteristic feature of Muscovite culture, where their scandalous idiom, like profane mockery, belonged to the unwritten laughter culture. The holy *jurodivyj* and the profane *šut* each expressed himself by means of his own variant of the code of this laughter culture. The differences between them in their application of this code depend on their different functions in society, even though the boundary line between them is somewhat blurred. Pančenko (1984) has observed that the laughter of the profane fools is more open, more of a liberating force. What they criticise, they annihilate by means of laughter, while the holy fools through their conduct provoke laughter in order to reveal a more profound meaning in the ridiculous and cause laughter to freeze, producing tears instead. This laughter through tears becomes highly ambivalent: the *jurodivye* mock worldly wisdom and the powerful of the world in the awareness that through their folly they possess a divine wisdom. This is the ambivalent laughter that we know from Avvakum's *Life*, where it underlies the account of his suffering and humiliation, and occasionally breaks through the surface of the narrative in such exclamations as "i smekh i gore," "i gore, i smekh."

It is only when we have established this distinction between a holy and a secular version of the old Russian laughter tradition that we shall be able to answer the paradoxical question once put by Vinogradov: "When criticising the art of the *skomorokhi* (jesters) on ideological grounds, did not Avvakum translate some of its forms into literature?" (1949:40n.).

Avvakum's representation of himself as *jurodivyj* is effected by means of the idiom of the holy fools, transformed into verbal signs. The uncovering of this process of transformation forms the basis of a rational, nonspeculative interpretation of the unofficial modes of expression in Russian seventeenth-century literature, which cannot have arisen spontaneously, as a mechanical reflex to historical events. These genres grew out of the endeavours of anonymous and known authors to translate the preliterary modes of expression of the laughter culture into writing. In this process the idiom of the fools was translated into writing and combined with elements of the traditional genres of early Russian literature. Thus the old idiom of pre-Petrine laughter was transformed, at the same time as the written genres were themselves transformed in the process.

# Afterword

The aim of this book has not been to reconstruct the historical development of the early Russian saint's Life. Considering that centuries of hagiographical literature have been lost, it is questionable whether such a reconstruction is even possible. At any rate, what is first required is publication of the extant texts.

Our examination of individual Lives from different periods of Russian history has, however, enabled us to draw some general conclusions about the historical development of early Russian hagiography.

The individual saints' Lives do not fall into line with the pattern of an historical evolution. We cannot compare Nestor's *Life of Saint Theodosius* with Avvakum's autobiographical *Life* and maintain that the former represents a primitive, the latter a more advanced stage in the history of the Russian *vita*.

Russian hagiographers took over a complete system of genres from the Slavs who had already been christianised, and from Byzantium. Their first task consisted in translating these genres into a Russian context.

In Kievan times the exemplars of Byzantine hagiography were introduced in Russia. A masterpiece like the *Life of Saint Theodosius* shows that even at this early stage a writer existed who had full command of the basic hagiographical patterns, which were not taken up mechanically, but transformed and combined into new, complex texts.

The comparison of works as different as the *Life of Saint Theodosius*, Cyprian's *Life of Peter*, the *Lives* of Saint Stephen of Perm and Sergius of Radonež, and the *Life of Avvakum* shows that the history of this genre does not take the form of a progressive evolution, but that we are faced with a variety of combinations and transformations of a set of traditional conventions. In this process the historical context is always a determining factor for the hierarchical order between the elements, in particular for the relationship between *vita* and *passio*, the basic patterns.

In my study of Avvakum's *vita* I have tried to demonstrate how the action pattern of the idealising *vita* is negated through its combination with the pattern of the *passio*. Avvakum used the pattern of the *passio* to shape his own story and give meaning to his life by representing it as a variant of a martyr's passion.

The *Life of Avvakum* is more complex than the other *Lives* examined. The interplay of hagiographical and nonhagiographical codes foreshadows the use of hagiographical elements in the second half of the last century, when the rediscovery of the old, pre-Petrine Russia led also to a rediscovery of the Saints' Lives.

Pushkin expressed his enthusiasm for the old legends, but it is above all in the works of the great prose writers that we recognise the traditional hagiographical elements. Turgenev, Leskov, Mel'nikov-Pečerskij, Tolstoy, and Dostoevsky, to mention only a few of the best-known writers of the last century, all used elements taken from the old Russian hagiography. Leskov's story of the Old Believers, the tale of the stone masons of the *Zapečatlennyj angel*, and the life story of the pilgrim Ivan Fljagin in the *Očarovannyj strannik*, are not easy to understand without some knowledge of the old legends.

The hagiographical element plays a prominent part also in Dostoevsky's contemporary novel about the brothers Karamazov. The connection with the *vita* emerges most clearly in the figure of his hero, Aleša, who is completely different from the *typical* characters of the realistic novel. Unlike them, Aleša is an "eccentric". In relation to the prevailing conventions his character is *atypical*.

According to the retrospective synopsis of Aleša's childhood given by the fictitious narrator, he was, from his early boyhood, "rather shy and taciturn." Even if he "loved people," and became popular everywhere, he usually kept to himself, and was fond of "retiring into some corner to read books." His shyness was due to an "inner preoccupation," which "did not concern others, but which was so important that he forgot others for its sake." From the time when he was a small boy, he consistently avoided judging his fellow men, although he often suffered under the mockery and insult of his school-fellows. When as a twenty-year old he returned to his father's house, this "dirty den of depravity," he never condemned anybody, but "simply withdrew in silence when it became unbearable to look on." Aleša is different from others also in his attitude to money and material values. According to the narrator, anybody who got to know him would be convinced that Aleša "was one of those youths, who like the *jurodivye* would not hesitate to give away all his money, should he suddenly come into possession of a large fortune."

The depiction of Aleša's childhood ends when he suddenly decides to leave school and return to his father. First he visits his mother's grave, and tells his father of his decision to enter a monastery in order to liberate his soul, which "strives out of darkness towards the light."

In Aleša's childhood Dostoevsky has not only used the traditional childhood *topoi* of the saintly Lives; he has also combined the individual *topoi* into a coherent whole in conformity with the invariant pattern of the hagiographical tradition. Like the saintly heroes of the old Russian Lives, Aleša carries in his heart a spiritual energy that strives after hypostatisation. His childhood and youth, like theirs, are marked by this process. The decision to become a monk means to Aleša, as to Saint Theodosius and to Saint Sergius of Radonež, a transition from the introspection of childhood and the passive attitude towards others to a self-realisation in action. Aleša is formed after the example of Christ. His figure joins the ranks of christophorous heroes, who from Late Antiquity until today have preserved in them the "very heart of the whole," to quote the author's preface to the novel.

The character of Aleša is formed according to a prototype which is not immediately familiar to modern readers of Dostoevsky, either in Russia or in Western Europe. Many critics have interpreted Aleša on the conventions of the realistic novel, and thereby misunderstood Dostoevsky's intentions. To read the story of Aleša in this way is like judging a Russian icon by the conventions of nineteenth-century realistic painting. In both cases the world-view of Realism will block a true understanding of this art.

The saintly figure of Aleša acquires its full significance only if we read *The Brothers Karamazov* as a carnivalised version of the old regeneration myth, in which the parricide marks the destruction of the old time on the threshold of a new world order (Børtnes 1968). Aleša, who "carries in him the very heart of the whole" at a time when all others "have been torn away from it, for the time being, as if by a gust of wind," represents the regenerative force in this drama. In the last chapter we meet him as he is about to found a new order among the schoolmates of the dead Iljušečka, a society of the future.

Against the background of what we know about protagonist and action pattern in early Russian hagiography, we realise that this connection between Aleša's saintly figure and the mythical structure of the novel is no coincidence. In *The Brothers Karamazov*, Dostoevsky has burst the conventions of the realistic novel. In his effort to express a vision of *the new society* he has revived codes that may be traced back to old Russian hagiography and early Christian passion literature. By means of these codes he created his own version of the *mythical novel*.

This connection between works of different genres and epochs shows that in literature as in other sign systems we are faced with basic invariant forms, and that these basic forms may be uncovered through comparative analyses of the structures underlying the individual variants, as these have been determined by their respective contexts. The function of the hagiographical elements in Dostoevsky's last novel shows also the significance of early Russian hagiography for the study of modern Russian literature.

# List of Abbreviations:

*ČOLDP: Čtenija v Obščestve ljubitelej dukhovnogo prosveščenija*
*Diss. Abs.: Dissertation Abstracts*
*IORJaS: Izvestija Otdelenija russkogo jazyka i slovesnosti Akademii nauk*
*Philos. Anz.: Philosophischer Anzeiger*
*SW:* Roman Jakobson's *Selected Writings*
*TODRL: Trudy Otdela drevnerusskoj literatury*
*VV: Vizantijskij Vremennik*
*ZfslPh: Zeitschrift für slavische Philologie*

# Bibliography

Abramovič, D.I. (1898), "K voprosu ob istočnikakh Nestorova žitija prepodobnogo Feodosija," *IORJaS*, III, 1, 243–246.
Adrianova-Peretc, V. P. (1937), *Očerki po istorii russkoj satiričeskoj literatury XVII v.*, Moscow.
(1947a), *Očerki poètičeskogo stilja drevnej Rusi*, Moscow.
(1947b), "Slovo o žitii i o prestavlenii velikogo knjazja Dmitrija Ivanoviča, carja Rus'skago," *TODRL*, V, 73–96.
(1948), "Literatura kanuna reformy," *Istorija russkoj literatury*, II, 2, Moscow, 150–157, 187–206.
(1954), *Russkaja demokratičeskaja satira XVII veka*, Moscow.
(1958), "Ob osnovakh khudožestvennogo metoda drevnerusskoj literatury," *Russkaja literatura*, 4, 61–70.
(1963), "Drevnerusskie literaturnye pamjatniki v jugoslavjanskoj pis'mennosti," *TODRL*, XIX, 5–27.
(1964), "Zadači izučenija "agiografičeskogo stilja" Drevnej Rusi," *TODRL*, XX, 41–71.
(1974), *Drevnerusskaja literatura i fol'klor*, Leningrad.
Ajnalov, D. (1913), *Istorija russkoj živopisi ot XVI po XIX vv.*, St. Petersburg.
Alpatov, M. (1967), *Ètjudy po istorii russkogo iskusstva*, I, Moscow.
(1971), *Andrej Rublev*, Moscow.
(1972), "Iskusstvo Feofana Greka i učenie isikhastov," *VV*, XXXIII, 190–202.
(1979), *Feofan Grek*, Moscow.
Alpatov, M., and N. Brunov (1932), *Geschichte der altrussischen Kunst*, Augsburg.
Amiranašvili, Š, (1966), *Gruzinskaja miniatjura*, Moscow.
(1971), "Feofan Grek i Andrej Rublev," *Andrej Rublev i ego èpokha*, ed. by M. V. Alpatov, Moscow, 171–180.
Ammann, A. M., (1938), *Ein Handbuch der spätbyzantinischen Mystik (Das östliche Christentum, 6/7)*, Würzburg.
Angyal, A. (1961), *Die slavische Barockwelt*, Leipzig.
Antonova, M. F. (1974), "Slovo o žitii i o prestavlenii velikogo knjazja Dmitrija Ivanoviča, carja Rus'skago," *TODRL*, XXVIII 140–154.
Assunto, R. (1963), *Die Theorie des Schönen im Mittelalter*, Cologne.
Auerbach, R. (1946), *Mimesis*, Bern.
(1967), *Gesammelte Aufsätze zur romanischen Philologie*, Bern.
(1973), *Scenes from the Drama of European Literature: Six Essays*, Gloucester (Mass.).

Avvakum Petrov, Archpriest (1927) *Žitie protopopa Avvakuma*, ed. by Ja. L. Barskov
    *(Pamjatniki istorii staroobrjadčestva XVII v.*, I, 1. = *Russkaja istoričeskaja
    biblioteka*, 39), Leningrad.
    (1934), *Žitie protopopa Avvakuma im samim napisannoe i drugie ego sočinenija*, ed.
    with an introd. and comm. by N. K. Gudzij, Moscow.
    (1938), *La vie de l'archiprêtre Avvakum écrite par lui-même*, transl. from the old
    Russian into French, with introd. and comm. by P. Pascal, Paris.
    (1960), *Žitie protopopa Avvakuma i drugie ego sočinenija*, ed. by N. K. Gudzij,
    Moscow.
    (1963), *Žizneopisanija Avvakuma i Epifanija: issledovanija i teksty*, by A. N.
    Robinson, Moscow.
    (1975), *Pustozerskij sbornik: Avtografy sočinenij Avvakuma i Epifanija*, ed. by N. S.
    Demkova, N. F. Droblenkova, and L. I. Sazonova, Leningrad. Reproduction of the
    Zavoloko manuscript with a transcription of the texts. The text of the *Life*, pp. 8–80.

Bakhtin, M. M. (1963), *Problemy poètiki Dostoevskogo*, Moscow.
    (1965), *Tvorčestvo Fransua Rablè i narodnaja kul'tura srednevekov'ja i renessansa*,
    Moscow.
    (1975),, *Voprosy literatury i èstetiki*, Moscow.
Bank, A. V. (1965), *Vizantijskoe iskusstvo v sobranijakh Sovetskogo Sojuza*, Moscow.
Bauer, A. (1901), "Heidnische Märtyrerakten," *Archiv für Papyrusforschung*, I, 29–47.
Beck, H.-G. (1959), *Kirche und theologische Literatur im byzantinischen Reich*, Munich.
Bédier, J. (1893), *Les Fabliaux*, Paris.
Birnbaum, H. (1972), "Byzantine Tradition Transformed," *Aspects of the Balkans*, ed. by
    H. Birnbaum and S. Vryonis, Jr. *(Slavistic Printings and Reprintings, 270)*, The
    Hague, 243–284.
    (1974), *On Medieval and Renaissance Slavic Writing (Slavistic Printings and
    Reprintings, 266)*, The Hague.
    (1978),"Altrussische Wortkunst in neuem Licht: Bemerkungen zu einer kritischen
    Neuausgabe der Klageschrift Daniels und zu einer Neuinterpretation des altrus-
    sischen Heiligenlebens," *Die Welt der Slaven*, XXIII, 1, N.F. II, 1, 187–215.
    (1984), "The Balkan Slavic Component of Medieval Russian Culture," *Medieval
    Russian Culture*, ed. by H. Birnbaum and M. S. Flier *(California Slavic Studies, XII)*,
    Berkeley, 3–30.
Booth, W. C. (1968), *The Rhetoric of Fiction*, Chicago [8].
Borozdin, A. K. (1898), *Protopop Avvakum. Očerk po istorii umstvennoj žizni russkogo
    obščestva v XVII v.*, St. Petersburg.
Bousset, W. (1922), *"Der verborgene Heilige,"* *Archiv für Religionswissenschaft*, XXI, 1–
    17.
Brinkmann, H. (1928), *Zu Wesen und Form mittelalterlicher Dichtung*, Halle (Saale).
Brown, P. (1978), *The Making of Late Antiquity*, Cambridge (Mass.).
    (1981), *The Cult of the Saints*, London.
Bugoslavskij, S. A. (1914), "K voprosu o kharaktere i ob"eme literaturnoj dejatel'nosti
    prepodobnogo Nestora", *IORJaS*, XIX, 1, 131–186; 3, 153–191.
    (1946), "Literatura vremeni ob"edinenija severo-vostočnoj Rusi (1380–1462)," *Istorija
    russkoj literatury*, II, 1, Moscow, 234–240.
Burkert, W. (1972), *Homo necans*, Berlin.
    (1979), *Structure and History in Greek Mythology and Ritual*, Berkeley.
Byčkov, V. V. (1977), *Vizantijskaja èstetika*,Moscow.
Børtnes, J. (1967), "Frame Technique in Nestor's Life of St. Theodosius," *Scando-
    Slavica*, XIII, 5–16.
    (1968), "To Dostoevskijstudier," *Edda*, 2–16.
    (1970), "Studier i gammelrussisk maleri," *Kunst og Kultur*, 161–180.
    (1972), "Hagiographical Transformation in the Old Russian Lives of Saints,"
    *Scando-Slavica*, XVIII, 5–12.
    (1975), *Det gammelrussiske helgenvita: dikterisk egenart og historisk betydning*,
    Oslo.
    (1978), "The Function of Hagiography in Dostoevskij's Novels," *Scando-Slavica*,

XXIV, 27-33. Repr. in *Critical Essays on Dostoevsky*, ed. by Robin Feuer Miller, Boston (Mass.), 1986, 188-193.

(1979), "Dissimilar Similarities: *Imitatio Christi* in the Life of Archpriest Avvakum," *To Honor Nikolay Andreyev (Canadian-American Slavic Studies*, 13, 1-2), 224-229.

(1981), "Orthodox Symbolism in Russian Literature," *Svantevit* VII, 1, 5-16.

(1984), "The Function of Word-weaving in the Structure of Epiphanius' *Life of Saint Stephen, Bishop of Perm'*," *Medieval Russian Culture*, ed. by H. Birnbaum and M. S. Flier (*California Slavic Studies*, XII), Berkeley, 311-342.

Camelot, P. Th. (1951), "Le martyr de Polycarpe," *Sources chrétiennes*, 10, Paris, 225-240.

Castro, A. (1969), "Perspektive des Schelmenromans," *Pikareske Welt (Wege der Forschung*, CLXIII), Darmstadt, 119-146.

Černykh, P. Ja. (1954), *Istoričeskaja grammatika russkogo jazyka*, Moscow.

Chambers, E. K. (1903),, *The Mediaeval Stage*, I-II, London.

Čiževsky, D. see Tschižewskij, D.

Cornford, F. (1934), *The Origin of the Attic Comedy*, Cambridge. 2nd ed. by Th. H. Gaster, Gloucester, Mass. 1968.

Ćorović. V. (1928), *Spisi sv. Save (Zbornik za istoriju, jezik i književnost srpskog naroda,* I, XVII, 1), Belgrade.

Curtius, E. R. (1954), *Europäische Literatur und lateinisches Mittelalter*, Bern[2].

(1960), *Gesammelte Aufsätze zur romanischen Philologie*, Bern.

Cyprian, Metropolitan og All Russia (1909), *Žitie i žizn' i malo ispovedanie ot čjudes iže vo svjatykh otca našego Petra mitropolita, arkhiepiskopa Kiev'skago i vseja Rusii. Spisano Kiprijanom mitropolitom smirenym Kiev'skym i vsjeja Rusii, Velikie Minei Četii*, fasc. 12, ed. by the Arkheografičeskaja kommissija, Moscow, cols. 1620-1646.

Dane, M. M. (1961), "Epiphanius' Image of St. Stefan," *Canadian Slavonic Papers*, V, 72-86.

Delehaye, H. (1921),, *Les passions des martyrs et les genres littéraires*, Brussels.

(1930), "La méthode historique et l'hagiographie," *Bulletins de l'Académie royale de Belgique*, XVI, 218-231.

(1962), *The Legends of the Saints*, with a memoir of the author by Paul Peeters, transl. by D. Attwater (orig. tit.: *Les légendes hagiographiques*, Brussels, 1905).

Demina, N. (1963), *Troica Andreja Rubleva*, Moscow.

Demkova, N. S. (1974), *Žitie protopopa Avvakuma, tvorčeskaja istorija proizvedenija*, Leningrad.

Dempf, A. (1964), *Geistesgeschichte der altchristlichen Kultur*, Stuttgart.

Deržavina, O. A. (1946), "Analiz obrazov povesti XVII v. o careviče Dimitrii Uglickskom," *Uč. zap. MGPI*, VII, Kaf. russ. lit., 1.

(1951), *Vremennik Ivana Timofeeva*, ed., transl. and notes by O. A. Deržavina, Moscow.

Devos, P. (1954-1955) "Chronique d'hagiographie slave," *Acta Bollandiana*, LXXII, 427-438, LXXIII, 214-236.

Dinekov, P. (1962), "Evtimij Tŭrnovskij," *Istorija na bŭlgarskata literatura*, I, Sofia, 285-306.

Dionysius the Areopagite (1970), *La hiérarchie céleste*, introd. by R. Roques, text by G. Heil, trad. by M. de Gandillac (*Sources chrétiennes*, 58), Paris.

Dmitriev, L. A. (1963), "Rol' i značenie mitropolita Kipriana v istorii drevnerusskoj literatury, *TODRL*, XIX, 215-254.

Dölger, F. (1967), "Byzantine Literature," *The Byzantine Empire*, II, ed. by J. M. Hussey (The Cambridge Medieval History, IV), Cambridge, 206-263.

Dorn, E. (1967), *Der sündige Heilige in der Legende des Mittelalters*, Munich.

Dubois, C.-G. (1973), *Le Baroque*, Paris.

Ejkhenbaum, B. (1969a), "Kak sdelana "Šinel'" Gogolja," *Texte der russischen Formalisten*, ed. with an introd. by J. Striedter, I, Munich, 122-158.

(1969b) "Illjuzija skaza," *Texte der russischen Formalisten*, ed. with an introd. by J. Striedter, I, 160-166.

(1969c), "Leskov i sovremennaja proza," *Texte der russischen Formalisten*, ed. with an introd. by J. Striedter, I, 208-242.

Eliade, M. (1957), *Das Heilige und das Profane*, Hamburg.

(1966), *Kosmos und Geschichte: der Mythos der ewigen Wiederkehr*, Hamburg.

Epifanij Premudryj (1897), *Žitie Svjatogo Stefana episkopa Permskogo*, ed. by V. G. Družinin, St. Petersburg.

(1981a), "Žitie Sergija Radonežskogo," *Pamjatniki literatury drevnej Rusi: XIV-seredina XV veka*, ed. by L. A. Dmitriev and D. S. Likhačev, Moscow, 256-429.

(1981b), "Pis'mo k Kirillu Tverskomu," *Pamjatniki literatury drevnej Rusi: XIV-seredina XV veka*, ed. by L. A. Dmitriev and D. S. Likhačev, Moscow, 444-447.

Eremin, I. P. (1953), "K istorii russko-ukrainskikh literaturnykh svjazej v XVII veke," *TODRL*, IX, 291-296.

(1955), *Ivan Višenskij: sočinenija*, ed. with introd. and notes by I. P. Eremin, Moscow.

(1966), *Literatura drevnej Rusi*, Moscow.

Evdokimov, P. (1965), *L'Orthodoxie*, Neuchâtel.

Fedotov, G. P. (1931), *Svjatye drevnej Rusi*, Paris.

(1952), *A Treasury of Russian Spirituality*, London.

(1960), *The Russian Religious Mind*, New York.

Fennell, J., and A. Stokes (1974), *Early Russian Literature*, London.

Fergusson, F. (1949), *The Idea of a Theater*, Princeton.

Florenskij, P. (1919), "Troice-Sergieva Lavra i Rossija," *Troice-Sergieva Lavra*, Sergiev Posad, 3-29.

Frejdenberg, O. (1936), *Poètika sjužeta i žanra*, Leningrad.

(1978), *Mif i literatura drevnosti*, Moscow.

Friis Johansen, H. (1955), *Den hellige Antonius' liv og andre skrifter om munke og helgener i Ægypten, Palæstina og Syrien*, transl. by Holger Friis Johansen with an introd. by Carsten Høeg, Copenhagen.

Gad, T. (1961), *Legenden i dansk middelalder*, Copenhagen.

Gasparov, M. L. (1969), "Raboty V. I. Jarkho po teorii literatury," *Trudy po znakovym sistemam*, IV, Tartu, 504-514.

Ginzburg, L. (1970), "O dokumental'noj literature i principakh postroenija kharaktera," *Voprosy literatury*, 7, 62-91.

Glubokovskij, N. (1892), "Sv. Kiprian, mitropolit vseja Rossii (1374-1406), kak pisatel'," *ČOLDP*, 1, 358-424.

Golejzovskij, N. K. (1964), "Zametki o tvorčestve Feofana Greka," *VV*, XXIV, 139-149.

Goleniščev-Kutuzov, I. N. (1973), *Slavjanskie literatury*, Moscow.

Golubinskij, E. (1900), *Istorija russkoj cerkvi*, II, 1, Moscow.

Gombrich, E. H. (1967), *The Story of Art*, London[11].

(1972), *Art and Illusion*, London[4].

Grabar, A. (1946), *Martyrium: recherches sur le culte des reliques et l'art chrétien antique*, II, *Iconographie*, Paris.

Gudzij, N. K. (1966), *Istorija drevnej russkoj literatury*, Moscow[7].

Günter, H. (1906), *Legenden-Studien*, Cologne.

(1910), *Die christliche Legende des Abendlandes*, Heidelberg.

(1922), *Buddha in der abendländischen Legende*, Leipzig.

(1949), *Psychologie der Legende. Studien zu einer wissenschaftlichen Heiligen-Geschichte*, Freiburg.

Gusev, V. E. (1957), "Zametki o stile "Žitija" protopopa Avvakuma," *TODRL*, XIII, 273-281.

(1960), "Protopop Avvakum Petrov, vydajuščijsja russkij pisatel' XVII veka," Avvakum (1960), 5-51.

Hägg, T. (1983), *The Novel in Antiquity*, Oxford.

Hafner, S. (1964), *Studien zur altserbischen dynastischen Historiographie (Südosteuropäische Arbeiten*, 62), Munich.

Hamann-MacLean, R., (1976), *Grundlegung zu einer Geschichte der mittelalterlichen Monumentalmalerei in Serbien und Makedonien (= Die Monumentalmalerei in*

*Serbien und Makedonien* by R. Hamann-MacLean and H. Hallensleben, IV), Giessen.

Hamburger, K. (1968), *Die Logik der Dichtung*, Stuttgart[2].

Hausherr, I. (1948), "L'imitation de Jésus Christ dans la spiritualité byzantine," *Mélanges offerts à R. P. Ferdinand Cavellera*, Toulouse, 231-259.

Holl, K. (1912), "Die schriftstellerische Form des griechischen Heiligenlebens," *Neue Jahrbücher für das klassische Altertum*, XXIX, 406-427.

Holthusen, J. (1967), "Epifanij Premudryj und Gregor von Nyssa," *Festschrift für Margarete Woltner*, Heidelberg, 64-82.

Hunger, H. (1965), *Reich der neuen Mitte*, Graz.

Il'in, M. A. (1959), "Kamennoe zodčestvo tret'ej četverti XVII veka," *Istorija russkogo iskusstva* IV, Moscow, 153-216.

(1966), "Nekotorye predloženija ob arkhitekture russkikh ikonostasov na rubeže XIV-XV vv.," *Kul'tura drevnej Rusi*, (Posvjaščaetsja 40-letiju naučnoj dejatel'nosti Nikolaja Nikolaeviča Voronina), Moscow, 79-88.

Ingham, N. W. (1984), "The Martyred Prince and the Question of Slavic Cultural Continuity in the Early Middle Ages," *Medieval Russian Culture*, ed. by H. Birnbaum and M. S. Flier *(California Slavic Studies*, XII), Berkeley, 31—53.

Ivanov, V. V. (1973), "Značenie idej M. M. Bakhtina o znake, vyskazyvanii i dialoge dlja sovremennoj semiotiki," *Trudy po znakovym sistemam*, VI, Tartu, 5-44.

Jablonskij, V. (1908), *Pakhomij Serb i ego agiografičeskie pisanija*, St. Petersburg.

Jagoditsch, R. (1934), "Der Stil der altrussischen Vitae: ein Beitrag zur Methodik und Systematik der altrussischen Literaturgeschichte," *Księga II międzynarodowy zjazd slavistów (filologów słowiańskich), Warsaw*, 62-68.

Jakobson, R. (1953), "The Kernel of Comparative Slavic Literature," *Harvard Slavic Studies*, I, 1-71. *(SW*, VI, 1, Berlin, 1985, 1-64).

(1954), "Minor Native Sources for the Early History of the Slavic Church," *Harvard Slavic Studies, II*, dedicated to F. Dvornik, 39-73. *(SW*, VI, 1, Berlin, 1985, 159-189.)

(1956), "Two Aspects of Language and Two Types of Aphasic Disturbances," *Fundamentals of Language*, by Roman Jakobson and Morris Halle *(Janua linguarum*, 1), The Hague, 55-82, *(SW*, II, The Hague, 1971, 239-259.)

(1958), "Medieval Mock Mystery (The Old Czech *Unguentarius*)," *Studia philologica et litteraria in honorem L. Spitzer*, Bern, 245-265. *(SW*, VI, 2, Berlin, 1985, 666-690.)

(1960), "Linguistics and Poetics," *Style in Languge*, ed. by Th. A. Sebeok, Cambridge (Mass.), 350-377, *(SW*, III, The Hague, 1981, 18-51.)

(1963), "St. Constantine's Prologue to the Gospels," *St. Vladimir's Seminary Quarterly*, VI, 1, *(SW*, VI, 1, Berlin 1985, 191-206.)

(1966a), "Linguistic Types of Aphasia," *Brain Function*, III, Berkeley, 67-91. *(SW*, II, The Hague, 1971, 307-333.)

(1966b), "Grammatical Parallelism and its Russian Facet," *Language*, 42, 399-429. *(SW*, III, The Hague, 1981, 98-135.)

(1970), "Pokhvala Konstantina Filosofa Grigoriju Bogoslovu," *Slavia*, XXXIX, 334-361. *(SW*, VI, 1,Berlin, 1985, 207-239.)

(1971), "Quest for the Essence of Language," *SW*, II, The Hague, 345-359.

(1973), *Questions de poétique*, Paris.

(1981), *Poetry of Grammar and Grammar of Poetry*, ed. by S. Rudy, The Hague (= *SW*, III).

(1985), "Retrospect," *SW*, VI, 2, Berlin, 889-897.

Jantzen, H. (1963), *Ottonische Kunst*, Hamburg.

Jolles, A. (1930), *Einfache Formen*, Tübingen.

Jommi, G. (1964), *Realität der irrealen Dichtung*, Hamburg.

Kadlubovskij, A. (1902), *Očerki po istorii drevnerusskoj literatury žitij svjatykh*, Warsaw.

Kagan, M. D. (1955), " 'Povest' o dvukh posol'stvakh'-legendarno-političeskoe proizvedenie načala XVII veka," *TODRL*, XI, 218-254.

(1957), "Legendarnaja perepiska Ivana IV s tureckim sultanom kak literaturnyj

pamjatnik pervoj četverti XVII v.," *TODRL*, XIII, 247-272.
(1958), "Legendarnyj cikl gramot tureckogo sultana k evropejskim gosudarjam—publicističeskoe proizvedenie vtoroj poloviny XVII v.," *TODRL*, XV, 225-250.
Kapterev, N. F. (1912), *Patriarkh Nikon i Car' Aleksej Mikhajlovič*, I-II:II, Sergiev Posad.
Kartašev, A. V. (1959), *Očerki po istorii russkoj cerkvi*, I-II, Paris.
Kayser, W. (1951), *Das sprachliche Kunstwerk*, Bern[2].
Kazakova, N. A. and Ja. S. Lur'e (1955), *Antifeodal'nye eretičeskie dviženija na Rusi XIV-načala XVI veka*, Moscow.
Kerényi, K. (1927), *Die griechisch-orientalische Romanliteratur in religionsgeschichtlicher Beleuchtung*, Tübingen.
Kitch, F. C. M. (1971), "Citaty iz knig svjaščennogo pisanija v sočinenijakh Epifanija Premudrogo," by F. Wigzell, *TODRL*, XXVI, 232-243.
(1976), *The Literary Style of Epifanij Premudryj: pletenije sloves (Slavistische Beiträge*, 96), Munich.
Klibanov, A. I. (1960), *Reformacionnye dviženija v Rossii v XIV-pervoj polovine XVI vv.*, Moscow.
(1971), "K kharakteristike mirovozzrenija Andreja Rubleva", *Andrej Rublev i ego èpokha*, ed. by M. Alpatov, Moscow, 62-102.
Ključevskij, V. O. (1871), *Drevnerusskie žitija svjatykh kak istoričeskij istočnik*, Moscow.
(1956), *Kurs russkoj istorii*, 1 (*Sočinenija v vos'mi tomakh*, I), Moscow.
(1957), *Kurs russkoj istorii*, 2 (*Sočinenija v vos'mi tomakh*, II), Moscow.
Kologriwow, I. (1958), *Das andere Russland*, Munich.
Komarovič, V. L. (1960), "Kul't roda i zemli v knjažeskoj srede XI-XIII vv.," *TODRL*, XVI, 84-104.
Konovalova, O. F. (1969), "Princip otbora faktičeskikh svedenij v 'Žitii Stefana Permskogo'," *TODRL*, XXIV, 136-138.
(1970), "Ob odnom tipe amplifikacii v žitii Stefana Permskogo," *TODRL*, XXV, 73-80.
Kossova, A. G. (1984), "Per una lettura analitica del *Žitie prepodobnago Feodosia Pečerskago* di Nestore," *Ricerche Slavistiche* (1980-1981), 27-28, 65-100.
Kovalevskij, I. (1900), *O jurodstve vo Khriste*, Moscow[2].
Krumbacher, K. (1897), *Geschichte der byzantinischen Literatur*, Munich[2].
Kruszewski, M. H. (1884 et seq.) "Prinzipien der Sprachentwicklung," *Internationale Zeitschrift für allgemeine Sprachwissenschaft*, I, 295-307; II, 258-268; III, 145-187; V, 339-360.
Kuev, K. (1962), "Kiprian," *Istorija na bŭlgarskata literatura*, I, Sofia, 308-314.
Kukčin, V. A. (1962), "Skazanie o smerti mitropolita Petra," *TODRL*, XVIII, 59-79.
Kuz'mina, V. D. (1971), "Drevnerusskie pis'mennye istočniki ob Andree Rubleve," *Andrej Rublev i ego èpokha*, ed. by M. V. Alpatov, Moscow, 103-124.

Lazarev, V. N. (1947), *Istorija vizantijskogo iskusstva*, I-II, Moscow.
(1959), "La Trinité d'André Roublev," *Gazette des Beaux-Arts*, December, 282-300.
(1960), *Mozaiki Sofii Kievskoj*, Moscow.
(1961), *Feofan Grek i ego škola*, Moscow.
(1966a), *Mikhajlovskie mozaiki*, Moscow.
(1966b), *Andrej Rublev i ego škola*, Moscow.
(1966c), *Old Russian Murals and Mosaics*, London.
(1970), *Russkaja srednevekovaja živopis'*, Moscow.
(1973), *Drevnerusskie mozaiki i freski*, Moscow.
Leclercq, J. (1957), *L'amour des lettres et le désir de Dieu*, Paris.
Lehmann, P. (1922), *Die Parodie im Mittelalter*, Munich.
Leonid, Archimandrite (1885), *Žitie prepodobnogo i bogonosnogo otca našego Sergija Čudotvorca i pokhval'noe emu slovo, napisannye učenikom ego Epifaniem Premudrym v XV veke*, St. Petersburg.
Lévi-Strauss, C. (1967), *Structural Anthropology*, New York.
Likhačev, D. S. (1958), *Nekotorye zadači izučenija vtorogo južnoslavjanskogo vlijanija v Rossii*, Moscow.
(1962), *Kul'tura Rusi vremeni Andreja Rubleva i Epifanija Premudrogo*, Moscow.

(1967), *Poètika drevnerusskoj literatury*, Leningrad.
(1969), "Semnadcatyj vek v russkoj literature," *XVII vek v mirovom literaturnom razvitii*, Moscow, 299-328.
(1970), *Čelovek v literature drevnej Rusi*, Moscow[2]. (1st ed. Moscow, 1958.)
(1973), *Razvitie russkoj literatury X-XVII vekov*, Leningrad.
(1984), "Smekh kak mirovozzrenie," *Smekh v drevnej Rusi*, by D. S. Likhačev, A. M. Pančenko, and N. V. Ponyrko, Moscow, 7-71.
List, J. (1930), "Das Antoniusleben des hl. Athanasius d. Gr. Eine literarhistorische Studie zu den Anfängen der byzantinischen Hagiographie," *Texte und Forschungen zur byzantinisch-neugriechischen Philologie*, 11, Athens.
Löwith, K. (1961), *Weltgeschichte und Heilsgeschehen*, Stuttgart.
L'Orange, H. P. (1958), *Fra prinsipat til dominat*, Oslo.
Lossky, V. (1957), *The Mystical Theology of the Eastern Church*, Cambridge.
Lotman, Ju. (1965a), "O probleme značenij vo vtoryčnykh modelirujuščikh sistemakh," *Trudy po znakovym sistemam*, II, 22-37.
(1965b), "O ponjatii geografičeskogo prostranstva v russkikh srednevekovykh tekstakh," *Trudy po znakovym sistemam*, II, 210-216.
(1967), "K probleme tipologii kul'tury," *Trudy po znakovym sistemam*, III, 30-38.
(1970a), *Struktura khudožestvennogo teksta*, Moscow.
(1970b), "Problema znaka i znakovoj sistemy i tipologija russkoj kul'tury XI-XIX vekov," *Stat'i po tipologii kul'tury*, Tartu, 12-35.

Mâle, É. (1924), *L'Art religieux du XIIe siècle en France*, Paris[2].
Mandel'štam, N. (1970), *Vospominanija*, New York.
Maranda, E. K. and P. (1971), *Structural Models in Folklore and Transformational Essays*, The Hague.
Mathauserová, S. (1968), "Baroko v ruské literatuře XVII. století," *Československé přednášky pro VI mezinárodní sjezd slavistu v Praze*, Prague, 253-259.
Mathew, G., (1963), *Byzantine Aesthetics*, London.
Mathiesen, R. (1965), "Nota sul genere acatistico e sulla letteratura agiografica slava," *Ricerche slavistiche*, XIII, 57-63.
Meletinskij, E. M. (1963), *Proiskhoždenie geroičeskogo èposa*, Moscow.
Mertel, H. (1909), *Die biographische Form der griechischen Heiligenlegenden*, Munich.
Meyendorff, J. (1964), *A Study of Gregory Palamas*, London.
(1981), *Byzantium and the Rise of Russia*, Cambridge.
Migne, J.-P., ed. (1887), "Bios kai politeia tou osiou patros emon Antoniou," *Patrologia græca*, XXVI, Paris, cols. 835-976.
Mirsky, D. S. (1949), *A History of Russian Literature*, London.
Morozov, A. (1962), "Problema barokko v russkoj literature XVII-načala XVIII veka (sostojanie voprosa i zadači izučenija)," *Russkaja literatura*, 3, 3-38.
(1967), "Nacional'noe svoeobrazie i problema stilej," *Russkaja literatura*, 3, 102-123.
(1968a), "Problema značitel'no složnee," *Russkaja literatura*, 4, 148-154.
(1968b), "Problemy evropejskogo barokko," *Voprosy literatury*, 12, 111-126.
Mošin, V. (1963), "O periodizacii russko-južnoslavjanskikh literaturnykh svjazej X-XV vv.," *TODRL*, XIX, 28-106.
Müller, G., (1929), "Bemerkungen zur Gattungspoetik", *Philos. Anz.*, 3, 129-147.
Müller, L., (1954 et seq.), "Studien zur altrussischen Legende der Heiligen Boris und Gleb", *ZfslPh*, XXIII, 60-77;XXV, 329-363; XXVII, 274-322; XXX, 14-44.
Mulić, M. (1963), "Srpsko 'pletenije sloves' do 14. stoljeća," *Radovi zavoda za slavensku filologiju*, 5, 117-129.
(1965), "Pletenije sloves i hesihazam," *Radovi zavoda za slavensku filologiju*, 7, 141-156.
(1968), "Serbskie agiografy XIII-XIV vv. i osobennosti ikh stilja," *TODRL*, XXIII, 127-142.
(1971), "Prilog pitanju ruskoga utjecaja na južnoslavenske književnosti u srednem vijeku," *Radovi zavoda za slavensku filologiju*, 12, 21-32.
(1975), *Srpski iztvori "pletenija sloves"* (*Djela* 4, Odjelenje za književnost i umjetnost, 2), Sarajevo.

Nestor, monk (1899), Žitie prepodobnaago otca našego Theodosija igoumena pečer'skago, Sbornik XII veka Moskovskogo Uspenskogo Sobora, ed. under the supervision of A. A. Šakhmatov and P. A. Lavrov, Moscow, 40-96.
   (1971), Žitie prepodobnaago otca našego Theodosija igoumena pečer'skago, Uspenskij sbornik XII-XIII vv., ed. prepared by O. A. Knjazevskaja, V. G. Demjanov, and M. V. Ljapon, ed. by S. I. Kotkov, Moscow, 71-135.
Nucubidze, Š. (1942), Tajna Psevdo-Dionisija Areopagita, Tbilisi.
Nygren, A. (1966), Eros och Agape, Stockholm.
Nykrog, P. (1957), Les Fabliaux, Copenhagen.

Obolensky, D. (1948), The Bogomils: A Study in Balkan Neo-Manichaeism, Cambridge.
   (1971a), The Byzantine Commonwealth: Eastern Europe, 500-1453, London.
   (1971b), Byzantium and the Slavs: Collected Studies, with a Preface by Ivan Dujčev, London.
   (1982), The Byzantine Inheritance of Eastern Europe, London.
Odincov, N. (1881), Porjadok obščestvennogo i častnogo bogosluženija v drevnej Rossii do XVI veka, St. Petersburg.
Okunev, N. (1928), Monumenta artis serbicae, I, Zagreb — Prague.
Onasch, K. (1961), Ikonen, Berlin.
   (1967), Grundzüge der russischen Kirchengeschichte (Die Kirche in ihrer Geschichte, ein Handbuch, ed. by K. D. Schmidt and E. Wolf, Vol. 3, fasc. M. part 1), Göttingen.
   (1968), Die Ikonenmalerei: Grundzüge einer systematischen Darstellung, Leipzig.
   (1977), Altrussische Heiligenleben, ed. by Konrad Onasch, Berlin.
   (1981), Kunst und Liturgie der Ostkirche in Stichworten, Vienna.
Orlov, A. S. (1945), Drevnjaja russkaja literatura XI-XVII vekov, Moscow.
Ostrogorskij, G. A. (1928), "Gnoseologičeskie osnovy vizantijskogo spora o sv. ikonakh," Seminarium Kondakovianum, II, Prague, 47-51.
Otto, R. (1917), Das Heilige, Breslau.

Pachomius the Serbian (1885), Žitie prepodobnogo i bogonosnogo otca našego Sergija-čudotvorca i pokhval'noe emu slovo, napisannye učenikom ego Epifaniem Premudrym v XV veke, published by Arkhimandrit Leonid (Pamjatniki drevnej pis'mennosti i iskusstva), St. Petersburg.
   (1981), see Epifanij Premudryj (1981a).
Palladius of Helenopolis (1974), La Storia Lausiaca, with an introd. by Christine Mohrmann, text and comm. by G. J. M. Bartelink, transl. by Marino Barchiesi, Verona.
Pančenko, A. M. (1973), Russkaja stikhotvornaja kul'tura XVII veka, Leningrad.
   (1984), "Smekh kak zrelišče," Smekh v drevnej Rusi, by D. S. Likhačev, A. M. Pančenko, N. V. Ponyrko, Moscow, 72-153.
Panofsky, E. (1955), Meaning in the Visual Arts, New York.
   (1965), Renaissance and Renaissances in Western Art, London.
Parker, A. A. (1967), Literature and the Delinquent, Edinburgh.
Pascal, P. (1938), Avvakum et les débuts du raskol, Paris.
Peeters, P. (1962), "Father Hippolyte Delehaye: A Memoir," H. Delehaye, The Legends of the Saints, London, 187-226.
Pelikan, J. (1974), The Spirit of Eastern Christendom (600-1700) (The Christian Tradition. A History of the Development of Doctrine, 2), Chicago.
Petrov, N. (1876), Istoričeskij vzgljad na vzaimnye otnošenija meždu serbami i russkimi v obrazovanii i literature, Kiev.
Petsch, R. (1932), "Die Lehre von den 'Einfachen Formen', 2. Die Legende," Deutsche Vierteljahrschrift für Litteraturwissenschaft und Geistesgeschichte, X, 346-357.
Philipp, W. (1940), Ansätze zum geschichtlichen und politischen Denken im Kiewer Russland (Jahrbücher für Geschichte Osteuropas, Beiheft 3), Breslau.
Picchio, R. (1958), " 'Prerinascimento esteuropeo' e 'Rinascita slava ortodossa.' (A proposito di una tesi di D. S. Lichačëv)," Ricerche slavistiche, VI, 185-199.
   (1977), "The Function of Biblical Thematic Clues in the Literary Code of Slavia Orthodoxa," Slavica Hiersolymitana, 1, 1-31.

(1984), "The Impact of Ecclesiastic Culture on Old Russian Literary Techniques," *Medieval Russian Culture*, ed. by H. Birnbaum and M. S. Flier *(California Slavic Studies*, XII), Berkeley, 247-279.

Platonov, S. F. (1891), *Pamjatniki drevnej russkoj pis'mennosti, otnosjaščiesja k Smutnomu vremeni (Russkaja istoričeskaja biblioteka*, XIII), St. Petersburg.

Plugin, V. A. (1974), *Mirovozzrenie Andreja Rubleva*, Moscow.

Podskalsky, G. (1982), *Christentum und theologische Literatur in der Kiever Rus' (988-1237)*, Munich.

Poljakova, S. V. (1972), *Vizantijskie legendy*, ed. by S. V. Poljakova, Leningrad.

Ponyrko, N. V. (1984), "Svjatočnyj i masleničnyj smekh", *Smekh v drevnej Rusi*, by D. S. Likhačev, A. M. Pančenko, N. V. Ponyrko, Moscow, 154-202.

Popov, A. (1869), *Izbornik slavjanskikh i russkikh sočinenij i statej, vnesennykh v khronografy russkoj redakcii*, Moscow.

Popović, P. (1912), *Obozrenie istorii serbskoj literatury*, St. Petersburg.

(1965), "Stare srpske biografije XV i XVII veka. Camblak, Konstantin i Pajsie," *Stara književnost*, ed. by Dj. Trifunović, Belgrade, 423-438, 449-475.

Poppe, A. (1965), "Chronologija utworów Nestora hagiografa," *Slavia orientalis*, XIV, 3, 287-305.

(1982), *The Rise of Christian Russia*, London.

Pozdneev, A. V. (1961), "Nikonovskaja škola pesennoj poèzii," *TODRL* XVII, 419-428.

Prokhorov, G. M. (1968), "Isikhazm i obščestvennaja mysl' v Vostočnoj Evrope v XIV v.," *TODRL*, XXIII, 86-108.

(1972), "K istorii liturgičeskoj poèzii: gimny i molitvy patriarkha Filofeja Kokkina," *TODRL*, XXVII, 120-149.

(1978), "Žitie mitropolita Petra," *Povest' o Mitjae: Rus' i Vizantija v èpokhu Kulikovskoj bitvy*, Leningrad, 204-215.

Propp, V. Ja.(1963), *Russkie agrarnye prazdniki*, Leningrad.

Radčenko, K. (1898), *Religioznoe i literaturnoe dviženie v Bolgarii v èpokhu pered tureckim zavoevaniem*, Kiev.

Radojčič, S. (1956), "Die serbische Ikonenmalerei vom 12. Jahrhundert bis zum Jahre 1459," *Jahrbuch der österreichischen byzantinischen Gesellschaft*, V, 61-83.

(1969), *Geschichte der serbischen Kunst von den Anfängen bis zum Ende des Mittelalters (Grundriss der slavischen Philologie und Kulturgeschichte*, 16), Berlin.

Radojičić, , Dj, Sp., (1963), *Actes du XII<sup>e</sup> congrès international d'études byzantines, Ochride 10-16 septembre 1961*, I, Belgrade, 431-436.

Reitzenstein, R. (1906), *Hellenistische Wundererzählungen*, Leipzig.

(1914), *Des Athanasius Werk über das Leben des Antonius - ein philolog. Beitrag zur Geschichte des Mönchtums (Sitzungsberichte der Heidelberger Akademie der Wissenschaften*, phil.-hist. Klasse, V. 8).

Rimscha, H. von (1970), *Geschichte Russlands*, Darmstadt².

Robinson, A. N. (1963), "Tvorčestvo Avvakuma i Epifanija, russkikh pisatelej XVII veka," *Žizneopisanija Avvakuma i Epifanija: issledovanija i teksty*, Moscow, 3-135.

(1967), "Ispoved'-propoved' (O khudožestvennosti "Žitija" Avvakuma)," *Istoriko-filologičeskie issledovanija: sbornik statej k 70-letiju akademika N. I. Konrada*, Moscow, 358-370.

(1974), *Bor'ba idej v russkoj literature XVII veka*, Moscow.

Rötzer, H. G. (1972), *Picaro-Landstörtzer-Simplicus: Studien zum niederen Roman in Spanien und Deutschland*, Darmstadt.

Roques, R. (1954), *L'Univers Dionysien*, Paris.

Rydén, L. (1981), "The Holy Fool," *The Byzantine Saint*, ed. by S. Hackel, London, 106-113.

Šakhmatov, A. (1896), "Neskol'ko slov o Nestorovom Žitii Feodosija," *IORJaS*, I, 1, 46-65.

Šambinago, S. K. (1948), "Literatura 1590-kh-1630-kh godov," *Istorija russkoj literatury*, II, 2, Moscow, 36-44.

Sasonova, L. I. (1974), "Princip ritmičeskoj organizacii v proizvedenijakh toržestvennogo krasnorečija staršej pory ("Slovo o zakone i blagodati" Ilariona,"Pokhvala sv. Simeonu i sv. Save" Domentiana)," *TODRL*, XXVIII, 30–46.

Saussure, F. de (1972), *Cours de linguistique générale*, crit. ed. by Tullio de Mauro, Paris.

Schöne, W. (1954), *Über das Licht in der Malerei*, Berlin.

Ševčenko, I. (1982), *Ideology, Letters and Culture in the Byzantine World*, London.

Sherrard, P. (1959), *The Greek East and the Latin West*, London.

Siefkes, F. (1970), *Zur Form des Žitije Feodosija (Frankfurter Abhandlungen zur Slavistik*, 12, *Osteuropastudien der Hochschulen des Landes Hessen*, Reihe III), Bad Homburg v.d.H.

Simoni, P. K. (1907), *"Povest' o Gore i Zločastii*, kak Gore-Zločastie dovelo molodca vo inočeskij čin, po edinstvennoj sokhranivšejsja rukopisi XVIII-go veka," *Sbornik Otdelenija russkogo jazyka i slovesnosti Akademii nauk*, LXXXIII, 1.

Simson, O. von (1964), *The Gothic Cathedral*, New York.

Skripil', M. O. (1947), "Povest'o Savve Grudcyne: teksty," *TODRL*, V, 225–308.

Smirnov, N. A. (1915), *"Orel rossijskij:* Tvorenie Simeona Polockogo," ed. by N. A. Smirnov, *Pamjatniki drevnej pis'mennosti*, CXXXIII.

Sobolevskij, A. I. (1894), *Južnoslavjanskoe vlijanie na russkuju pis'mennost' v XIV-XV vv.*, St. Petersburg.

*(1903), Perevodnaja literatura Moskovskoj Rusi XIV–XVII vekov*, St. Petersburg.

Solov'ev, A. V. (1961), "Epifanij Premudryj kak avtor' Slova o žitii i prestavlenii velikago knjazja Dmitrija Ivanoviča, carja rus'skago'" *TODRL*, XVII, 85–106.

Speirs, J. (1951), "Some Towneley Cycle Plays," *Scrutiny*, XVIII.

Sreznevskij, I. I. (1958), *Materialy dlja slovarja drevnerusskogo jazyka*, I–III, Moscow. 1st ed. SPb, 1893–1903.

Stanojević, St., and D. Glumac (1932), *Sv. Pismo u našim starim spomenicima*, Belgrade.

Stender-Petersen, Ad. (1952), *Den russiske litteraturs historie*, I–III: I, Copenhagen.

(1963), "Menneskeskildringen i den oldrussiske litteratur," *På tærsklen til en ny tid*, Aarhus, 35-58.

Stokes, A. D. (1969), "Russian Literature of the 17th Century," *The Penguin Companion to Literature*, II, ed. by A. Thorlby, London, 675–680.

Syrku, P. (1901), *Očerki iz istorii literaturnykh snošenij bolgar i serbov v XIV-XVII vekakh*, St. Petersburg.

Talev, I. V. (1972), *The Impact of Middle Bulgarian on the Russian Literary Language (Post-Kievan Period)*, Doct. diss., UCLA, *Diss. Abs.*

(1973), *Some Problems of the Second South Slavic Influence in Russia (Slavistische Beiträge*, 67), Munich.

Tikhonravov, N. S., (1892), *Drevnie žitija Sergija Radonežskogo*, Moscow.

(1898), *Sočinenija*, I–II, Moscow.

Timofeev, Ivan, see Platonov (1891), Deržavina (1951).

Trifunović, Dj. (1965), "Biografske beleške o piscima pomenutim u ovoj knjizi," *Stara književnost*, ed. by Dj. Trifunović, Belgrade, 557f.

Trubetzkoy, N. S. (1973), *Vorlesungen über die altrussische Literatur*, with an afterword by R. O. Jakobson *(Studia historica et philologica. Sectio slavica*, I), Florence.

Tschiževskij, D. (1948), *Geschichte der altrussischen Literatur im 11., 12., und 13. Jahrhundert: Kiever Epoche*, Frankfurt (Main).

(1950), "Anklänge and die Gumpoldslegende des hl. Václav in der altrussischen Legende des hl. Feodosij und das Problem der 'Originalität' der slavischen mittelalterlichen Werke," *Wiener slavistisches Jahrbuch*, I, 71–86.

(1952), *Outline of Comparative Slavic Literatures (Survey of Slavic Civilization*, I, American Academy of Arts and Sciences), Boston (Mass.).

(1956a), *Aus zwei Welten (Slavistic Printings and Reprintings*, 10), The Hague.

(1956b), *Istorija ukraïns'koï literatury*, New York.

(1956c), "Zur Stilistik der altrussischen Literatur: Topik," *Festschrift für Max Vasmer zum 70. Geburtstag*, Wiesbaden, 105-113.

(1957), *Sbornik XII veka Moskovskogo Uspenskogo sobora*, vyp., 1-yj, ed. by A. A. Šakhmatov and P. A. Lavrov. Photofacs. repr. with an introd. by D. Čiževskij *(Apophoreta Slavica*, I), The Hague.

(1959a), *Das Heilige Russland: Russische Geistesgeschichte,* I, Hamburg.
(1959b), "Epiphanius the Wise, Medieval Russian Hagiographer," *Žitije Sv. Stefana Episkopa Permskogo,* ed. by V. Družinin, repr. with an introd. by Dmitrij Čiževskij (*Apophoreta Slavica,* II), The Hague, V-XVIII.
(1960), *History of Russian Literature from the 11th Century to the End of the Baroque (Slavistic Printings and Reprintings,* 12) The Hague.
(1964), *Das Paterikon des Kiever Höhlenklosters,* new ed. by D. Tschiževskij of D. Abramovič's ed. (*Slavische Propyläen, 2),* Munich.
(1970), "Das Barock in der russischen Literatur," *Forum Slavicum,* 23, 9-40.
Tvorogov, O. V. (1964), "Zadači izučenija literaturnykh formul drevnej Rusi," *TODRL,* XX, 29-40.
Tynjanov, Ju. (1929), *Arkhaisty i novatory,* Leningrad.

Usener, H. (1879), *Die Legende der heiligen Pelagia,* Bonn.
*Uspenskij sbornik XII-XIII vv.,* (1971), ed. by O. A. Knjazevskaja, V. G. Dem'janov, and M. V. Ljapon, Moscow.
Uspensky, B. (1973), *A Poetics of Composition,* Berkeley.

Vernadsky, G. (1969), *The Tsardom of Moscow 1547-1682: A History of Russia,* V, 1, New Haven.
Veselovskij, A. N. (1875), "Otryvki vizantijskogo èposa v russkom," *Vestnik Evropy,* 52, 750-775.
(1880), "Pamjatniki literatury povestvovatel'noj," *Istorija russkoj slovestnosti, drevnej i novoj,* by A. Galakhov, St. Petersburg², I, 394-517.
(1940), *Istoričeskaja poètika,* ed. with introd. and notes by V. M. Žirmunskij, Leningrad.
Vinogradov, V. V. (1923), "O zadačakh stilistiki. Nabljudenija nad stilem žitija protopopa Avvakuma," *Russkaja reč',* I, 195-293.
(1949), *Očerki po istorii russkogo literaturnogo jazyka XVII-XIX vv.,* Leyden.
(1959), *O jazyke khudožestvennoj literatury,* Moscow.
(1969), "Problema skaza v stilistike." *Texte der russischen Formalisten,* I, ed. with an introd. by J. Striedter, Munich. 168-206.
Vyšens'kyj, Ivan, see Eremin (1955).
Vološinov, V. N. (1930), *Marksizm i filosofija jazyka,* Moscow².
Walter, Ch. (1977), *Studies in Byzantine Iconography,* London.
Weimann, R. (1966), "Erzählsituation und Romantypus," *Sinn und Form,* 18, 109-133.
(1972), *Literaturgeschichte und Mythologie,* Berlin.
(1973), "French Structuralism and Literary History," *New Literary History,* IV, 3, 437-469.
(1977), *Structure and Society: Studies in the History and Theory of Historical Criticism,* London.
Weingarten, H. (1877), *Der Ursprung des Mönchtums im nachkonstantinischen Zeitalter,* Gotha.
Wölfflin, H. (1915), *Kunstgeschichtliche Grundbegriffe,* Munich.
Wyller, E. A. (1970), *Der späte Platon,* Hamburg.

Zabelin, I. (1872), *Domašnij byt russkikh caric v XVI i XVII st.,* Moscow².
Ždanov, I. N. (1892), "Beseda trekh svjatitelej i Jocha monachorum," *Žurnal Ministerstva narodnogo prosveščenija,* 279, 157-194.
Zenkovsky, S. A. (1956), "Der Mönch Epifanij und die Entstehung der altrussischen Autobiographie," *Die Welt der Slaven,* I, 3, 276-292.
Zimin, A. A., (1953), "O političeskoj doktrine Iosifa Volockogo," *TODRL,* IX, 159-177.
Živov, V. M. (1982), "'Mistagogija' Maksima Ispovednika i razvitie vizantijskoj teorii obraza," *Khudožestvennyj jazyk srednevekov'ja,* ed. by V. A. Karpušin, Moscow, 108-127.
Zubov, V. P. (1953), "Epifanij Premudryj i Pakhomij Serb", *TODRL,* IX, 145-158.

# INDEX

302

# SLAVICA NORVEGICA

Published by the Norwegian Association of Slavists.
Editors: Erik Egeberg (Tromsø), Siri Sverdrup Lunden (Oslo)
and Per Restan (Bergen).

1. Geir Kjetsaa, Sven Gustavsson, Bengt Beckman & Steinar
   Gil: The Authorship of *The Quiet Don.* (1984)
2. Alf Grannes, Arnvid Lillehammer & Egil Pettersen:
   Documents russes sur la pêche et le commerce russes en
   Norvège au XVIII$^e$ siècle. (1984)
3. Geir Kjetsaa: Dostoevsky and His New Testament. (1984)
4. Гейр Хетсо: Принадлежность Достоевскому: К вопросу об
   атрибуции Ф.М. Достоевскому анонимных статей в
   журналах *Время и Эпоха* (1986).
5. Jostein Børtnes: Visions of Glory: Studies in Early Russian
   Hagiography. (1988).